Microsoft Azure AI Fundamentals (AI-900) Certification Guide

Master AI, Machine Learning, and Azure Cloud Intelligence to Earn Your Microsoft Azure AI-900 Certification

Higor Luis Barbosa

AVA

www.orangeava.com

First Published: January 2026

Published By: Orange Education Pvt Ltd, AVA®

Address: 9, Daryaganj, Delhi, 110002, India

275 New North Road Islington Suite 1314 London,
N1 7AA, United Kingdom

ISBN (PBK): 978-93-49887-15-2
ISBN (E-BOOK): 978-93-49887-96-1

Scan the QR code to explore our entire catalogue

www.orangeava.com

Dedicated To

My Beloved Parents:

Luis Carlos Barbosa
Maria Martins – In Memoriam
Núria Barbosa,

My Wife, Gabriele Fleck and My Dog, Lebron.

About the Author

Higor Luis Barbosa is an experienced Cloud Platform Engineer, Enterprise Architect and Instructor, with deep expertise in Microsoft Azure, Amazon Web Services (AWS), and DevOps practices. Over a career spanning more than 20 years, he has built a strong foundation in both software development and cloud architecture, combining technical excellence with a passion for innovation and lifelong learning.

Higor began his professional journey as a .NET developer, dedicating his early years to creating robust and scalable applications. Over time, his curiosity for infrastructure and automation led him to specialize in cloud computing, mastering technologies such as Azure Kubernetes Service (AKS), Amazon Elastic Kubernetes Service (EKS), and Azure DevOps. His work focuses on designing secure, efficient, and resilient architectures that help organizations modernize their systems, and accelerate digital transformation.

In recent years, Higor has become a strong advocate for Artificial Intelligence (AI) adoption within enterprise environments. He has explored and implemented solutions using Azure OpenAI Service and Azure Cognitive Services, applying them to improve productivity, enhance decision-making, and promote innovation through responsible AI practices. His approach bridges traditional software engineering with the new frontiers of generative AI, highlighting how cloud platforms can unlock business value through intelligent automation.

As an educator, Higor has impacted the lives of over 50,000 students worldwide through his online courses on Azure, DevOps, and Kubernetes. His teaching style blends clarity, practicality, and real-world insight, helping professionals of all backgrounds build confidence in cloud and AI technologies. He is deeply passionate about democratizing technical education, making advanced topics accessible to anyone eager to grow in the digital era.

As the author of *Microsoft Azure AI Fundamentals* (AI-900), Higor combines his technical expertise with his commitment to teaching. His goal is to help learners understand not just how to use Azure AI services, but also how to apply them ethically, responsibly and effectively in real-world scenarios.

About the Technical Reviewer

Shanthababu Pandian is a distinguished technology leader with more than 23 years of experience in IT industry, specializing in Artificial Intelligence (AI), Machine Learning (ML), Generative AI (GenAI), and Data Science. He holds a Bachelor's degree in Electronics and Communication Engineering, three Master's degrees– M. Tech, MBA, and M.S.–from premier Indian institutions, a Postgraduate Program in AI and ML from the University of Texas, and a Postgraduate Certification in Data Science from IIT Guwahati. He is currently pursuing a Ph.D. in Artificial Intelligence from Anna University, Chennai, reflecting his unwavering commitment to advancing research, innovation, and responsible AI.

Throughout his career, Shanthababu has delivered transformative, enterprise-scale solutions for clients in the UK and US across healthcare, finance, and retail. His expertise spans architecting complex data ecosystems, implementing AI governance and compliance frameworks, and developing BI and AI-driven platforms that bridge cutting-edge technology with strategic business goals. As a seasoned leader, he has steered globally distributed teams, collaborated with executive stakeholders, and ensured seamless delivery through agile practices and modern cloud technologies.

A respected thought leader and mentor, Shanthababu has delivered more than 50 keynote talks at national and international forums, sharing deep insights with both academic and industry communities. He is the author of over 100 publications and books, and a trusted Technical Reviewer for leading global publishers, having reviewed over 75 titles across AI, data engineering, cloud computing, and software development.

Through his leadership, mentorship, and academic contributions, Shanthababu continues to inspire the next generation of AI and data professionals–championing innovation, ethical AI adoption, and a culture of data literacy, quality, and governance across global technological ecosystems.

Acknowledgments

First and foremost, I want to thank my wife for her unconditional support, patience, and constant encouragement throughout the entire writing process. Without her love, understanding, and companionship, this project would never have been completed.

I am deeply grateful to my sister, who has always encouraged me to study, and continuously improve my technical skills. Her example and support have been essential in motivating me to pursue knowledge with determination and curiosity.

I also express my eternal gratitude to my mother, who is no longer with us, for all the education, values, and principles she instilled in me. I also offer my heartfelt gratitude to my father for always being present and continuing to be a source of inspiration, strength, and pride. Everything I am—both professionally and personally—is a reflection of what I learned from them.

A special thanks to my loyal companion, Lebron, the best dog and friend in the world, who stayed by my side through long hours of writing. His constant presence brought lightness, joy, and inspiration to the entire process.

I would also like to thank my dear friend, Márcio Martins, who encouraged me more than 25 years ago to begin my journey in the IT field. His influence was a defining moment that shaped my entire career path.

Finally, I extend my gratitude to Microsoft and to the global community of Azure instructors and professionals, whose dedication to promoting responsible, accessible, and ethical AI continues to inspire educators and developers around the world.

Preface

This book covers many different aspects of **Artificial Intelligence (AI)** and its practical applications using Microsoft Azure. It introduces the importance of AI in today's world, and explains how intelligent technologies are reshaping industries by automating decisions, understanding natural language, analyzing images, and generating meaningful insights from data. This book helps readers build a strong foundation in AI workloads such as Machine Learning, Computer Vision, and Natural Language Processing. It also emphasizes the role of Azure services in simplifying AI adoption through ready-to-use models and cloud-based tools.

This book takes a practical and learner-friendly approach. It connects fundamental AI concepts with real-world business scenarios, demonstrating how AI can be used responsibly to drive innovation, and improve decision-making. Readers will also gain awareness of Responsible AI principles such as fairness, transparency, reliability, and inclusiveness – essential values when developing ethical AI systems.

Throughout the book, you will explore Microsoft Azure services, including **Azure Machine Learning**, **Azure AI Services**, and **Azure OpenAI Service**. You will also learn how these services enable automation, data analysis, image recognition, and content generation, while minimizing the complexity of AI model development.

This book is divided into **14 chapters**, each focusing on a key domain of AI, and its implementation in Microsoft Azure. The details are listed as follows:

Chapter 1 introduces Artificial Intelligence workloads and considerations, explaining how AI is used in different contexts, and highlighting the importance of ethical and responsible use.

Chapter 2 identifies the main features of common AI workloads, including computer vision, natural language processing, and conversational AI, establishing a foundation for later chapters.

Chapter 3 explores the guiding principles of Responsible AI, discussing fairness, transparency, inclusiveness, and accountability within the Microsoft Azure ecosystem.

Chapter 4 explains the fundamentals of Machine Learning, covering concepts such as training data, features, models, and evaluation techniques.

Chapter 5 introduces Azure tools and services for Machine Learning, including Azure Machine Learning, AutoML, and the designer interface for model building and deployment.

Chapter 6 focuses on Computer Vision fundamentals, showing how machines can analyze and interpret visual data from images and videos.

Chapter 7 dives deeper into the types of Computer Vision solutions–such as object detection, classification, and OCR–and their real-world applications.

Chapter 8 describes Azure tools and services for Computer Vision, including Azure AI Vision, Custom Vision, and Form Recognizer, showing how these can be integrated into enterprise solutions.

Chapter 9 explores Natural Language Processing (NLP) workloads, such as sentiment analysis, key phrase extraction, and translation, and their importance in modern communication.

Chapter 10 examines Azure tools and services for NLP workloads, including Azure AI Language, Translator, and Speech Services, with examples of conversational and text-based AI systems.

Chapter 11 introduces Generative AI, explaining how models such as GPT and DALL-E create new content, such as text, code, and images, and how these technologies are transforming industries.

Chapter 12 focuses on the capabilities of Azure OpenAI Service and Azure AI Foundry, highlighting natural language, code, and image generation as well as providing hands-on guidance for real deployments.

Chapter 13 provides a comprehensive practice test and sample questions to help learners assess their understanding, and become familiar with the AI-900 exam format.

Chapter 14 concludes the book with the best practices, emerging AI trends and practical tips for preparing for the exam. It connects all concepts to real-world scenarios, and encourages responsible and continuous learning.

Thus, by the end of this book, readers will have the knowledge and confidence to understand Azure AI workloads, apply responsible AI principles, and successfully achieve the **Microsoft Azure AI Fundamentals (AI-900)** certification. More importantly, they will be ready to apply these concepts in real business environments—creating intelligent, ethical, and impactful AI solutions.

Get a Free eBook

We hope you are enjoying your recently purchased book! Your feedback is incredibly valuable to us, and to all other readers looking for great books.

If you found this book helpful or enjoyable, we would truly appreciate it, if you could take a moment to leave a short review with a 5 star rating on Amazon. It helps us grow, and lets other readers discover our books.

As a thank you, we would love to send you a free digital copy of this book, and a **30%** discount code on your next cart value on our official websites:

www.orangeava.com

www.orangeava.in (For Indian Subcontinent)

☑ Here's how:

Leave a review for the book on Amazon.

Take a screenshot of your review, and send an email to **info@orangeava.com** (it can be just the confirmation screen).

Once, we receive your screenshot, we will send you the digital file, within 24 hours.

Thank you so much for your support – it means a lot to us!

Colored Images

Please follow the links or scan the QR codes to download the *Images* of the book:

You can find code bundles of our books on our official Github Repository. Go to the following link to and QR code to explore the further:

https://github.com/orgs/ava-orange-education/repositories

Please follow the link to download the Colored Images of the book:
https://rebrand.ly/629e5f

In case there's an update to the code, it will be updated on the existing GitHub repository.

Errata

We take immense pride in our work at **Orange Education Pvt Ltd,** and follow best practices to ensure the accuracy of our content to provide an indulging reading experience to our subscribers. Our readers are our mirrors, and we use their inputs to reflect and improve upon human errors, if any, that may have occurred during the publishing processes involved. To let us maintain the quality and help us reach out to any readers who might be having difficulties due to any unforeseen errors, please write to us at :

errata@orangeava.com

Your support, suggestions, and feedback are highly appreciated.

DID YOU KNOW

Did you know that Orange Education Pvt Ltd offers eBook versions of every book published, with PDF and ePub files available? You can upgrade to the eBook version at **www.orangeava.com** and as a print book customer, you are entitled to a discount on the eBook copy. Get in touch with us at: **info@orangeava.com** for more details.

At **www.orangeava.com**, you can also read a collection of free technical articles, sign up for a range of free newsletters, and receive exclusive discounts and offers on Print Books and eBooks.

PIRACY

If you come across any illegal copies of our works in any form on the internet, we would be grateful if you would provide us with the location address or website name. Please contact us at **info@orangeava.com** with a link to the material.

ARE YOU INTERESTED IN AUTHORING WITH US?

If there is a topic that you have expertise in, and you are interested in either writing or contributing to a book, please write to us at **business@orangeava.com**. We are on a journey to help developers and tech professionals to gain insights on the present technological advancements and innovations happening across the globe and build a community that believes Knowledge is best acquired by sharing and learning with others. Please reach out to us to learn what our audience demands and how you can be part of this educational reform. We also welcome ideas from tech experts and help them build learning and development content for their domains.

REVIEWS

Please leave a review. Once you have read and used this book, why not leave a review on the site that you purchased it from? Potential readers can then see and use your unbiased opinion to make purchase decisions. We at Orange Education would love to know what you think about our products, and our authors can learn from your feedback. Thank you!

For more information about Orange Education, please visit **www.orangeava.com**.

Table of Contents

Chapter 1
Introduction to Exam AI-900

Introduction

In this chapter, we will provide a comprehensive introduction to the AI-900 exam and the fundamental concepts of Artificial Intelligence (AI) in Microsoft Azure. We will begin by discussing the growing relevance of AI in today's world and its impact across various industries. Next, we will explore the range of AI services available on Azure, while offering an overview of key tools like Azure AI Services and Azure Machine Learning. We will also dive into core AI concepts such as machine learning, neural networks, and natural language processing, illustrating how these technologies are applied in real-world scenarios.

Additionally, we will discuss the practical benefits of AI across different sectors and provide a detailed roadmap to help you prepare for the AI-900 certification exam. Finally, we will guide you through the first steps to implementing AI solutions on Azure and equip you with the tools and knowledge necessary for building intelligent applications.

By the end of this chapter, you will have a solid understanding of the key AI principles and Azure services, as well as the strategies required to succeed in the AI-900 exam.

Structure

In this chapter, we will discuss the following topics:

- Introduction to Artificial Intelligence and the AI-900 Exam
- Understanding AI
- Overview of Azure and main services
- AI Services on Azure
- Key concepts in artificial intelligence
- Benefits and applications of AI
- Azure AI Certification Roadmap
- How to Study for the AI-900 Certification
- Registering for the AI-900 exam
- Create your Azure account
- Benefits of the Azure Free Account

Introduction to Artificial Intelligence and the AI-900 Exam

We live in an era where Artificial Intelligence (AI) is radically transforming the world around us.

From facial recognition on our smartphones to advanced recommendation systems used by major streaming platforms, AI is already a part of our daily lives, often in ways we do not even notice.

In this context, it is essential to understand how Microsoft helps professionals validate their foundational AI knowledge through certification.

The **Microsoft Azure AI-900: Azure AI Fundamentals exam** is designed to help learners understand the core principles of artificial intelligence and how these concepts are implemented through Azure services. It introduces key topics like **machine learning**, **Natural Language Processing (NLP)**, **computer vision**, and **conversational AI**, while providing a strong foundation for building intelligent solutions on the Azure platform.

Exam Topic	Weight (%)	Key Focus Area
Describe AI Workloads and Considerations	15 - 20 %	Vision, NLP, Responsible AI
Describe Machine Learning Principles on Azure	15 - 20 %	Model training and deployment
Describe Computer Vision Workloads	15 - 20 %	Azure AI Vision, Face API
Describe Natural Language Processing (NLP) Workloads	15 - 20 %	Azure AI Language, LUIS
Describe Generative AI Workloads	20 - 25 %	Azure Open AI, DALL·E

Table 1.1: *AI-900 Exam Topic Distribution*

By the end of this certification journey, you will not only gain theoretical knowledge but also practical experience in applying Azure AI services to solve real-world problems. This foundational understanding sets the stage for deeper learning in Artificial Intelligence, and will ultimately lead us to explore, next, what AI truly is and how it works.

Understanding AI

In simple terms, Artificial Intelligence refers to the ability of machines to perform tasks that would normally require human intelligence. These tasks can range from solving complex problems and making decisions to recognizing patterns and learning from data. By mimicking aspects of human reasoning, AI not only streamlines processes but also opens new possibilities across various fields—from healthcare and economics to entertainment and transportation.

This book has a clear goal: to prepare you for the **AI-900: Microsoft Azure AI Fundamentals exam,** while demystifying the fundamental concepts of AI. The AI-900 exam is a gateway for professionals seeking to build skills in Artificial Intelligence and its applications within Microsoft's Azure platform. Throughout the following pages, you will find accessible explanations, practical examples, and valuable tips to help you master the exam topics, from AI fundamentals to key Microsoft solutions.

Whether your interest is personal or professional, understanding AI and earning the AI-900 certification will give you a competitive edge in the job market and a solid foundation to further explore this innovative technology. Get ready to embark on a fascinating journey through the world of artificial intelligence and empower yourself to transform this technology into real and impactful solutions.

Overview of Azure and Main Services

Microsoft Azure is a robust cloud computing platform that offers a wide range of services, from basic IT infrastructure to advanced Artificial Intelligence (AI) solutions. Cloud computing enables businesses and developers to access and use resources such as storage, servers, and databases over the internet without the need to maintain physical infrastructure. This flexibility allows organizations to scale operations, balance costs, and allocate resources based on demand.

Before diving into Azure's AI services, it is important to understand the broader scope of key services Azure provides, as many of them serve as the foundation for building and implementing AI solutions.

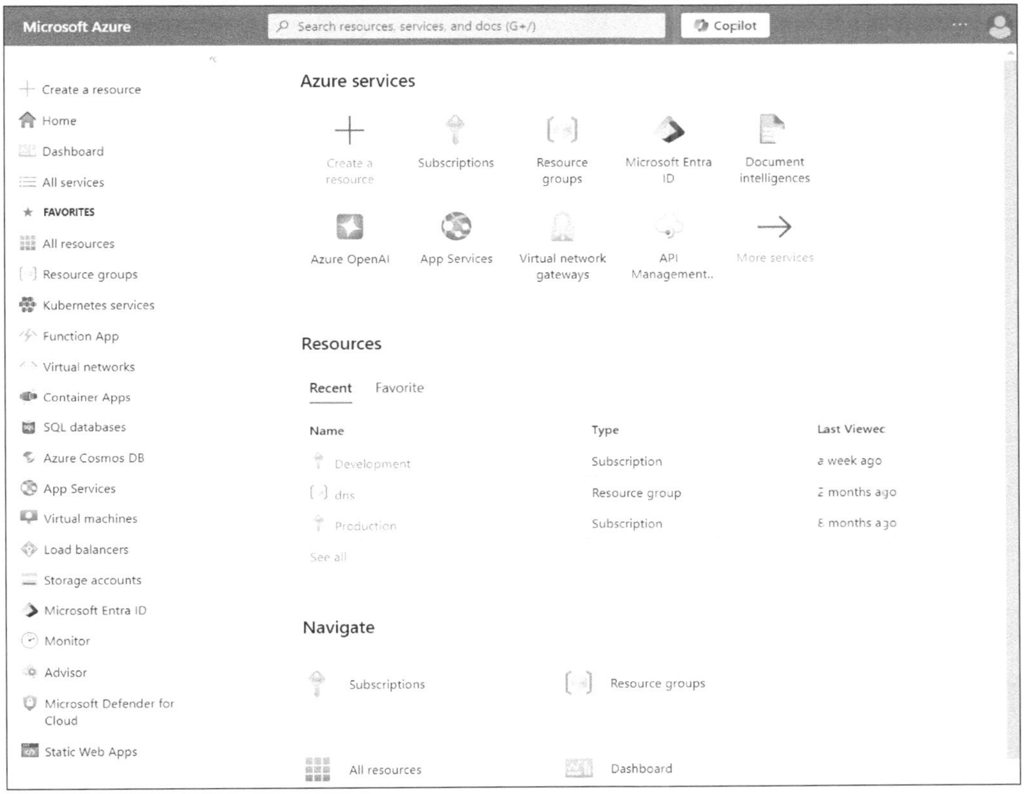

Figure 1.1: *Azure Portal*

Here are some of the primary categories of services available on Azure:

Compute Services

Azure offers the following options for hosting and managing your applications in the cloud:

- **Azure Virtual Machines (VMs):** Virtual machines that allow you to run custom operating systems in the cloud, thus giving you full control over the hosting environment
- **Azure App Service:** A fully managed platform for building and deploying web applications and APIs with automatic scaling
- **Azure Kubernetes Service (AKS):** A managed container orchestration service based on Kubernetes, which allows you to deploy and manage containerized applications at scale

Storage Services

Cloud storage is a key element of modern infrastructure, and Azure offers the following solutions to meet various needs:

- **Azure Blob Storage:** Object storage for handling large volumes of unstructured data such as media files and backups

- **Azure Disk Storage:** Managed disk storage providing high durability and performance; is ideal for supporting virtual machines
- **Azure Files:** A fully managed file share service accessible via SMB protocol, allowing data sharing across instances

Networking Services

Azure provides a range of services for creating, connecting, and securing networks:

- **Azure Virtual Network (VNet):** Allows you to create private networks in the cloud with control over IP addressing, security, and routing
- **Azure Load Balancer:** Distributes network traffic efficiently across different resources to ensure high availability
- **Azure VPN Gateway:** Provides secure connections between on-premises networks and Azure's virtual networks

Database Services

Data management is critical to most cloud solutions, and Azure offers a variety of database services:

- **Azure SQL Database:** A fully-managed relational database service based on SQL Server, offering automatic scaling and high availability
- **Azure Cosmos DB**: A globally distributed NoSQL database designed for high performance and scalability
- **Azure Database for MySQL/PostgreSQL:** Fully managed solutions for MySQL and PostgreSQL databases

Monitoring and Management Services

To ensure your systems are running efficiently, Azure provides the following monitoring and management tools:

- **Azure Monitor:** A service that helps you monitor the performance and health of your applications and infrastructure
- **Azure Automation:** Automates repetitive cloud management tasks such as VM maintenance or running scheduled scripts
- **Azure Security Center:** A unified security solution that provides threat prevention and visibility into the security state of your workloads

DevOps Services

Azure supports the software development lifecycle with the following services that make continuous integration and delivery easier:

- **Azure DevOps:** A suite of tools for agile planning, version control, CI/CD pipelines, and automated testing
- **GitHub Actions:** Integrates with GitHub to automate development workflows, enabling continuous delivery directly from your code repository

Identity and Security Services

Security and identity management are crucial for any cloud application. Therefore, Azure provides the following services for users to achieve this goal:

- **Microsoft Entra ID (formerly known as Azure AD):** A service for identity and access management that provides user authentication and integrates with Single Sign-On (SSO)
- **Azure Key Vault:** A secure storage solution for managing keys, secrets, and certificates, essential for protecting sensitive data

These foundational services enable the implementation of many robust cloud solutions which are crucial while integrating Artificial Intelligence. In the upcoming modules, we will dive deeper into Azure's AI services and explore how they build on these core solutions to create intelligent and innovative applications.

Now that you understand the core Azure services, let us explore how Azure brings intelligence to these foundations through its AI capabilities.

AI Services on Azure

Azure also offers a comprehensive suite of AI services, enabling businesses to build intelligent applications that can perceive, reason, and learn from data. The following services empower organizations to implement advanced AI without needing deep expertise in data science or machine learning:

Azure AI Services

Azure AI Services is a set of pre-built AI models that allow applications to interact with users in more human-like ways and tackles the following key areas:

- **Vision:** Services such as image recognition, object detection, and Optical Character Recognition (OCR)
- **Speech:** Speech-to-text, text-to-speech, and speech translation capabilities
- **Language:** Text analytics, Natural Language Processing (NLP), and sentiment analysis
- **Decision:** Services like anomaly detection and personalization recommendations
- **Search:** Enhances applications with powerful search capabilities through Azure Cognitive Search

Exam Tip: *Remember that Azure AI Services include pre-built models for vision, speech, language, and decision-making workloads.*

Azure Machine Learning

Azure Machine Learning is a cloud-based service that enables data scientists and developers to build, train, and deploy machine learning models at scale. It includes key features like automated ML, model interpretability, and real-time deployment of predictive models.

Azure AI Bot Services

Build intelligent bots that can interact with users across multiple channels, including websites, messaging apps, and virtual assistants.

In the upcoming modules, we will dive deeper into Azure's AI services and explore how they build on these core solutions to create intelligent and innovative applications.

Key Concepts in Artificial Intelligence

Artificial Intelligence (AI) is a broad and constantly evolving field that encompasses various technologies and approaches designed to simulate human intelligence. To build a solid foundation in AI, it is essential to understand its key concepts, which serve as the pillars for more advanced systems. Below, we highlight some of the most important concepts in AI:

Machine Learning (ML)

Machine learning is a subset of AI that enables systems to learn from data and improve over time without being explicitly programmed. It involves training algorithms on large volumes of data to make predictions or decisions based on the patterns identified. Key ML techniques include:

- **Supervised Learning:** Involves training a model with labeled data, where the desired outcome is known (for example, classifying images as "cat" or "dog").
- **Unsupervised Learning:** The model learns from unlabeled data, identifying patterns or clusters without explicit instructions (such as in data clustering).
- **Reinforcement Learning:** A system learns by interacting with the environment and receiving feedback in the form of rewards or penalties, while optimizing its actions over time.

Neural Networks

Neural networks are algorithms inspired by the structure of the human brain. They consist of layers of interconnected "neurons" that process and transmit information. **Deep learning**, a subset of machine learning, uses deep neural networks (with many layers) to handle large and complex data volumes, such as in image and speech recognition. These models can automatically extract features from raw data and perform tasks like classification and prediction with high accuracy.

Natural Language Processing (NLP)

NLP is the area of AI focused on enabling machines to understand, interpret, and generate human language. NLP powers applications such as chatbots, language translation services, and voice virtual assistants. Key concepts include:

- **Text Processing:** Techniques for analyzing and understanding texts, such as tokenization, stemming, and entity recognition
- **Sentiment Analysis:** Determining the sentiment or emotional tone of a text, such as identifying whether a review is positive or negative
- **Language Models:** Models like GPT (Generative Pre-Trained Transformer), which can generate text, answer questions, or engage in conversations based on input data
- **Computer Vision:** This field of AI allows machines to interpret and understand visual data, such as images and videos. Computer vision tasks include object detection, facial recognition, and image classification. Neural networks, especially Convolutional Neural Networks (CNNs), play a crucial role in processing and analyzing visual information.
- **Robotics:** Robotics integrates AI to enable machines to perceive their environment, make decisions, and perform actions autonomously. AI-powered robots can be utilized in industries such as manufacturing, healthcare, and logistics to perform tasks like object manipulation, navigation, and problem-solving.
- **Expert Systems:** Expert systems are AI programs that mimic the decision-making ability of a human expert. These systems rely on a knowledge base (facts and rules) and an inference engine that applies logic to make decisions or solve problems in specific domains like medical diagnosis or financial analysis.

- **Generative AI:** Generative AI refers to AI models that create new data or content based on the input data received. These models, such as GANs (Generative Adversarial Networks) or large language models (like GPT), can generate images, text, music, and more. Generative AI has applications in creative industries, data augmentation, and AI-assisted design.
- **Ethics and Bias in AI:** As AI becomes more integrated into society, ethical concerns arise, particularly regarding privacy, fairness, and bias. It is crucial to develop AI systems that are transparent, fair, and responsible to avoid unintended consequences, such as discrimination or misuse. Understanding and mitigating bias in AI models, ensuring data privacy, and adhering to ethical guidelines are fundamental challenges in AI development.

These key concepts form the foundation of AI and are the starting point for more complex topics and applications. In this book, we will explore in depth how these principles apply to AI solutions within the Microsoft Azure platform to help you create and implement AI models effectively.

After learning the main principles, let us see how AI transforms these concepts into real business value.

Applications and Benefits of AI

Artificial Intelligence (AI) is transforming industries and redefining how businesses operate. Its ability to analyze large volumes of data, automate processes, and make intelligent decisions is driving innovations across various sectors. Understanding the benefits and applications of AI is important for recognizing its potential in current and future technologies. Below, we explore the main advantages and real-world use cases of AI.

Applications of AI

Artificial Intelligence is applied across numerous industries, enabling innovations that enhance efficiency, improve decision-making, and create more personalized and intelligent experiences.

- **Healthcare:** AI is revolutionizing healthcare with diagnostic tools, personalized treatment plans, and drug discovery. AI algorithms analyze medical images (like X-rays or MRIs), predict disease progression, and even assist in robotic surgeries. AI-enabled wearable devices monitor patient health in real-time and alert doctors to potential issues.
- **Finance:** In the financial sector, AI is used for fraud detection, risk assessment, and automated trading. ML models identify suspicious transactions, assess credit risks, and help financial institutions offer more personalized products. AI-based robot-advisors are becoming popular in investment portfolio management.
- **Retail and E-commerce:** AI is transforming retail by enabling personalized shopping experiences through recommendation engines. E-commerce platforms use AI to analyze customer behavior, suggesting products based on their preferences. Additionally, AI-powered chatbots assist in customer service and AI is also used in inventory management and demand forecasting.
- **Manufacturing:** AI plays a significant role in automating manufacturing processes, quality control, and predictive maintenance. AI-powered robots are used to assemble products, while machine learning models analyze sensor data to predict when machines will require repairs, reducing downtime.
- **Transportation:** AI is crucial for the development of autonomous vehicles, helping cars navigate and make real-time decisions. AI is also improving logistics by optimizing routes, managing fleet operations, and reducing fuel consumption Additionally, AI aids in traffic management to make cities smarter and more efficient.

- **Education:** In education, AI enables personalized learning experiences through adaptive platforms that adjust content based on student progress. AI-powered tutors provide additional support, while administrative tasks like grading can be automated. AI is also used for educational data analysis, helping institutions improve curriculum design and student outcomes.
- **Entertainment and Media:** AI is being applied to create content, recommend media, and enhance production in the entertainment industry. Streaming services use AI algorithms to suggest movies, shows, or music based on user preferences. AI is also used in video game development, animation, and even music composition.
- **Agriculture:** AI is transforming agriculture by enabling precision farming. AI-powered drones and sensors monitor crop health, soil conditions, and weather patterns, allowing farmers to optimize irrigation, planting, and harvesting. AI also helps predict yields and prevent pest infestations.
- **Human Resources:** AI is being used to streamline recruitment by analyzing resumes, conducting initial interviews through chatbots, and predicting candidate success based on historical data. AI is also helpful in tasks like employee engagement, performance tracking, and even creating personalized training plans.
- **Energy:** AI is helping energy companies optimize consumption and improve grid management. AI systems analyze energy usage patterns to make real-time adjustments, thereby reducing waste and enhancing efficiency. In the renewable energy sector, AI plays a role in predicting weather patterns to optimize energy generation.

Benefits of AI

Artificial Intelligence offers several advantages that help organizations improve efficiency, make better decisions, and unlock new opportunities for innovation.

- **Increased Efficiency and Automation:** AI excels at automating repetitive and time-consuming tasks and reduces human intervention in processes like data entry, scheduling, and customer service. This leads to greater productivity and fewer errors.
- **Improved Decision-Making:** By analyzing large volumes of data in real-time, AI systems provide valuable insights and forecasts, allowing businesses to make more informed, data-driven decisions. This contributes to better risk management and strategic planning.
- **Cost Reduction:** AI helps lower operational costs by optimizing workflows, enhancing process efficiency, and automating labor-intensive tasks. AI-powered solutions also identify inefficiencies, resulting in significant savings.
- **Enhanced Customer Experiences:** AI is used to create personalized interactions with customers, whether through chatbots, virtual assistants, or tailored recommendations. By providing quick and accurate responses, AI improves customer satisfaction.
- **Innovation and Creativity:** AI enables companies to innovate by providing tools for advanced problem-solving and product development. The ability of AI to generate content, design, and even uncover new insights powers creativity in areas like art, entertainment, and product design.
- **Scalability:** AI-powered solutions can be easily scaled to handle large volumes of data and high-demand environments. This allows businesses to serve more customers or users without compromising performance or accuracy.
- **24/7 Availability:** AI-based systems, such as virtual assistants and chatbots, can operate continuously without interruptions. This ensures that support and services are available around the clock, enhancing operational efficiency.

These benefits and applications showcase the transformative potential of AI across various sectors, enhancing everyday life and business operations. Throughout this book, we will explore how Microsoft Azure offers AI solutions that can drive innovation and efficiency in different areas.

Azure AI Certification Roadmap

As Artificial Intelligence (AI) continues to transform the tech landscape, earning Azure AI certifications can significantly enhance your career opportunities. Microsoft provides a clear certification path that supports professionals at every stage—from foundational learning to advanced solution design.

The Azure AI certification journey follows a natural flow that helps learners build knowledge step by step:

1. **Start with AI-900: Microsoft Azure AI Fundamentals:** Learn the foundational AI concepts and how they are implemented with Azure services.
2. **Advance to AI-102: Designing and Implementing an Azure AI Solution:** Gain hands-on experience building and deploying AI solutions.
3. *(Optional)* **AZ-900: Microsoft Azure Fundamentals:** Strengthen your overall understanding of Azure before diving deeper into AI.
4. *(Optional)* **DP-900 / DP-500 / AZ-305:** Expand your expertise in data and cloud architecture for complete, enterprise-level AI solutions.

This roadmap provides a clear learning path that begins from understanding basic AI principles and ends at designing and deploying intelligent systems using Microsoft Azure.

Microsoft Certified: Azure AI Fundamentals (AI-900)

Figure 1.2: *AI-900 Fundamentals Badge*

The **Microsoft Certified: Azure AI Fundamentals** certification is the perfect starting point for anyone interested in understanding the core AI concepts and how these technologies are applied within the Microsoft Azure ecosystem.

This entry-level certification validates your foundational knowledge of AI principles, including **machine learning**, **computer vision**, **natural language processing**, and **conversational AI**. It also introduces you to key Azure services such as **Azure AI Services**, **Azure Machine Learning**, and **Azure Cognitive Search** and demonstrates how these components integrate to create intelligent, scalable solutions in the cloud.

By earning this certification, candidates gain the ability to identify the most appropriate Azure AI services for various business needs, describe responsible AI principles, and understand how AI can transform real-world processes across different industries.

Key Topics Covered:

- **AI Workloads and Use Cases:** Learn about the different types of AI workloads (vision, speech, language, and decision-making) and the way they address real-world challenges.
- **Machine Learning Fundamentals:** Understand supervised, unsupervised, and reinforcement learning, (including how models are trained, evaluated, and deployed using Azure Machine Learning).
- **Core Azure AI Services:** Explore services such as **Azure AI Vision**, **Azure AI Language**, **Azure AI Speech**, and **Azure AI Search** to understand their capabilities and integration points.
- **Responsible AI and Ethics:** Gain awareness of Microsoft's six principles for responsible AI – fairness, reliability, privacy, inclusiveness, transparency, and accountability.
- **Common AI Scenarios:** Identify business applications for AI across industries like finance, healthcare, retail, and manufacturing.

Ideal for:

- **Beginners in AI and Cloud Computing:** No prior experience with programming or data science required
- **Business Professionals:** Those seeking to understand how AI can enhance organizational processes and decision-making
- **Technical Professionals:** Developers, IT specialists, or analysts who want a foundational overview of Azure's AI capabilities

Exam Information:

- **Exam Name:** AI-900: *Microsoft Azure AI Fundamentals*
- **Exam Format:** Multiple-choice and scenario-based questions
- **Duration:** 60 minutes (approximately)
- **Question Count:** Around 40–60 questions
- **Languages Available:** English, Portuguese, Spanish, Japanese, German, and others
- **Cost:** Varies by region (typically around USD 99)
- **Passing Score:** 700 (out of 1,000)

Learning Outcomes

By completing this certification, you will be able to:

- Explain key AI concepts and their business relevance.
- Identify Azure services that support AI workloads.
- Recognize the role of machine learning in AI solutions.
- Describe the principles of responsible AI.
- Build a strong foundation for more advanced certifications such as **AI-102: Designing and Implementing an Azure AI Solution**.

In summary, the **AI-900 certification** not only establishes your understanding of artificial intelligence in Azure but also prepares you to confidently explore more advanced AI technologies and certifications in the Microsoft ecosystem.

Microsoft Certified: Azure AI Engineer Associate (AI-102)

Figure 1.3: *AI-102 Associate Badge*

The **Microsoft Certified: Azure AI Engineer Associate** certification is designed for professionals who want to **design, build, and deploy AI solutions using Microsoft Azure AI services**. It validates your ability to translate business requirements into scalable, production-ready AI systems that integrate natural language processing, computer vision, and conversational intelligence.

This certification goes beyond theory – it focuses on **hands-on implementation** of AI models, demonstrating how to operationalize machine learning pipelines, integrate APIs, and deliver intelligent applications using Azure resources.

Key Topics Covered:

- **Designing AI Solutions:** Plan, architect, and select the right Azure AI services for different workloads like vision, language, and decision-making.
- **Implementing Azure AI Services:** Use **Azure AI Vision**, **Azure AI Language**, and **Azure AI Speech** for image analysis, understanding text, and voice recognition.
- **Building Conversational Bots:** Create intelligent chatbots and virtual assistants using the **Azure AI Bot Service** integrated with **Azure AI Language** and **Azure OpenAI**.
- **Integrating Machine Learning Models:** Connect custom ML models from **Azure Machine Learning** into AI-powered applications.
- **Securing, Monitoring, and Scaling Solutions:** Apply best practices for authentication, performance optimization, and responsible AI deployment.

Ideal for:

- **AI Engineers and Developers:** Professionals building end-to-end intelligent applications on Azure
- **Data Scientists and Solution Architects:** Those integrating machine learning models with enterprise systems
- **Technical Professionals:** Developers who have already completed the AI-900 and want to move into implementation and solution design

Exam Information:

- **Exam Name:** AI-102: *Designing and Implementing an Azure AI Solution*
- **Level:** Associate
- **Format:** Multiple-choice and practical scenario-based questions

- **Duration:** ~100 minutes
- **Question Count:** 40–60 questions
- **Passing Score:** 700 / 1000
- **Languages Available:** English, Portuguese, Japanese, Chinese (Simplified), and others
- **Prerequisites:** No mandatory prerequisites, but completing **AI-900** is highly recommended.

Optional: Microsoft Certified: Azure Fundamentals (AZ-900)

The **Microsoft Certified: Azure Fundamentals (AZ-900)** certification is an excellent starting point for professionals who are new to cloud computing and want to understand the core concepts, services, and pricing models of Microsoft Azure.

Although it is not AI-specific, this certification provides the **foundational cloud knowledge** necessary to fully grasp how Azure supports AI workloads, data solutions, and modern applications. It helps candidates build confidence in navigating the Azure portal, understanding its global infrastructure, and identifying the services to use in different scenarios.

Key Topics Covered:

- **Cloud Concepts:** Understand the fundamentals of cloud computing, including scalability, elasticity, high availability, fault tolerance, and disaster recovery.
- **Core Azure Services:** Learn about Azure's main service categories such as compute, networking, storage, and databases, along with their role in modern applications.
- **Azure Governance and Management:** Explore Azure Resource Manager (ARM), management groups, and cost control tools like Azure Pricing Calculator and Cost Management.
- **Security, Privacy, and Compliance:** Learn how Azure protects data through network security, identity management, and encryption.
- **Azure Pricing and Support:** Understand subscription models, Service-Level Agreements (SLAs), and available support plans.

Ideal for:

- **Beginners in Cloud Computing:** Individuals exploring cloud concepts for the first time
- **Business and Non-Technical Professionals:** Managers, analysts, or sales teams looking to understand cloud solutions conceptually
- **Technical Professionals Transitioning to Azure:** Developers, IT administrators, or engineers coming from other cloud platforms or on-prem environments

Exam Information:

- **Exam Name:** AZ-900: *Microsoft Azure Fundamentals*
- **Level:** Fundamental
- **Format:** Multiple-choice and scenario-based questions
- **Duration:** ~60 minutes
- **Passing Score:** 700 / 1000
- **Languages Available:** English, Portuguese, Spanish, Japanese, Korean, German, and others
- **Cost:** Varies by region (typically USD 99)
- **Prerequisites:** None – this certification is entry-level.

Therefore, **AZ-900** serves as the **foundation of the Microsoft certification ecosystem**, as it provides professionals with the essential cloud knowledge to build and scale intelligent solutions using Microsoft Azure.

Optional Certifications to Expand Your AI Expertise

Beyond the core AI certifications, there are optional paths that can further enhance your expertise, depending on your role and focus. Below are some additional certifications for AI professionals to expand their skill set and improve their career prospects.

- **DP-900: Microsoft Azure Data Fundamentals:** Provides foundational knowledge of core data concepts and how they are implemented using Microsoft Azure data services; ideal for those new to data management
- **DP-500: Azure Enterprise Data Analyst Associate:** Focuses on designing and implementing enterprise-scale data analytics solutions using Microsoft Azure and Power BI; ideal for professionals working with data modeling, reporting, and business intelligence
- **AZ-305: Designing Microsoft Azure Infrastructure Solutions:** Focuses on designing cloud and hybrid solutions on Azure, covering areas like governance, security, and cost management; ideal for solution architects looking to implement infrastructure solutions on the platform

Through these optional certifications, AI professionals can expand their expertise beyond AI and explore related areas like data science, engineering, and infrastructure design. This broader skill set not only enhances their technical capabilities but also opens up new career opportunities in fields such as cloud architecture, data engineering, and solution design, thus, making them more versatile and competitive in the rapidly evolving AI and cloud landscape.

How to Study for the AI-900 Certification

The **Microsoft Azure AI Fundamentals (AI-900)** certification is a great opportunity to build a solid foundation in artificial intelligence and its key services on the Azure cloud. To succeed in the exam, it is essential to adopt an organized and focused study strategy. Here are some tips on how to prepare for the exam:

Understand the Exam Content

The first step is to familiarize yourself with the topics covered in the AI-900 certification. The exam is divided into five main areas, as follows:

- Describe Artificial Intelligence workloads and considerations (15–20%).
- Describe fundamental principles of machine learning on Azure (20–25%).
- Describe features of computer vision workloads on Azure (15–20%).
- Describe features of Natural Language Processing (NLP) workloads on Azure (15–20%).
- Describe features of generative AI workloads on Azure (15–20%).

Each topic has a different weight in the exam, so it is important to prioritize those with higher percentages. To check the weights and exam content updates, access the official documentation link here: https://learn.microsoft.com/en-us/credentials/certifications/resources/study-guides/ai-900.

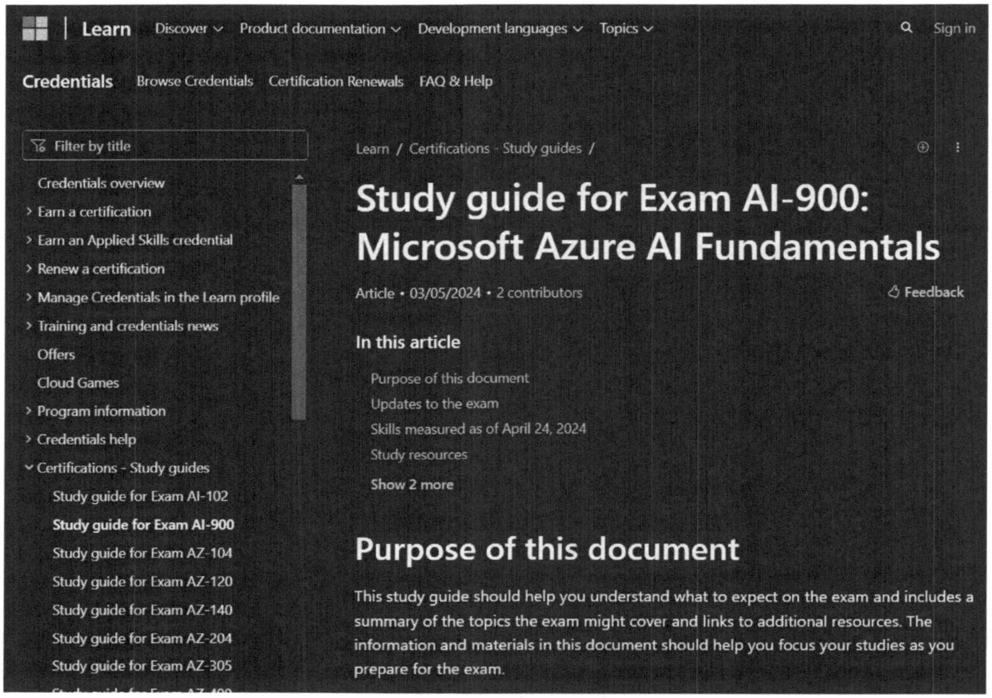

Figure 1.4*: AI-900 Official Documentation*

Here is a quick summary of each of the five AI-900 certification topics:

- **Describe Artificial Intelligence workloads and considerations (15–20%)**

  Introduces fundamental AI concepts, including types of workloads (vision, speech, language, decision-making) and the ethical and governance considerations involved in implementing AI solutions.

- **Describe fundamental principles of machine learning on Azure (20–25%)**

  Explains the basic concepts of machine learning, including the distinction between supervised and unsupervised learning, and how ML models are trained and deployed via Azure Machine Learning.

- **Describe features of computer vision workloads on Azure (15–20%)**

  Focuses on Azure's computer vision services such as Azure Computer Vision and Face API, which enable image analysis, object detection, and facial recognition in applications.

- **Describe features of Natural Language Processing workloads on Azure (15–20%)**

  Covers Azure's natural language processing services, such as Text Analytics and Language Understanding (LUIS), used for sentiment analysis, translation, and extracting insights from text.

- **Describe features of generative AI workloads on Azure (15–20%)**

  Presents the use of generative AI on Azure, including text and image generation models based on machine learning, highlighting services like Azure OpenAI and Azure Cognitive Services.

In this book, we will guide you through the learning journey for the AI-900 certification by following the official Microsoft curriculum. You will gain a solid understanding of each topic, reinforced with practical examples and insights. Together, we will cover all the essential areas step by step to help you prepare well, pass the exam, and apply AI concepts effectively using Microsoft Azure.

Leverage Microsoft's Official Resources

Microsoft Learn offers a series of **free courses** that cover all the content required for the AI-900 certification. These courses are well-structured and include hands-on labs where you can apply what you are learning in real-world environments.

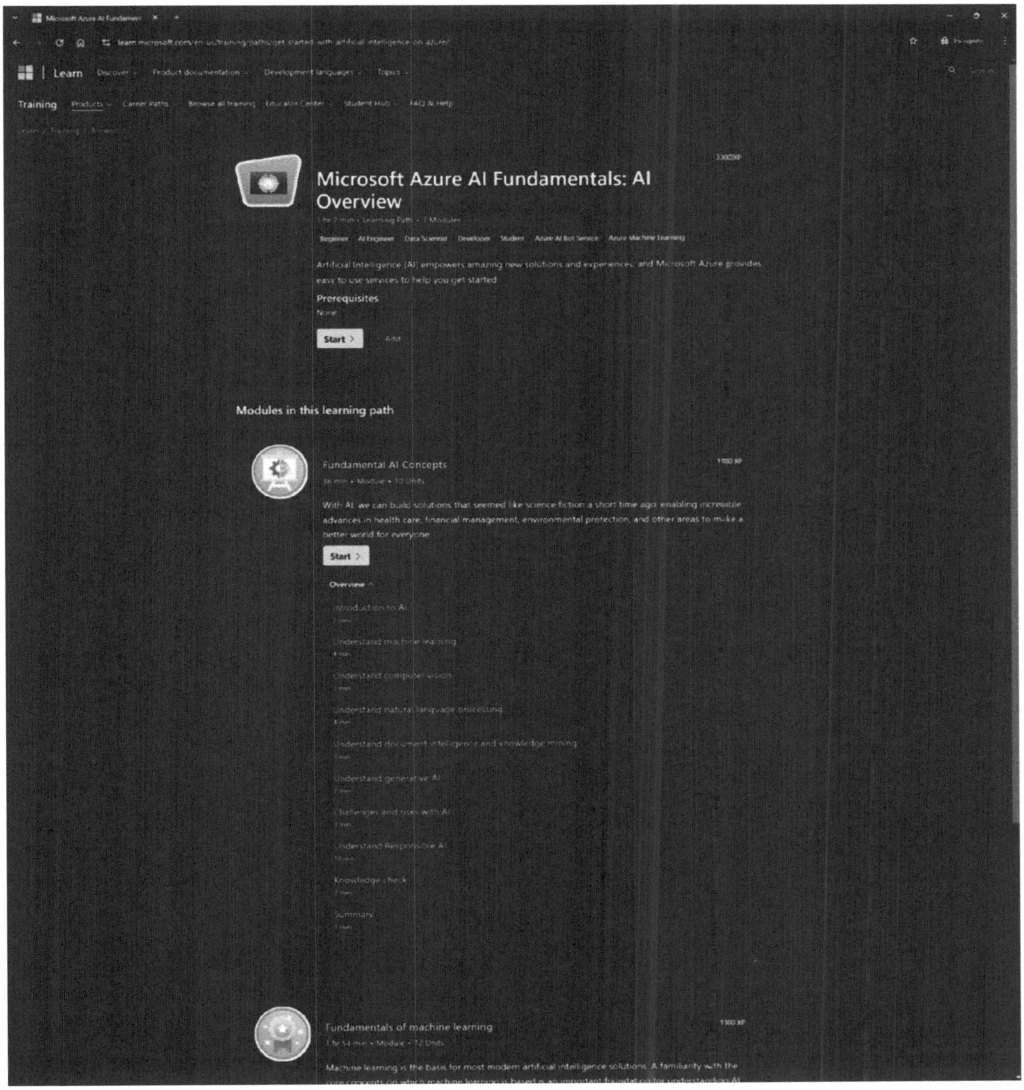

Figure 1.5: *Microsoft Learn*

Practice with Azure AI Services

Hands-on practice is crucial for consolidating concepts. Create a free **Azure** account and try out key services such as:

- **Azure Machine Learning** to build, train, and deploy machine learning models
- **Azure AI Services** to explore image analysis, speech, and text recognition

- **Azure Bot Service** to build smart, interactive bots

This practical experience will reinforce theoretical knowledge and help you understand how to apply these services in real-world scenarios.

Practice Tests and Mock Exams

One of the best ways to prepare for the exam is by taking mock exams. Use platforms like **Whizlabs**, **MeasureUp**, or other specialized sites offering **practice tests** for the AI-900. These mock exams can help you identify areas for improvement and familiarize you with the format of the questions you might see in the exam.

To complement your preparation, Microsoft also provides official study resources and practice assessments. Some of these are mentioned as follows:

- **Microsoft Learn – AI-900 Official Study Path:** https://learn.microsoft.com/en-us/training/paths/get-started-with-artificial-intelligence-on-azure/

  This free learning path covers all exam objectives through guided modules, practical examples, and hands-on labs.

- **Microsoft Practice Assessment for AI-900:** https://learn.microsoft.com/en-us/credentials/certifications/practice-assessments-for-microsoft-certifications

  This official Microsoft page provides free practice assessments that simulate real exam questions and help evaluate your readiness for the AI-900 exam.

- **MeasureUp – Microsoft Official Practice Test (AI-900):** https://www.measureup.com/microsoft-practice-test-ai-900-microsoft-azure-ai-fundamentals.html

  The official MeasureUp test offers a large bank of realistic questions with detailed explanations, timed sessions, and exam simulation features.

By combining these resources with consistent study and hands-on practice in Azure, you will be able to build the confidence and gain the knowledge required to pass the **AI-900 certification exam** successfully.

Organize Your Study Schedule

Setting up a study schedule is essential for maintaining consistency. Break down your preparation time into focused blocks to ensure that you cover all key topics of the AI-900 exam in a balanced and structured way. A well-organized plan will help you maintain discipline and allocate time effectively for both study and practice.

Here are two example study plans you can follow or adapt depending on your availability and prior experience:

Two-Week Intensive Plan (for experienced learners)

If you already have some experience with Azure or AI concepts, a two-week plan allows for focused and accelerated preparation. This might look like the following:

- **Days 1–2:** Review fundamental AI concepts, workloads, and responsible AI principles. Explore the Azure Portal to understand its structure.
- **Days 3–4:** Study the basics of machine learning, including supervised and unsupervised learning. Complete Microsoft Learn modules on Azure Machine Learning.
- **Days 5–6:** Explore Azure Cognitive Services such as Vision, Speech, and Language. Perform hands-on exercises in AI Studio or Azure Portal.

- **Days 7–8:** Build a simple chatbot using Azure AI Bot Service and understand how it integrates with Azure AI Language.
- **Days 9–10:** Review Microsoft's Responsible AI framework and principles for ethical AI use.
- **Days 11–12:** Take practice exams using MeasureUp or Microsoft Practice Assessments. Review your results and focus on weak areas.
- **Days 13–14:** Revisit key concepts, services, and exam objectives. Conduct a final self-assessment before the test.

Four-Week Standard Plan (recommended for beginners)

If you are new to AI or Azure, a four-week schedule provides more time for comprehension and practical exercises.

- **Week 1:** Begin with the fundamentals of AI, common workloads, and Responsible AI. Familiarize yourself with the Azure Portal and core services.
- **Week 2:** Focus on machine learning and cognitive services. Explore Azure Machine Learning, Vision, and Language capabilities through guided labs.
- **Week 3:** Study conversational AI concepts and develop a basic chatbot project using Azure AI Bot Service. Review real-world AI use cases.
- **Week 4:** Dedicate time to practice exams and revision. Review incorrect answers and reinforce areas needing improvement before scheduling your certification test.

By following a structured study plan—whether over two weeks or four, you will be able to maintain a steady pace and ensure full coverage of the exam material. Combine theoretical study with hands-on experimentation in Azure to build practical understanding and confidence for the **AI-900 certification exam**.

Exam Tip: *The AI-900 exam emphasizes practical understanding: practice with Azure AI Services to reinforce your knowledge.*

Registering for AI-900 exam

Registering for the AI-900 exam is a straightforward process that involves a few key steps. Here is a simple guide to help you navigate through the registration:

1. **Visit the Microsoft Certification Page**
    a. Go to the official Microsoft Learn website: https://learn.microsoft.com/en-us/credentials/.
    b. Search for the **AI-900: Microsoft Azure AI Fundamentals** exam or visit the specific: https://learn.microsoft.com/en-us/credentials/certifications/azure-ai-fundamentals/?practice-assessment-type=certification.

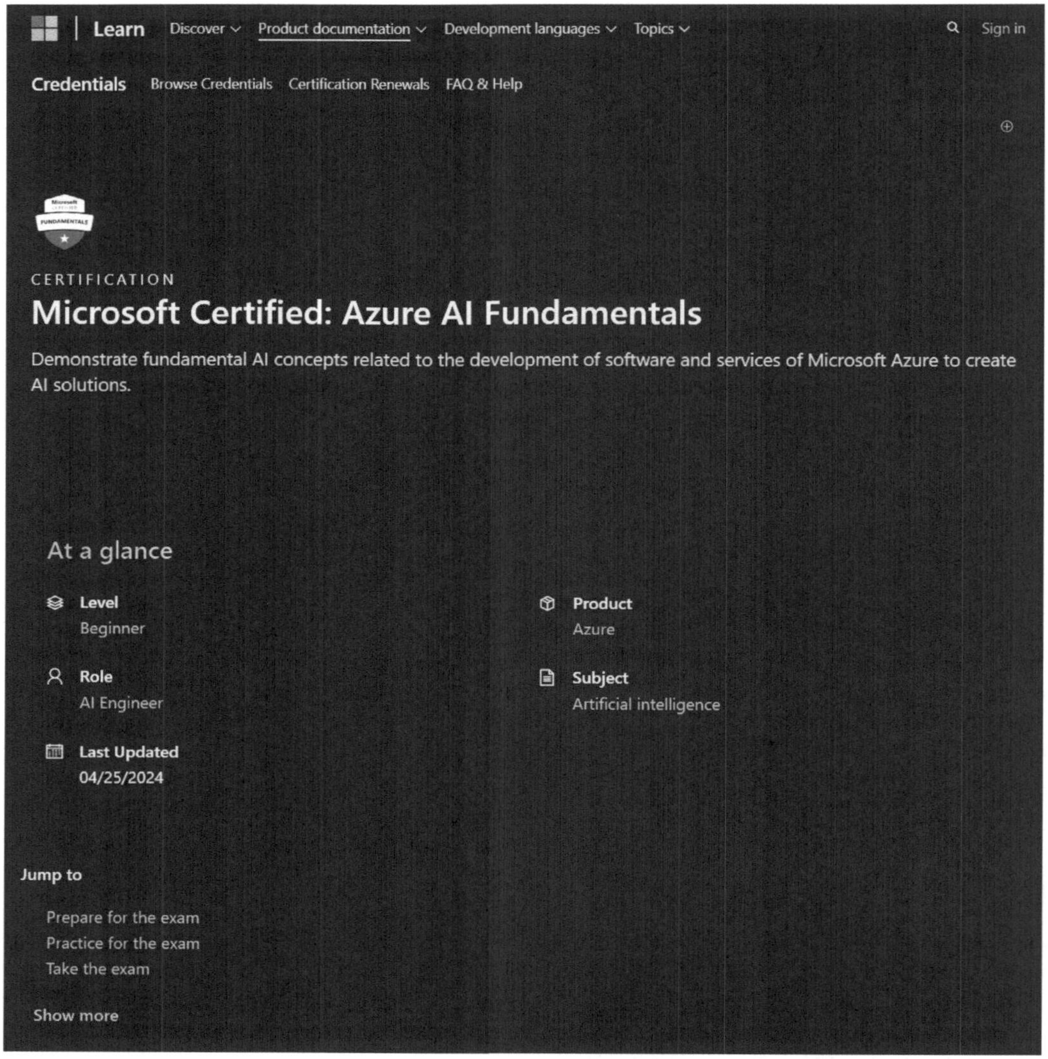

Figure 1.6: *AI-900: Microsoft Azure AI Fundamentals Official Page*

 c. Search for the **AI-900: Microsoft Azure AI Fundamentals** exam or visit the specific page at: https://learn.microsoft.com/en-us/credentials/certifications/azure-ai-fundamentals/?practice-assessment-type=certification.

2. **Sign in to Your Microsoft Account**

 a. You will now need a Microsoft account to register for the exam. If you do not have one, you can create it for free on the Microsoft website.

 b. After signing in, navigate to the AI-900 exam page and click "`Take the Exam`". This will take you to the registration process.

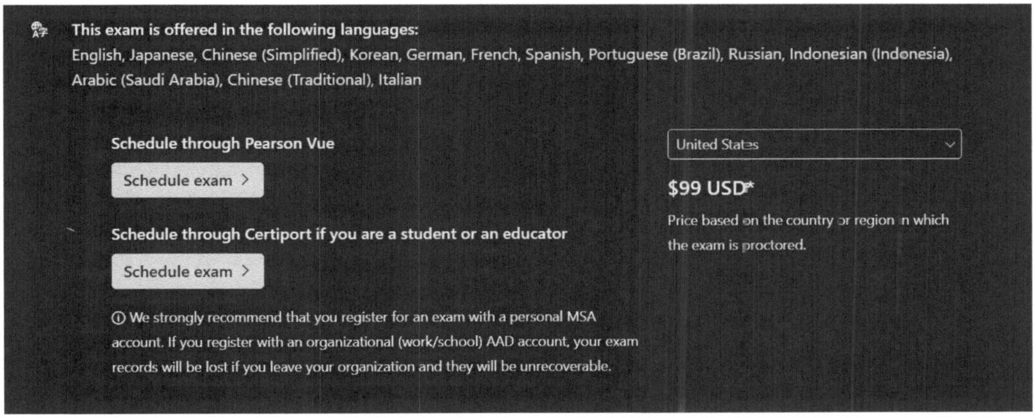

Figure 1.7: *AI-900: Microsoft Azure AI Fundamentals Schedule Exam*

3. **Select Your Exam Format**
   a. Microsoft offers different options to take the exam such as:
      i. **Online Proctored**: Take the exam from home or another location, with a proctor monitoring you via webcam.
      ii. **In-Person**: Visit a testing center near you. Pearson VUE and Certiport are Microsoft's two main partners for in-person testing.
4. **Choose Your Preferred Date and Time**
   a. Once you have selected the exam format, you can view available dates and times. Be sure to choose a time that gives you enough space to review your study materials.
5. **Select Your Preferred Language**
   a. Microsoft offers the AI-900 exam in multiple languages. You will need to select the language in which you prefer to take the exam. Ensure that you are comfortable with the language you choose as the exam questions will be presented in that language.
6. **Apply a Discount Code (If Available)**
   a. If you have a **discount code or voucher**, there is an option to apply for it during the payment process. Be sure to enter the code in the designated field before proceeding to payment and check if the discount has been applied.
7. **Pay for the Exam**
   a. The cost of the AI-900 exam varies by country or region. You can see the exact price when registering. Be sure to verify the final price, especially if you have applied for a discount code.
   b. There may also be discounts available, such as student discounts or vouchers provided by your organization.
8. **Prepare for Exam Day**
   a. If you are taking the online proctored exam, ensure you have a quiet space, a working webcam, and a stable internet connection. Microsoft also recommends running a system test to ensure your computer is ready.

9. **Take the Exam**
    a. On exam day, whether in person or online, make sure that you have a valid ID ready. For online exams, you will also need to show your surroundings to the proctor.

To conclude, after completing the registration and payment process, you will be officially enrolled in the AI-900 exam. Make sure you are well-prepared by reviewing study materials and practicing with mock exams. In the upcoming chapters, you will find everything you need to master the topics covered in the exam and ensure your success in achieving the **Microsoft Azure AI Fundamentals** certification. Best of luck on your certification journey!

Exam Tip: *You can retake the AI-900 exam after 24 hours if you do not pass on your first attempt.*

Create Your Azure Account

To follow along with the hands-on exercises in this book and better understand Azure AI services, it is essential to have access to a Microsoft Azure account. Fortunately, Microsoft offers a free plan that allows you to explore many of its features, including AI services, without upfront costs. You can create your Azure account via the following steps:

Steps to Create Your Azure Account

1. **Visit the Azure Website**
    a. Navigate to page https://azure.microsoft.com/en-us/.
2. **Click "`Get Started with Azure`"**
    a. This will guide you to the registration process.
3. **Click "`Try Azure for free`"**
    a. If you have never created an Azure account, select `Try Azure for Free` option. If you have had an account in the past, you'll get the benefits of the free account.
4. **Sign in or Create a Microsoft Account**
    a. If you already have a Microsoft account, sign in. If you do not have one, create a new account by following the prompts.

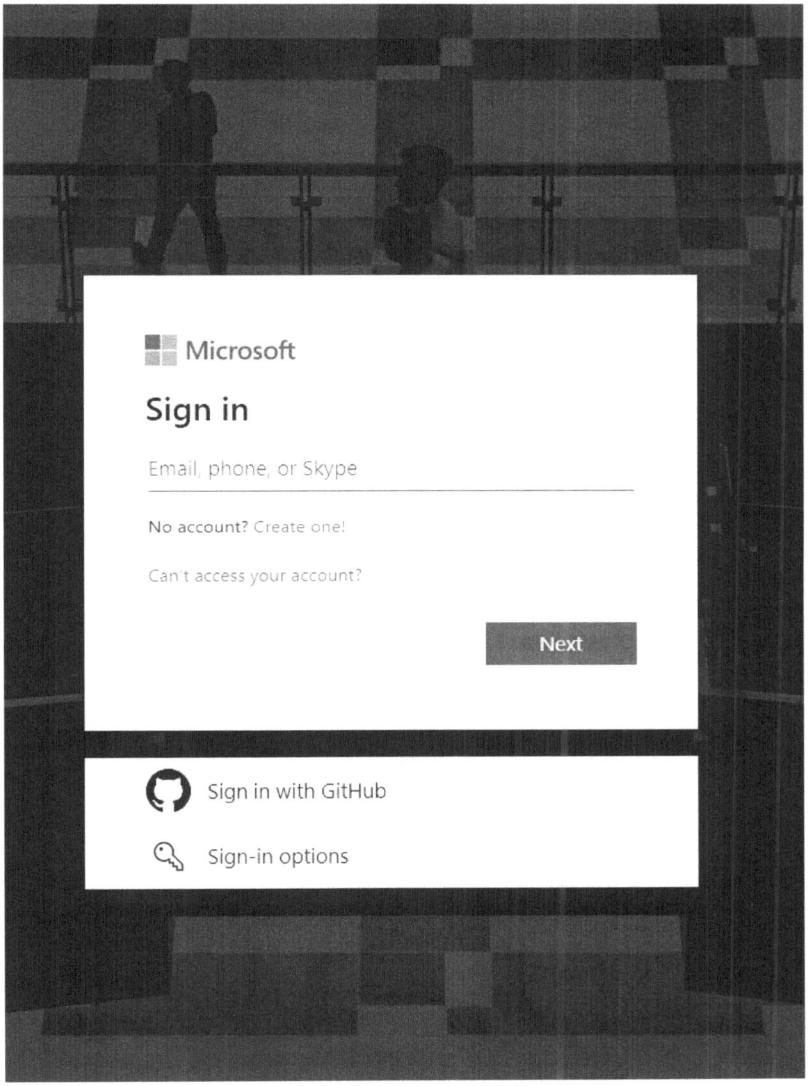

Figure 1.8: *Sign in Page for a Microsoft Account*

5. **Provide Personal Information**
    a. Fill in your name, email, and the country of residence.

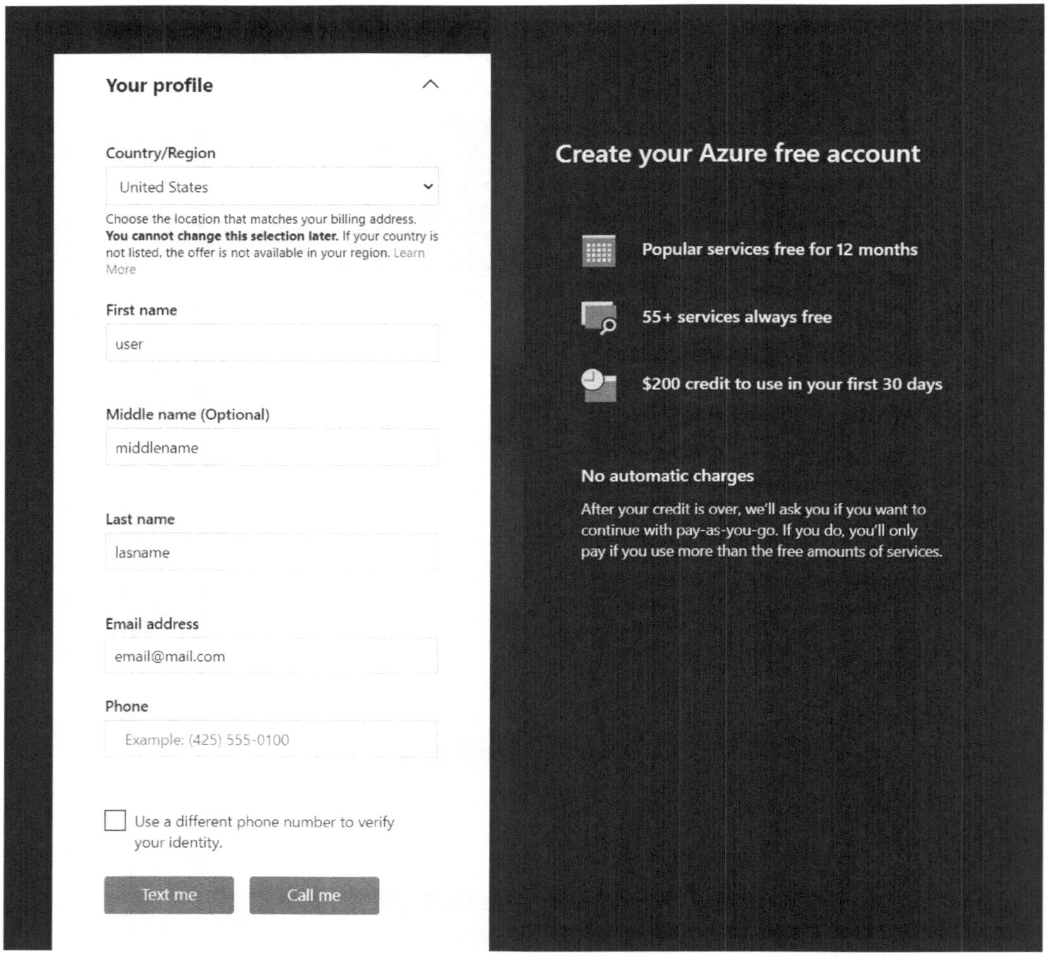

Figure 1.9: *Provide Personal Information*

6. **Phone Verification**
   a. Microsoft will ask for a phone number to send a verification code via SMS or a call. Enter the code to proceed.
7. **Payment Details**
   a. You will need to add a credit or debit card. No charges will be made unless you exceed the free services or credits available.
8. **Activate the Free Subscription**
   a. Microsoft provides:
      i. $200 in credits for the first 30 days
      ii. Access to more than 25 services, including AI services, for free
      iii. 12 months of free services like virtual machines, databases, and storage

9. **Access the Azure Portal**
    a. Once the setup is complete, you will be directed to the Azure portal where you can begin exploring services.

Benefits of the Azure Free Account

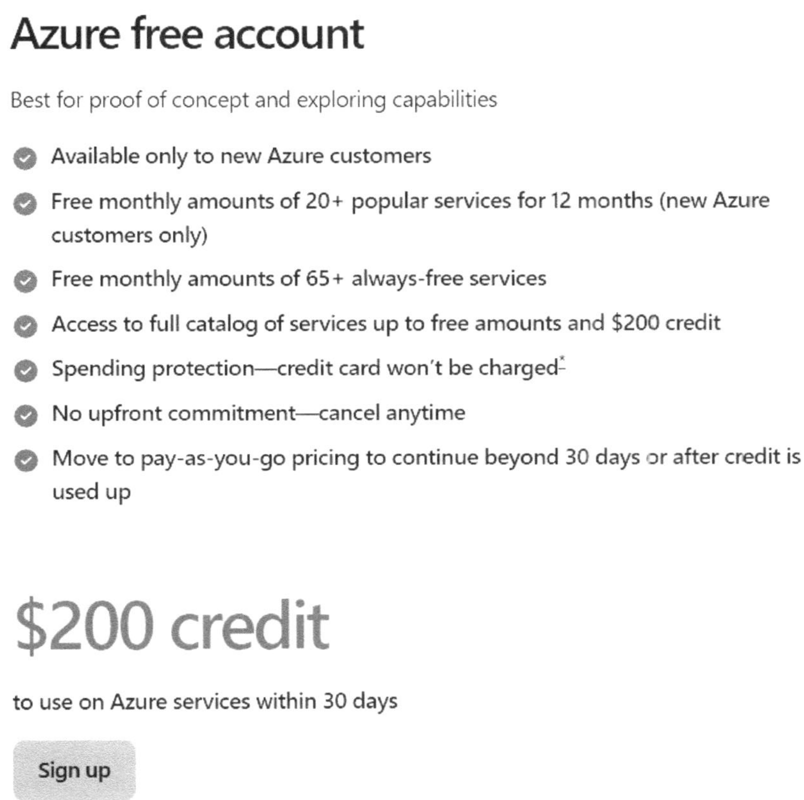

Figure 1.10: *Azure Free Account*

The Azure Free Account offers a valuable opportunity for individuals and organizations to explore the Microsoft Azure cloud platform without any initial financial commitment. Whether you are preparing for certification like the AI-900 or simply want to experiment with Azure's services, the free account provides access to a wide range of tools and features that help you build, deploy, and manage applications. Here are some key benefits:

- **Free Credits to Get Started**
    - Upon signing up, you receive $200 in free credits, valid for 30 days. This allows you to explore various Azure services, from virtual machines tc AI tools without worrying about costs during your initial experiments and learning period.

- **Access to Popular Services for 12 Months**
  - Azure's free account includes access to over 25 services at no cost for 12 months. These include virtual machines, storage, databases, and more, thereby giving you ample time to learn and develop solutions.
  - Some key free services include:
    - **Linux and Windows Virtual Machines** for development and testing
    - **Azure SQL Database** for building and managing databases
    - **Blob Storage** for storing unstructured data like images and videos
- **Always-Free AI Services**
  - Along with the $200 credits and 12-month free services, Azure offers certain AI services that are always free within certain usage limits. This includes:
    - **Azure AI Services** for tasks such as natural language processing, image recognition, and speech analysis
    - **Azure Machine Learning** for building, training, and deploying machine learning models
- **No Charges Until You Choose**
  - The Azure free account ensures you will not be billed unless you choose to upgrade or exceed the free usage limits. This pay-as-you-go model offers flexibility and peace of mind, which allows you to explore Azure services without the fear of unexpected costs.
- **Learn in a Real Cloud Environment**
  - By using the free account, you gain hands-on experience in a production-grade cloud environment. This is invaluable for learning how to manage cloud resources, automate processes, and build scalable applications, which are crucial skills to master for certifications and real-world projects.
- **Scalability and Flexibility**
  - Azure's free account allows you to test and build small-scale applications with the potential to scale as needed. Once your needs grow, you can easily transition to paid plans without starting over, thus ensuring smooth continuity.
- **Global Availability**
  - Azure operates across a large network of data centers worldwide and ensures that you can build projects with excellent performance, while ensuring scalability and eliminating redundancy. You can experiment with Azure's global infrastructure to better understand how it benefits real-world solutions.
- **Security and Compliance**
  - Even with a free account, you will have access to Azure's enterprise-grade security features, including network security groups, identity and access management, and encryption. This ensures that even your test projects are built with security in mind.

Why This is Important

Throughout this book, you will find hands-on examples and exercises that use Azure's AI services. Having an Azure account allows you to practice and understand these services in a real-world setting, thus helping you solidify the concepts and skills needed for the AI-900 certification.

By creating your account now, you will be prepared to engage with these practical exercises as you progress through the chapters.

Conclusion

We are now familiar with the essential concepts of artificial intelligence and Azure's comprehensive services. We have explored the range of Azure offerings, including compute, storage, networking, databases, and AI services, as well as the benefits and applications of AI. With this knowledge, you are now prepared to dive deeper into Azure AI solutions and navigate the Azure certification roadmap. You also have the tools to create your Azure account, understand the Azure Portal, and effectively prepare for the AI-900 certification exam.

In the next chapter, we will begin studying for the AI-900 certification by focusing on the ***Describe Artificial Intelligence workloads and considerations (15–20%)*** domain. This section introduces key AI concepts, such as different types of AI workloads (vision, speech, language, and decision-making) and the ethical and governance considerations involved in implementing AI solutions.

Points to Remember

- Azure provides a wide range of services, including compute, storage, networking, and AI services, all crucial for developing AI solutions.
- Artificial intelligence offers immense benefits that are widely applicable across industries.
- An Azure certification, especially the AI-900, is an excellent starting point to anhance your AI skills.

Key Terms

- **Artificial Intelligence (AI):** The ability of machines to perform tasks that typically require human intelligence, such as problem-solving, decision-making, and pattern recognition
- **Azure AI Services:** A suite of pre-built AI models in Microsoft Azure that enable applications to interact with users in human-like ways, while encompassing areas like vision, speech, language, decision-making, and search
- **Machine Learning (ML):** A subset of AI that enables systems to learn from data and improve over time without explicit programming. It includes supervised learning, unsupervised learning, and reinforcement learning.
- **Neural Networks:** Algorithms inspired by the human brain's structure, consisting of interconnected layers of "neurons" used for complex tasks like image and speech recognition
- **Natural Language Processing (NLP):** The field of AI focused on enabling machines to understand, interpret, and generate human language, while powering applications like chatbots and language translation
- **Computer Vision:** A branch of AI that allows machines to interpret and understand visual data, including tasks like object detection and facial recognition
- **Robotics:** The integration of AI in machines to enable them to perceive their environment, make decisions, and perform tasks autonomously
- **Expert Systems:** AI programs that mimic the decision-making ability of human experts using a knowledge base and an inference engine to solve problems in specific domains
- **Generative AI:** AI models that create new data or content based on input data, with applications in areas such as image and text generation
- **Ethics and Bias in AI:** The study of ethical concerns related to AI, including privacy, fairness, and bias, thereby emphasizing the importance of transparent and responsible AI development
- **Azure Machine Learning:** A cloud-based service that allows data scientists and developers to build, train, and deploy machine learning models at scale

- **Azure AI Bot Services:** Services for creating intelligent bots that interact with users across various channels, enhancing customer engagement and support

Multiple Choice Questions

1. What is the primary benefit of cloud computing?
    a. Requires physical infrastructure
    b. Limited scalability
    c. Access to resources over the internet
    d. Higher costs than on-premises solutions
2. Which Azure service allows you to run custom operating systems in the cloud?
    a. Azure App Service
    b. Azure Virtual Machines (VMs)
    c. Azure Blob Storage
    d. Azure Kubernetes Service (AKS)
3. What type of storage does Azure Blob Storage provide?
    a. Managed disk storage for virtual machines
    b. Object storage for unstructured data
    c. Fully managed file share service
    d. Structured storage for relational databases
4. What does Azure Virtual Network (VNet) allow you to do?
    a. Distribute network traffic across resources
    b. Create private networks in the cloud
    c. Provide secure connections between on-premises networks and Azure
    d. Monitor the performance of applications
5. Which Azure service is designed for identity and access management?
    a. Azure Key Vault
    b. Azure Automation
    c. Microsoft Entra ID
    d. Microsoft Defender for Cloud
6. What is the purpose of Azure Monitor?
    a. To store large volumes of unstructured data
    b. To provide user authentication
    c. To automate cloud management tasks
    d. To monitor the performance and health of applications and infrastructure

7. Which of the following is a type of AI service offered by Azure?
    a. Azure DevOps
    b. Azure Blob Storage
    c. Azure AI Service
    d. Azure Virtual Machines
8. What does Machine Learning (ML) enable systems to do?
    a. Operate without human input
    b. Learn from data and improve over time
    c. Create new data or content
    d. Mimic human decision-making
9. In the context of AI, what is Natural Language Processing (NLP) focused on?
    a. Understanding and generating human language
    b. Managing and storing large datasets
    c. Automating business processes
    d. Analyzing network traffic
10. What is one of the key benefits of using AI in business?
    a. Decreased operational costs
    b. Increased human intervention
    c. Reduced availability of services
    d. Limited data processing capabilities

Answers

1. c
2. b
3. b
4. b
5. c
6. d
7. c
8. b
9. a
10. a

CHAPTER 2
Identify Features of Common AI Workloads

Introduction

In the previous chapter, you learned about the fundamental concepts of Artificial Intelligence (AI), including how AI systems learn from data to recognize patterns, make predictions, and support decision-making. Building on that foundation, this chapter will focus on the main types of AI workloads and their applications in real-world scenarios.

An AI workload refers to a specific type of task that an AI system is designed to perform, such as analyzing images, understanding language, and generating content. Each workload relies on specialized techniques and models that allow machines to process information intelligently and efficiently.

In this chapter, we will explore five major categories of AI workloads: **computer vision**, **natural language processing**, **knowledge mining**, **document intelligence**, and **generative AI**. Each section introduces the key features, common use cases, and Azure services that support these workloads.

By the end of this chapter, you will be able to understand how these workloads function individually and how they can be combined to create intelligent, scalable, and secure AI solutions in Microsoft Azure, thereby helping organizations automate processes, gain insights, and deliver more personalized experiences.

Structure

In this chapter, we will discuss the following topics:

- Identifying Features of Content Moderation and Personalization Workloads
- Identifying Computer Vision Workloads
- Identifying Natural Language Processing Workloads
- Identifying Knowledge Mining Workloads
- Identifying Document Intelligence Workloads
- Identifying Features of Generative AI Workloads

Identifying Features of Content Moderation and Personalization Workloads

In today's digital landscape, where billions of users interact daily on social media, e-commerce platforms, and streaming services, content moderation and personalization have become essential to ensure a safe and enjoyable user experience. Imagine opening your news feed to find only posts that genuinely interest you or accessing a shopping site that recommends products based on your browsing history. These are clear examples of how content moderation and personalization technologies shape our interactions with online content.

As user-generated content continues to grow, ensuring its safety and relevance poses a constant challenge. This is where content moderation and personalization workloads come into play as they leverage AI to manage online interactions and meet user needs effectively.

Content Moderation

Content moderation is a critical artificial intelligence workload that uses machine learning and Natural Language Processing (NLP) models to automatically detect, classify, and manage user-generated content. Its goal is to maintain safe, respectful, and compliant environments on digital platforms. By leveraging AI models trained on large datasets, moderation systems can analyze text, images, videos, and live streams to identify inappropriate or harmful material.

Key Features of Content Moderation Workloads

- **Automated Image and Text Analysis:** AI models automatically identify and flag unsafe or inappropriate content like explicit imagery, hate speech, violence, or spam. This automation helps platforms reduce the spread of harmful content quickly.
- **Sentiment and Tone Analysis:** NLP techniques enable AI systems to analyze the tone and emotional intent behind posts, comments, or reviews, while helping moderators detect hostile interactions and maintain a positive online environment.
- **Language Filtering:** AI supports multilingual moderation, ensuring consistent enforcement of content policies across languages and regions.
- **Customizable Filters and Policies:** Moderation models can be tailored to the specific guidelines of each organization. For instance, a children's educational platform may enforce stricter content filters than a general social media network.
- **Contextual Understanding:** Advanced AI models use contextual cues to distinguish between satire, humor, or harassment, enhancing accuracy and reducing false positives.
- **Real-Time Moderation:** AI-powered systems can analyze and flag content instantly, which makes them essential for high-traffic environments such as social media feeds, live chats, or gaming platforms.

Practical Example of Content Moderation

On a large social media platform, AI-based moderation systems review millions of posts every day. When a post contains potentially harmful content, the AI flags it for human review or automatically hides offensive comments. By learning from moderator feedback, the system continuously improves accuracy, thereby balancing freedom of expression with community safety.

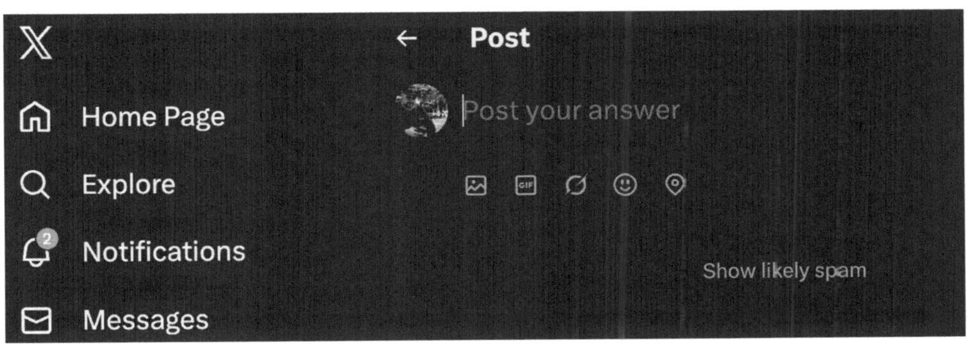

Figure 2.1: *Spam Detection Mechanisms in X (formerly Twitter)*

Azure Services and Implementation of Content Moderation

Microsoft Azure provides the following AI services to design and deploy intelligent and scalable moderation systems:

- **Azure AI Content Safety:** Detects and classifies potentially offensive, risky, or harmful content across text and images. It supports adjustable sensitivity levels and can be integrated into moderation pipelines or apps.
- **Azure AI Language:** Performs text-based analysis for sentiment detection, key phrase extraction, and text classification, thereby improving the precision and efficiency of moderation workflows
- **Azure OpenAI Service:** Enables advanced contextual moderation through generative models that recognize nuanced forms of harmful content, thus reducing false positives and improving reliability

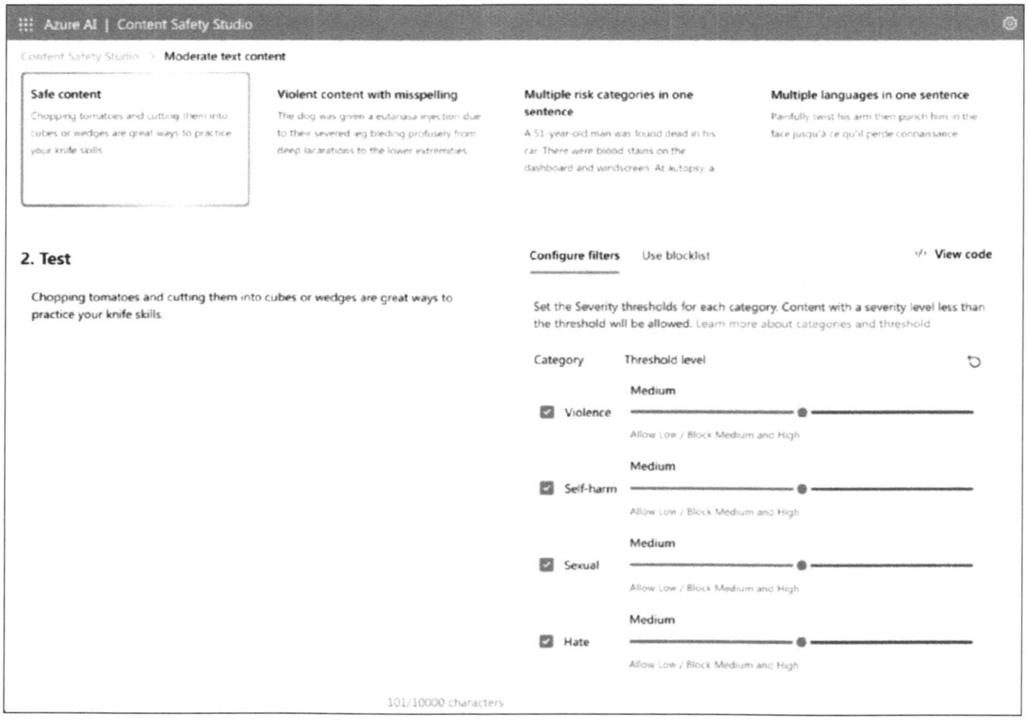

Figure 2.2: *Moderate Text Content with Azure Content Safety Studio*

Content moderation workloads combine data analytics, computer vision, and language understanding to automatically analyze user-generated content. With Azure's AI ecosystem, organizations can build scalable, real-time moderation systems that strengthen user trust, ensure compliance, and create safer digital experiences.

Personalization

Personalization workloads leverage AI to deliver tailored user experiences by analyzing user behaviors, preferences, and contextual data. These workloads power recommendation systems, adaptive interfaces, and dynamic content delivery by creating more engaging and relevant interactions. From streaming platforms that suggest your next favorite series to e-commerce sites that anticipate your next purchase, personalization enhances user satisfaction and loyalty.

Key Features of Personalization Workloads

- **Behavioral Analysis:** AI examines user activity like browsing history, clicks, and purchase patterns to predict preferences and recommend relevant content.
- **Recommendation Engines:** These engines are central to personalization systems as they suggest items like videos, products, or articles based on user interactions. They are widely used by e-commerce, media, and entertainment platforms.
- **Dynamic Content Customization:** Websites and applications adapt their content in real time according to user profiles, location, or interests. For instance, a news app might display different headlines for each reader based on engagement patterns.
- **Location and Context Awareness:** Personalization algorithms use contextual signals like device type, location, or time to refine recommendations and improve relevance.
- **Continuous Learning and A/B Testing:** AI models test multiple recommendation variations by learning from user responses to continuously optimize engagement.
- **User Segmentation:** AI identifies clusters of users with similar behaviors or demographics, thereby enabling targeted campaigns and personalized promotions.

Practical Example of Personalization

An e-commerce retailer uses AI to personalize its shopping experience. When a user frequently browses electronic devices, the homepage automatically highlights the latest gadgets and accessories in that category. The platform also suggests complementary items (such as smartwatches or chargers) and presents limited-time offers for returning customers. These personalized experiences boost sales conversions and foster customer loyalty.

Figure 2.3: *Product Recommendation on Ebay*

Azure Services and Implementation of Personalization

Microsoft Azure provides the following AI services that enable the creation of personalized and adaptive experiences:

- **Azure Machine Learning:** Provides an environment for building and training custom recommendation models using historical data, behavioral analysis, and machine learning pipelines
- **Azure OpenAI Service:** Enables advanced personalization by generating context-aware text, summaries, and recommendations based on user profiles or interactions
- **Azure Cognitive Search:** Enhances personalization by retrieving contextually relevant information from large datasets, enabling smarter, user-specific search experiences

- **Azure Synapse Analytics:** Integrates and analyzes user data from multiple sources, supporting large-scale personalization strategies with real-time insights

Personalization workloads combine **data analytics**, **machine learning**, and **natural language understanding** to adapt content for each individual user. With Azure's AI ecosystem, organizations can implement scalable, intelligent recommendation systems that increase engagement, improve satisfaction, and create more meaningful digital experiences.

Identifying Computer Vision Workloads

Imagine walking into a store and being recognized by a facial recognition system that greets you by name, or taking a picture of a flower and having your smartphone instantly identify the species. These scenarios, which were once the stuff of science fiction, are becoming increasingly common in our daily lives, thanks to the advancements in computer vision technology. Computer vision, which is a subfield of artificial intelligence, allows machines to interpret and understand visual information just like humans do. In this section, we will identify the key computer vision workloads and explore their applications across various industries.

Exam Tip: *In the AI-900 exam, Computer Vision questions often ask you to match workloads such as image classification, object detection, or facial recognition to the correct Azure service. Examples can be* ***Azure AI Vision*** *or* ***Custom Vision****.*

Image Classification

Image classification is a foundational computer vision workload that enables machines to categorize images into predefined classes or labels. By leveraging AI and deep learning models trained on large datasets, this process allows systems to automatically recognize and organize visual content, while helping organizations extract meaningful insights and streamline operations. From identifying defective products in manufacturing to tagging photos on social media, image classification is one of the most common and versatile AI applications.

Key Features of Image Classification Workloads

- **Automated Image Labeling:** AI models analyze visual patterns and assign predefined labels such as "car," "tree," or "person," thereby eliminating the need for manual tagging.
- **Feature Extraction:** Deep learning models extract and learn distinctive features (like shape, color, and texture) to distinguish one object class from another.
- **High Accuracy Through Model Training:** Classification accuracy improves as models are trained with large, diverse, and well-labeled datasets, while enhancing generalization across multiple use cases.
- **Real-Time Classification:** Image classification can be applied in real-time scenarios such as quality control systems in factories or automated sorting in logistics.
- **Custom Model Development:** AI services allow organizations to build and train custom models tailored to specific categories such as identifying medical scans, branded products, or wildlife species.

Practical Example of Image Classification

An online retail platform uses image classification to automatically organize product photos uploaded by sellers. Whenever a new image is added, the AI model identifies the item's category (for example, "electronics" or "clothing") and applies the correct labels. This automation improves inventory organization, enhances product search, and creates a more efficient shopping experience for customers.

Azure Services and Implementation of Image Classification

Microsoft Azure provides the following tools and services to design and deploy image classification solutions:

- **Azure AI Vision:** Offers prebuilt and customizable computer vision models capable of classifying images, detecting objects, and analyzing visual features like color and composition
- **Azure Machine Learning:** Enables the training and deployment of custom image classification models using frameworks like PyTorch and TensorFlow that can be integrated with scalable compute environments
- **Azure Cognitive Services Custom Vision:** Provides a user-friendly interface for building and fine-tuning models specific to organizational needs, while supporting image tagging and classification through drag-and-drop workflows
- **Azure AI Studio:** Allows developers to manage datasets, label images, and monitor model performance throughout the machine learning lifecycle.

Image classification workloads combine computer vision, deep learning, and data analytics to extract insights from visual data. With Azure's AI ecosystem, organizations can implement scalable, accurate, and efficient image classification solutions that improve automation, enhance decision-making, and drive innovation across industries.

Object Detection

Object detection is an advanced computer vision workload that identifies and locates specific objects within an image or video frame. Unlike image classification, which assigns a single label to an entire image, object detection classifies and also provides spatial localization by drawing bounding boxes around detected items. This capability enables a wide range of real-world applications such as autonomous driving, security monitoring, manufacturing quality control, and retail analytics.

Key Features of Object Detection Workloads

- **Object Localization:** Detects and pinpoints multiple objects within a single image using bounding boxes, thus enabling detailed spatial awareness
- **Multi-Class Detection:** Identifies different object types (such as vehicles, people, or traffic signs) simultaneously, even in complex visual environments
- **Real-Time Processing:** Advanced models can process video feeds in real time, which is used in surveillance systems and self-driving cars to react instantly.
- **Model Training and Customization:** AI developers can train models on domain-specific datasets (for example, medical images or industrial machinery) to improve precision in specialized use cases.
- **Edge and Cloud Deployment:** Object detection can be executed in the cloud for large-scale processing or deployed on edge devices (like cameras or drones) for faster, localized inference.
- **Integration with Other AI Workloads:** Object detection can be combined with tracking, image segmentation, or anomaly detection to build more sophisticated vision systems.

Practical Example of Object Detection

An AI-based vision system analyzes outdoor scenes to detect multiple objects and activities in real time. In this example, the system identifies a man wearing a yellow apron cooking at a grill, while two girls play nearby with hula hoops. Using object detection, the model recognizes people, clothing items, and accessories such as the spatula and hoops, assigning bounding boxes to each element. This capability demonstrates how computer vision can interpret complex environments, classify objects accurately, and support applications like surveillance, safety monitoring, and automated scene analysis.

Figure 2.4: *Object Detection in Practice*

Azure Services and Implementation of Object Detection

Microsoft Azure offers the following AI services to design and deploy powerful object detection solutions:

- **Azure AI Vision:** It provides prebuilt models capable of detecting and locating objects in images and videos. It supports bounding box generation and detailed object metadata extraction.
- **Azure Cognitive Services Custom Vision:** Allows users to train and deploy custom object detection models with minimal code. It does so while using labeled datasets tailored to specific business needs.
- **Azure Machine Learning:** It supports the development, training, and deployment of custom deep learning models using frameworks like PyTorch and TensorFlow, that are integrated with scalable GPU-based compute environments.
- **Azure AI Studio:** It simplifies data labeling, experiment tracking, and model versioning, thereby streamlining the entire object detection development lifecycle.

Object detection workloads combine **computer vision**, **deep learning**, and **real-time analytics** to identify and locate multiple objects simultaneously. With Azure's AI ecosystem, organizations can deploy intelligent vision solutions that enhance automation, improve safety, and optimize decision-making across industries such as transportation, retail, and manufacturing.

Facial Recognition

Facial recognition is a specialized computer vision workload that identifies or verifies individuals based on their unique facial features. Using deep learning and image analysis, these systems can detect faces in photos, videos, or live camera streams and compare them against stored data for authentication or identification purposes. Facial recognition is widely used in security systems, access control, digital identity verification, and to generate personalized user experiences.

Key Features of Facial Recognition Workloads

- **Face Detection:** Identifies and locates human faces in images or videos, thus serving as the foundation for recognition and analysis tasks
- **Feature Extraction:** Analyzes distinctive facial characteristics such as eye spacing, jawline structure, or skin texture to create unique digital representations known as facial embeddings
- **Face Matching and Verification:** Compares detected faces with existing records in a database to verify identity or find matches, while supporting both one-to-one and one-to-many recognition
- **Liveness Detection:** Uses visual cues (like blinking or movement) to differentiate between real human faces and spoofing attempts such as photos or masks, while enhancing security
- **Emotion and Attribute Analysis:** Some models can detect emotions, age group, or other facial attributes, thereby enabling richer analytics for marketing or customer experience use cases.
- **Privacy and Ethical Controls:** Modern facial recognition systems integrate features for data protection, consent management, and compliance with privacy regulations such as GDPR.

Practical Example of Facial Recognition

An international airport uses facial recognition to streamline passenger identification during check-in and boarding. When a traveler approaches a security gate, the system matches their facial data with the airline's database to confirm their identity within seconds. This process reduces wait times, enhances security, and improves the overall travel experience.

Azure Services and Implementation of Facial Recognition

Microsoft Azure provides a set of AI services designed to develop and manage secure and ethical facial recognition solutions:

- **Azure AI Vision:** Offers prebuilt facial detection and recognition models capable of identifying faces, detecting emotions, and extracting facial landmarks from images and video feeds.
- **Azure Cognitive Services Face API:** Provides high-accuracy face detection, verification, and grouping capabilities. It supports identifying multiple faces within a single image and comparing them across datasets for authentication and analysis.
- **Azure Machine Learning:** Enables organizations to train and fine-tune custom facial recognition models using domain-specific datasets to ensure compliance and accuracy across different use cases.
- **Azure Responsible AI Dashboard:** Helps monitor and evaluate fairness, bias, and transparency in facial recognition applications, while supporting ethical AI development and deployment.

Figure 2.5: *Facial Recognition with Azure AI Face API*

Facial recognition workloads combine computer vision, deep learning, and biometric analysis to accurately identify or verify individuals in various scenarios. With Azure's AI ecosystem, organizations can build secure, ethical, and scalable facial recognition systems that enhance security, streamline user verification, and enable personalized digital experiences.

Image Segmentation

Image segmentation is a computer vision workload that divides an image into multiple meaningful segments and allows machines to analyze each section independently. Unlike image classification or object detection, which focus on identifying or locating objects, segmentation provides a pixel-level understanding of visual content. This capability is essential in fields such as medical imaging, autonomous driving, and precision agriculture, where detailed analysis of visual data is required to make accurate decisions.

Key Features of Image Segmentation Workloads

- **Pixel-Level Classification:** Assigns a label to every pixel in an image for a fine-grained analysis of shapes, textures, and object boundaries
- **Semantic Segmentation:** Groups pixels into classes such as "road," "tree," or "building" to help the system understand the overall composition of a scene
- **Instance Segmentation:** Differentiates between multiple objects of the same class (for example, separating individual cars in a parking lot) to provide object-level precision
- **Panoptic Segmentation:** Combines semantic and instance segmentation for comprehensive scene understanding and offers both class and instance information simultaneously
- **Edge Detection and Boundary Refinement:** Uses deep learning models to accurately define the contours of objects, thereby improving visual clarity and measurement accuracy
- **Integration with Other Vision Tasks:** Can be combined with object detection and image classification to create end-to-end visual analysis systems

Practical Example of Image Segmentation

In healthcare, doctors often use image segmentation to analyze MRI or CT scans. The AI system highlights specific regions of interest, like tumors or damaged tissue, at the pixel level to help medical professionals diagnose conditions more accurately and plan targeted treatments.

Azure Services and Implementation of Image Segmentation

Microsoft Azure provides the following AI tools for building and deploying image segmentation models:

- **Azure AI Vision:** Offers pretrained models that can perform semantic segmentation and object boundary detection on images and video streams
- **Azure Machine Learning:** Enables the development and training of custom segmentation models using deep learning frameworks such as PyTorch and TensorFlow, while supporting distributed training and GPU acceleration
- **Azure Cognitive Services Custom Vision:** Allows users to create domain-specific segmentation models through an intuitive interface, while streamlining dataset labeling and model iteration
- **Azure AI Studio:** Provides tools for labeling images, managing datasets, and monitoring segmentation performance during experimentation and deployment

Image segmentation workloads combine computer vision, deep learning, and image analysis to deliver pixel-level understanding of visual data. With Azure's AI ecosystem, organizations can deploy accurate and efficient segmentation solutions that improve diagnostics, enhance automation, and enable intelligent decision-making across industries such as healthcare, manufacturing, and autonomous systems.

Optical Character Recognition (OCR)

Optical Character Recognition (OCR) is a computer vision workload that converts text contained in images, scanned documents, or PDFs into machine-readable and editable formats. By using deep learning and image processing techniques, OCR systems can recognize printed or handwritten characters, which makes it easier to digitize and organize information from paper-based sources. This capability is widely applied across industries like finance, law, logistics, and healthcare to automate data entry and improve document accessibility.

Key Features of Optical Character Recognition (OCR) Workloads

- **Text Detection and Extraction:** Identifies regions of an image that contain text and converts them into editable digital formats like plain text or structured data
- **Handwritten and Printed Text Recognition:** Supports both handwritten and printed character recognition, thus enhancing flexibility for processing diverse document types
- **Language and Font Adaptability:** Recognizes text across multiple languages, fonts, and writing styles, thereby improving accuracy and usability in global applications
- **Layout and Structure Analysis:** Preserves formatting elements such as tables, columns, and headers to maintain document structure during digitization
- **Searchable Document Generation:** Converts images or PDFs into searchable documents, thereby allowing users to easily locate information within large archives
- **Integration with Other AI Workloads:** OCR can be combined with document classification, knowledge mining, or natural language processing to create intelligent document processing pipelines

Practical Example of Optical Character Recognition (OCR)

A law firm uses OCR technology to convert printed legal contracts and case files into digital text. Once scanned, the system extracts key clauses and client information and then stores them in a searchable database. This automation accelerates document retrieval, enhances accuracy, and reduces the need for manual data entry, which allows lawyers to focus on higher-value tasks.

Azure Services and Implementation of Optical Character Recognition (OCR)

Microsoft Azure offers the following services to build and deploy OCR solutions:

- **Azure AI Vision:** Provides pretrained models which are capable of extracting printed and handwritten text from images, forms, and scanned documents with high accuracy
- **Azure Cognitive Services Read API:** Delivers advanced OCR capabilities optimized for large-scale document digitization, including layout detection and structured data extraction
- **Azure Form Recognizer (Document Intelligence):** Extends OCR with form and table recognition, thereby efficiently capturing data from receipts, invoices, and identity documents
- **Azure Machine Learning:** Supports the training of custom OCR models and post-processing pipelines to adapt recognition workflows to specific business needs

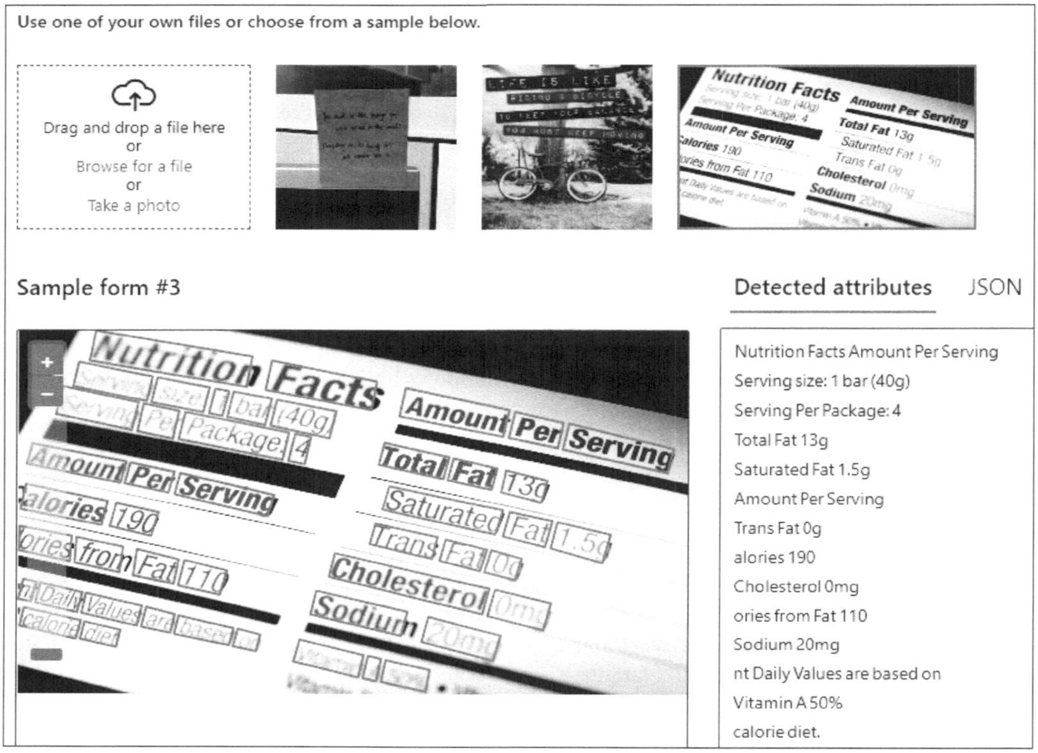

***Figure 2.6**: OCR with Azure AI Vision*

OCR workloads combine **computer vision**, **machine learning**, and **language understanding** to transform unstructured documents into usable, structured data. With Azure's AI ecosystem, organizations can automate manual document workflows, enhance data accuracy, and create information management systems that are more accessible and efficient.

Video Analysis

Video analysis uses AI models to interpret video frames in real time, detecting objects, identifying activities, and understanding environmental context. These capabilities support applications like surveillance, traffic management, safety monitoring, and operational analytics.

Key Features of Video Analysis Workloads

- **Real-Time Object Detection and Tracking:** Continuously identifies and tracks multiple objects or people across video frames, while enabling real-time monitoring and alerting
- **Event and Activity Recognition:** Detects specific actions or events such as unauthorized access, crowd formation, or abnormal movement patterns to improve safety and situational awareness.
- **Scene and Context Understanding:** Analyzes environmental context like lighting conditions, motion, and object relationships to interpret complex video scenes accurately
- **Facial and Identity Recognition:** Integrates facial recognition models to identify individuals within live or recorded footage, thereby enhancing access control and law enforcement operations

- **Behavioral Analytics:** Uses AI models to identify behavioral trends, customer flow, or dwell times, supporting data-driven decision-making in retail and marketing environments
- **Integration with Other AI Systems:** Video analysis can be combined with IoT sensors, knowledge mining, or natural language processing to build end-to-end intelligent monitoring solutions.

Practical Example of Video Analysis

A professional sports team uses video analysis to evaluate player performance during matches. The AI system tracks players' positions, speed, and actions, providing coaches with detailed metrics for each athlete. By analyzing this data, the team can optimize training programs, improve strategies, and reduce injury risks.

Figure 2.7: *An Example of Video Analysis Using AI-Powered Object Tracking*

Azure Services and Implementation of Video Analysis

Microsoft Azure provides a range of AI services and tools for building and deploying scalable video analysis solutions:

- **Azure AI Vision:** Offers video analytics capabilities to detect, track, and analyze movement within video streams, while supporting real-time event detection
- **Azure Video Indexer:** Provides comprehensive video analysis, including object detection, facial recognition, scene segmentation, and speech-to-text transcription, while transforming video content into searchable insights
- **Azure Machine Learning:** Enables training and deployment of custom video analysis models using deep learning frameworks like PyTorch and TensorFlow, along with GPU-based compute support
- **Azure Media Services:** Integrates with AI workloads to process, encode, and analyze video files at scale, thereby enabling content indexing and metadata generation for media libraries

Video analysis workloads combine **computer vision**, **motion tracking**, and **machine learning** to extract insights from video content in real time. With Azure's AI ecosystem, organizations can deploy intelligent video analytics solutions that enhance safety, optimize operations, and generate valuable insights across industries such as security, transportation, sports, and retail.

Computer Vision Workloads in Azure

Microsoft Azure provides a comprehensive suite of AI services that enable organizations to build, train, and deploy computer vision workloads at scale. These workloads help businesses extract insights from images and videos, recognize objects, detect faces, and analyze visual data for automation and decision-making. Azure's tools combine prebuilt AI capabilities with options for custom model development, thus making it possible to create intelligent applications tailored to address specific business needs.

Key Capabilities of Azure Computer Vision Workloads

- **Image and Video Analysis:** Detects, classifies, and labels objects within images and videos, enabling automated visual understanding for a wide range of applications
- **Optical Character Recognition (OCR):** Extracts printed and handwritten text from documents, forms, and images, thereby allowing organizations to digitize and structure unorganized data
- **Facial Detection and Recognition:** Identifies and verifies individuals in images and video feeds, while supporting authentication, personalization, and security use cases
- **Object Detection and Localization:** Identifies multiple objects and their positions within visual content by using bounding boxes and metadata for accurate spatial mapping
- **Image Segmentation:** Divides an image into distinct regions or layers for fine-grained visual analysis, which is useful in medical imaging, autonomous navigation, and industrial inspection
- **Custom Model Training:** Provides flexible tools to build, label, and deploy models trained on proprietary datasets, thus enabling the creation of industry-specific solutions

Practical Example of Computer Vision Workloads in Azure

A retail company uses Azure computer vision services to monitor in-store activity and optimize customer experiences. Cameras connected to Azure AI Vision analyze customer traffic patterns, detect product interactions, and identify frequently visited areas. Insights from this analysis help store managers adjust layouts, improve staff allocation, and enhance marketing strategies based on real-time behavior data.

Azure Services and Implementation of Computer Vision

Microsoft Azure offers several AI tools and services to develop, customize, and manage computer vision workloads:

- **Azure AI Vision:** It provides prebuilt models for image and video analysis as well as other applications like object detection, facial recognition, and text extraction. It supports real-time processing and can be integrated with edge devices for live monitoring.
- **Azure Cognitive Services Custom Vision:** It allows users to build and train custom vision models using labeled datasets. The drag-and-drop interface makes it easy to adapt models to specific business scenarios without requiring deep AI expertise.
- **Azure Machine Learning:** It supports custom computer vision workflows, including data preparation, training, evaluation, and deployment of deep learning models built with frameworks like PyTorch and TensorFlow.
- **Azure AI Studio:** It offers a unified workspace for dataset management, labeling, and experiment tracking, while enabling streamlined model development and collaboration.
- **Azure Cognitive Search:** It integrates with vision services to make visual content searchable by extracting metadata, labels, and textual information from images and videos.

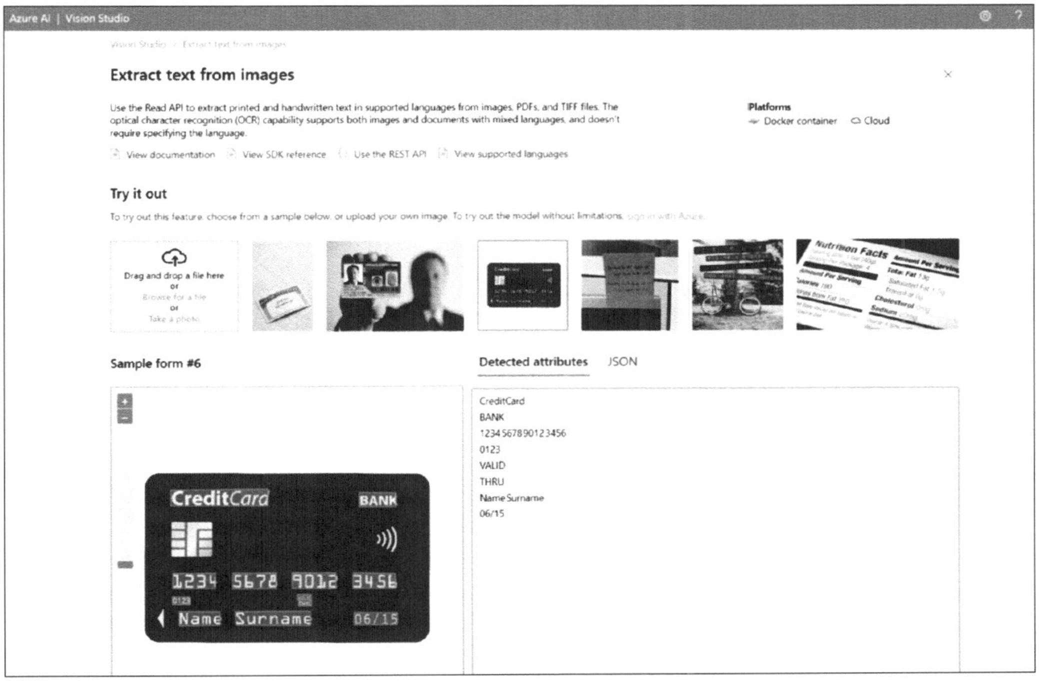

Figure 2.8: *Using Azure AI Vision Studio to Extract Text from Images*

Computer vision workloads in Azure combine **AI-driven image processing**, **deep learning**, and **data analytics** to turn visual information into actionable insights. With Azure's AI ecosystem, organizations can develop intelligent solutions that automate operations, improve safety, and enable data-driven innovation across various industries.

Identifying Natural Language Processing Workloads

In our digitally-driven world, communication occurs at lightning speed. Whether it is a text message, a social media post, or an email, the volume of written language generated every day is staggering. Natural Language Processing (NLP) is a branch of artificial intelligence that enables machines to understand, interpret, and generate human language in a way that is both valuable and meaningful. In this section, we will identify key NLP workloads and explore their applications across various industries.

Text Classification

Text classification is a core Natural Language Processing (NLP) workload that categorizes text into predefined groups based on its content. By leveraging AI and machine learning models, systems can automatically organize, filter, and interpret large volumes of text data like emails, reviews, or support tickets. This capability is essential for applications like spam detection, topic tagging, sentiment analysis, and document organization, and helps organizations improve automation and decision-making.

Key Features of Text Classification Workloads

- **Automated Text Categorization:** Classifies documents, messages, or paragraphs into predefined categories such as "support," "billing," or "feedback", thereby reducing the need for manual sorting
- **Supervised and Unsupervised Learning:** Supports model training with labeled datasets (supervised) or discovers hidden topics and groupings in unlabeled data (unsupervised)
- **Multi-Label Classification:** Allows a single document to belong to multiple categories at once, which reflects the complexity of real-world text analysis
- **Sentiment and Intent Detection:** Identifies emotional tone or intent behind text, while providing valuable insights for customer feedback and brand reputation management
- **Real-Time Processing:** Enables instant classification of incoming text streams such as live chats, emails, or social media posts for immediate routing and analysis
- **Custom Model Training:** Lets organizations fine-tune models to specific use cases or industries, thus improving accuracy through domain-specific language understanding

Practical Example of Text Classification

A customer service platform uses text classification to automatically categorize incoming support tickets. When a message arrives, the AI model analyzes its content and assigns it to the appropriate department such as technical support, billing, or general inquiries. This automation reduces response times, ensures faster problem resolution, and ends up improving the overall customer experience.

Azure Services and Implementation of Text Classification

Microsoft Azure provides the following AI services to build, deploy, and enhance text classification solutions:

- **Azure AI Language:** Offers prebuilt and customizable text classification models to detect topics, categories, and sentiment across different languages and domains
- **Azure Machine Learning:** Supports custom NLP model training with frameworks such as Hugging Face Transformers, PyTorch, and TensorFlow, thereby enabling organizations to fine-tune text classification models with their own data
- **Azure OpenAI Service** – Leverages Large Language Models (LLMs) such as GPT to classify text based on context, intent, or sentiment with high precision
- **Azure AI Studio:** Provides tools for data labeling, model monitoring, and deployment, while simplifying the end-to-end workflow of building classification systems

Text classification workloads combine **natural language processing**, **machine learning**, and **semantic analysis** to organize and interpret text data automatically. Thus, with Azure's AI ecosystem, organizations can implement scalable, accurate, and intelligent classification systems that enhance productivity, streamline workflows, and unlock valuable insights from unstructured information.

Sentiment Analysis

Sentiment analysis is a natural language processing (NLP) workload that determines the emotional tone or attitude expressed in a piece of text. By analyzing words, phrases, and linguistic patterns, AI models can assess whether the sentiment behind a message is positive, negative, or neutral. This workload is widely used in customer feedback systems, market research, brand monitoring, and social media analytics, which helps organizations understand how people feel about their products, services, or content.

Key Features of Sentiment Analysis Workloads

- **Emotion Detection:** Identifies the polarity of text as positive, negative, or neutral; can also extend to detecting emotions such as happiness, frustration, or excitement
- **Aspect-Based Analysis:** Breaks down text into specific components (for example, "delivery," "price," "customer service") to determine which aspects users feel positively or negatively about
- **Contextual Understanding:** Uses advanced language models to interpret sentiment in context, distinguishing between literal meaning and sarcasm or idiomatic expressions
- **Multilingual Support:** Analyzes text written in multiple languages for accurate sentiment detection across global audiences
- **Real-Time Analysis:** Processes live data streams such as tweets or chat messages to identify and respond to customer sentiment as it happens
- **Integration with Business Intelligence:** Combines sentiment results with dashboards or analytics tools to visualize trends and guide strategic decisions

Practical Example of Sentiment Analysis

A retail company uses sentiment analysis to monitor customer reviews across social media platforms. When negative comments about shipping delays appear, the AI system automatically flags them for the support team, while positive reviews are used in marketing campaigns. This real-time insight helps the company respond quickly to issues, improve customer satisfaction, and strengthen its brand image.

Azure Services and Implementation of Sentiment Analysis

Microsoft Azure provides the following AI services to develop and deploy sentiment analysis models:

- **Azure AI Language:** It offers prebuilt models to analyze sentiment and opinion mining across multiple languages. It can extract sentiment scores at both document and sentence levels, while providing fine-grained emotional insights.
- **Azure Machine Learning:** It supports training and fine-tuning of custom sentiment models using large datasets, thus enabling domain-specific emotion recognition.
- **Azure OpenAI Service:** It leverages advanced language models like GPT to analyze sentiment in context, while capturing nuances, irony, and cultural variations in expression.
- **Azure AI Studio:** It simplifies dataset management, annotation, and deployment of sentiment analysis solutions while integrating seamlessly with other Azure AI tools.

Sentiment analysis workloads combine **natural language processing**, **machine learning**, and **linguistic analysis** to uncover emotions and opinions within text data. With Azure's AI ecosystem, organizations can build intelligent systems that monitor customer sentiment in real time, enhance engagement strategies, and make data-driven decisions to improve user experience and brand perception.

Named Entity Recognition (NER)

Named Entity Recognition (NER) is a Natural Language Processing (NLP) workload that identifies and classifies key elements within text like names of people, organizations, locations, dates, and numerical values. By extracting this information automatically, NER transforms unstructured text into structured data that can be easily analyzed and integrated into databases, analytics systems, or search tools. It is widely used in areas like news aggregation, compliance monitoring, and customer data analysis.

Key Features of Named Entity Recognition (NER) Workloads

- **Entity Identification:** Detects and highlights entities such as people, places, products, companies, or dates within sentences and documents
- **Entity Classification:** Categorizes recognized entities into predefined types (for example, "Organization," "Person," "Location," "Date," or "Monetary Value") to improve information organization and retrieval
- **Contextual Disambiguation:** Uses contextual cues to distinguish between entities with similar names (for example, differentiating "Amazon" the company from "Amazon" the rainforest)
- **Custom Entity Recognition:** Enables training of models to detect domain-specific entities such as medical terms, financial instruments, or legal clauses, which are tailored to cater to industry needs
- **Integration with Knowledge Graphs:** Connects recognized entities to external data sources or knowledge bases, while enriching contextual understanding and supporting semantic search
- **Scalable Processing:** Handles large text volumes efficiently while extracting entities in real-time from continuous data streams such as news feeds or customer interactions

Practical Example of Named Entity Recognition (NER)

A news aggregation platform uses NER to automatically identify and tag names of people, companies, and countries mentioned in articles. This tagging allows readers to click an entity and instantly access related stories or background information. The system enhances content organization, improves searchability, and helps users discover relevant insights faster.

Azure Services and Implementation of Named Entity Recognition (NER)

Microsoft Azure provides the following AI services to develop, deploy, and integrate entity recognition capabilities:

- **Azure AI Language:** It offers prebuilt NER models that can detect standard entities (like names, locations, and dates) across multiple languages. It also supports custom entity extraction tailored to specific business domains.
- **Azure Machine Learning:** It enables organizations to train and fine-tune custom entity recognition models using labeled datasets, while leveraging frameworks like spaCy, PyTorch, and Transformers.
- **Azure OpenAI Service:** It uses Large Language Models (LLMs) such as GPT to identify and contextualize entities even in complex or unstructured text, thus enhancing accuracy in real-world scenarios.
- **Azure AI Studio:** It provides an integrated environment for labeling entities, training models, and monitoring performance, while ensuring efficient lifecycle management for NER projects.

Named Entity Recognition workloads combine **natural language processing**, **machine learning**, and **semantic analysis** to extract structured insights from raw text. With Azure's AI ecosystem, organizations can develop intelligent text analytics solutions that enhance data discovery, automate information extraction, and drive smarter decision-making across industries such as journalism, finance, healthcare, and law.

Machine Translation

Machine translation is a Natural Language Processing (NLP) workload that automatically converts text or speech from one language to another. Using deep learning and large multilingual datasets, these systems can understand context, grammar, and meaning to produce accurate and fluent translations. Machine translation plays a vital role in breaking language barriers and facilitates global communication across industries such as education, e-commerce, customer service, and international collaboration.

Key Features of Machine Translation Workloads

- **Neural Machine Translation (NMT):** Uses advanced deep learning architectures to capture context and semantics, thereby producing more natural and accurate translations than traditional rule-based systems
- **Contextual Understanding:** Goes beyond word-for-word translation by interpreting sentence meaning, idioms, and cultural nuances for better readability
- **Bidirectional Translation:** Supports two-way translation between multiple language pairs, thus enabling dynamic communication across regions
- **Domain Adaptation:** Allows customization of models to specific domains such as healthcare, finance, or technology, while ensuring more precise terminology and consistency.
- **Multilingual and Multimodal Support:** Translates across dozens of languages and can process both text and speech, integrating with applications like chatbots and voice assistants
- **Real-Time Translation:** Enables instant translation in live conversations, video captions, or customer support chats to facilitate global engagement

Practical Example of Machine Translation

A multinational company integrates machine translation into its customer support system to assist users worldwide. When customers submit inquiries in different languages, the AI system automatically translates their messages into English for support agents and translates responses back into the customer's native language. This approach brings about seamless global communication without requiring human translators.

Azure Services and Implementation of Machine Translation

Microsoft Azure provides the following AI services for building and deploying machine translation solutions:

- **Azure AI Translator:** It is a prebuilt service that provides text and speech translation across more than 100 languages. It supports real-time translation, custom terminology, and domain-specific models.
- **Azure AI Language:** It complements translation workloads by detecting language, extracting entities, and analyzing sentiment before or after translation to develop a better contextual understanding.
- **Azure OpenAI Service:** It uses large language models like GPT to generate context-aware translations that preserve tone, intent, and fluency in complex or creative content.
- **Azure Machine Learning:** It enables developers to train and fine-tune custom translation models with specialized vocabularies, ensuring consistent results across industry-specific use cases.

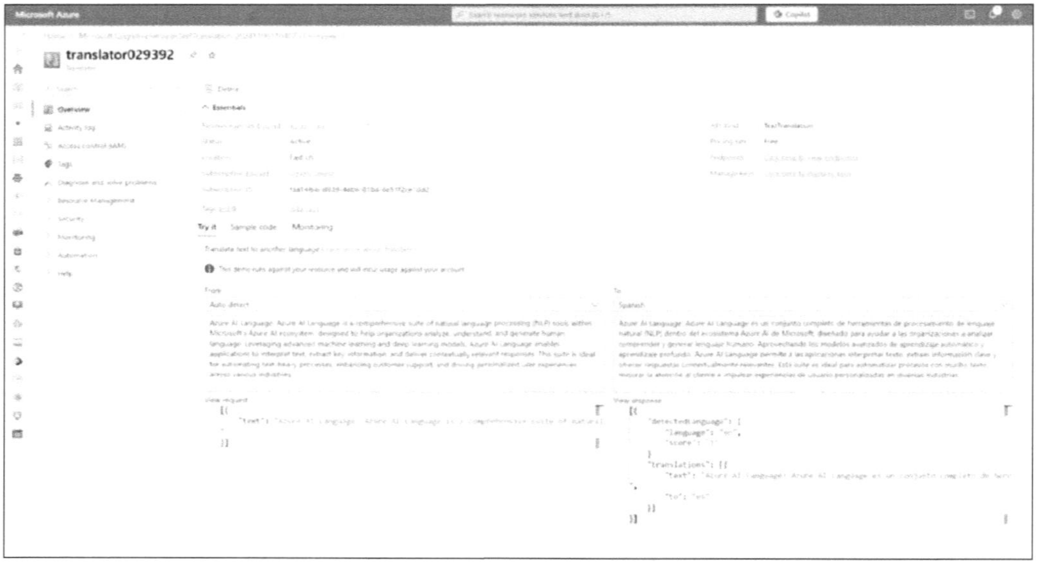

Figure 2.9: *Using Azure AI Translator to Translate Texts*

Machine translation workloads combine **natural language processing**, **deep learning**, and **contextual analysis** to enable seamless multilingual communication. With Azure's AI ecosystem, organizations can deliver real-time, high-quality translations that enhance accessibility, improve collaboration, and connect users across languages and cultures.

Text Generation

Text generation is a natural language processing (NLP) workload that enables machines to automatically create human-like text based on a given input or prompt. Through Large Language Models (LLMs) and deep learning techniques, these systems can produce coherent, contextually relevant, and grammatically accurate sentences across a wide range of tasks. Text generation powers applications such as chatbots, content creation, report summarization, and code generation, which radically transforms how humans interact with AI systems.

Key Features of Text Generation Workloads

- **Contextual Understanding:** Analyzes the input prompt to generate text that follows the correct context, tone, and intent of the user's request
- **Coherence and Continuity:** Produces logically consistent and flowing text over multiple sentences or paragraphs, mimicking natural human writing
- **Creativity and Style Adaptation:** Adapts writing style, tone, and structure to different contexts such as technical documentation, storytelling, or marketing content
- **Summarization and Expansion:** Can condense large pieces of text into summaries or expand short inputs into detailed, informative outputs
- **Multilingual Text Generation:** Supports generation in multiple languages, enabling global applications such as multilingual chatbots and content localization
- **Customization and Fine-Tuning:** Models can be fine-tuned on domain-specific datasets to align with organizational tone, vocabulary, and use cases.

Practical Example of Text Generation

A content marketing platform uses AI-based text generation to assist copywriters in creating blog posts and social media content. By providing a short description or topic, the system generates a complete draft with headlines, sections, and calls to action. Writers can then refine the text, which reduces content creation time while maintaining brand voice and quality.

Azure Services and Implementation of Text Generation

Microsoft Azure provides the following AI tools to build and deploy advanced text generation solutions with flexibility and control:

- **Azure OpenAI Service:** Offers access to state-of-the-art language models such as GPT, that are capable of generating high-quality text for chatbots, creative writing, summarization, and documentation tasks
- **Azure AI Language:** Provides text analysis and summarization features that complement generation workloads by extracting insights and structuring generated content
- **Azure Machine Learning:** Supports the training and fine-tuning of custom language models for specific domains, while generating tailored text that is aligned with organizational needs
- **Azure AI Studio:** Facilitates prompt engineering, experimentation, and deployment of generative AI models, while streamlining workflow management and performance tracking

Text generation workloads combine **deep learning**, **natural language processing**, and **contextual reasoning** to create high-quality human-like text. With Azure's AI ecosystem, organizations can implement intelligent systems that automate content creation, enhance communication, and unlock new opportunities for creativity and productivity.

Speech Recognition

Speech recognition is a Natural Language Processing (NLP) workload that converts spoken language into written text. By leveraging deep learning, acoustic modeling, and language modeling, these systems can accurately interpret speech in real time or from recorded audio. Speech recognition is widely used in applications such as virtual assistants, automated transcription, voice-enabled devices, and accessibility tools, thus allowing users to interact with technology naturally and efficiently.

Key Features of Speech Recognition Workloads

- **Automatic Speech-to-Text Conversion:** Transcribes spoken words into digital text with high accuracy, thus enabling documentation and data processing from audio sources
- **Multilingual and Multimodal Support:** Recognizes speech in multiple languages, dialects, and accents, thereby facilitating global deployment across industries
- **Real-Time and Batch Processing:** Supports both live transcription for streaming applications and batch processing for recorded audio or video files
- **Noise Reduction and Speaker Separation:** Uses signal processing and AI models to filter background noise and distinguish between multiple speakers in the same recording
- **Domain-Specific Adaptation:** Models can be fine-tuned with custom vocabularies to recognize industry-specific terminology (for example, legal, medical, or technical).
- **Integration with Voice Interfaces:** Seamlessly integrates with chatbots, customer service systems, and virtual assistants to enable hands-free, voice-driven interaction

Practical Example of Speech Recognition

A healthcare organization uses speech recognition to transcribe doctor-patient consultations in real time. The AI system captures spoken notes and automatically converts them into structured medical records. This reduces manual data entry, minimizes transcription errors, and allows healthcare professionals to focus more on patient care.

Azure Services and Implementation of Speech Recognition

Microsoft Azure provides a suite of the following AI services to build and deploy scalable, high-accuracy speech recognition systems:

- **Azure AI Speech:** It offers Automatic Speech Recognition (ASR) capabilities that transcribe real-time or recorded audio. It supports multiple languages, noise reduction, and custom speech models for domain-specific optimization.
- **Azure AI Language:** It enhances speech workloads by applying Natural Language Understanding (NLU) to extract meaning, sentiment, or intent from transcribed text.
- **Azure OpenAI Service:** It enables conversational intelligence by combining transcription with generative models for creating contextual responses or summaries.
- **Azure Machine Learning:** It supports the training and evaluation of custom speech models, thereby allowing developers to improve accuracy for specialized applications or industries.

Speech recognition workloads combine **acoustic modeling**, **natural language processing**, and **machine learning** to transform spoken input into actionable text. With Azure's AI ecosystem, organizations can build intelligent, voice-driven applications that enhance accessibility, streamline operations, and deliver more natural human-computer interactions.

Conversational Agents (Chatbots)

Conversational agents, or chatbots, are Natural Language Processing (NLP) workloads designed to simulate human conversation and interact with users through text or voice. Powered by artificial intelligence and Large Language Models (LLMs), chatbots can understand intent, respond contextually, and assist users with tasks such as answering questions, providing recommendations, or resolving issues. They are widely used across industries in customer service, e-commerce, education, and healthcare to improve engagement and operational efficiency.

Key Features of Conversational Agent Workloads

- **Intent Recognition:** Identifies the purpose of a user's message to determine the most relevant response or action
- **Contextual Understanding:** Maintains conversation history and context, while allowing multi-turn interactions that feel natural and coherent
- **Natural Language Generation (NLG):** Produces human-like responses that adapt to tone, emotion, and conversation flow
- **Integration with External Systems:** Connects with APIs, databases, and enterprise systems to retrieve information or perform actions (for example, checking an order status or scheduling an appointment)
- **Omnichannel Deployment:** Operates across multiple platforms such as websites, mobile apps, messaging services, and voice assistants
- **Continuous Learning and Improvement:** Uses feedback and interaction data to retrain and optimize models, thereby enhancing accuracy and user satisfaction over time

Practical Example of Conversational Agents

An e-commerce company implements a chatbot to help customers find products, track orders, and resolve common issues. Whenever a user asks about shipping status, the chatbot accesses order data through an API and provides real-time updates. If the query becomes complex, the conversation can be seamlessly transferred to a human agent. This system reduces support costs and improves customer response time.

Azure Services and Implementation of Conversational Agents

Microsoft Azure provides a comprehensive set of the following tools and AI services to develop and deploy conversational agents:

- **Azure OpenAI Service:** It offers advanced large language models like GPT that enable natural, context-aware, and dynamic conversations. These models can power both text and voice-based assistants.
- **Azure AI Language:** It provides intent recognition, entity extraction, and sentiment analysis features that enhance chatbot understanding and dialogue flow.
- **Azure Bot Service:** It is a managed platform for building, connecting, and deploying chatbots across multiple communication channels and is integrated with Azure Cognitive Services.
- **Azure AI Speech:** It adds voice interaction capabilities, allowing chatbots to support spoken input and audio responses for a more immersive user experience.
- **Azure Machine Learning:** It enables continuous improvement of chatbot performance by supporting model training, evaluation, and fine-tuning.

Conversational agent workloads combine **natural language understanding**, **machine learning**, and **dialogue management** to create intelligent systems capable of natural and efficient human-computer interaction. With Azure's AI ecosystem, organizations can deploy scalable, multilingual, and context-aware chatbots that enhance customer engagement, automate support, and deliver personalized user experiences across digital channels.

Exam Tip: *You may expect AI-900 questions about Natural Language Processing and Conversational AI that test your ability to recognize services like* ***Azure AI Language****,* ***Azure OpenAI Service****, and* ***Azure Bot Service*** *that are used to build chatbots and language applications.*

Identifying Knowledge Mining Workloads

In today's data-driven world, organizations face a growing challenge: how to extract meaningful value from vast amounts of unstructured and semi-structured data. Knowledge mining is a technique that allows businesses to discover insights, patterns, and hidden relationships within data, thereby facilitating informed decision-making. In this section, we will identify key knowledge-mining workloads and explore their applications across various industries.

Exam Tip: *Knowledge Mining is typically associated with* ***Azure Cognitive Search*** *and* ***Form Recognizer****. On the exam, remember that these workloads focus on extracting insights from unstructured data, not on training machine-learning models.*

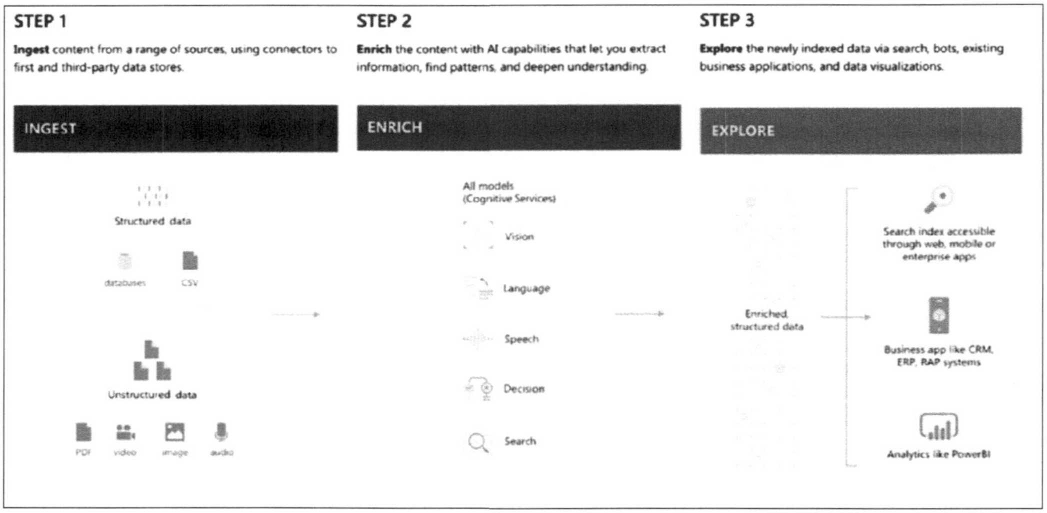

Figure 2.10: *How Knowledge Mining Works in Azure Architecture*

Information Extraction

Information extraction is a knowledge mining workload that automatically identifies and retrieves relevant data from large collections of unstructured or semi-structured documents. By using Artificial Intelligence (AI), Natural Language Processing (NLP), and machine learning, this process converts raw text into structured, searchable, and actionable information. Information extraction is essential in industries such as law, finance, healthcare, and government, where organizations must process massive volumes of documents to uncover insights efficiently.

Key Features of Information Extraction Workloads

- **Entity and Keyword Identification:** Detects key terms, names, dates, monetary values, and other important entities from unstructured text
- **Relationship Detection:** Identifies associations between entities–such as "customer-purchase," "doctor-patient," or "company-contract"–to reveal patterns and dependencies
- **Custom Schema Mapping:** Converts extracted data into structured formats such as tables, JSON, or databases for easy integration with analytics systems
- **Domain-Specific Customization:** Supports training of models on specialized vocabularies for industries such as healthcare, law, or banking, improving recognition accuracy
- **Integration with Knowledge Bases:** Links extracted data to external databases or knowledge graphs, enriching insights and enabling advanced search functionality
- **Scalable Processing:** Handles large document sets efficiently through parallelization and distributed computing, enabling real-time or batch extraction at scale

Practical Example of Information Extraction

A financial institution uses AI-powered information extraction to analyze thousands of loan agreements. The system automatically identifies and extracts key fields such as borrower names, loan amounts, interest rates, and expiration dates. This structured data is then fed into an internal analytics dashboard, reducing manual review time and improving compliance reporting accuracy.

Azure Services and Implementation of Information Extraction

Microsoft Azure offers a comprehensive ecosystem of the following AI tools for developing and implementing information extraction solutions:

- **Azure AI Language:** Provides prebuilt and customizable text analytics features such as entity recognition, key phrase extraction, and relation detection for structured data generation
- **Azure Form Recognizer (Document Intelligence):** Uses advanced OCR and layout analysis to extract data from forms, invoices, and contracts, converting them into machine-readable formats
- **Azure Machine Learning:** Enables training of custom extraction models tailored to specific document types or business processes using supervised and unsupervised learning techniques
- **Azure OpenAI Service:** Leverages large language models to interpret context, extract relationships, and summarize information across complex, unstructured documents

Figure 2.11: *Azure AI Language*

Information extraction workloads combine **natural language processing**, **machine learning**, and **data modeling** to transform unstructured information into organized insights. With Azure's AI ecosystem, organizations can automate manual data handling, accelerate decision-making, and unlock the value hidden in a massive volume of documents.

Text Analysis

Text analysis is a knowledge mining workload that processes and interprets large volumes of unstructured text to extract patterns, trends, and insights. By applying Artificial Intelligence (AI) and Natural Language Processing (NLP), text analysis enables organizations to understand customer feedback, monitor brand perception, detect emerging topics, and make data-driven decisions. This capability is widely used in business intelligence, marketing analytics, customer service, and social media monitoring.

Key Features of Text Analysis Workloads

- **Keyword and Phrase Extraction:** Identifies significant terms, topics, and expressions within documents, helping summarize and categorize large datasets

- **Topic Modeling and Trend Detection:** Analyzes text to uncover recurring themes and evolving trends across customer reviews, articles, or support tickets
- **Sentiment and Opinion Mining:** Determines emotional tone or customer sentiment to assess satisfaction and brand perception
- **Entity and Relationship Analysis:** Detects entities such as names, products, or organizations and identifies their relationships to uncover deeper insights
- **Multilingual Processing:** Supports text analysis across multiple languages, ensuring consistent results for global operations
- **Integration with Visualization Tools:** Provides structured outputs that can be connected to analytics dashboards or business intelligence platforms for deeper reporting

Practical Example of Text Analysis

A global retail company uses text analysis to process customer feedback from multiple channels, including social media posts and online reviews. The AI system identifies recurring complaints about delivery times and extracts key themes related to customer satisfaction. As a result, the insights drawn from this analysis helps the company optimize logistics operations and improve the overall quality of their service.

Azure Services and Implementation of Text Analysis

Microsoft Azure provides a variety of AI tools to design and deploy text analysis solutions efficiently:

- **Azure AI Language:** Offers prebuilt models for entity recognition, key phrase extraction, sentiment analysis, and language detection across multiple languages
- **Azure Cognitive Search:** Combines text analysis with search capabilities, allowing users to query, filter, and rank relevant results based on semantic understanding
- **Azure OpenAI Service:** Uses large language models to perform advanced text summarization, classification, and insight extraction with contextual precision
- **Azure Machine Learning:** Enables the development and customization of text analysis pipelines using NLP frameworks and labeled datasets for domain-specific analysis

Text analysis workloads combine **natural language processing**, **machine learning**, and **semantic understanding** to transform unstructured text into actionable business insights. With Azure's AI ecosystem, organizations can automate data interpretation, improve decision-making, and uncover valuable trends hidden within textual information.

Pattern Discovery

Pattern discovery is a knowledge mining workload that uses AI and machine learning to uncover hidden relationships, correlations, and trends within large datasets. By analyzing structured and unstructured data, these systems can detect recurring behaviors, anomalies, and predictive indicators that may not be visible through traditional analytics. Pattern discovery helps organizations make data-driven decisions, improve forecasting, and identify opportunities or risks across multiple domains such as finance, healthcare, retail, and cybersecurity.

Key Features of Pattern Discovery Workloads

- **Anomaly Detection:** Identifies unusual behaviors or data points such as fraudulent transactions, equipment failures, or security breaches by recognizing deviations from normal patterns
- **Association and Correlation Analysis:** Reveals relationships between variables such as customer purchasing habits or medical symptom connections to enhance strategic decision-making

- **Trend and Sequence Analysis:** Tracks evolving behaviors or event sequences over time and enables predictive modeling and demand forecasting
- **Clustering and Grouping:** Uses unsupervised learning to group similar data points or customers based on shared characteristics to improve segmentation and personalization
- **Data Visualization and Interpretability:** Converts complex patterns into visual representations, while making insights accessible to both technical and non-technical users
- **Continuous Learning:** Continuously refines models as new data becomes available and ensures adaptive and up-to-date pattern detection

Practical Example of Pattern Discovery

A cybersecurity company applies pattern discovery to detect potential data breaches. The AI system continuously monitors network traffic and identifies unusual activity patterns such as repeated failed login attempts or large outbound data transfers. These alerts enable the security team to respond proactively, thereby reducing the risk of cyberattacks and data loss.

Azure Services and Implementation of Pattern Discovery

Microsoft Azure provides the following AI and analytics services to build and deploy pattern discovery workloads:

- **Azure Machine Learning:** Enables the creation of custom models for clustering, anomaly detection, and predictive analytics using supervised and unsupervised learning techniques
- **Azure Synapse Analytics:** Integrates data from multiple sources, providing powerful querying and visualization capabilities for identifying hidden patterns across structured and unstructured data
- **Azure Data Explorer:** Offers fast and scalable analytics for real-time data streams, thus enabling instant detection of anomalies or emerging trends
- **Azure OpenAI Service:** Uses large language models to analyze textual data and uncover semantic patterns or relationships across complex datasets

Pattern discovery workloads combine **data mining**, **machine learning**, and **statistical analysis** to reveal meaningful insights hidden within data. With Azure's AI ecosystem, organizations can detect trends earlier, predict outcomes more accurately, and make smarter, data-informed decisions across a wide range of business applications.

Sentiment Analysis in Knowledge Mining

Sentiment analysis in knowledge mining focuses on extracting emotional and opinion-based insights from large volumes of unstructured text within documents, reviews, and communications. By integrating sentiment analysis into knowledge mining pipelines, organizations can evaluate public perception, monitor customer satisfaction, and identify emerging issues hidden in their data. This workload transforms qualitative feedback into quantifiable metrics that can drive strategic business decisions, and enhance customer experience.

Key Features of Sentiment Analysis in Knowledge Mining

- **Document-Level and Sentence-Level Sentiment Detection:** Evaluates the overall tone of entire documents, while also analyzing individual sentences for more detailed emotional understanding
- **Aspect-Based Sentiment Analysis:** Identifies specific topics or attributes (such as "delivery," "quality," or "pricing") and measures the sentiment expressed toward each one, thereby pointing out areas for improvement

- **Multilingual Processing:** Analyzes sentiment across multiple languages, which allows global organizations to monitor feedback consistently in international markets
- **Contextual Understanding:** Uses large language models to interpret sarcasm, idiomatic expressions, and cultural nuances that might influence emotional meaning
- **Integration with Search and Visualization Tools:** Combines sentiment data with Azure Cognitive Search and Power BI to present intuitive dashboards for trend monitoring and decision support
- **Automation and Continuous Learning:** Continuously refines models through user feedback and new data, thereby improving accuracy and adaptability over time

Practical Example of Sentiment Analysis in Knowledge Mining

A hospitality company uses knowledge mining with sentiment analysis to evaluate guest feedback from surveys, social media, and online reviews. The AI pipeline extracts customer opinions and classifies them by sentiment and topic, for example, "room cleanliness," "staff friendliness," and "breakfast quality." Insights from this analysis are visualized in Power BI dashboards, which allow the management to identify recurring complaints, recognize positive trends, and improve service quality proactively.

Azure Services and Implementation of Sentiment Analysis in Knowledge Mining

Microsoft Azure provides the following integrated AI services that enable sentiment analysis as part of a knowledge mining architecture:

- **Azure AI Language:** Offers sentiment and opinion mining models that can analyze feedback across multiple languages and contexts, thus producing sentiment scores and confidence levels
- **Azure Cognitive Search:** Integrates sentiment results as searchable metadata, thereby allowing users to filter or rank documents based on emotional tone or customer satisfaction levels
- **Azure Machine Learning:** Enables users to train domain-specific sentiment models to analyze industry-related feedback, thus improving precision for specialized contexts such as healthcare or finance
- **Azure OpenAI Service:** Utilizes large language models to enhance contextual understanding, summarize sentiment trends, and interpret nuanced human expressions
- **Power BI and Azure Synapse Analytics:** Visualize and analyze sentiment results from large datasets, thus supporting data-driven insights and executive reporting

Thus, sentiment analysis in knowledge mining combines **natural language processing**, **machine learning**, and **data visualization** to transform subjective opinions into actionable insights. With Azure's AI ecosystem, organizations can monitor public perception, identify opportunities for improvement, and enhance strategic decision-making at scale through real-time emotional intelligence.

Automatic Summarization

Automatic summarization is a Natural Language Processing (NLP) workload that uses artificial intelligence to generate concise summaries of large volumes of text while preserving the original meaning and key information. By analyzing context, structure, and relevance, summarization models can condense lengthy documents, articles, or reports into clear and readable overviews. This capability is valuable in business intelligence, legal analysis, healthcare, and media monitoring, where professionals must process large amounts of information quickly and efficiently.

Key Features of Automatic Summarization Workloads

- **Extractive Summarization:** Selects the most relevant sentences or phrases from the original text to create a shorter version that retains key points
- **Abstractive Summarization:** Generates new sentences that paraphrase and rephrase the source text to produce more natural and human-like summaries
- **Contextual Understanding:** Uses deep learning models to identify relationships between concepts and maintain coherence in condensed outputs
- **Multilingual Summarization:** Supports summarization in multiple languages, allowing global organizations to process multilingual documents consistently
- **Topic Prioritization:** Focuses summaries on specific themes, entities, or keywords to tailor content for different audiences or business goals
- **Integration with Knowledge Mining Pipelines:** Works with document indexing and sentiment analysis tools to provide summarized insights for decision-making

Practical Example of Automatic Summarization

A legal firm uses automatic summarization to process lengthy case files and court decisions. The AI system analyzes each document and generates a one-page summary highlighting key arguments, rulings, and dates. Lawyers can quickly review these summaries to identify relevant precedents and prepare cases more efficiently and save hours of manual reading time.

Azure Services and Implementation of Automatic Summarization

Microsoft Azure offers a suite of the following AI tools to build and deploy automatic summarization systems:

- **Azure AI Language:** Provides prebuilt extractive summarization models and customizable options for generating concise summaries from long-form text
- **Azure OpenAI Service:** Uses advanced large language models like GPT to perform abstractive summarization and is capable of paraphrasing and synthesizing complex information
- **Azure Machine Learning:** Supports the training and fine-tuning of custom summarization models using domain-specific datasets to improve precision and relevance
- **Azure Cognitive Search:** Integrates summarization outputs into knowledge mining pipelines, enabling users to quickly preview and explore large document collections
- **Azure AI Studio:** Simplifies the experimentation, evaluation, and deployment of summarization models, while tracking performance metrics and fine-tuning outputs

Thus, automatic summarization workloads combine **natural language processing**, **machine learning**, and **semantic understanding** to transform lengthy content into concise, actionable summaries. With Azure's AI ecosystem, organizations can accelerate information discovery, enhance productivity, and improve decision-making by delivering clear and contextually accurate summaries at scale.

Mining Unstructured Data

Mining unstructured data is a knowledge mining workload that focuses on extracting insights, relationships, and patterns from information that lacks a predefined structure such as emails, PDFs, reports, social media posts, images, and videos. By using artificial intelligence (AI), Natural Language Processing (NLP), and computer vision, these systems transform raw, unorganized data into structured, searchable knowledge. This capability is essential for organizations that need to derive value from vast repositories of unstructured information.

Key Features of Mining Unstructured Data Workloads

- **Data Ingestion and Processing:** Collects and preprocesses data from multiple unstructured sources, including text, audio, and visual formats
- **Entity and Keyword Extraction:** Identifies key terms, people, locations, and topics to structure data for easier indexing and retrieval
- **Semantic Search and Categorization:** Uses AI models to understand meaning and context for more accurate document classification and to create intelligent search experiences
- **Document Classification and Tagging:** Automatically categorizes files based on content, metadata, or detected entities, while simplifying information management
- **Integration of Multimodal AI:** Combines text analytics, computer vision, and OCR to analyze diverse data types such as images with embedded text or scanned documents
- **Knowledge Graph Generation:** Builds interconnected representations of extracted data which shows relationships between entities and uncovers hidden insights

Practical Example of Mining Unstructured Data

A global consulting firm uses unstructured data mining to analyze client reports, emails, and presentations stored in its internal repository. The AI pipeline extracts topics, identifies frequently mentioned organizations, and summarizes trends across documents. The resulting insights help consultants find relevant expertise, identify emerging market patterns, and support data-driven strategic recommendations.

Azure Services and Implementation of Mining Unstructured Data

Microsoft Azure provides a comprehensive set of AI and data services to build unstructured data mining pipelines:

- **Azure Cognitive Search:** Enables intelligent search across large collections of unstructured content using AI-driven indexing, entity recognition, and semantic ranking
- **Azure AI Language:** Performs text analytics, key phrase extraction, and entity recognition to structure textual data for knowledge discovery
- **Azure AI Vision:** Analyzes images and video content, detecting text, objects, and scenes to integrate visual data into searchable formats
- **Azure Form Recognizer (Document Intelligence):** Extracts structured information from scanned documents, invoices, and forms, converting them into machine-readable data
- **Azure Synapse Analytics:** Aggregates and analyzes structured and unstructured data, integrating insights into dashboards and business intelligence tools
- **Azure OpenAI Service:** Leverages large language models to interpret unstructured content, summarize documents, and generate contextual insights

Mining unstructured data workloads combine **natural language processing**, **computer vision**, and **machine learning** to transform raw information into organized knowledge. With Azure's AI ecosystem, organizations can unlock hidden insights, automate content discovery, and make better-informed decisions by harnessing the full value of their unstructured data.

Social Media Analytics

Social media analytics is a knowledge mining workload that uses Artificial Intelligence (AI), Natural Language Processing (NLP), and data analytics to collect, process, and interpret data from social media platforms. By analyzing posts, comments, hashtags, and user interactions, organizations can gain real-time insights into public sentiment, brand perception, and market trends. This capability helps businesses measure campaign performance, identify influencers, and detect emerging opportunities or risks.

Key Features of Social Media Analytics Workloads

- **Data Collection and Aggregation:** Gathers public data from platforms such as X (formerly Twitter), Facebook, LinkedIn, and Instagram for analysis
- **Sentiment and Emotion Analysis:** Identifies positive, negative, or neutral opinions expressed in posts and comments to assess brand reputation or public response
- **Trend and Topic Detection:** Monitors emerging topics, hashtags, and keywords to understand audience interests and market shifts
- **Audience Segmentation:** Groups users based on behaviors, demographics, or engagement levels to optimize marketing and communication strategies
- **Influencer Identification:** Detects key individuals or accounts that drive discussions and shape public opinion around specific topics
- **Real-Time Monitoring and Alerts:** Provides live dashboards that notify organizations of sudden sentiment changes or viral events that might impact their brand

Practical Example of Social Media Analytics

A consumer electronics company uses social media analytics to monitor reactions to a new smartphone launch. The AI system collects thousands of comments from different platforms, classifies them by sentiment, and identifies trending topics like "camera quality" or "battery life." This information helps the marketing team adjust future campaigns, address user concerns, and highlight popular features in real time.

Azure Services and Implementation of Social Media Analytics

Microsoft Azure provides a wide range of AI and data services to implement effective social media analytics pipelines:

- **Azure AI Language:** Performs sentiment analysis, key phrase extraction, and topic detection on social media text data across multiple languages
- **Azure Cognitive Search:** Indexes and makes social data searchable by enabling filtering by sentiment, topic, or source
- **Azure OpenAI Service:** Uses large language models to summarize trends, interpret nuanced social discussions, and identify emerging public themes
- **Azure Synapse Analytics:** Integrates and visualizes social media data from multiple sources, supporting advanced reporting and predictive modeling
- **Power BI:** Creates interactive dashboards for real-time visualization of sentiment trends, engagement metrics, and audience segmentation results
- **Azure Logic Apps and Event Hubs:** Automate social media data ingestion, transformation, and streaming analytics for continuous monitoring

Social media analytics workloads combine **natural language processing**, **data mining**, and **real-time analytics** to transform social interactions into actionable business insights. With Azure's AI ecosystem, organizations can track brand performance, understand audience sentiment, and make informed marketing decisions that strengthen engagement and reputation.

Identifying Document Intelligence Workloads

In today's data-driven world, businesses are inundated with documents ranging from contracts to invoices. Document intelligence workloads harness the power of AI to process, analyze, and extract meaningful insights from these vast amounts of unstructured data. This section will explore the key features of document intelligence workloads, their applications, and how they can streamline operations across various industries.

Exam Tip: *Document Intelligence is most closely tied to* ***Azure Form Recognizer****. Questions may describe automated data extraction from invoices or forms. Make sure to recognize this as a Document Intelligence workload.*

Document Classification

Document classification is a key **Document Intelligence Workload** that enables organizations to automatically categorize and organize large volumes of digital and scanned documents. By leveraging AI, NLP, and machine learning, document classification models analyze text content, layout, and metadata to assign documents to predefined categories. This workload streamlines information management, improves compliance, and reduces manual processing efforts.

Key Features of Document Classification Workloads

- **Automated Categorization:** Classifies documents into defined categories such as "invoice," "contract," or "policy document" based on their textual content and structure
- **Multi-Class and Multi-Label Classification:** Supports assigning one or multiple labels to a single document, which reflects its complexity or multiple contextual roles
- **Layout and Structural Analysis:** Uses AI models to identify visual patterns such as headers, tables, or form fields to enhance classification accuracy, even in scanned or semi-structured documents
- **Content and Metadata Integration:** Combines textual analysis with metadata (author, date, and format) to improve precision and contextual understanding
- **Scalability and Automation:** Handles thousands of documents simultaneously, thus minimizing human intervention and accelerating document workflows
- **Integration with Data Extraction Pipelines:** Works alongside Optical Character Recognition (OCR) and Information Extraction workloads to create end-to-end intelligent document processing systems.

Practical Example of Document Classification

A global insurance company uses document classification to process customer claims. The AI system automatically distinguishes between "claim forms," "supporting documents," and "payment receipts." Each file is routed to the appropriate workflow for validation or approval, significantly reducing manual sorting time and improving response efficiency.

Azure Services and Implementation of Document Classification

Microsoft Azure provides specialized tools within its Document Intelligence ecosystem to build and deploy document classification workloads:

- **Azure Form Recognizer (Document Intelligence):** Analyzes document layouts, identifies fields, and classifies document types using both content and structure
- **Azure AI Language:** Performs text classification and key phrase extraction, thereby enhancing document understanding and enabling precise categorization
- **Azure Machine Learning:** Supports custom model training with labeled datasets for domain-specific document classification, improving accuracy in regulated industries
- **Azure Cognitive Search:** Indexes and organizes classified documents for fast retrieval, while integrating with knowledge mining and analytics tools

- **Azure OpenAI Service:** Uses large language models to understand semantic meaning to enable classification of complex or ambiguous documents through contextual reasoning

Document classification workloads within **Azure Document Intelligence** combine **computer vision**, **natural language processing**, and **machine learning** to automate document organization and streamline digital workflows. With Azure's AI ecosystem, organizations can create scalable, intelligent document management systems that can enhance accuracy, efficiency, and compliance across their operations.

Entity Recognition

Entity recognition is a core **Document Intelligence workload** that automatically identifies and extracts key pieces of information, also known as *entities*, from documents. These entities may include names, organizations, dates, monetary amounts, or other domain-specific data relevant to business operations. By using Natural Language Processing (NLP) and machine learning, entity recognition transforms unstructured or semi-structured documents into structured, searchable information, thereby enabling faster analysis and automation.

Key Features of Entity Recognition Workloads

- **Entity Detection and Classification:** Recognizes and categorizes important information such as people, companies, locations, or financial values within documents
- **Custom Entity Models:** Supports training custom models to detect industry-specific entities such as product names, legal clauses, or medical terms
- **Contextual Understanding:** Uses advanced language models to interpret entities in context–for example, distinguishing between "Apple" the company and "apple" the fruit
- **Integration with Document Pipelines:** Works alongside other Document Intelligence workloads like OCR and Document Classification to enhance data extraction accuracy
- **Scalability and Automation:** Processes thousands of documents simultaneously, while automatically tagging and structuring data for use in databases or analytics platforms
- **Linking to Knowledge Graphs:** Connects extracted entities to external data sources or internal knowledge bases, hence enriching context and enabling advanced search experiences

Practical Example of Entity Recognition

A legal services company uses entity recognition to process large volumes of contracts. The AI system identifies and extracts key entities such as party names, contract values, and renewal dates. These entities are then stored in a structured database, allowing lawyers to search and filter contracts by client, term, or status. This automation reduces manual review time and enhances compliance tracking.

Azure Services and Implementation of Entity Recognition

Microsoft Azure provides the following AI services to implement entity recognition within Document Intelligence pipelines:

- **Azure AI Language:** Offers prebuilt and customizable Named Entity Recognition (NER) models that identify standard and domain-specific entities across multiple languages
- **Azure Form Recognizer (Document Intelligence):** Extracts text and layout data from documents using OCR and can be integrated with entity recognition models for deeper analysis
- **Azure Machine Learning:** Enables organizations to train custom entity extraction models tailored to specific document types or regulatory requirements

- **Azure Cognitive Search:** Indexes extracted entities and allows users to perform semantic or entity-based searches across document repositories
- **Azure OpenAI Service:** Leverages large language models to perform advanced entity extraction and contextual linking across complex or unstructured content

Entity recognition workloads within **Azure Document Intelligence** combine **natural language processing**, **machine learning**, and **data modeling** to transform text-heavy documents into structured, meaningful insights. With Azure's AI ecosystem, organizations can automate information extraction, accelerate document analysis, and enhance knowledge discovery across large-scale business operations.

Document Summarization

Document summarization is a key **Document Intelligence workload** that uses AI and NLP to generate concise summaries of lengthy documents while preserving the most relevant information. This workload enables organizations to quickly and efficiently process large volumes of content such as contracts, reports, or research papers. By automating the summarization process, teams can reduce manual reading time, accelerate decision-making, and focus on critical insights.

Key Features of Document Summarization Workloads

- **Extractive Summarization:** Selects the most important sentences or paragraphs directly from the original document, while ensuring factual accuracy and key point preservation
- **Abstractive Summarization:** Generates new, paraphrased sentences that capture the essence of the document in a more natural, human-like style
- **Contextual Understanding:** Leverages deep learning models to recognize relationships, priorities, and intent within a document, while ensuring coherent and relevant summaries
- **Domain Adaptation:** Can be fine-tuned for specific industries such as legal, healthcare, or finance to highlight the most relevant sections based on context
- **Integration with Document Pipelines:** Works alongside other Document Intelligence workloads such as OCR and Entity Recognition to create complete document understanding workflows
- **Scalable Processing:** Processes large document collections simultaneously and allows organizations to summarize hundreds of files within seconds

Practical Example of Document Summarization

A financial institution uses document summarization to process regulatory filings and compliance reports. The AI system scans each document and automatically produces a short summary highlighting key findings, financial figures, and deadlines. These summaries are then shared with compliance officers, thereby enabling faster reviews and reducing manual workload.

Azure Services and Implementation of Document Summarization

Microsoft Azure provides the following AI services to implement document summarization as part of a broader Document Intelligence pipeline:

- **Azure AI Language:** Provides prebuilt extractive summarization capabilities and customizable models to generate summaries from long-form text
- **Azure OpenAI Service:** Uses advanced Large Language Models (LLMs) such as GPT to perform abstractive summarization that captures meaning and context in a human-like manner
- **Azure Machine Learning:** Enables organizations to train and fine-tune custom summarization models for domain-specific use cases or specialized document types

- **Azure Cognitive Search:** Integrates with summarization workflows to provide users with concise document previews in search results, thereby enhancing knowledge discovery
- **Azure AI Studio:** Offers tools for prompt engineering, experimentation, and evaluation of summarization models, thus streamlining deployment and optimization

Document summarization workloads within **Azure Document Intelligence** combine **machine learning**, **natural language processing**, and **semantic understanding** to distill complex content into actionable insights. With Azure's AI ecosystem, organizations can automate document review, improve productivity, and enable faster, more informed decision-making across departments.

Information Extraction

Information extraction is a fundamental **Document Intelligence workload** that focuses on identifying, capturing, and structuring relevant data from unstructured or semi-structured documents. By combining artificial intelligence (AI), natural language processing (NLP), and machine learning, this workload enables organizations to automatically extract key information such as names, amounts, dates, and entities from complex files like invoices, forms, and contracts. It plays a crucial role in automating document workflows, enhancing data accuracy, and accelerating decision-making.

Key Features of Information Extraction Workloads

- **Structured Data Capture:** Extracts essential information from documents such as invoice totals, client names, or contract dates and organizes it into structured formats like tables or databases
- **Layout and Format Awareness:** Uses document layout analysis to interpret complex structures including tables, fields, and checkboxes, even in scanned or handwritten documents
- **Custom Extraction Models:** Allows training of models tailored to domain-specific data fields, improving accuracy in specialized industries such as finance, insurance, or healthcare
- **Integration with OCR and Entity Recognition:** Works in conjunction with Optical Character Recognition (OCR) to extract text and with Entity Recognition to identify meaningful terms within that text
- **Validation and Confidence Scoring:** Provides confidence metrics for extracted data to ensure accuracy before integrating results into business systems
- **Scalable Automation:** Processes large document collections efficiently, while reducing manual entry and accelerating data processing across the organization

Practical Example of Information Extraction

A healthcare organization uses information extraction to process patient admission forms. The AI system automatically extracts fields like patient name, admission date, diagnosis, and insurance details. This data is then validated and integrated into the hospital's Electronic Health Record (EHR) system, which significantly reduces administrative workload and minimizes human-made errors.

Azure Services and Implementation of Information Extraction

Microsoft Azure provides a comprehensive suite of the following AI tools and services to implement information extraction within Document Intelligence pipelines:

- **Azure Form Recognizer (Document Intelligence):** Extracts key-value pairs, tables, and fields from forms, invoices, and receipts using OCR and layout-based AI models
- **Azure AI Language:** Identifies and extracts key phrases, entities, and relationships from text, threby transforming unstructured content into structured insights

- **Azure Machine Learning:** Enables custom model development for domain-specific extraction tasks, thus improving precision and adaptability across unique datasets
- **Azure Cognitive Search:** Indexes and organizes extracted information for easy querying, filtering, and integration with analytics dashboards
- **Azure OpenAI Service:** Uses Large Language Models (LLMs) to understand document context and extract complex relationships or implicit data that traditional models might overlook

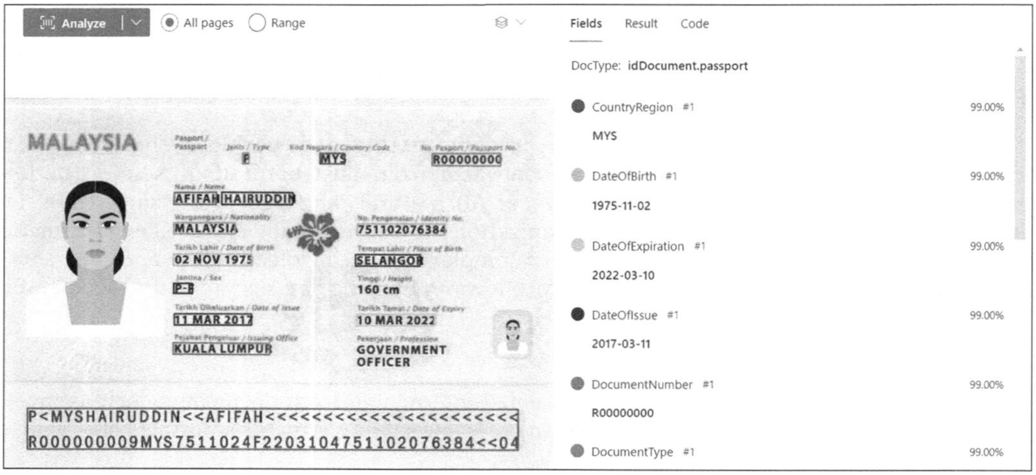

Figure 2.12: *Using Azure AI Document Intelligence to Process Data from an Identity (ID)*

Information extraction workloads within **Azure Document Intelligence** combine **natural language processing**, **computer vision**, and **machine learning** to transform unstructured documents into structured, actionable data. With Azure's AI ecosystem, organizations can automate manual information capture, reduce errors, and improve operational efficiency across data-intensive business processes.

Identifying Features of Generative AI Workloads

Generative AI represents one of the most transformative areas in artificial intelligence, which enables machines to create new and original content rather than simply analyze existing data. It powers applications that range from content creation to customer support and produces outputs that are coherent, contextually relevant, and adaptable across multiple tasks.

Exam Tip: *Generative AI questions typically mention* **Azure OpenAI Service** *and models like* **GPT** *or* **DALL·E**. *These workloads create new content (text, images, or code) instead of analyzing existing data.*

A well-known example is **ChatGPT**, which generates human-like text responses in real time. As a result, it has reshaped how people interact with technology. From drafting emails and writing stories to answering queries and summarizing information, generative AI demonstrates how machines can replicate aspects of human creativity and reasoning.

As organizations continue to adopt generative AI solutions, understanding the key features and practical applications of these workloads becomes essential. The following sections explore the defining characteristics of generative AI and how Azure services enable these capabilities across different domains.

Content Generation

Content generation is a core **Generative AI workload** that enables machines to create original, human-like content based on input prompts or contextual data. Using Large Language Models (LLMs) and deep learning techniques, this workload can produce text, images, audio, or video that reflects creativity, coherence, and intent. It is widely used in marketing, education, journalism, customer support, and software development, which helps organizations scale production while maintaining quality and consistency.

Key Features of Content Generation Workloads

- **Natural Language Generation (NLG):** Produces written text such as articles, reports, blog posts, or emails that align with a given tone, topic, or purpose
- **Multimodal Generation:** Extends beyond text to include images, audio, and video content, leading to richer, more engaging creative outputs
- **Prompt-Based Creation:** Uses natural language prompts to guide AI systems in generating contextually relevant and coherent content tailored to user intent
- **Context Awareness:** Understands the meaning, tone, and structure of prompts to ensure generated content is accurate, logical, and aligned with the target audience
- **Customization and Fine-Tuning:** Models can be adapted to specific industries or brand guidelines, thus producing outputs consistent with company voice or domain expertise
- **Human-AI Collaboration:** Supports iterative refinement, allowing users to review, edit, and improve generated content through interactive feedback loops

Figure 2.13: *Image Generation with ChatGPT and DALL-E*

Practical Example of Content Generation

A digital marketing agency uses content generation to create blog articles and social media posts for clients. By providing a short prompt such as "Top 5 cybersecurity practices for small businesses," the AI system can generate a complete, SEO-optimized article with headers, key insights, and call-to-action phrases. This allows the agency to deliver more content in less time while maintaining quality and brand alignment.

Azure Services and Implementation of Content Generation

Microsoft Azure provides the following AI services that enable organizations to design and deploy content generation solutions:

- **Azure OpenAI Service:** Provides access to powerful language models like GPT that are capable of generating high-quality text, code, or conversational content based on natural language prompts
- **Azure AI Vision:** Supports image generation and analysis, resulting in creative workloads that combine textual and visual content
- **Azure Machine Learning:** Facilitates fine-tuning of generative models using domain-specific datasets, ensuring that outputs align with organizational needs and tone
- **Azure AI Studio:** Offers an intuitive environment for prompt engineering, experimentation, and model management, while allowing teams to refine and control generative outputs
- **Azure Cognitive Search:** Integrates with generative AI workflows to supply contextual information, and enables Retrieval-Augmented Generation (RAG) for factual and relevant content creation

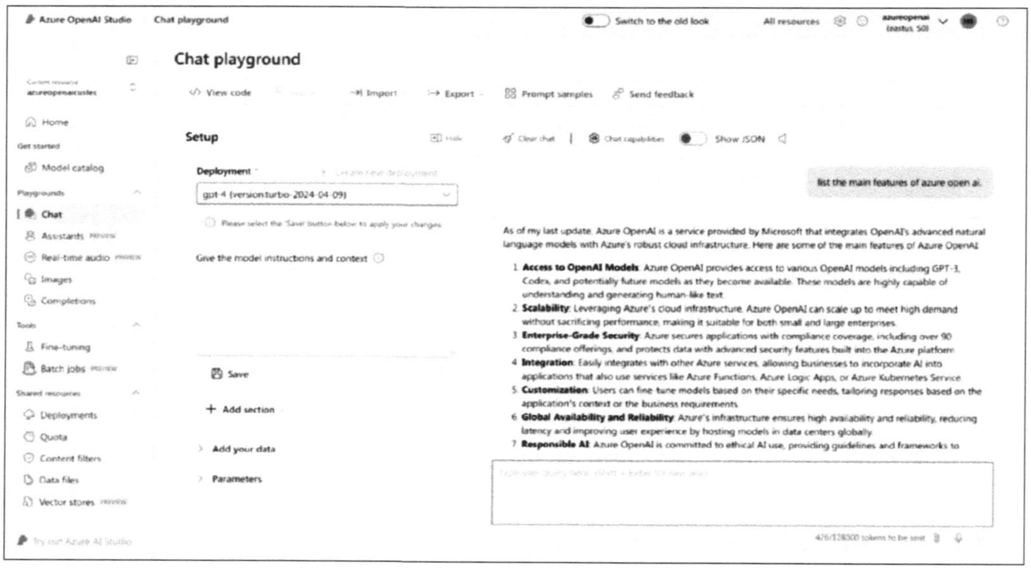

***Figure 2.14:** Using Azure AI Open AI Chat*

Content generation workloads within **Azure Generative AI** combine **deep learning**, **natural language processing**, and **contextual reasoning** to create meaningful and high-quality digital assets. With Azure's AI ecosystem, organizations can accelerate creativity, automate communication, and deliver personalized content at scale, which transforms the way ideas are produced and shared.

Data Augmentation

Data augmentation is a critical **Generative AI workload** that enhances the size, diversity, and quality of datasets by creating new, synthetic data samples derived from existing information. This process improves model accuracy, robustness, and generalization, especially when real-world data is limited, imbalanced, or expensive to collect. Generative models such as Variational Autoencoders (VAEs), Generative Adversarial Networks (GANs), and Large Language Models (LLMs) are often used to produce realistic synthetic data for training machine learning and AI systems.

Key Features of Data Augmentation Workloads

- **Synthetic Data Generation:** Creates artificial data that mimics real-world samples such as images, text, or sensor readings to expand and balance datasets
- **Data Diversity and Balance:** Addresses class imbalances by generating additional examples for underrepresented categories, which improves fairness and accuracy in model training
- **Noise Injection and Variation:** Introduces controlled modifications (for example, rotations, translations, or paraphrasing) to make models more resilient to real-world variability
- **Domain-Specific Augmentation:** Uses contextual or industry-specific knowledge to generate relevant data such as synthetic patient records, manufacturing defects, or financial transactions
- **Privacy Preservation:** Produces synthetic datasets that retain statistical characteristics of real data without exposing sensitive or Personally Identifiable Information (PII)
- **Integration with Model Training Pipelines:** Seamlessly combines with existing training workflows in Azure Machine Learning to continuously enrich datasets and improve performance

Practical Example of Data Augmentation

A healthcare research organization uses data augmentation to enhance its training dataset for medical image analysis. Since acquiring labeled X-ray images is expensive and time-consuming, a generative model can create realistic synthetic images showing various disease patterns. These additional samples allow the diagnostic AI system to achieve higher accuracy, while reducing overfitting.

Azure Services and Implementation of Data Augmentation

Microsoft Azure provides a range of tools and services that enable data augmentation as part of generative AI and machine learning workflows:

- **Azure Machine Learning:** Supports data augmentation pipelines with automated transformations, synthetic data generation, and integration into training workflows
- **Azure OpenAI Service:** Leverages large language models (LLMs) to create synthetic text, dialogues, or code data for augmenting natural language or software development datasets
- **Azure AI Vision:** Generates and manipulates synthetic image data to improve computer vision models through controlled visual variations
- **Azure Synapse Analytics:** Facilitates large-scale storage, management, and analysis of both real and synthetic datasets for continuous model improvement
- **Azure AI Studio:** Provides an environment for creating, managing, and validating augmented datasets to ensure consistency and alignment with ethical AI principles

Data augmentation workloads within Azure Generative AI use synthetic data generation and machine learning strategies to broaden and improve training datasets. This approach helps organizations address data scarcity, boost model robustness, and ensure more dependable and fair AI outcomes in various applications.

Style Transfer

Style transfer is a **Generative AI workload** that applies the artistic or structural characteristics of one piece of content such as an image, video, or text to another, while preserving its original meaning or composition. Using deep learning techniques, particularly Convolutional Neural Networks (CNNs) and transformer-based models, this workload enables AI systems to blend creative styles and produce visually or linguistically unique outputs. Style transfer is widely used in design, entertainment, marketing, and digital art to automate creative transformations and enhance personalization.

Key Features of Style Transfer Workloads

- **Image-to-Image Style Adaptation:** Transfers the visual characteristics of one image (like color palette, brushstroke, or texture) onto another while retaining the original content structure
- **Text Style Transformation:** Adjusts the tone, formality, or writing style of a text such as converting casual language into professional writing, or translating prose into poetic form
- **Audio and Video Style Conversion:** Applies tonal or rhythmic patterns from one audio source to another and can be used in voice synthesis, film editing, and music production
- **Content Preservation:** Ensures that the underlying meaning or spatial structure of the original content remains intact during the transformation process
- **Cross-Domain Creativity:** Combines visual, textual, or audio data to create hybrid content such as turning sketches into photorealistic images, or adapting one artist's style to another medium
- **Customizable Model Training:** Allows organizations to train models with specific artistic, linguistic, or cultural influences, while tailoring outputs to desired creative outcomes

Practical Example of Style Transfer

A digital art studio uses style transfer to transform photographs into images that mimic famous painting styles, such as those of Van Gogh or Monet. The AI system analyzes the texture and color patterns of the artist's work and applies them to modern photographs. This enables the studio to produce unique and stylized artwork for marketing campaigns and exhibitions.

Azure Services and Implementation of Style Transfer

Microsoft Azure provides the following AI and compute services to implement and scale style transfer workloads:

- **Azure Machine Learning:** Supports training and deployment of custom neural networks for image, text, and video style transfer, while leveraging GPU-accelerated environments
- **Azure OpenAI Service:** Enables text-based style transformation using Large Language Models (LLMs), allowing tone, sentiment, or format adjustments in generated content
- **Azure AI Vision:** Facilitates visual style analysis and transformation in image and video data, integrating with generative pipelines for automated creative workflows
- **Azure AI Studio:** Provides an environment for experimentation, fine-tuning, and version control of style transfer models, while supporting iterative creative development
- **Azure Cognitive Services for Media:** Processes and transforms multimedia content (audio, video, and images) to apply specific stylistic features at scale

Style transfer workloads within **Azure Generative AI** combine **deep learning**, **neural network modeling**, and **creative computation** to transform how content is generated and personalized. With Azure's AI ecosystem, organizations can automate artistic and stylistic adaptation, which results in new forms of digital creativity, brand consistency, and innovation across industries.

Text-to-Image and Image-to-Text Generation

Text-to-image and image-to-text generation are complementary **Generative AI workloads** that enable bidirectional understanding and creation between visual and textual information. These are explained as follows:

- **Text-to-Image Generation** creates original images from textual descriptions, while translating language into detailed visual outputs.
- **Image-to-Text Generation**, also known as image captioning, interprets and describes the content of images in natural language.

Together, these workloads bridge the gap between vision and language, allowing AI systems to both visualize ideas and articulate visual content. They are widely used in digital design, accessibility, education, and creative industries.

Key Features of Text-to-Image and Image-to-Text Workloads

- **Cross-Modal Understanding:** Combines Natural Language Processing (NLP) and computer vision to translate information between text and image domains
- **Text-to-Image Generation:** Uses deep learning diffusion models (such as DALL·E or Stable Diffusion) to generate realistic, contextually accurate images from descriptive prompts
- **Image Captioning and Description:** Employs visual understanding models to generate natural language descriptions of image content, supporting accessibility and metadata creation
- **Prompt Engineering and Control:** Allows users to guide generation through text prompts, style keywords, or composition parameters to influence the final output
- **Multimodal Integration:** Supports complex scenarios that involve both text and visual reasoning, such as answering questions about images or generating illustrations from narratives
- **Creativity and Personalization:** Enables users to produce custom visuals or descriptive text that aligns with specific styles, tones, or branding requirements

Practical Example of Text-to-Image and Image-to-Text Generation

An educational publishing company uses text-to-image generation to create custom illustrations for science textbooks. The AI system transforms textual descriptions like "a cross-section of a volcano showing magma flow" into detailed visuals. Simultaneously, the same system uses image-to-text generation to create captions and alt-text for accessibility compliance. This dual workflow enhances content creation speed, consistency, and inclusivity.

Azure Services and Implementation of Text-to-Image and Image-to-Text Generation

Microsoft Azure provides several AI services that enable the implementation of these multimodal generative workloads:

- **Azure OpenAI Service:** Supports multimodal generative models such as DALL·E for text-to-image creation and GPT-based models for image captioning and text generation
- **Azure AI Vision:** Analyzes images to identify objects, scenes, and actions, thus forming the foundation for accurate image-to-text generation
- **Azure Machine Learning:** Enables training and fine-tuning of custom multimodal models that combine vision and language understanding for domain-specific applications
- **Azure AI Studio:** Provides an environment for prompt experimentation and model integration, which allows developers to orchestrate both text-to-image and image-to-text pipelines
- **Azure Cognitive Search:** Enhances generative workflows by indexing and retrieving visual or textual data for creating content with a rich context

Text-to-image and image-to-text generation workloads within **Azure Generative AI** combine **computer vision**, **natural language processing**, and **deep learning** to connect the visual and linguistic worlds. With Azure's AI ecosystem, organizations can create more inclusive, creative, and intelligent applications that both visualize ideas and describe the world with precision.

Retrieval-Augmented Generation (RAG)

Retrieval-Augmented Generation (RAG) is an advanced **Generative AI workload** that enhances Large Language Models (LLMs) by combining text generation with external information retrieval. Instead of relying solely on pre-trained model knowledge, RAG systems dynamically access relevant documents, databases, or APIs during the generation process to produce accurate, up-to-date, and contextually grounded responses. This hybrid approach significantly improves factual reliability and domain specificity, which makes RAG ideal for enterprise knowledge applications, customer support, and research environments.

Key Features of Retrieval-Augmented Generation (RAG) Workloads

- **Dynamic Knowledge Retrieval:** Accesses external data sources such as document repositories, websites, or vector databases at query time to enrich responses with real-world information
- **Context-Aware Generation:** Uses retrieved content as context for the language model, ensuring that generated outputs are both accurate and relevant to the user's query
- **Vector Embedding and Semantic Search:** Employs embedding models to represent text as vectors, thereby enabling precise semantic matching between user prompts and stored information
- **Factual Consistency and Transparency:** Reduces hallucinations and improves trustworthiness by grounding generated text in verifiable sources
- **Scalable Knowledge Integration:** Allows continuous updates of external knowledge bases without retraining the underlying language model
- **Customizability for Enterprises:** Supports secure integration with private datasets, ensuring compliance with data governance and privacy requirements

Practical Example of Retrieval-Augmented Generation (RAG)

A global consulting firm deploys a RAG-based assistant to help analysts generate reports using internal documentation and research papers. When an employee asks, "What are the latest cybersecurity regulations in the EU?", the system retrieves recent documents from the company's compliance database and generates a summarized, source-cited response. This workflow ensures accuracy, saves research time, and allows organizations to make informed business decisions.

Azure Services and Implementation of Retrieval-Augmented Generation (RAG)

Microsoft Azure provides a robust ecosystem consisting of the following tools to build and deploy RAG-based applications using AI and search services:

- **Azure OpenAI Service:** Provides large language models such as GPT that can generate contextually relevant text when supplied with retrieved external information
- **Azure Cognitive Search:** Acts as the retrieval layer for indexing, searching, and ranking relevant content, powering the "retrieve" component of RAG pipelines
- **Azure AI Studio:** Offers orchestration tools for building and testing RAG workflows, while managing prompt templates, and evaluating response quality
- **Azure Machine Learning:** Enables the development of custom embedding models and fine-tuning pipelines for domain-specific retrieval and generation tasks

- **Azure Cosmos DB and Azure Data Explorer:** Store and manage structured and unstructured data efficiently, thereby supporting large-scale knowledge retrieval with low latency

Retrieval-Augmented Generation workloads within **Azure Generative AI** combine **natural language processing**, **information retrieval**, and **knowledge grounding** to deliver responses that are both creative and factual. With Azure's AI ecosystem, organizations can build intelligent, trustworthy, and domain-aware assistants that generate accurate insights powered by their own data.

Conclusion

Having explored the foundational features of common AI workloads, you now have a solid understanding of the diverse applications of artificial intelligence. We have examined content moderation and personalization workloads, as well as computer vision, natural language processing, knowledge mining, document intelligence, and generative AI workloads. This chapter has provided insights into how these workloads function and their impact across various industries. With this knowledge, you will be prepared to recognize the value AI can bring to different scenarios and how to leverage these workloads effectively.

In the next chapter, we will shift our focus to the guiding principles for responsible AI, essential for creating fair, reliable, and secure AI solutions. We will explore considerations for fairness, reliability and safety, privacy and security, inclusiveness, transparency, and accountability in AI solutions. These principles are crucial for developing ethical AI applications that prioritize trust, inclusivity, and accountability, while aligning with best practices for the implementation of responsible AI.

Points to Remember

- Content moderation ensures platforms remain safe and adhere to guidelines by using AI to analyze, filter, and manage user-generated content.
- Personalization uses AI to analyze user behaviors and preferences to create customized experiences.
- Computer vision workloads encompass a variety of tasks that enable machines to analyze and understand visual data.
- NLP workloads encompass a variety of tasks that allow machines to understand and manipulate human language.
- Knowledge mining workloads are essential for transforming raw data into valuable information that can guide decision-making.
- Document intelligence workloads are crucial for transforming unstructured data into structured insights in order to drive business efficiency and decision-making.
- Generative AI workloads offer a range of powerful features that enable the creation of new and innovative content.

Key Terms

- **Content Moderation Workloads:** Automated processes for analyzing and managing user-generated content to maintain platform safety and guideline adherence
    - **Automated Image and Text Analysis:** Flags explicit, hateful, or spammy content in images and text
    - **Sentiment Analysis:** Identifies tone to manage offensive or harmful posts
    - **Language Filtering:** Applies moderation in multiple languages for global consistency

  - **Customizable Filters and Policies:** Enables tailored settings, such as stricter rules for children's content
  - **Contextual Understanding:** Distinguishes content based on context to enhance accuracy
  - **Real-Time Moderation:** Instantly processes high-volume content for immediate response
- **Personalization Workloads:** AI-driven techniques for customizing user experiences based on behaviors and preferences
  - **Behavioral Analysis:** Recommends content aligned with user interests
  - **Recommendation Engines:** Suggest products or content based on user history
  - **Dynamic Content Customization:** Adapts content to user profiles
  - **Location and Context Awareness:** Provides context-based recommendations
  - **A/B Testing and Continuous Learning:** Refines recommendations based on performance
  - **User Segmentation:** Groups users by preferences for targeted content
- **Computer Vision Workloads:** AI processes for analyzing and understanding visual data in images and video
  - **Image Classification:** Categorizes images into predefined classes
  - **Object Detection:** Identifies and locates objects in images
  - **Facial Recognition:** Verifies identities based on facial features
  - **Image Segmentation:** Divides images for detailed analysis
  - **Optical Character Recognition (OCR):** Converts paper-based text to digital
  - **Video Analysis:** Extracts insights from video streams
- **Natural Language Processing (NLP) Workloads:** Techniques enabling machines to process and interact with human language
  - **Text Classification:** Groups text for tasks like spam detection
  - **Sentiment Analysis:** Assesses emotional tone in text
  - **Named Entity Recognition (NER):** Extracts key entities (names, dates) from text
  - **Machine Translation:** Translates text between languages
  - **Text Generation:** Creates human-like text from prompts
  - **Speech Recognition:** Converts spoken language to text
  - **Conversational Agents (Chatbots):** Engages users in natural language for support
- **Knowledge Mining Workloads:** Processes for transforming raw data into structured insights
  - **Information Extraction:** Identifies relevant data from large datasets
  - **Text Analysis:** Converts unstructured text into structured data
  - **Pattern Discovery:** Detects trends and relationships in data
  - **Sentiment Analysis:** Analyzes text for opinions and emotions
  - **Automatic Summarization:** Generates summaries of lengthy documents
  - **Mining Unstructured Data:** Analyzes unformatted data for insights
  - **Social Media Analytics:** Extracts consumer insights from social data
- **Generative AI Workloads:** AI models that create new content or enhance existing data
  - **Content Generation:** Produces new text, images, or music
  - **Data Augmentation:** Enhances datasets with synthetic data
  - **Style Transfer:** Applies artistic styles to content

- **Text-to-Image and Image-to-Text Generation:** Links text and visuals for better searchability
- **Retrieval-Augmented Generation (RAG):** Integrates generative AI with retrieval systems for dynamic information access

Multiple Choice Questions

1. What is the primary purpose of content moderation in digital platforms?
   a. Increasing user engagement through targeted ads
   b. Ensuring compliance with platform guidelines and maintaining a safe environment for users
   c. Generating revenue from user interactions
   d. Promoting user-generated content without restrictions
2. How does sentiment analysis contribute to content moderation?
   a. Classifying content based on geographic location
   b. Analyzing the tone and emotional impact of posts to identify potentially harmful content
   c. Generating automated responses to user comments
   d. Tracking user login times for performance metrics
3. What is the benefit of real-time moderation in content moderation workloads?
   a. Reducing the need for user feedback on content
   b. Allowing for slower content analysis to ensure accuracy
   c. Enabling immediate action against harmful content as it is posted
   d. Creating more opportunities for user interaction and engagement
4. How does user segmentation enhance personalization?
   a. Limiting content availability based on the user's age
   b. Preventing users from seeing unrelated content
   c. Allowing targeted content delivery based on specific user behaviors or preferences
   d. Tracking all user activities for analytical purposes
5. What is the primary purpose of image classification in computer vision?
   a. To convert images into editable formats
   b. To categorize images into predefined classes or labels
   c. To enhance video quality for streaming
   d. To detect objects within an image using bounding boxes
6. Which computer vision workload is essential for real-time detection of objects such as pedestrians and traffic signs in autonomous vehicles?
   a. Image Segmentation
   b. Facial Recognition

   c. Object Detection
   d. Video Analysis

7. What is the primary purpose of text classification in NLP?
   a. To analyze the emotional tone of the text
   b. To categorize text into predefined groups or labels based on content
   c. To translate text from one language to another
   d. Implementing and classifying key entities within text

8. What is the focus of Named Entity Recognition (NER)?
   a. To assess customer satisfaction through feedback
   b. To generate human-like text based on prompts
   c. To identify and classify key entities in text, such as names and dates
   d. To categorize text for spam detection

9. What roles do conversational agents (chatbots) play in customer service?
   a. They convert spoken language into text for documentation.
   b. They interact with users using natural language to provide support and assistance.
   c. They categorize text for sentiment analysis.
   d. They identify key entities within user queries.

10. What is the primary function of information extraction in knowledge mining?
   a. To create condensed versions of documents
   b. To analyze social media posts for trends
   c. To identify and classify relevant data from large sets of information
   d. To transform unstructured text into structured data

11. What is the purpose of pattern discovery in knowledge mining?
   a. To classify data into specific categories
   b. To summarize lengthy reports
   c. To find relationships and trends within large datasets
   d. To analyze customer feedback for sentiment

12. How does document classification benefit organizations?
   a. By summarizing lengthy documents
   b. By automatically categorizing documents for efficient retrieval
   c. By extracting monetary amounts from invoices
   d. By automating workflow processes

13. What is the primary function of content generation in generative AI workloads?
    a. To analyze existing data
    b. To classify documents into categories
    c. To create new content such as text, images, and audio from existing data
    d. To automate workflow processes
14. What is Retrieval-Augmented Generation (RAG) in generative AI?
    a. A feature that generates random content without context.
    b. A combination of generative models with retrieval systems for dynamic access to external information.
    c. A technique for generating images from text.
    d. A method for analyzing customer feedback.

Answers

1. b
2. b
3. c
4. c
5. b
6. c
7. b
8. c
9. b
10. c
11. c
12. b
13. c
14. b

CHAPTER 3
Identify Guiding Principles for Responsible AI

Introduction

In this chapter, we will explore the concept of **Responsible AI** and its importance for the development of ethical, safe, and reliable AI systems. Artificial intelligence is transforming the way we live and work, bringing unprecedented opportunities across industries. However, as AI becomes more integrated into our daily lives, it also presents new ethical and security challenges. To address these, it is crucial to ensure that AI is developed and applied responsibly, with a focus on transparency, safety, and fairness.

Responsible AI is a framework designed to guide each stage of an AI system's life cycle by grounding it in human values and ethical principles. This approach places people and their needs at the center of design decisions, while encouraging developers to create technology that respects and promotes core values. Responsible AI emphasizes impartial treatment, reliable and secure operations, respect for privacy, and inclusiveness to ensure that AI serves the greater good.

To support this commitment to ethical and safe AI, Microsoft has established the **Responsible AI Standard**, which is built on six core principles: **Fairness**, **Reliability and Safety**, **Privacy and Security**, **Inclusiveness**, **Transparency**, and **Accountability**. These principles lay the foundation for developing trustworthy AI and ensure that as technology evolves, it should continue to uphold ethical standards and respect human values.

By the end of this chapter, you will have a strong understanding of the foundational principles of Responsible AI, including fairness, transparency, accountability, and other core values that are necessary for the development of ethical AI.

Structure

In this chapter, we will discuss the following topics:

- Responsible AI
- Fairness in an AI Solution
- Reliability and Safety in an AI Solution
- Privacy and Security in an AI Solution
- Inclusiveness in an AI Solution
- Transparency in an AI Solution
- Accountability in an AI Solution

Responsible AI

Artificial Intelligence (AI) continues to transform the way we live, work, and make decisions, thus creating both new opportunities and new responsibilities. As AI systems become more integrated into everyday life, it is important that they should be designed and operated ethically, safely, and transparently. **Responsible AI** is the framework that ensures that these goals are met. It guides the entire AI lifecycle–from data collection and model design to deployment and monitoring–so that systems are **fair, reliable, secure, and centered on human values**.

Responsible AI goes beyond technical compliance. It reflects a deep commitment to **human ethics and societal well-being**. By prioritizing fairness, transparency, inclusiveness, and accountability, developers ensure that AI benefits everyone, instead of a select few. This approach helps prevent harm, builds trust, and ensures that AI contributes positively to people and communities.

Microsoft's Responsible AI Principles

Microsoft has formalized its ethical approach through the **Responsible AI Standard**, which is built on **six guiding principles** that define how AI should be developed and used:

- **Fairness:** AI systems must treat all people equitably, while mitigating bias and ensuring that algorithms do not unfairly favor or disadvantage any individual or group.

  Example: In **Computer Vision workloads**, fairness is essential to prevent **bias in facial recognition models**, which could otherwise misidentify people from certain ethnic backgrounds.
- **Reliability and Safety:** AI must operate in a consistent and predictable way, protecting users from malfunction, misuse, or harm. For example, in **Conversational AI or NLP systems**, reliability ensures that a chatbot responds appropriately without generating **offensive or harmful language**.
- **Privacy and Security:** AI solutions must safeguard personal data and ensure that sensitive information is handled responsibly. For example, in **Healthcare AI workloads**, privacy and security are vital to **protect patient data** and maintain confidentiality in diagnostic models.
- **Inclusiveness:** AI should empower and represent all people, especially those from underrepresented or marginalized groups. For example, inclusive design in **Computer Vision** or **voice recognition** allows people with disabilities or diverse accents to interact equally with AI systems.
- **Transparency:** Users should be able to understand how AI systems work and why certain outcomes occur. For example, in **Generative AI**, transparency helps identify the instances when a model creates **synthetic or copyrighted content**, promoting awareness and trust.
- **Accountability:** Human oversight must always remain central to the development of Responsible AI. Developers, operators, and organizations are responsible for the actions and outcomes of their AI systems. For example, in **Generative AI** and **Conversational AI**, accountability ensures that humans remain responsible for detecting and correcting **misinformation or ethical violations**.

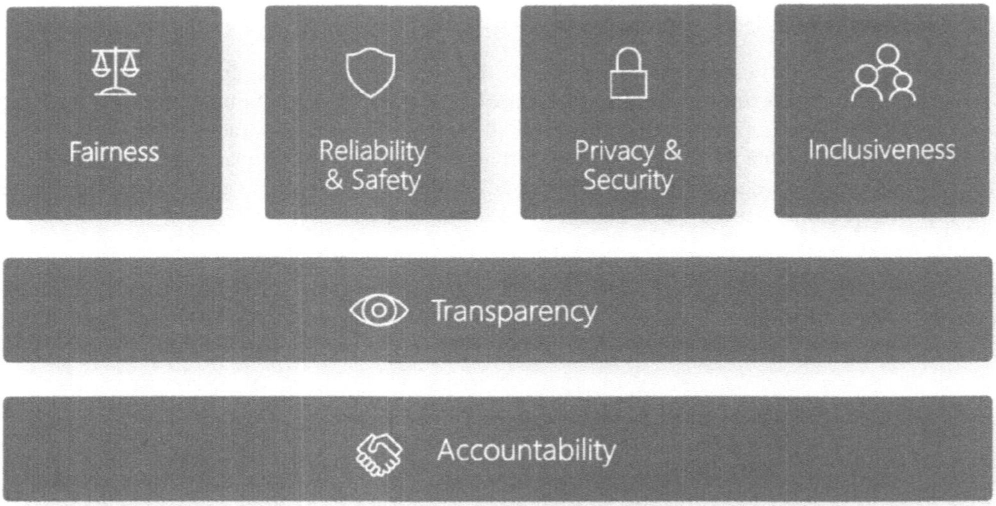

Figure 3.1: *Microsoft's Responsible AI Principles*

Together, these six principles establish the foundation for **trustworthy AI**. They ensure that as technology evolves, innovation must align with ethics, privacy, and inclusiveness.

The Importance of Responsible AI

Applying these principles is not just about meeting regulations–it is about building a better future through technology. Responsible AI ensures that innovation supports **human progress, fairness, and safety** rather than amplifying bias or risk.

For the **AI-900 exam**, understanding these principles is essential: you will often need to identify which **Responsible AI principle** applies to a given **workload scenario**, such as bias in Computer Vision, data protection in healthcare, or transparency in Generative AI.

Fairness in an AI Solution

Fairness is one of the core principles of Responsible AI and addresses a critical question: **How can an AI system allocate opportunities, resources, and information equitably to all users?**

In essence, *fairness* means ensuring that AI systems treat all individuals impartially, without any discrimination based on attributes such as gender, race, or disability. For example, consider an AI model used to **approve loan applications**. It must evaluate applicants solely on objective criteria, ensuring no group is unfairly favored or disadvantaged.

This principle is not only a technical requirement but an **ethical commitment** to equality and social justice. Fairness protects individual rights and prevents technology from amplifying historical or cultural biases that may exist in datasets.

Fairness in AI Workloads

In the **AI-900 exam**, you will need to recognize that fairness plays a crucial role in many AI scenarios.

- In **Computer Vision workloads**, fairness helps **prevent bias in facial recognition systems**, where inaccurate performance across gender or ethnicity groups could lead to misidentification.

- In **Natural Language Processing (NLP)** systems, fairness ensures that chatbots or content filters do not produce discriminatory or offensive responses.

By addressing fairness, developers help build systems that serve all users equitably, and uphold trust in AI solutions.

Tools for Ensuring Fairness in AI

Microsoft Azure provides several tools to help developers **detect and mitigate bias** in AI models. Within **Azure Machine Learning**, the **Responsible AI dashboard** includes a **Fairness assessment component** that allows teams to evaluate model performance across different demographic groups.

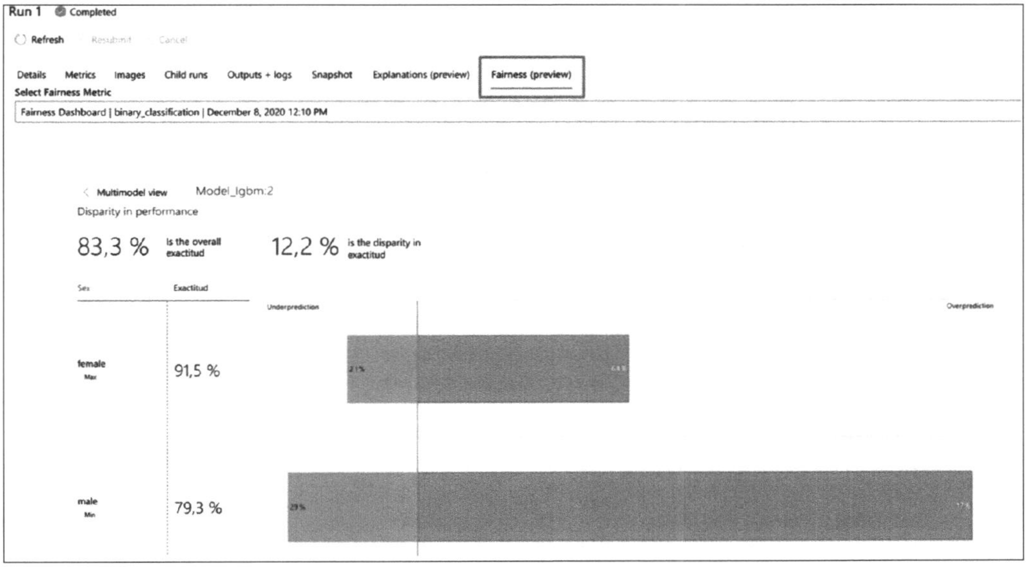

***Figure 3.2**: Fairness in Azure Machine Learning*

This feature helps identify whether certain populations experience higher error rates or less favorable predictions, enabling corrective action. By examining fairness metrics, data scientists can refine both the dataset and the algorithm, thereby ensuring that models take decisions rooted in equality rather than inherited bias.

Example: A fairness evaluation can reveal if a facial recognition model performs better for lighter-skinned individuals than darker-skinned ones, prompting retraining with more diverse data.

Reliability and Safety in an AI Solution

While fairness ensures equal treatment, **reliability and safety** guarantee consistent and secure performance under diverse conditions. These principles answer the question:

How can an AI system perform reliably for different users and scenarios—even those it was not originally trained for?

Reliable AI systems operate predictably and safely, handling errors or unexpected inputs without causing harm. For instance, **autonomous vehicles** must adapt to sudden weather changes or road obstacles, while **healthcare diagnostic models** must maintain accuracy especially when analyzing rare or complex cases.

Achieving reliability requires **rigorous testing and validation** throughout the AI lifecycle to ensure models perform effectively across varied environments.

Planning for the Unexpected

To achieve true reliability, AI systems should be designed to:

- **Perform as intended**, while consistently meeting design specifications
- **Respond safely to unforeseen conditions** without endangering users
- **Resist manipulation or adversarial attacks** that could compromise performance or integrity

A system's ability to handle unexpected inputs reflects the quality of planning, testing, and governance during development. By anticipating failure modes, developers ensure that AI systems are dependable and become more resilient over time.

Tools for Ensuring Reliability and Safety

To help developers build reliable and safe AI systems, Microsoft provides specific tools within **Azure Machine Learning**. One such resource is the error analysis component within the Responsible AI dashboard. This tool enables data scientists and developers to gain a deeper understanding of where and how errors occur in an AI model.

Error analysis, for example, can identify data groups with higher-than-expected error rates. This type of analysis is essential for recognizing potential performance issues, especially regarding specific demographic groups or input conditions that may not have been initially considered. With these insights, developers can adjust the model to make it more robust and equitable across diverse situations and users.

Reliability and Safety in AI Workloads

In the context of **Conversational AI** or **chatbots**, reliability ensures that responses are accurate, consistent, and safe for end-users. This helps prevent issues like **offensive or misleading answers**, which could harm an organization's reputation.

In **autonomous or industrial AI**, safety mechanisms ensure that the system reacts appropriately to hazards, reducing the risk of physical or operational damage.

Tools for Ensuring Reliability and Safety

Azure Machine Learning supports reliability and safety through built-in analysis and monitoring tools, including:

- **Error Analysis within the Responsible AI dashboard:** Helps identify patterns where the model underperforms or makes incorrect predictions for specific data groups.
- **Model Monitoring and Drift Detection:** Continuously evaluates model accuracy over time to detect changes in data patterns.

Figure 3.3: *Error Analysis in Azure Machine Learning*

For example, *error analysis* can reveal if a predictive model for customer satisfaction consistently misclassifies younger users. Developers can then retrain or adjust the model to improve performance consistency.

Exam Tip: *Reliability and safety are often tested in* ***Conversational AI*** *scenarios, such as preventing a chatbot from generating inappropriate or unsafe responses.*

Privacy and Security in an AI Solution

As Artificial Intelligence (AI) becomes increasingly integrated into our lives–from healthcare systems and financial services to education and entertainment–**data privacy and security** have become essential pillars of responsible innovation. Since AI relies on vast amounts of information to learn and make decisions, ensuring that this data is handled safely and ethically is a fundamental responsibility for developers and organizations, alike.

This principle focuses on one of the most important questions in modern AI development: ***How can an AI system protect sensitive information while still providing accurate and valuable insights?***

Privacy and security are ultimately about building **trust**. Users need to feel confident that their personal data is treated responsibly and that AI systems will not expose, misuse, or share their information without consent. For instance, in **Healthcare AI workloads**, models that process patient records or medical images must guarantee confidentiality by encrypting data, controlling access, and meeting strict compliance requirements such as **GDPR** or **HIPAA**. Protecting this type of data is not only a legal obligation, but also a way to preserve human dignity and respect the individuals whose data enriches AI.

Challenges of Privacy and Security in AI

Protecting data in AI systems is an ongoing challenge. Modern privacy regulations demand transparency and accountability, requiring organizations to disclose how data is collected, stored, and used. However, because AI models depend on data to improve their accuracy, developers must balance the need for large datasets with the responsibility to safeguard personal information.

Common risks include **data leakage**, **unauthorized access**, and **adversarial attacks**, where malicious actors attempt to exploit model vulnerabilities to extract private information. These threats highlight the need for strong privacy mechanisms and careful system design. Ethical AI requires anticipating these risks rather than reacting to them after harm occurs.

Exam Tip: *On the AI-900 exam, privacy and security often appear in* **Healthcare AI** *examples. Questions may describe systems analyzing patient data and ask which Responsible AI principle ensures confidentiality and compliance.*

Microsoft's Privacy and Security Tools

Microsoft Azure provides a comprehensive set of tools and services that protect data throughout the AI lifecycle. These solutions allow teams to apply privacy-by-design principles in every stage of model development and are mentioned as follows:

- **Resource Access Restriction:** Defines who can view or modify datasets and AI models, ensuring that only authorized personnel can handle sensitive data
- **Network Communication Control:** Uses **Private Endpoints** and **Virtual Networks** to isolate data traffic and prevent exposure to the public internet
- **Data Encryption:** Secures information both *at rest* and *in transit*, with **Azure Key Vault** managing encryption keys safely and centrally
- **Security Policy Auditing:** Continuously evaluates system configurations to ensure compliance with internal and external data protection standards

These mechanisms help organizations minimize risks, prevent data breaches, and maintain compliance with privacy laws—making it possible to innovate with AI responsibly.

Additionally, developers can use the **Responsible AI Toolbox**, an open-source suite from Microsoft that provides diagnostic and evaluation tools for Responsible AI practices. Within this toolkit, privacy-related assessments can help identify data exposure risks and evaluate model behavior under sensitive data conditions, thereby strengthening end-to-end governance and ethical compliance.

Open-Source Initiatives to Strengthen Privacy and Security

Microsoft is also committed to fostering robust privacy and security practices through open-source initiatives, providing tools to help protect data and strengthen AI system security:

- **SmartNoise:** Developed in collaboration with Microsoft, SmartNoise implements **differential privacy**, which refers to a technique that keeps individual data safe and anonymous in machine learning analyses. This approach is essential for regulatory compliance and data security in AI solutions.
- **Counterfit:** A tool that simulates cyberattacks on AI systems, allowing developers to test the robustness of their models. By simulating attacks, Counterfit enables teams to evaluate and strengthen the security of AI models deployed across various environments.

These initiatives highlight Microsoft's commitment to ensuring privacy and security in the AI era, benefiting both developers and end-users. By offering advanced security tools and developing ethical guidelines, Microsoft fosters a more secure and trustworthy AI ecosystem.

Inclusiveness in an AI Solution

An essential element of Responsible AI is **inclusiveness**, which refers to the commitment to design technology that serves everyone, regardless of background, ability, or circumstance. As AI becomes more embedded in daily life, inclusiveness ensures that innovation benefits the widest possible range of people and avoids unintentionally excluding any group.

This principle addresses a fundamental design question: ***How can we build AI systems that empower people of all abilities to participate equally in a digital world?***

Inclusiveness means going beyond eliminating bias. It's about actively creating solutions that are accessible, fair, and empowering. By considering diverse needs during development such as language differences, accessibility features, or cultural contexts, AI can become a force for equity rather than division.

This principle aligns closely with the concept of **Human-Centered Design**, which emphasizes creating technology around people's real needs, abilities, and experiences. Designing with empathy and inclusion in mind ensures that AI systems are not only technically sound but also ethically grounded and truly useful for everyone.

Examples of Inclusive AI

Inclusive AI design directly impacts real users.

- In **Speech AI**, voice-controlled assistants can allow individuals with motor impairments to interact with devices more independently.
- In **Computer Vision**, models can interpret visual information and provide **audio descriptions** for users who are blind or visually impaired.
- **Educational platforms powered by AI** can adjust between reading levels and languages to support learners with different backgrounds or cognitive needs.

These examples show that inclusiveness improves not only accessibility but also usability and innovation, because when systems are designed for more people, everyone benefits from them.

Exam Tip: *On the AI-900 exam, inclusiveness often appears alongside fairness in scenarios involving* **Computer Vision** *(for example, facial recognition that must work equally well for all skin tones) or* **Speech AI** *(for example, ensuring accurate recognition across different accents and speech patterns).*

Tools for Building Inclusive AI

Microsoft embeds inclusiveness into its AI ecosystem through Azure Machine Learning and its **Responsible AI dashboard**. Within this suite, developers can use the **Fairness assessment component** to analyze how models perform across different user groups, such as the ones differentiated on the basis of gender, ethnicity, or age.

This evaluation helps teams identify imbalances in performance and make the necessary adjustments to achieve equity. By applying these insights early, developers ensure that AI models do not reinforce existing social inequalities but instead create experiences that are welcoming and effective for all users.

Inclusiveness also extends beyond model metrics. Azure's commitment includes accessible documentation, multilingual interfaces, and integration with assistive technologies, so both developers and end-users can participate fully in AI innovation.

Importance of Inclusiveness

Designing for inclusiveness transforms AI from a purely technical achievement into a social one. When systems are built with accessibility in mind, they reflect empathy, fairness, and respect for human difference–values that are central to Responsible AI. For anyone working with Azure or preparing for the AI-900 exam, understanding this principle means recognizing that **ethical technology must include everyone**. Inclusive AI does not just expand reach; it strengthens trust and ensures technology truly serves humanity.

Transparency in an AI Solution

Another fundamental principle of Responsible AI is **transparency**. As AI systems become more common in daily life, users must be able to understand **how** these systems make decisions, **what** data they rely on, and **where** their limitations lie. This clarity is essential for preventing misunderstanding, misuse, or blind trust in automated outcomes.

Transparency addresses an important design question: ***How can we help users clearly understand the reasoning behind AI decisions?***

Being transparent means providing open, honest information about how an AI system operates and why it produces certain results. For example, a mobile application that uses **Computer Vision** to detect water damage on walls should be clearly able to explain its detection limits and possible error rates, while reminding users that professional verification may still be required. Documenting the system's behavior clearly builds realistic expectations and prevents overreliance on automation.

Importance of Transparency

Transparency is especially vital when AI influences **major life decisions**, such as loan approvals, job recruitment, or medical diagnoses. In these situations, users and those affected by AI decisions must understand the logic behind the outcomes. When organizations communicate how models are built, tested, and validated, they promote fairness, accountability, and user confidence.

In the context of **Generative AI**, transparency also involves disclosing when content like text, images, or audio has been **AI-generated**, in order to prevent the spread of misinformation or the unintentional use of copyrighted material. Similarly, in **Conversational AI**, being transparent about a chatbot's capabilities and limitations helps users distinguish between automated responses and human input, thereby reducing confusion and building trust.

Exam Tip: *On the AI-900 exam, transparency is often linked to **Generative AI workloads**. For example, a question might deal with identifying the need to disclose when content was produced by an AI model or explaining how model limitations can lead to misinformation.*

Transparency Tools in Azure Machine Learning

Microsoft places transparency at the core of its AI development philosophy. Within **Azure Machine Learning**, several tools and features help teams build explainable and auditable AI systems:

- **Model Interpretability:** Provides explanations for how models make predictions. Developers can view **global explanations**, showing how features influence the overall model, or **local explanations**, while describing the reasoning behind a specific prediction.
- **Counterfactual Testing:** Allows developers to test how small changes in input data affect

model outputs. This helps uncover patterns and ensures that models behave consistently and predictably.

- **Responsible AI Scorecard:** Generates detailed reports on data quality, model performance, and fairness metrics. The scorecard serves as a transparency report for both technical and non-technical audiences, supporting compliance and stakeholder communication.

Figure 3.4: *Responsible AI Scorecard Overview in Azure ML*

Together, these tools make AI systems **interpretable, verifiable, and accountable**, ensuring that they are not only effective but also understandable and trustworthy.

Accountability in an AI Solution

A fundamental aspect of Responsible AI is **accountability**, which ensures that humans remain responsible for the design, deployment, and outcomes of AI systems. As AI increasingly supports or automates decision-making, organizations must maintain **clear oversight** and **traceability** so that technology operates ethically and under human control.

This principle raises a central question: ***How can AI systems maintain transparency and human oversight throughout their lifecycle?***

Accountability means that the individuals and teams who create and operate AI systems must take responsibility for their impact. This involves establishing governance frameworks, performing regular audits, and documenting every stage of model development to ensure compliance with ethical and legal standards.

For example, in **Generative AI**, accountability requires verifying that generated content does not spread misinformation or violate copyright laws. In **Conversational AI**, it means ensuring that chatbot interactions remain safe, respectful, and aligned with organizational guidelines. In all cases, humans must stay in the loop by reviewing, validating, and approving AI decisions that affect people.

Human Oversight and Responsible AI Practices

True accountability depends on both **human governance** and **technical transparency**. Developers, data scientists, and decision-makers must collaborate to define who is responsible for each stage of the AI lifecycle—from data sourcing to model monitoring. Documentation, interpretability, and ethical review are not optional, but are core to maintaining trust in AI systems.

Exam Tip: *For the AI-900 exam, accountability often relates to* ***explainability and governance tools*** *in Azure such as the* ***Responsible AI Dashboard***, ***Model Interpretability***, *and* ***Datasheets for Datasets***.

Accountability Tools in Azure Machine Learning

Microsoft Azure provides a range of integrated features and open-source toolkits that promote accountability by improving **traceability**, **explainability**, and **documentation** across the AI lifecycle.

Here are five of the most relevant tools and frameworks:

- **Responsible AI Dashboard:** This is a unified interface that brings together several Responsible AI components, including fairness, error analysis, and interpretability. It enables developers to evaluate models holistically—tracking how they perform across user groups and identifying potential risks or biases.
- **Model Interpretability:** Provides insights into how a model makes predictions by showing the relative importance of features (global view) and the reasoning behind individual predictions (local view). This transparency helps teams explain AI outcomes to stakeholders and auditors.
- **Fairlearn (Fairness Assessment):** An open-source toolkit integrated into Azure Machine Learning that measures and mitigates bias across different demographic groups. It allows practitioners to visualize disparities in model performance and apply corrective strategies for equitable outcomes.
- **Error Analysis Tool:** Identifies patterns of incorrect predictions by examining which data subgroups experience higher error rates. This diagnostic insight helps teams understand model weaknesses and improve reliability and fairness before deployment.
- **Datasheets for Datasets and Model Cards:** These documentation frameworks provide structured, human-readable reports describing dataset origins, intended use, limitations, and known biases. Similarly, Model Cards summarize how an AI model was trained, validated, and tested, thereby offering transparency to users, reviewers, and regulators.

Additional accountability resources include **Counterfactual and What-If Analysis**, which help visualize how small data changes impact predictions, and the **Responsible AI Toolbox**, a collection of open-source libraries designed to evaluate models ethically and systematically.

Importance of Accountability

Accountability ensures that **AI remains guided by human values**. By combining transparent documentation, interpretability tools, and fairness assessments, organizations can demonstrate control and compliance, while fostering trust among users and stakeholders.

When AI systems are explainable and auditable, responsibility is never lost—it is traceable, measurable, and shared across every person involved in their design and deployment. This balance of innovation and oversight is what defines truly **Responsible AI**.

Conclusion

Having explored the foundational principles of Responsible AI, you now have a clear understanding of how to create AI systems that are ethical, safe, and inclusive. We examined key values such as fairness, reliability and safety, privacy and security, inclusiveness, transparency, and accountability—principles that are essential for building AI that aligns with societal and ethical standards.

Across Computer Vision, NLP, Generative AI, and Healthcare, these principles ensure that AI innovation remains fair, transparent, secure, and human-centered. They connect ethical design with real-world workloads, guiding developers to build solutions that respect users and deliver trustworthy outcomes.

With a solid grasp of these ethical foundations, you're now ready to explore how these principles translate into practical machine learning applications. In the next chapter, we will shift our focus to the fundamental principles of machine learning on Azure. We will cover essential concepts and tools that Azure provides to support machine learning workflows—from data preparation to model deployment and monitoring. This will give you a strong foundation for understanding how to leverage Azure's machine learning capabilities to build scalable, efficient, and effective machine learning solutions.

Points to Remember

- **Responsible AI Principles:** These principles ensure AI is developed and applied in ways that are ethical, safe, and fair. Key principles include fairness, reliability and safety, privacy and security, inclusiveness, transparency, and accountability.
- **Fairness:** AI systems should treat all individuals impartially, avoiding biases based on characteristics like gender, race, or disability.
- **Reliability and Safety:** AI systems must operate predictably and safely, handling errors or unexpected situations responsibly.
- **Privacy and Security:** Protecting user data is essential. AI systems should ensure data privacy, and prevent unauthorized access, aligning with regulatory standards.
- **Inclusiveness:** AI should be accessible and useful to everyone, considering the needs of people of different backgrounds, abilities, and characteristics.
- **Transparency:** Users should understand how AI systems work, including their decision-making processes and limitations, to foster trust and clarity.
- **Accountability:** Developers and organizations must assume responsibility for AI systems, ensuring oversight, compliance with regulations, and adherence to ethical standards.
- **Azure Machine Learning Tools:** Microsoft's Azure Machine Learning offers features like MLOps, data governance, monitoring, and Responsible AI Scorecards, which help implement these principles in AI workflows.

Key Terms

- **Responsible AI:** An approach to developing, evaluating, and implementing AI systems that emphasize ethical, safe, and fair practices. Key principles include fairness, reliability and safety, privacy and security, inclusiveness, transparency, and accountability.
- **Fairness:** A principle of Responsible AI that ensures all individuals are treated impartially, while avoiding biases based on characteristics such as race, gender, or disability.

- **Reliability and Safety:** This principle requires AI systems to operate predictably and securely, handling unexpected situations and errors responsibly to protect users.
- **Privacy and Security:** The protection of user data from unauthorized access and misuse, while ensuring compliance with privacy laws and safeguarding personal information.
- **Inclusiveness:** A focus on making AI accessible and useful to people from diverse backgrounds and abilities, promoting equity in technology.
- **Transparency:** The principle that AI systems should be understandable to users, with clear explanations of how decisions are made and if the system has any limitations.
- **Accountability:** The responsibility held by developers and organizations for the actions and impact of their AI systems, ensuring human oversight and adherence to legal and ethical standards.

Multiple Choice Questions

1. What is the primary purpose of Responsible AI?
   a. Ensure AI systems operate ethically and safely
   b. Improve computational speed
   c. Increase data storage
   d. Enhance the visual quality of applications
2. What does the principle of Fairness in AI aim to prevent?
   a. High system performance
   b. Improved data processing
   c. Discrimination based on characteristics like race or gender
   d. Cost reduction in AI projects
3. Which of the following is a key focus of Reliability and Safety in AI?
   a. Boosting computational power
   b. Reducing human input in AI development
   c. Ensuring AI systems operate securely and predictably
   d. Enhancing UI/UX design
4. Why is Privacy and Security essential in AI?
   a. To streamline application processing time
   b. To improve the accuracy of AI predictions
   c. To make AI systems fully autonomous
   d. To safeguard user data and prevent unauthorized access

5. What does Inclusiveness in AI aim to achieve?
    a. Ensuring accessibility and usefulness to a diverse range of people
    b. Allowing AI systems to self-optimize without human input
    c. Reducing the complexity of AI models
    d. Focusing on computational efficiency over accessibility
6. What is the purpose of Transparency in AI?
    a. Enhancing the speed of AI systems
    b. Minimizing the use of cloud storage
    c. Allowing users to understand how decisions are made by AI systems
    d. Reducing the need for ongoing model training
7. How does Accountability contribute to Responsible AI?
    a. By automating AI model updates
    b. By allowing AI systems to operate independently
    c. By lowering computational costs
    d. By ensuring developers and organizations are responsible for AI decisions

Answers

1. a
2. c
3. c
4. d
5. a
6. c
7. d

CHAPTER 4
Identify Common Machine Learning Techniques

Introduction

In this chapter, we will explore the fundamental concepts of **machine learning techniques** and how they are applied to solve real-world problems. Machine Learning (ML) has become a cornerstone of modern technology and has enabled systems to analyze data, identify patterns, and make predictions with minimal human intervention. By mastering these techniques, organizations and individuals can unlock innovative solutions to complex challenges across industries such as healthcare, finance, and manufacturing.

Machine learning models can be grouped into several categories based on their objectives and methods. **Regression techniques** are used to predict continuous outcomes, such as while forecasting sales or estimating temperature changes. **Classification techniques** categorize data into predefined classes, for example, detecting spam emails or diagnosing diseases. **Clustering techniques** identify natural groupings within data, making them ideal for tasks like customer segmentation or market analysis. Finally, **deep learning**, which is a subset of machine learning, leverages neural networks to process large volumes of unstructured data, achieving remarkable accuracy in areas such as image recognition, speech analysis, and natural language processing.

Understanding when and how to use these techniques is the key to knowing about how to apply them effectively. By recognizing the strengths of each approach, you will be able to select the most appropriate solution for tasks such as predicting future trends, grouping related data, or uncovering hidden patterns in complex datasets.

By the end of this chapter, you will have a solid understanding of the most common machine learning techniques and their practical applications. You will also explore the unique capabilities of deep learning and learn how these methods power modern AI solutions.

Structure

In this chapter, we will discuss the following topics:

- The Basics of Machine Learning
- Identifying Regression Machine Learning Scenarios
- Identifying Classification Machine Learning Scenarios
- Identifying Clustering Machine Learning Scenarios
- Identifying Features of Deep Learning Techniques

The Basics of Machine Learning

Machine Learning (ML) is a subset of **Artificial Intelligence (AI)** that enables computers to learn from data and make predictions or decisions without being explicitly programmed for every task. Instead of relying on predefined rules, machine learning models identify patterns within data and use those patterns to draw insights or forecast outcomes, which is similar to how humans learn from experience.

Figure 4.1: *Visual Representation of Machine Learning Concepts*

Machine learning transforms raw data into **actionable insights** by analyzing it, detecting relationships, and recognizing trends. It has applications ranging from **movie recommendations** and **fraud detection**, to **healthcare diagnostics** and **predictive maintenance**. Its versatility makes it one of the most impactful technologies in today's digital landscape.

The Machine Learning Process

At its core, machine learning operates on the principle of training a model. A model is essentially a mathematical representation of data relationships. This process allows the system to identify patterns and make predictions based on examples, rather than relying on explicit programming instructions.

The machine learning process generally unfolds in four key stages:

1. **Input Data:** The process begins with data collection. This may include numerical values, text, or images that represent the problem domain.

2. **Training the Model:** Algorithms analyze the input data to identify meaningful patterns and correlations. This stage is similar to showing examples to a student to help them understand a concept.
3. **Prediction:** Once trained, the model can apply what it has learned to new, unseen data, generating predictions or classifications.
4. **Feedback and Improvement:** The model's performance is evaluated and refined over time. Developers may adjust parameters, add new data, or improve algorithms to enhance accuracy and reliability.

Example: To train a system that detects spam emails, you would provide examples of both spam and non-spam messages. The algorithm learns the distinctive features of each category, such as keywords, sender reputation, or link patterns, and uses this knowledge to classify new incoming emails automatically.

Understanding the Types of Machine Learning

Machine Learning is a branch of artificial intelligence that enables computational systems to learn from data, adjusting automatically without the need for explicit programming. This learning capability is broadly categorized into two main approaches: **Supervised Learning** and **Unsupervised Learning**. Each of these methods addresses distinct problems and uses specific techniques to extract value from data.

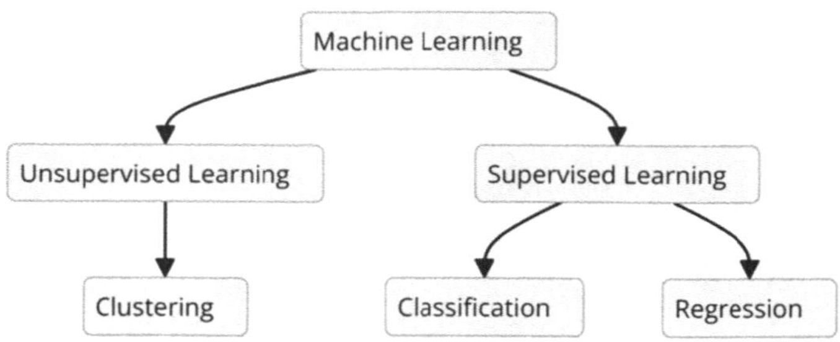

Figure 4.2: *Types of Machine Learning*

Supervised Learning: Predictions Guided by Labeled Data

In supervised learning, the model is trained using a dataset where both the **inputs** (input data) and the **outputs** (expected results) are known. The goal is for the model to learn to associate these inputs with the outputs, allowing it to generalize this knowledge to new, unseen data.

The main types of problems addressed by supervised learning are:

- **Classification:** The objective here is to categorize data into predefined groups. For example, determining whether an email is spam or not, or classifying images as "cat" or "dog."
- **Regression:** In this task, the goal is to predict continuous values. A common example is estimating the price of a house based on variables like size, location, and number of bedrooms.

These techniques are widely used in areas such as medical diagnostics, recommendation systems, and market forecasting.

Unsupervised Learning: Discovering Patterns in Data

While supervised learning works with labeled data, unsupervised learning operates in scenarios where only input data is available, without any indication of what the output should be. The idea is for the algorithm to identify patterns or hidden structures within the data on its own.

Two of the most common problems tackled by unsupervised learning are:

- **Clustering:** This technique groups similar data points into clusters. For example, in marketing, clustering can be used to segment customers based on their purchasing behaviors.
- **Dimensionality Reduction:** Though not explicitly discussed here, this is another important application, where large volumes of data are simplified to highlight the most relevant features.

This approach is widely used for data exploration, behavior analysis, and information compression.

Key Differences between the Methods

The distinction between supervised and unsupervised learning goes beyond the type of data used. While supervised learning is focused on a specific objective such as predicting or categorizing future data, unsupervised learning is exploratory and aims to understand the inherent structure of the data.

Practical Applications and Impact

Both methods are indispensable across various industries. Supervised learning excels at tasks like predicting financial outcomes or diagnosing diseases based on medical histories. Meanwhile, unsupervised learning plays a critical role in areas such as market segmentation and exploratory analysis of large datasets.

In the next sections of this chapter, we will explore these types of machine learning in more detail, delving into their methods, applications, and real-world examples.

Regression: Predicting Numerical Values

Regression is one of the most fundamental and versatile techniques in machine learning, and is designed to predict continuous numerical values by analyzing historical data. It plays a vital role in solving various real-world problems like forecasting sales, predicting house prices, and modeling stock market trends. The following section will explore the key concepts, types, applications, and challenges of regression; while explaining why it remains a cornerstone in the field of data science.

Understanding Regression

At its core, regression is a supervised learning technique used to model the relationship between one or more input features (independent variables) and a target output (dependent variable). Unlike classification, which predicts discrete categories (for example, spam or not spam), regression focuses on predicting a continuous numerical value.

For example, predicting the price of a car involves analyzing features such as brand, model, mileage, and year of manufacture to estimate a numerical target: the car's price. By identifying patterns in historical data, regression models can generalize these relationships to provide accurate predictions for new, unseen data.

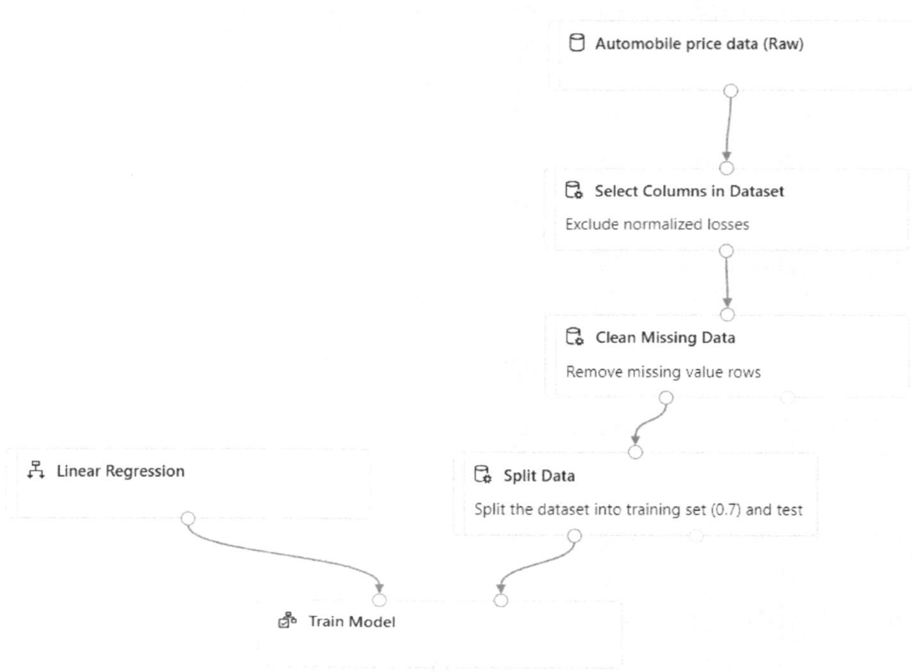

Figure 4.3: *Regression Example in Azure Machine Learning*

Understanding Regression Mechanism

The process of regression involves several steps such as:

Features and Labels

- **Features:** These are independent variables or attributes that influence the outcome. For instance, in predicting house prices, features could include square footage, the number of bedrooms, and location.
- **Labels:** The dependent variable or the value that will be predicted. For a house pricing model, this price of the house is a label.

Model Training

- The regression algorithm analyzes historical data to find the mathematical relationship between the features and the label. This relationship is typically represented as an equation such as a linear function for linear regression.

Prediction

- Once trained, the regression model can predict the label for new input data. For example, it might predict the price of a new house given its size, location, and age.

Evaluation

- The performance of a regression model is evaluated using metrics such as Mean Squared Error (MSE) or Root Mean Squared Error (RMSE), which measure how close the predictions are to the actual values.

Types of Regression

Regression can be categorized into several types, each suited to specific data types and relationships:

- **Linear Regression:** Assumes a straight-line relationship between features and the target variable. For example, predicting housing prices based on square footage and number of rooms.
- **Multiple Linear Regression:** Extends linear regression to include multiple features. For example, predicting car prices based on mileage, engine size, and age.
- **Polynomial Regression:** Captures non-linear relationships by introducing polynomial terms. For example, modeling population growth over time.
- **Logarithmic Regression:** Suitable for data that grows or decays exponentially. For example, predicting website traffic that decreases after a marketing campaign.
- **Ridge and Lasso Regression:** Used for datasets with many features to prevent overfitting by adding regularization terms. For example, modeling customer preferences based on hundreds of product attributes.
- **Logistic Regression (for Classification):** While named "regression", it is commonly used for binary classification tasks, such as predicting whether a customer will churn or not.

Advantages of Regression

Regression provides a number of practical benefits that make it suitable for a wide range of predictive analytics tasks.

- **Simplicity and Interpretability:** Regression models, especially linear regression, are easy to understand and interpret, which makes them ideal for explaining relationships between variables.
- **Predictive Accuracy:** Regression provides precise numerical predictions which are essential for tasks like sales forecasting or budget planning.
- **Versatility:** Regression works well with both small and large datasets, thus making it adaptable to various industries and use cases.
- **Feature Insights:** Regression analysis reveals the importance of each feature, thereby providing actionable insights into which factors drive the target variable.

Regression Example: Predicting Real Estate Prices

Regression is a cornerstone technique in machine learning, as it allows the user to predict continuous numerical values. In this example, we will explore how regression can be applied to **real estate price prediction**, which is a practical and common scenario that demonstrates the effectiveness of this approach.

The following figure illustrates a regression scenario used to predict housing prices:

Figure 4.4: *Predicting Real Estate Prices*

Implementing Regression in Azure Machine Learning

This regression example can be reproduced using **Azure Machine Learning Studio**, which is a visual, low-code environment that allows users to train, evaluate, and deploy models.

Within the Azure Machine Learning environment, you can use two main options to build regression models, which are explained as follows:

- **Azure Machine Learning Designer:** Provides a drag-and-drop interface where you can connect data preparation, model training, and evaluation modules.

  Some exemplar modules are: *Select Columns in Dataset*, *Split Data*, *Linear Regression*, and *Evaluate Model*.

- **Automated ML (AutoML):** Automatically tests multiple regression algorithms and parameters to identify the best model for your dataset. This approach is ideal for users who want accurate results without configuring the algorithms manually.

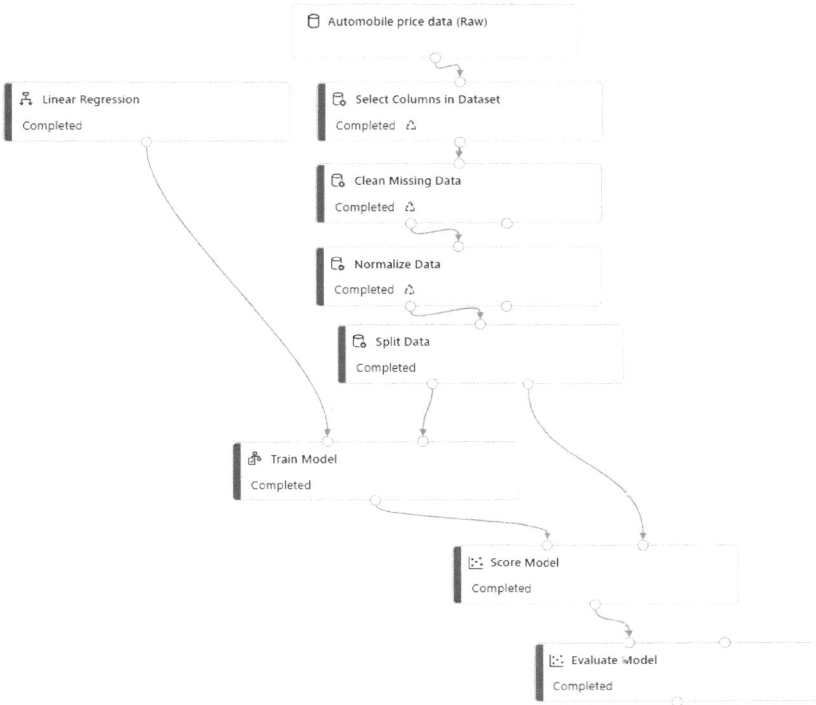

Figure 4.5: *Regression Model Creation in Azure Machine Learning Designer*

This integration with Azure allows you to observe model performance visually, compare algorithms, and deploy the model as a web service to make real-time predictions.

Scenario: Predicting Real Estate Prices

A real estate agency wants to forecast house prices based on various features such as:

- **Size (in square feet):** The total area of the house
- **Number of Bedrooms:** The count of bedrooms in the house
- **Location Index:** A categorical representation of the neighborhood
- **Year Built:** The year the house was constructed

Thus, by analyzing all the historical data, the agency can automate property valuation, which will result in more efficient pricing, and better customer service.

Dataset Example

Size (sq. ft.)	Bedrooms	Location Index	Year Built	Price (USD)
2.000	3	1	2005	350,000
2.500	4	2	2010	450,000
1.800	3	1	2000	300,000
3.000	4	3	2015	550,000
1.200	2	1	1995	200,000

Table 4.1: *Sample Dataset for Real Estate Price Prediction*

In the preceding table, the **Price (USD)** column is the target variable and the other columns are features used to predict it.

Step-by-Step Implementation

1. **Data Preprocessing**

   Before building the model:

   a. **Handle Missing Data:** Fill or drop missing values to ensure data integrity.

   b. **Normalize Numerical Features:** Scale numerical data (for example, Size and Year Built) to ensure uniformity.

   c. **Encode Categorical Data:** Convert categorical features such as *Location Index* into numerical values using encoding techniques (for example, label or one-hot encoding) if they are not already numeric.

   d. **Split the Data:** Divide the dataset into training (80%) and testing (20%) sets to evaluate model performance.

2. **Choosing the Algorithm**

   Linear regression is selected due to its simplicity and interpretability. It assumes a linear relationship between the features and the target variable.

Model Training and Regression Equation

The linear regression algorithm finds the best-fit line that minimizes the error between predicted and actual prices. After training, the model produces the following regression equation:

Price = (150 * Size) + (20,000 * Bedrooms) + (30,000 * Location Index) - (1,000 * Year Built) + 100,000

Prediction Example

Using the equation:

- **Size:** 2,500 sq. ft.
- **Bedrooms:** 4
- **Location Index:** 2
- **Year Built:** 2010

Therefore, the predicted price is:

Price = (150 * 2500) + (20,000 * 4) + (30,000 * 2) - (1,000 * 2010) + 100,000 = 450,000

The model predicts a price of **$450,000** for this house.

Evaluating the Model

The model is evaluated using key metrics such as:

- **Mean Absolute Error (MAE):** Average absolute error between predictions and actual prices
- **Mean Squared Error (MSE):** Average squared difference between predictions and actual prices, penalizing large errors
- **R^2 (R-Squared):** Measures how well the model explains the variance in the data (value close to 1 indicates a good fit)

Exam Tip: *For the AI-900 exam, remember that regression is used for predicting continuous numerical values such as prices, sales, or temperatures.*

Visualization: Predicted versus Actual Prices

The following figure illustrates a scatter plot comparing predicted and actual house prices:

***Figure 4.6**: Predicted versus Actual House Prices*

A scatter plot is used to visualize the performance of the model, where:

- **X-axis:** Represents actual prices
- **Y-axis:** Represents predicted prices
- **Red Line:** Represents perfect predictions (where actual = predicted).

The following is the plot showcasing the comparison between the X and the Y axes:

Scatter Plot:

Feature	**Details**
X-axis: Actual Prices	Represents real values from the dataset.
Y-axis: Predicted Prices	Represents values predicted by the regression model.

***Table 4.2**: Description of Scatter Plot Features for Regression Model Evaluation*

Key Takeaways

- **Interpretability:** The linear regression equation provides insight into how each feature influences the price. For instance, increasing the size by 1 sq. ft. adds $150 to the predicted price.
- **Practicality:** Automating house price prediction saves time and ensures consistency in valuations.
- **Room for Improvement:** Refining the model with more features, such as proximity to amenities or market trends, can enhance accuracy.

Regression is a powerful technique for predicting numerical outcomes. In this example, it allowed a real estate agency to efficiently and accurately estimate house prices based on key features. By understanding the relationships between features and prices, the agency can now make data-driven decisions, improve customer satisfaction, and streamline its operations.

Having explored regression techniques for predicting numerical values, let us now move to **classification**, which focuses on predicting discrete categories.

Classification: Predicting Categorical Outcomes

Classification is one of the most widely used techniques in machine learning, and is designed to predict discrete categories or classes based on input features. It is the backbone of numerous applications, from detecting spam emails to diagnosing diseases. This chapter explores the fundamentals, types, applications, and challenges of classification, while emphasizing its role as a cornerstone of modern data science.

Implementing Classification in Azure Machine Learning

Classification models can be easily created using **Azure Machine Learning Studio**, which provides both a visual interface and automated tools to train and evaluate classification algorithms.

Two main approaches are available to do so:

- **Azure Machine Learning Designer:** A drag-and-drop workspace where you can connect modules such as *Split Data*, *Two-Class Logistic Regression*, and *Evaluate Model* to build classification pipelines.
- **Automated ML (AutoML):** Automatically selects the best algorithm for classification tasks, including logistic regression, decision trees, and support vector machines

The following figure illustrates the classification report generated in Azure Machine Learning Studio:

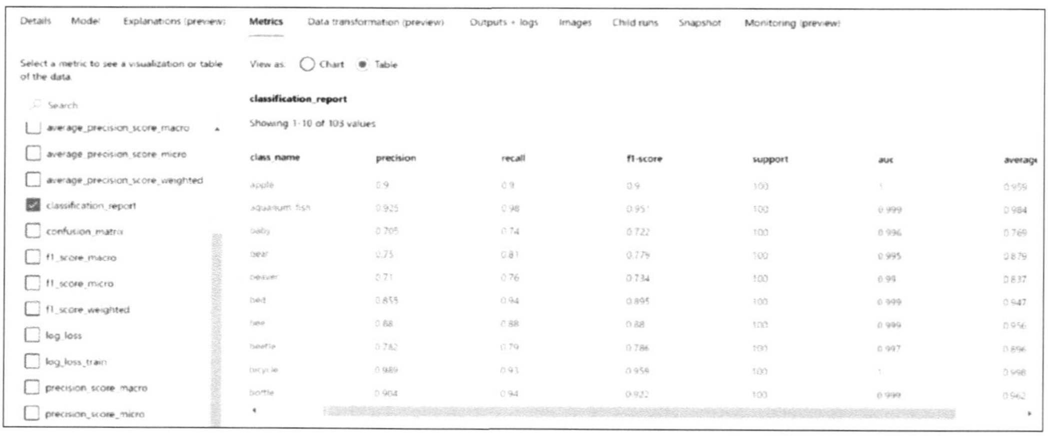

Figure 4.7: *Classification Report in Azure Machine Learning Studio*

The Azure Machine Learning environment allows you to easily visualize results, compare accuracy and recall metrics, and deploy models as REST endpoints for real-time predictions.

Understanding Classification

At its core, classification is a supervised learning technique that maps input features to predefined labels. Unlike regression, which predicts continuous numerical values, classification focuses on assigning data points to discrete categories.

For instance, consider predicting whether an email is **spam** or **not spam**. The model analyzes features like the presence of keywords, the number of links, and the sender's reliability to classify the email. By recognizing patterns in historical labeled data, classification models can generalize these relationships to make accurate predictions for new, unseen data.

Working of Classification

The classification process involves several steps such as:

Features and Labels

- **Features:** Independent variables or attributes that influence the classification outcome. For example, in email classification, features might include the frequency of certain keywords, the presence of links, or the email length.
- **Labels:** The dependent variable or category to predict. For spam detection, the labels could be **Spam** or **Not Spam**.

Model Training

- The classification algorithm is trained on historical data, learning to associate patterns in features with specific labels.

Prediction

- Once trained, the model can classify new data points. For instance, in a new email, the model can predict whether it is spam or not spam.

Evaluation

- The model's performance is evaluated using metrics such as accuracy, precision, recall, and F1-score, which measure the quality of the classifications.

Types of Classification

Classification methods can be broadly categorized into several types, with each being suited to specific use cases:

- **Binary Classification:** Assigns data points to one of two possible classes. Example: Predicting whether an email is spam or not spam. The following figure illustrates a binary classification problem, where data points are divided into two categories and are illustrated in blue and orange:

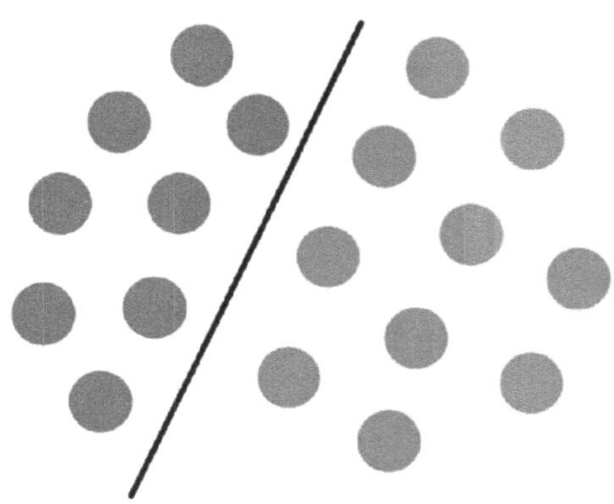

Figure 4.8: *Binary Classification*

- **Multiclass Classification:** Assigns data points to one of several possible classes. Example: Classifying handwritten digits (0–9). The following figure illustrates a multiclass classification scenario, where each instance belongs to one of several classes shown in blue, orange, and green:

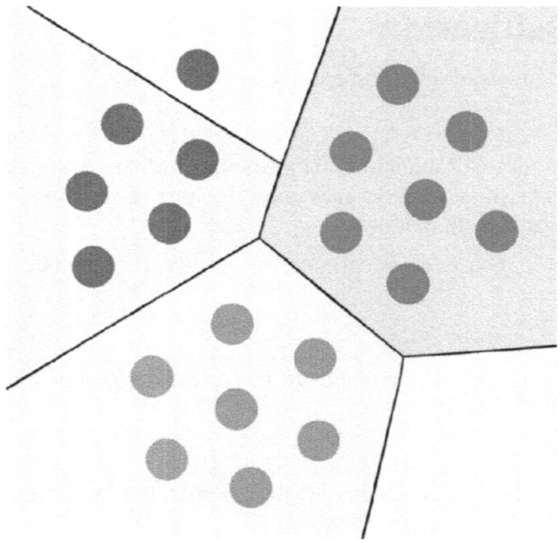

Figure 4.9: Multiclass Classification

- **Multi-Label Classification:** Assigns multiple labels to a single data point. Example: Tagging images with multiple labels such as "dog" and "outdoors." The following figure demonstrates a multi-label classification example, where a single data point can belong to more than one category:

Figure 4.10: Multi-Label Classification

- **Imbalanced Classification:** Focuses on datasets where one class significantly outweighs others. Example: Fraud detection, where fraudulent transactions are rare compared to legitimate ones. The following figure illustrates an imbalanced classification problem, where one class has far more examples than the others. The class with majority of the points is shown in blue, while the other one is shown in orange:

Figure 4.11: *Imbalanced Classification*

Advantages of Classification

Classification algorithms offer several benefits that make them essential for tasks involving decision-making, pattern recognition, and data categorization.

- **Versatility:** Classification works across a wide variety of domains and data types, including text, images, and structured data.
- **Decision-Making Support:** Classification provides actionable insights by categorizing data, thus enabling businesses to automate processes and improve efficiency.
- **Model Simplicity:** Many classification algorithms, such as logistic regression, are simple to implement and interpret.
- **Adaptability:** Classification models can handle both binary and multiclass problems, making them highly adaptable.

Classification Example: Detecting Spam Emails

Classification is a foundational technique in machine learning and allows the user to categorize data into distinct groups. In this example, we will explore how classification can be applied to detect spam emails, a practical use case that highlights its importance in improving email management and user experience.

The following figure illustrates the spam detection example used in the classification section:

***Figure 4.12:** Detecting Spam Emails*

Scenario: Spam Detection in Emails

An email service provider wants to implement a spam detection system to automatically filter spam emails from users' inboxes. The goal is to analyze incoming emails and classify them as either **Spam** or **Not Spam** based on their characteristics, thereby reducing the burden of manually managing unwanted messages.

Key Features for Classification

- **Keyword Frequency:** Measures the number of times certain words (for example, "win," "free," "offer") appear in the email. Spam emails often contain specific keywords to attract attention.
- **Number of Links:** Indicates the number of hyperlinks embedded in the email. Spam emails tend to include multiple links to redirect users to malicious websites.
- **Sender Reputation:** Evaluates the trustworthiness of the email sender. A low sender reputation may indicate spam activity.
- **Length (in words):** The total word count of the email. Spam emails might be unusually short or excessively long to manipulate users.

Thus, by leveraging historical data of labeled emails (Spam/Not Spam), the system aims to train a classification model to automatically identify and filter spam emails. This automation enhances user experience by ensuring a cleaner inbox.

Dataset Example

Keyword Frequency	Number of Links	Sender Reputation	Length (words)	Label
3	5	Low	200	Spam
0	1	High	50	Not Spam
2	10	Low	300	Spam
0	2	High	70	Not Spam
1	4	Medium	150	Spam

***Table 4.3:** Sample Dataset for Email Spam Classification*

In this dataset:

- **Features:** Keyword Frequency, Number of Links, Sender Reputation, Length
- **Label:** Spam or Not Spam (binary classification)

Step-by-Step Implementation

1. **Data Preprocessing**
    a. Handle missing values by filling in or removing incomplete records.
    b. Encode categorical features such as "Sender Reputation" into numerical values (for example, Low = 1, Medium = 2, High = 3).
    c. Normalize numerical features like "Keyword Frequency" to ensure consistent scaling.
2. **Splitting the Data**
    a. Divide the dataset into training (80%) and testing (20%) sets to evaluate the model's performance.
3. **Choosing the Algorithm**
    a. Logistic Regression is selected for its simplicity and effectiveness in binary classification problems.

Model Training and Prediction

The logistic regression algorithm learns the relationship between the features and the label. After training, the model generates probabilities for each class. A threshold of 0.5 is typically used to decide:

- **Spam:** If the probability is greater than 0.5
- **Not Spam:** If the probability is less than or equal to 0.5

Prediction Example: Given a new email with the following characteristics:

- **Keyword Frequency:** 2
- **Number of Links:** 6
- **Sender Reputation:** Low (1)
- **Length:** 180 words

The model predicts:

- **Spam Probability:** 0.78 (78%)
- **Final Classification:** Spam

Evaluating the Model

The model's performance is assessed using the following metrics:

- **Accuracy:** Proportion of correct predictions
- **Precision:** Proportion of correctly identified spam emails out of all emails classified as spam
- **Recall:** Proportion of actual spam emails correctly identified by the model
- **F1-Score:** Harmonic means of precision and recall

Confusion Matrix Example:

Actual Class	**Predicted Spam**	**Predicted Not Spam**
Actual Spam	90	10
Actual Not Spam	5	95

Table 4.4: *Confusion Matrix for Email Spam Classification*

Exam Tip: *In the exam, you might be asked to identify the scenarios when classification is used, which is typically when the output belongs to predefined categories such as spam detection or disease diagnosis.*

Visualization: Model Performance

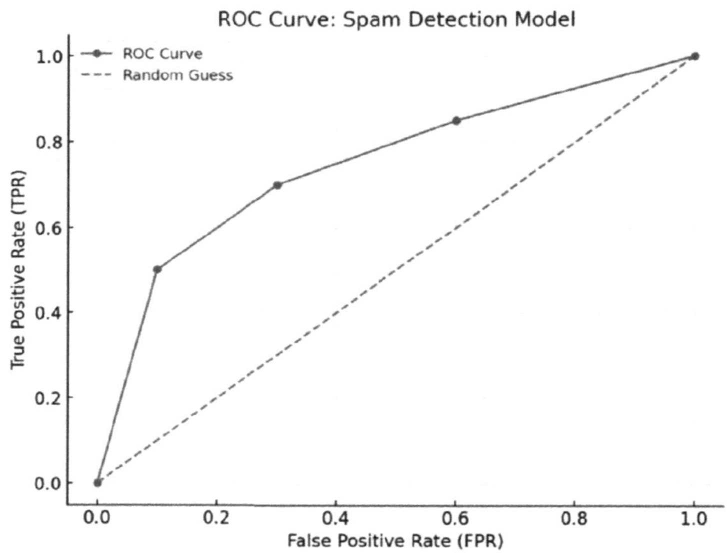

Figure 4.13: *ROC Curve–Spam Detection Model*

The ROC Curve (Receiver Operating Characteristic) provides a visual representation of the spam detection model's performance.

- **Blue Curve (Model Performance):** Represents the spam detection model's ability to distinguish between spam and non-spam emails. The closer the curve is to the top-left corner, the better will be the model's performance. A steep curve indicates a high True Positive Rate with a low False Positive Rate.
- **Red Dashed Line (Random Guess):** Acts as a baseline and represents the performance of a model making random guesses. For example, a random classifier would have a 50% chance of correctly classifying spam or non-spam, resulting in a diagonal line.
- **X-axis (False Positive Rate):** Indicates the proportion of legitimate (non-spam) emails incorrectly classified as spam.
- **Y-axis (True Positive Rate):** Shows the proportion of spam emails correctly identified by the model.
- **AUC (Area Under the Curve):** Quantifies the model's overall performance. A value closer to 1 indicates a highly effective model, while a value near 0.5 reflects performance no better than random guessing.

In this figure, the blue curve clearly outperforms the red dashed line and demonstrates the model's strong ability to correctly classify spam emails while minimizing false positives.

Classification is a powerful tool for solving problems that involve categorizing data into predefined groups. In the example of spam detection, it automates email filtering, thereby saving time and improving user experience. By leveraging classification models, organizations can streamline processes, enhance decision-making, and gain insights across various domains.

Thus, beyond supervised learning methods like classification, some problems involve unlabeled data where categories are unknown. In such cases, **clustering** helps uncover hidden patterns and natural groupings within data.

Clustering: Grouping Data by Similarities

Clustering is an essential technique in machine learning used to group data points based on their similarities. Unlike classification or regression, which rely on labeled data to predict outputs, clustering is an **unsupervised learning** method. It identifies patterns and structures within a dataset by organizing data points into clusters where members of a cluster share more common traits with each other than with members of other clusters.

Understanding Clustering

Clustering is a process of organizing data into groups, or "clusters," where data points within the same cluster share similar characteristics, while data points in different clusters are dissimilar. It uncovers hidden patterns or relationships in datasets that lack predefined labels.

For example, in a dataset of customer transactions, clustering can segment customers into groups based on their purchase behavior such as frequent buyers, occasional shoppers, and discount seekers. These insights can guide marketing strategies, personalized recommendations, and business decisions.

Working of Clustering

The clustering process involves the following steps:

Data Preprocessing

- **Feature Selection:** Identify relevant attributes that capture the characteristics of the data.
- **Normalization:** Scale the data to ensure that all features contribute equally to the clustering process.
- **Handling Missing Data:** Remove or impute missing values to maintain data consistency.

Choosing the Clustering Algorithm

The choice of algorithm depends on a dataset's size, structure, and the clustering objective. Popular algorithms include K-Means, Hierarchical Clustering, and DBSCAN.

Defining the Number of Clusters

Some algorithms, like K-Means, require specifying the number of clusters (k) beforehand. Techniques like the Elbow Method or Silhouette Score can help determine the optimal k.

Running the Clustering Algorithm

The algorithm groups data points into clusters based on their similarity. For instance:

- K-Means assigns data points to the nearest cluster center.

- DBSCAN groups data points based on density.

Evaluating the Clustering

Clustering results are evaluated using metrics such as:

- **Silhouette Score:** Measures the quality of clustering by evaluating how similar a data point is to its own cluster compared to others
- **Inertia:** Sum of squared distances of data points from their cluster centers (used in K-Means)
- **Cluster Visualization:** Helps interpret clustering results visually

Types of Clustering

Clustering can be categorized into the following types based on how the clusters are formed:

Centroid-Based Clustering (for example, K-Means): Clusters are represented by a central point, or "centroid." For example, segmenting customers based on purchase behavior. The following figure illustrates centroid-based clustering, where clusters are represented by a central point.

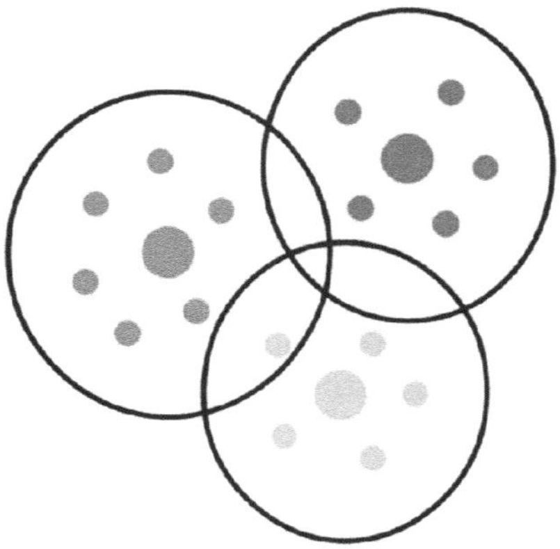

Figure 4.14: *Centroid-Based Clustering*

Density-Based Clustering (for example, DBSCAN): Clusters are formed based on regions of high data density. For instance, identifying hotspots in geographical data. The following figure illustrates density-based clustering, where clusters form in regions of high data density:

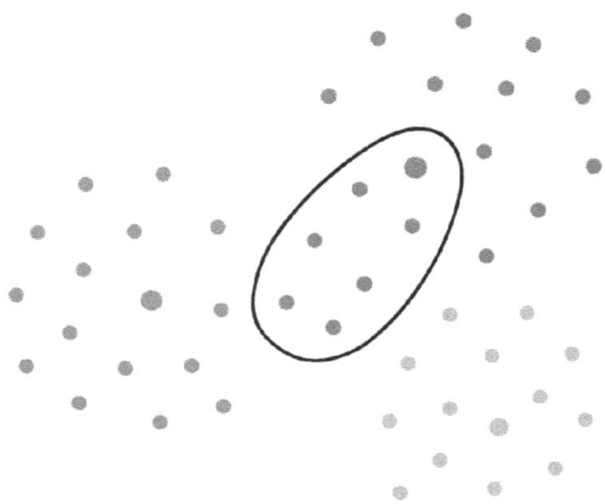

Figure 4.15: *Density-Based Clustering*

Hierarchical Clustering: Clusters are formed in a tree-like structure, starting with individual data points and merging them based on similarity. For example, organizing books in a library based on genre and subgenre. The following figure illustrates hierarchical clustering in a tree-like structure.

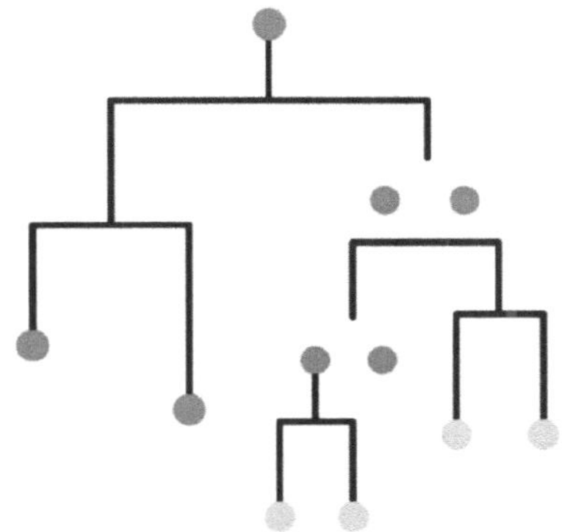

Figure 4.16: *Hierarchical Clustering*

Distribution-Based Clustering (for example, Gaussian Mixture Models): Clusters are modeled as probabilistic distributions. For example, identifying customer preferences based on probabilistic behaviors. The following figure demonstrates distribution-based clustering using probabilistic models:

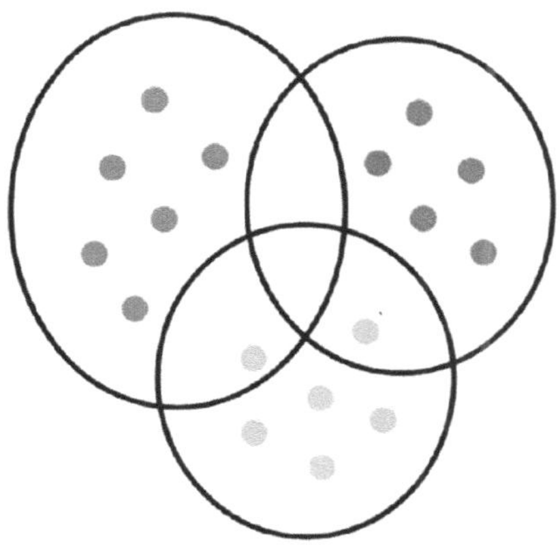

Figure 4.17: *Distribution-Based Clustering*

Advantages of Clustering

Clustering offers several important benefits that make it a valuable technique for uncovering structure within unlabeled datasets and supporting exploratory analysis.

- **Unsupervised Learning:** Does not require labeled data; is ideal for exploratory analysis.
- **Pattern Discovery:** Reveals hidden patterns and relationships in the data.
- **Flexibility:** Works with diverse data types such as numerical, categorical, and mixed datasets.

Exam Tip: *Clustering scenarios in the AI-900 exam may involve unlabeled data and tasks such as customer segmentation or anomaly detection.*

Applications of Clustering

Clustering is widely used across different domains to uncover natural groupings in data, enabling organizations to better understand patterns, behaviors, and relationships within their datasets.

- **Customer Segmentation:** Groups of customers based on purchasing behavior or preferences
- **Image Segmentation:** Divides images into regions based on pixel similarity
- **Biological Research:** Identifies species or genetic groupings based on DNA sequences
- **Anomaly Detection:** Detects outliers in data, such as fraudulent transactions
- **Recommendation Systems:** Groups of users with similar preferences to recommend products

Clustering is a versatile and powerful technique for discovering patterns and structures in unlabeled data. Whether used for customer segmentation, anomaly detection, or exploratory data analysis, clustering provides valuable insights that drive decision-making. Hence, by grouping data points based on their similarities, organizations can uncover hidden opportunities and optimize processes.

Clustering Example: Clustering Customer Transactions

Clustering can be applied to analyze customer behavior and segment them into meaningful groups, based on their purchasing patterns. This approach helps businesses tailor their marketing strategies, provide personalized recommendations, and make informed decisions.

The following figure illustrates customer transactions which are clustered based on purchase behavior:

Figure 4.18: *Clustering Customer Transactions*

Scenario: Segmenting Customers by Purchase Behavior

A retail company has a dataset of customer transactions, including information such as the **frequency of purchases**, **total spending**, and **average discount used**. The company wants to segment customers into three distinct groups:

- **Frequent Buyers:** Customers who shop often and spend consistently.
- **Occasional Buyers:** Customers who shop infrequently but may spend significantly on specific occasions.
- **Discount Seekers:** Customers who primarily buy discounted items.

Dataset Example

Customer ID	Frequency of Purchases (per month)	Total Spending (USD)	Average Discount Used (%)	Cluster
1	15	500	10	Frequent Buyers
2	3	200	50	Discount Seekers
3	7	350	20	Occasional Buyers
4	18	600	5	Frequent Buyers
5	5	150	40	Discount Seekers
6	8	400	15	Occasional Buyers

Table 4.5: *Sample Dataset for Customer Clustering Analysis*

Implementing Clustering in Azure Machine Learning

Clustering tasks can be performed directly in **Azure Machine Learning Studio**, which provides a visual interface for creating, training, and evaluating clustering models. The most common algorithm used for this purpose is **K-Means Clustering**, which is available as a built-in module in the **Designer** workspace.

In Azure Machine Learning Designer, you can:

- Drag and drop modules such as **Select Columns in Dataset**, **Normalize Data**, **K-Means Clustering**, and **Evaluate Model**.
- Configure parameters like the number of clusters (*k*) and the distance metric (for example, Euclidean).
- Run the experiment to visualize how data points are grouped into distinct clusters.

After training, Azure Machine Learning displays visualizations like **cluster assignments**, **distance metrics**, and **silhouette scores**, which can help users in evaluating the quality of segmentation.

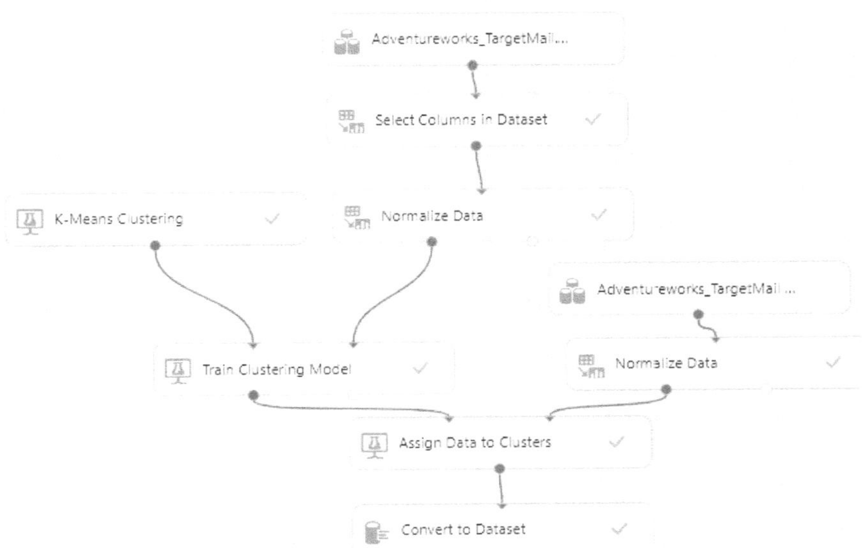

Figure 4.19: *K-Means Clustering Workflow in Azure Machine Learning Designer*

Step-by-Step Implementation

1. **Preprocessing the Data**
    a. **Feature Selection:** Use relevant features such as purchase frequency, total spending, and discount usage.
    b. **Normalization:** Scale the features to ensure all attributes contribute equally to the clustering.
        i. For example: Normalize "Total Spending" and "Frequency of Purchases", so that they are on the same scale as "Average Discount Used."
2. **Choosing the Clustering Algorithm**
    a. **K-Means Algorithm:** Is chosen for its simplicity and effectiveness in partitioning data into distinct groups
    b. Specify k = 3 clusters (Frequent Buyers, Occasional Buyers, and Discount Seekers)
3. **Running the Clustering Algorithm**
    a. Initialize k centroids.
    b. Assign each customer to the nearest centroid based on their feature values.
    c. Update centroids iteratively until they stabilize to ensure that customers are grouped accurately.
4. **Evaluating the Clusters**
    a. Use the **Silhouette Score** to assess clustering quality.
    b. Visualize clusters in a 2D or 3D scatter plot to interpret the segmentation.

Visualization: Scatter Plot of Customer Clusters

This scatter plot visualizes the clustering of customers based on their **purchase frequency** (how often they buy) and **total spending** (how much they spend). Each point represents a customer and the colors indicate the cluster to which a customer might belong.

Figure 4.20: *Scatter Plot–Customer Clusters*

A scatter plot can be created with:

- **X-axis (Frequency of Purchases):**
  - Represents how often a customer makes a purchase per month
  - Higher values indicate frequent buyers, while lower values represent less frequent shoppers
- **Y-axis (Total Spending):**
  - Shows the total amount a customer spends, measured in USD
  - Higher values suggest customers who spend more, whereas lower values indicate lower spenders
- **Cluster 1 (Blue Dots - Frequent Buyers):**
  - These customers shop frequently (for example, 15–18 purchases per month) and spend a significant amount (for example, $500–$600).
  - They are highly engaged shoppers and might benefit from loyalty programs, exclusive offers, or premium product recommendations.
- **Cluster 2 (Green Dots - Occasional Buyers):**
  - Customers in this group shop less frequently (for example, 7–8 purchases per month) but have moderate spending levels (for example, $350–$400).
  - They may make purchases for specific occasions or events, making them ideal for seasonal promotions or targeted campaigns.
- **Cluster 3 (Orange Dots - Discount Seekers):**
  - These customers shop infrequently (for example, 3–5 purchases per month) and spend less overall (for example, $150–$200).
  - However, they tend to purchase during sales or when discounts are available.
  - Engaging them with discount-focused campaigns or flash sales can increase their loyalty.

This scatter plot demonstrates how clustering can effectively segment customers into actionable groups based on their behaviors. By identifying these clusters, businesses can create targeted strategies to enhance customer engagement, maximize revenue, and improve customer satisfaction.

Key Insights from Clustering

Frequent Buyers:

- Shop frequently and spend significantly
- Ideal for loyalty programs or premium product recommendations

Occasional Buyers:

- Shop less often but may make high-value purchases
- Target with seasonal promotions or event-based offers

Discount Seekers:

- Shop mainly for discounted items
- Engage with special discount campaigns or flash sales

Clustering customer transactions provides actionable insights into buying behaviors. By segmenting customers into meaningful groups, businesses can personalize their offerings, optimize marketing efforts, and improve customer satisfaction. This approach not only enhances decision-making, but also drives revenue growth through tailored strategies.

Having explored how clustering organizes data based on similarity, we now move to **deep learning**, which is a technique capable of understanding far more complex and unstructured information like images, speech, and natural language.

Deep Learning: The Revolution of Artificial Intelligence

Deep Learning is a subfield of machine learning that uses artificial neural networks to model complex patterns and make decisions based on large volumes of data. Inspired by the workings of the human brain, Deep Learning has been the driving force behind recent advancements in Artificial Intelligence (AI) and has enabled machines execute complex tasks, such as speech recognition, computer vision, and machine translation, with remarkable precision.

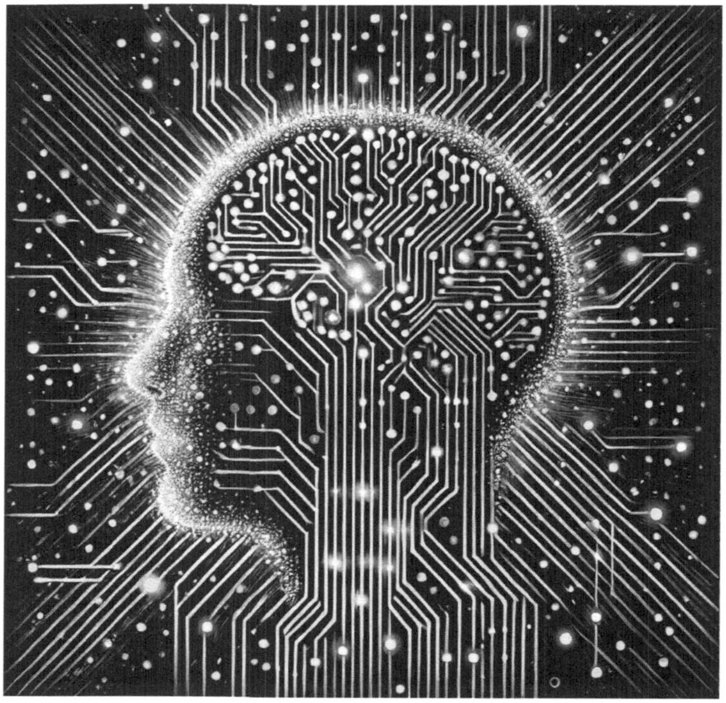

Figure 4.21: *Conceptual Illustration of Deep Learning Architecture*

Understanding Deep Learning

Deep Learning is based on deep artificial neural networks that consist of multiple layers of interconnected artificial neurons. Each layer has a specific function, which is explained as follows:

- **Input layer:** Receives raw data, such as an image or a sentence
- **Hidden layers:** Process and transform data, extracting increasingly abstract features
- **Output layer:** Produces the final result, such as a classification or prediction

The term "deep" refers to the large number of layers in these networks, allowing the learning of hierarchical data representations. This capability enables Deep Learning to detect complex patterns that would be otherwise difficult or impossible to identify using traditional methods.

Deep Learning Process Overview

Deep Learning is a subset of machine learning that replicates the way the human brain processes information by leveraging artificial neural networks. These networks are composed of interconnected layers of nodes or neurons that work collaboratively to learn from data. By structuring these layers hierarchically, Deep Learning models (also referred to as Deep Neural Networks (DNNs), are capable of extracting complex features and making accurate predictions on a wide variety of tasks.

The Architecture of a Neural Network

A neural network is composed of multiple layers that work together to process and transform data. The following diagram illustrates the basic structure of a feedforward neural network, showing how information flows from the input layer through the hidden layers to the output layer.

The following figure illustrates the architecture of a neural network:

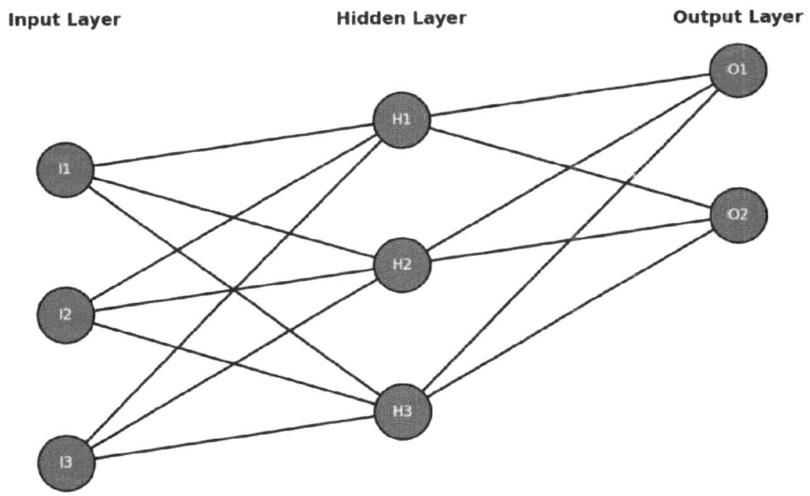

Figure 4.22: *Neural Network Diagram*

At the heart of deep learning lies the **neural network**, which consists of three primary layers: the input layer, one or more hidden layers, and the output layer. Each layer serves a distinct purpose as it helps the network to transform raw data into meaningful insights.

Input Layer: The Gateway to Data:

The input layer receives the raw data to be analyzed. Each node (neuron) in this layer represents a specific feature of the input data like the intensity of pixels in an image or numerical attributes in a dataset. The role of the input layer is purely to pass data to the next layer without altering it.

Hidden Layers: The Learning Engine

Hidden layers are where the actual learning occurs. Each node in a hidden layer takes input from the previous layer, processes it, and passes the results to the next layer. This is achieved through two critical steps which are explained as follows:

1. **Weighted Summation and Bias:** Each input to a neuron is multiplied by a weight that determines its importance, summed up with other inputs, and adjusted by a bias value. Mathematically, this is expressed as: $\Sigma\ (input * weight) + bias$

2. **Activation Function:** The result of the weighted summation is passed through a mathematical function called an activation function (for example, ReLU, Sigmoid, or Tanh). This introduces non-linearity into the model, enabling the network to learn complex patterns and relationships that go beyond simple linear mappings.

The number of neurons and layers significantly impacts the model's ability to capture intricate details in the data. However, excessive complexity can lead to overfitting, where the model becomes too specialized to the training data.

Output Layer: Delivering Results

The output layer provides the final prediction or classification based on the data processed through the hidden layers. Depending on the task, this could be a single numerical value (for example, in regression tasks), probabilities (for example, in classification tasks), or multi-dimensional outputs (for example, in object detection tasks).

The Learning Process

The core of Deep Learning lies in its iterative training process, which involves the following steps:

Forward Propagation: Data is fed through the network from the input layer to the output layer. Each neuron processes its input, applies the activation function, and passes its output to the neurons in the next layer. This hierarchical transformation enables the network to gradually extract more abstract and meaningful features from the data.

Loss Calculation: The network's output is compared to the true values using a loss function, which quantifies the error. For instance, in a classification problem, cross-entropy loss is commonly used, while mean squared error is suitable for regression tasks.

Backward Propagation and Weight Adjustment: The model minimizes the error by adjusting the weights of the connections between neurons. This is achieved through backpropagation, which computes the gradient of the loss function with respect to each weight. An optimization algorithm, such as Stochastic Gradient Descent (SGD) or Adam, then updates the weights to reduce the error.

Repetition (Training Epochs): The forward and backward propagation steps are repeated for multiple iterations (epochs), until the model converges to an optimal state where loss is minimized and predictions are as accurate as possible.

Applications of Deep Learning

Deep Learning is present in the following areas of our daily lives:

- **Computer Vision:** Facial recognition, medical image diagnostics, video analysis, and so on
- **Natural Language Processing (NLP):** Virtual assistants, machine translation, sentiment analysis, and so on
- **Autonomous Systems:** Self-driving cars, intelligent drones, and so on
- **Gaming and Entertainment:** Virtual characters, personalized content recommendations, and so on
- **Science and Healthcare:** Drug discovery, genomic analysis, and so on

Key Strengths of Deep Learning

Several factors contribute to the prominence of Deep Learning and are mentioned as follows:

- **Unsupervised Learning Capability:** It can leverage unlabeled data, which was a significant challenge for traditional machine learning.

- **Scalability:** It can perform well with large datasets.
- **Automated Feature Engineering:** While classical methods require manual feature selection, deep networks automatically learn the most relevant features.

Exam Tip: *Deep Learning is usually referenced in the exam for tasks involving unstructured data–images, speech, or natural language processing.*

Challenges of Deep Learning

Despite its power, Deep Learning faces the following challenges:

- **Requirement for Large Data Volumes:** Deep networks often need extensive datasets for training.
- **High Computational Cost:** Training and execution demand advanced resources.
- **Explainability:** The models often function as a "black box," making it difficult to understand the reasons behind their decisions.

Machine Learning versus Deep Learning: Understanding the Differences

Machine Learning (ML) and Deep Learning (DL) are two essential pillars of Artificial Intelligence (AI), each offering unique capabilities for solving problems across industries. While they share common goals, their approaches, requirements, and applications differ significantly.

Feature	Machine Learning	Deep Learning
Data Requirement	Small to medium datasets	Large datasets
Computational Requirements	Low; works on standard machines	High; requires GPUs or TPUs
Feature Engineering	Manual; requires domain expertise Automatic;	learns features from raw data
Training Time	Fast	Slow
Best for	Structured data	Unstructured data (for example, images, text, audio)

Table 4.6: *Comparison between Machine Learning and Deep Learning*

Exam Tip: *In the AI-900 exam, expect questions comparing machine learning and deep learning. Remember that machine learning handles structured data and smaller datasets, while deep learning excels with unstructured data like images and text.*

Machine learning and deep learning represent two distinct approaches to artificial intelligence. While ML is better suited for simpler, structured tasks with smaller datasets, DL excels in handling large, complex, and unstructured data. By understanding their differences, strengths, and limitations, you can make informed decisions about which technique to use for a given problem. As AI continues to evolve, both ML and DL will remain indispensable tools in driving innovation and solving real-world challenges.

The Future of Deep Learning Techniques

The future of Deep Learning is promising, with continuous advances in areas such as deep reinforcement learning, convolutional neural networks, and transformers. Additionally, combining

Deep Learning with other technologies such as quantum computing, can further transform industries and science.

Thus, by understanding the full spectrum of machine learning techniques like regression, classification, clustering, and deep learning, you will be able to identify the right approach for each scenario, and leverage Azure tools effectively.

Conclusion

Having explored how to select the right machine learning algorithms, you now have a solid foundation for aligning problem types, data structures, and algorithm characteristics. These are core competencies assessed in the **AI-900 Exam–Microsoft Azure AI Fundamentals**, helping you recognize which Azure Machine Learning techniques apply to each scenario.

In the next chapter, we will delve into the **core concepts of machine learning**, starting with how to identify features and labels within datasets, which is a crucial step in designing effective models. Additionally, we will examine the importance of training and validation datasets in the model development process, exploring how they contribute to building accurate, reliable, and generalizable machine learning solutions. This knowledge will strengthen your ability to manage data and evaluate models effectively and lay the groundwork for hands-on machine learning workflows.

Points to Remember

- **Machine Learning Techniques:** These techniques enable systems to analyze data, identify patterns, and make predictions. The key categories of this technique include regression, classification, clustering, and deep learning.
- **Regression:** Focuses on predicting continuous numerical values by modeling relationships between variables.
    - Example: Predicting house prices based on size, location, and year built.
    - Types of Regression include Linear Regression, Polynomial Regression, and Ridge Regression.
- **Classification:** Assigns data points to predefined categories using labeled data.
    - Example: Detecting spam emails or diagnosing diseases.
    - Types include Binary Classification, Multiclass Classification, and Multi-Label Classification.
- **Clustering:** Groups data into clusters based on similarities, revealing hidden patterns in unlabeled datasets.
    - Example: Customer segmentation or anomaly detection
    - Important types of clustering include Centroid-Based Clustering (K-Means) and Density-Based Clustering (DBSCAN).
- **Deep Learning:** A subset of machine learning using neural networks to solve complex problems with large, unstructured datasets.
    - Examples: Image recognition, natural language processing, and autonomous vehicles
    - Key components of deep learning include Input Layers, Hidden Layers, and Output Layers.

Key Terms

- **Machine Learning (ML):** A subset of artificial intelligence that enables systems to learn from data and make predictions without explicit programming. The key techniques include regression, classification, clustering, and deep learning.

- **Supervised Learning:** A machine learning approach that uses labeled data to train models for tasks like classification and regression
- **Unsupervised Learning:** A learning method that identifies patterns or structures in unlabeled data, commonly used for clustering and dimensionality reduction
- **Regression:** A supervised learning technique used to predict continuous numerical values based on input features. An illustration of this technique is found in predicting house prices.
- **Classification:** A supervised learning approach that categorizes data into predefined groups. A practical example of its use is while detecting spam emails.
- **Clustering:** An unsupervised learning method that groups data points into clusters based on similarities, often used for customer segmentation and anomaly detection.
- **Deep Learning (DL):** A subset of machine learning that leverages artificial neural networks with multiple layers to model complex patterns in large datasets; is common in applications like image recognition and natural language processing.
- **Neural Networks:** Computational models inspired by the human brain that consist of layers (input, hidden, and output) that process data and extract patterns

Multiple Choice Questions

1. What is the primary goal of regression in machine learning?
   a. Classify data into categories
   b. Predict continuous numerical values
   c. Group similar data points into clusters
   d. Identify anomalies in datasets
2. Which of the following is an example of a clustering application?
   a. Predicting house prices
   b. Detecting spam emails
   c. Segmenting customers based on purchasing behavior
   d. Classifying handwritten digits
3. What is the purpose of the hidden layers in a neural network?
   a. Receive raw data inputs
   b. Produce final predictions or classifications
   c. Process and extract abstract features from data
   d. Visualize model performance
4. Which of the following is a key characteristic of unsupervised learning?
   a. Uses labeled data for training
   b. Focuses on predicting outcomes
   c. Explores hidden patterns in unlabeled data
   d. Requires predefined categories for analysis

5. What type of machine learning technique is commonly used for spam detection?
    a. Regression
    b. Clustering
    c. Classification
    d. Deep Learning
6. Which of the following best describes deep learning?
    a. A technique for grouping similar data into clusters
    b. A subset of machine learning that uses neural networks to model complex patterns
    c. A method for predicting continuous numerical values
    d. A supervised learning approach using labeled data
7. What is the main advantage of classification models?
    a. Predicting continuous numerical values
    b. Automatically discovering hidden patterns
    c. Categorizing data into predefined groups
    d. Modeling non-linear relationships

Answers

1. b
2. c
3. c
4. c
5. c
6. b
7. c

Chapter 5
Describe Core Machine Learning Concepts

Introduction

In this chapter, we will explore the fundamentals of machine learning, which is an area of artificial intelligence that allows systems to learn from data and improve continuously. Machine learning has become a driving force behind innovation across industries like healthcare, finance, retail, and technology. From personalized recommendations to predictive analytics, its applications are shaping how businesses operate and solve problems.

At the core of machine learning lies the ability to extract meaningful insights from data. This process involves two key components: **features**, which describe the attributes or characteristics of the data, and **labels**, which represent the outcomes or targets the model aims to predict. Understanding and preparing these components effectively is vital for creating reliable and high-performing machine learning workflows.

Additionally, this chapter emphasizes the importance of **training and validating models**. These processes ensure that models not only learn patterns from historical data but also generalize effectively to new scenarios, while avoiding common pitfalls like overfitting and underfitting. Through iterative improvements, machine learning models can be fine-tuned to tackle complex real-world challenges with confidence.

By the end of this chapter, you will have a solid understanding of the core principles of machine learning and how to apply them to design, evaluate, and optimize models for diverse scenarios.

Structure

In this chapter, we will discuss the following topics:

- Core Machine Learning Concepts
- Identifying Features and Labels in a Dataset
- Designing Robust Training and Validation Workflows
- Key Metrics to Evaluate and Optimize Model Performance

Core Machine Learning Concepts

As we move forward in our journey of understanding machine learning, it is crucial to delve deeper into the mechanics and strategies that make machine learning models effective. Moving beyond the basics, we will explore how machine learning systems transform raw data into actionable insights, while focusing on the roles of features and labels, the training-validation workflow, and the strategies to optimize model performance.

Selecting the Right Machine Learning Algorithm

Selecting the right machine learning algorithm is a critical step in solving any problem effectively. The choice of algorithm depends on the type of data, the problem, and the expected results. This section of the chapter will guide you through the key considerations and criteria for selecting an appropriate machine learning algorithm.

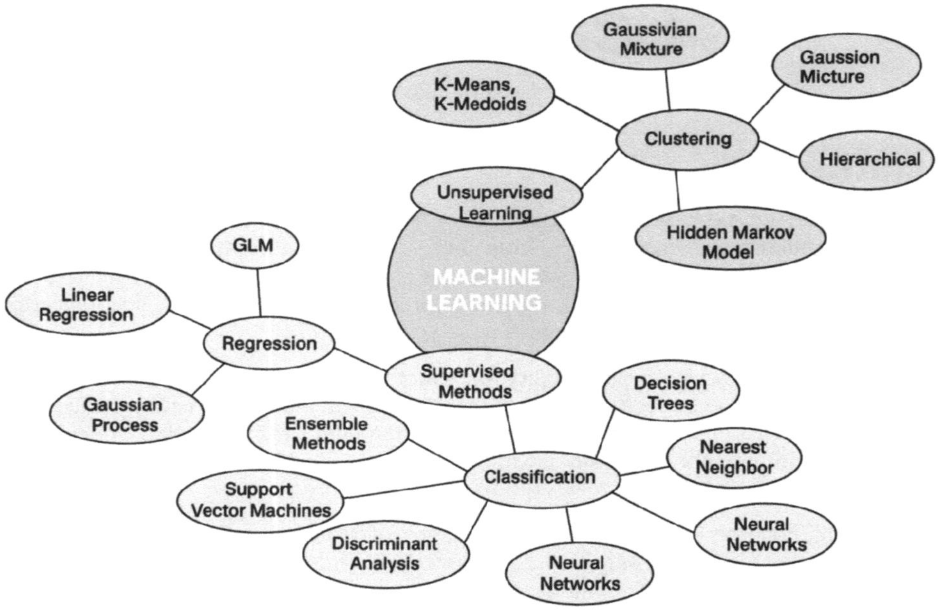

Figure 5.1: *Machine Learning Algorithms*

Exam Tip: *The AI-900 exam often asks you to match algorithm types with their problem categories like classification, regression, or clustering.*

Define the Problem Type

The first step in algorithm selection is to determine the type of problem you are solving. Machine learning problems typically fall into the following categories:

- **Regression:** Predicts continuous numerical values
  - Example: Predicting house prices based on features like size, location, and age
- **Classification:** Categorizes data into discrete classes
  - Example: Detecting spam emails or classifying transactions as fraudulent or non-fraudulent
- **Clustering:** Groups data into clusters based on similarities
  - Example: Segmenting customers into behavioral groups for targeted marketing
- **Dimensionality Reduction:** Reduces the number of features while retaining essential information
  - Example: Using Principal Component Analysis (PCA) to simplify high-dimensional data for visualization
- **Sequence Modeling:** Predicts or classifies sequences of data over time
  - Example: Forecasting stock prices or performing speech recognition

Understanding the problem type will help you narrow down the list of suitable algorithms.

Now that we understand how to define the problem type, let's explore how the nature of data influences algorithm selection.

Consider the Nature of the Data

The structure and quality of your data significantly influence algorithm selection. Key considerations include:

- **Labeled vs. Unlabeled Data:**
  - **Supervised Learning Algorithms** (for example, linear regression and decision trees) require labeled data with known input-output pairs.
    - Example: Predicting house prices using historical sales data
  - **Unsupervised Learning Algorithms** (for example, K-means clustering and PCA) work with unlabeled data to uncover hidden patterns.
    - Example: Identifying customer segments without prior labels
- **Feature Types:**
  - **Numerical Data:** Algorithms like linear regression and support vector machines perform well with numerical features.
    - Example: Predicting temperature trends based on historical data
  - **Categorical Data:** Requires preprocessing (for example, one-hot encoding); suitable algorithms include decision trees and Naive Bayes
    - Example: Predicting product categories (Electronics, Furniture).
  - **Mixed Data:** Flexible algorithms like neural networks and gradient boosting can handle both numerical and categorical data.
- **Data Volume:**
  - **Small Datasets:** Algorithms like linear regression or Naive Bayes are efficient for limited data.
    - Example: Analyzing small-scale survey data for customer feedback
  - **Large Datasets:** Deep learning models and ensemble methods like XGBoost are better-suited for large-scale data.
    - Example: Training image recognition systems on millions of labeled photos
- **Data Quality:**
  - If data contains missing values or outliers, algorithms like decision trees or ensemble methods handle these challenges effectively.

Beyond data quality, computational resources also play a key role in algorithm selection.

Evaluate Computational Resources

The computational cost of training and deploying models varies by algorithm:

- **Low Resource Algorithms:** Linear regression, logistic regression, and Naive Bayes are computationally efficient.
  - Example: Developing a simple recommendation engine for small businesses
- **High Resource Algorithms:** Neural networks and ensemble methods require substantial computational power and may benefit from GPUs or TPUs.
  - Example: Training a deep learning model for image classification

Balance Model Complexity and Interpretability

When selecting an algorithm, it is important to understand how its complexity affects the level of interpretability it can offer.

Consider the trade-off between model complexity and interpretability:

- **High Interpretability:** Algorithms like linear regression and decision trees are easy to explain and ideal for regulated industries like healthcare and finance.
- **Low Interpretability:** Neural networks and ensemble methods often function as "black boxes," which makes them less transparent but more powerful for complex tasks.

Consider Scalability

The scalability of an algorithm is essential for large-scale problems:

- **Algorithms suited for small-scale problems:** Support vector machines, k-nearest neighbors, or Naive Bayes
- **Algorithms suited for large-scale problems:** Neural networks, gradient boosting, and scalable versions of linear models (for example, SGDClassifier)

Leverage Domain Knowledge

Understanding the problem domain provides the following valuable insights for algorithm selection:

- **Time Series Forecasting:** Use ARIMA models or recurrent neural networks (RNNs) to analyze sequential data.
  - Example: Predicting seasonal sales trends for retail businesses
- **Image Recognition:** Convolutional neural networks (CNNs) are the industry standard.
  - Example: Automating quality control in manufacturing using defect detection
- **Natural Language Processing:** Transformers (for example, BERT) or recurrent architectures (for example, LSTMs) are preferred.
  - Example: Building a chatbot for customer support

Experimentation and Validation

There is no one-size-fits-all algorithm. To ensure that a model performs reliably, the experimentation and validation process must include several key steps, such as the following:

- **Cross-Validation:** Ensure that the model generalizes well to unseen data.
- **Performance Metrics:** Choose metrics aligned with the problem type, such as accuracy for classification or RMSE for regression.
- **Hyperparameter Tuning:** Optimize parameters to improve model performance.

Combine Algorithms When Necessary

In some cases, combining multiple algorithms can yield better results like:

- **Ensemble Methods:** Techniques like random forests and XGBoost aggregate predictions from multiple models for higher accuracy.
- **Hybrid Models:** Combine unsupervised and supervised approaches, such as clustering for feature preprocessing, followed by classification.

Algorithm Recommendations for Common Scenarios

Choosing the appropriate machine learning algorithm depends on the type of problem you are trying to solve and the characteristics of your data.

Each algorithm has its own strengths and best-fit scenarios. The following table summarizes common problem types and the algorithms most frequently used to address them:

Problem Type	Recommended Algorithms
Regression	Linear Regression, Random Forest, Gradient Boosting
Binary Classification	Logistic Regression, SVM, Neural Networks
Multiclass Classification	Decision Trees, Naive Bayes, Gradient Boosting
Clustering	K-Means, Gaussian Mixture Models, Hierarchical Clustering
Time Series Forecasting	ARIMA, LSTM, Prophet
Dimensionality Reduction	PCA, t-SNE, Autoencoders

Table 5.1: *Algorithm Recommendations for Common Scenarios*

Choosing the right machine learning algorithm involves evaluating the problem type, data characteristics, computational resources, and desired interpretability. While guidelines can help narrow down options, experimentation and validation remain critical steps in identifying the most effective solution. With careful consideration and iterative testing, you can ensure that your chosen algorithm aligns with your technical constraints as well as your business objectives.

Identifying Features and Labels in a Machine Learning Dataset

In machine learning, the concept of features and labels is essential for developing an effective model. A dataset is composed of different attributes, which are classified as features (characteristics) and labels (tags or outputs).

Features

Features are the input variables that provide information to the machine learning model. They represent attributes or properties that can influence the model's final output. For example, in a house price prediction problem, features may include:

- **Square Footage:** Represents the size of the property in square meters
- **Location:** Can indicate the neighborhood or proximity to areas of interest, such as schools or shopping centers
- **Number of Bedrooms:** Indicates how many bedrooms the property has
- **Age of the Property:** The older the property, the greater the impact it may have on its value.
- **Type of Property:** Whether it is an apartment, house, or townhouse, which can affect the value
- **Proximity to Public Transport:** The distance to subway stations or bus stops can be an important factor

Each of these variables is used by the algorithm to understand the relationships within the data and make accurate predictions. The quality and relevance of the selected features directly impact the model's ability to identify meaningful patterns and make accurate predictions.

Types of Features

Features can vary in type and are listed as follows:

- **Numerical Features:** Continuous or discrete values, such as the square footage of a house, the age of a car, or temperature readings. These values are often normalized or scaled for better performance with certain machine learning algorithms.
  - **Example:** Square footage of a house, age of a vehicle
- **Categorical Features:** Discrete categories or groups, such as the type of neighborhood (urban, suburban, rural). These are encoded into numerical values, often using techniques like one-hot encoding.
  - **Example:** Product categories, day of the week
- **Boolean Features:** Binary variables represented as True/False or Yes/No.
  - **Example:** "Is the house new?" (Yes = 1, No = 0).
- **Derived Features:** Features created from existing ones to add additional context, such as "price per square foot," are calculated by dividing the total house price by its square footage.
  - **Example:** Population density of a city

Importance of Features

Careful analysis of the features is required to ensure that only relevant attributes are used in training. For example, features that have no correlation with the desired outcome can be removed to avoid unnecessarily increasing the model's complexity. Methods such as correlation analysis or feature importance can be used to identify which features have the most influence on the target variable (label).

To facilitate understanding of how features are used in a model, consider the example of a scatter plot where each point represents a property; square footage is located on the X-axis and price on the Y-axis. This type of graph helps visualize the correlation between a feature (square footage) and the label (price).

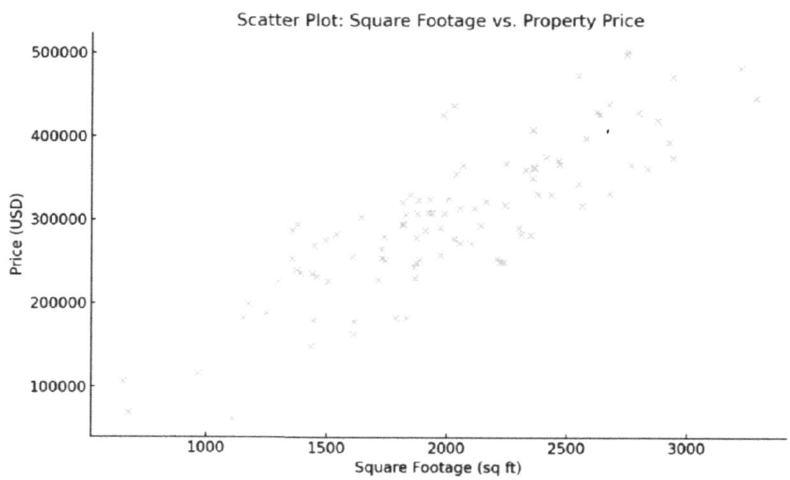

Figure 5.2: *Features in Scatter Plot Example*

Another visual example could be a **histogram** to show the distribution of property ages, which can help you understand how this feature varies within the dataset, as shown in the following figure:

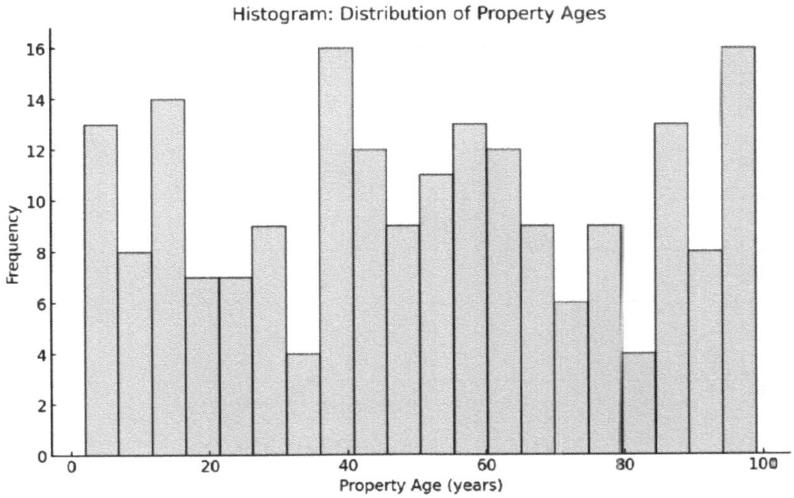

Figure 5.3: *Features in Histogram Example*

Feature Selection

Not all features available in a dataset are equally useful. **Feature selection** is used to choose those that contribute most to the model's prediction, eliminating irrelevant or redundant ones. This helps reduce the complexity of the model and improve its efficiency and interpretability. Techniques such as **RFE (Recursive Feature Elimination)** or **LASSO (Least Absolute Shrinkage and Selection Operator)** are commonly used for this purpose.

Labels

Labels are the output variables that the model attempts to predict. They represent the response or expected result based on the provided features. Continuing with the house price example, the **label** would be the actual price of the property. During training, the model uses the features to learn how to predict the labels. Once the model is properly trained, it will be able to estimate labels for new data.

- **Example:** In an email classification scenario, where the goal is to identify whether an email is spam or not, the label could be a binary category: **spam** or **not spam**.
- **In a regression problem**, such as sales prediction, the label could be a continuous value, for example, the number of units sold.

A useful visual example for understanding labels is a **line graph** that shows the relationship between the model's predictions and the actual values. If the model is functioning correctly, the prediction line will be close to the actual values line, thereby indicating that the predictions are aligned with the expected results. Here is an example of a line graph:

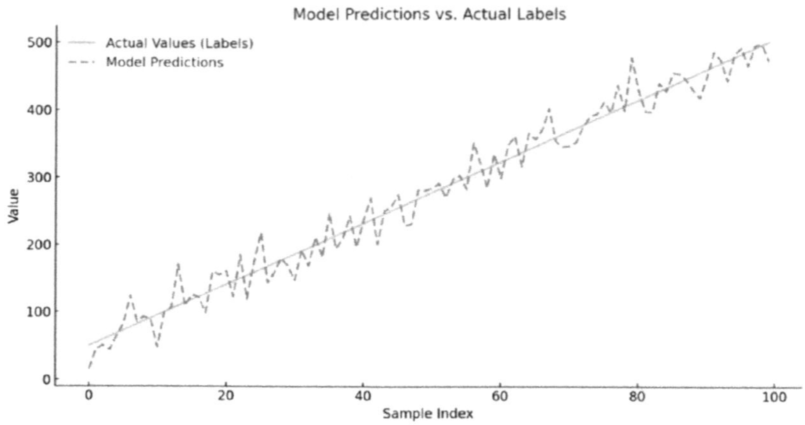

Figure 5.4: *Labels in Line Graph Example*

This graph helps visualize how the model's predictions compare to the actual values, highlighting whether the model is making accurate predictions.

Clearly identifying features and labels is fundamental to building an effective machine learning model. If the selected features are not relevant to the problem at hand, the model will not be able to make accurate predictions, directly impacting the quality of the results.

Importance of Preprocessing Features and Labels

Features and labels need to be preprocessed before training the model. This can include:

- **Normalization and Standardization:** Adjusting features so that they have a similar scale, avoiding high-value variables dominating the training process. This is especially important for models that depend on distances, such as logistic regression and K-means.
- **Encoding:** Categorical variables (such as "neighborhood" in a house price problem) need to be converted into a form that the model can understand, such as **One-Hot Encoding** or **Label Encoding**.
- **Handling Missing Data:** Missing data can be filled (imputed) or discarded depending on the amount of missing information. Common techniques include filling with the mean, median, or mode of the available values, or using more complex methods such as imputation with decision tree-based algorithms.
- **Outlier Detection:** Extreme values can affect model quality. Techniques such as **Z-score** or **IQR (Interquartile Range)** can be used to identify and handle outliers.

Use of Training and Validation Datasets in Machine Learning

To build a machine learning model, it is necessary to use different datasets to train and evaluate the model's quality. These datasets are generally divided into three main types: the training set, validation set, and test set.

Training Set

The **training set** is used to teach the model to identify patterns in the data. It consists of labeled examples, where each feature is associated with a label. During training, the model attempts to learn the relationships between features and labels by adjusting its parameters to minimize prediction errors. The more training data is used, the greater the model's ability to learn different variations in the data, although this does not necessarily guarantee better generalization ability.

A common graph used during training is the **loss graph**, which shows how the model's error decreases over training epochs. Visualizing this graph helps understand whether the model is learning adequately or showing signs of overfitting or underfitting.

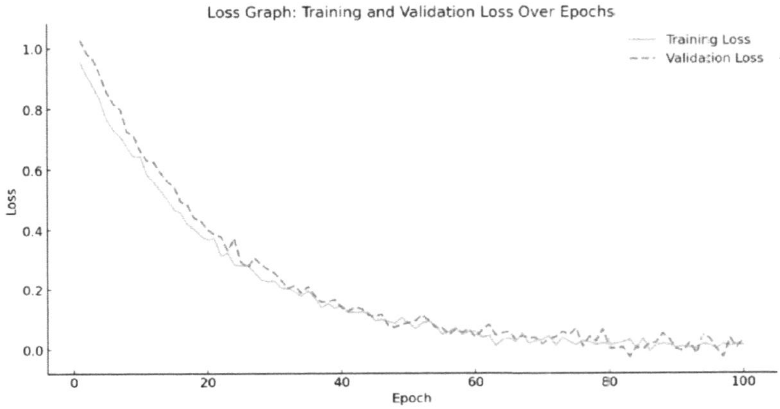

Figure 5.5: *Training Set in Loss Graph Example*

Validation Set

After training the model, it is necessary to evaluate its performance on unseen data to ensure that it is not just "memorizing" the training data but is also generalizing to new data. The **validation set** is a subset of the original dataset that was not used during training. It is used to tune the model's hyperparameters and measure its performance before final deployment. This process helps avoid overfitting, which refers to how the model over-adjusts to the training data and performs poorly on new data.

A **comparison graph between training and validation error** is often used to verify the model's performance. If the validation error starts to increase while the training error continues to decrease, it indicates that the model is overfitting to the training data.

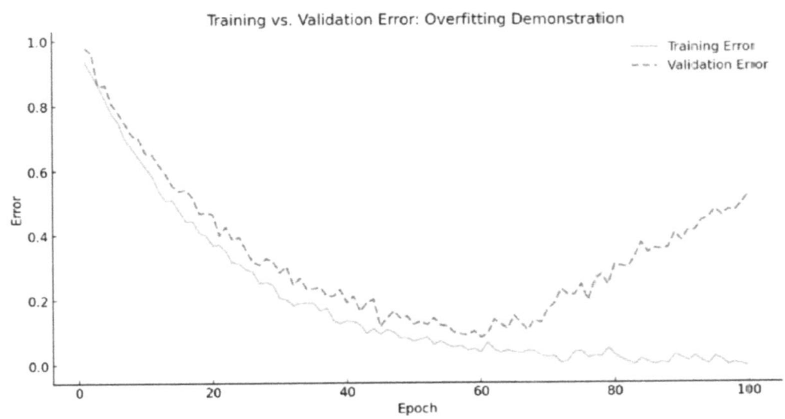

Figure 5.6: *Validation Set Example*

Test Set

In addition to training and validation sets, a **test set** is generally used to evaluate the model's final performance. This dataset is never used during training or hyperparameter tuning and is reserved exclusively for measuring the model's ability to generalize in real-world situations. This ensures that you receive an honest evaluation of the model's performance without any bias that may have been caused by prior adjustments.

Overfitting and Underfitting

It is important to remember that separating training and validation sets helps avoid two common problems in machine learning: **overfitting** and **underfitting**.

- **Overfitting** occurs when the model fits the training data so well that it cannot generalize to new data. As a result, it has high accuracy on training data but low performance on validation data. Overfitting usually happens when the model is too complex relative to the problem it is trying to solve. This can include using too many parameters or layers in neural network models.
  - **Visual Example - Overfitting Graph:** A fitting curve graph where a very complex line (fitting all data points) indicates overfitting. In the graph, the fitting line is extremely close to each data point in the training set but fails to adequately predict new data. The following is an example graph illustrating overfitting:

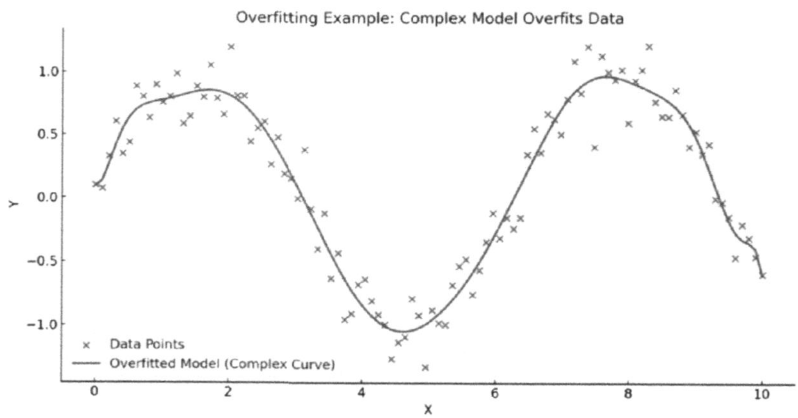

Figure 5.7: *Overfitting*

- **Underfitting** occurs when the model fails to capture relevant patterns in the data, which results in poor performance on both training and validation. This typically happens when the model is too simple for the data's complexity or when an inadequate number of iterations is used during training. Underfitting models tend to have low predictive capacity and cannot learn significant relationships from the data.
  - **Visual Example - Underfitting Graph:** A very simple line that does not capture the data trend indicates underfitting. This graph shows that the model does not fit the data points well, which has resulted in large errors for both training and new data. The following is an example graph demonstrating underfitting:

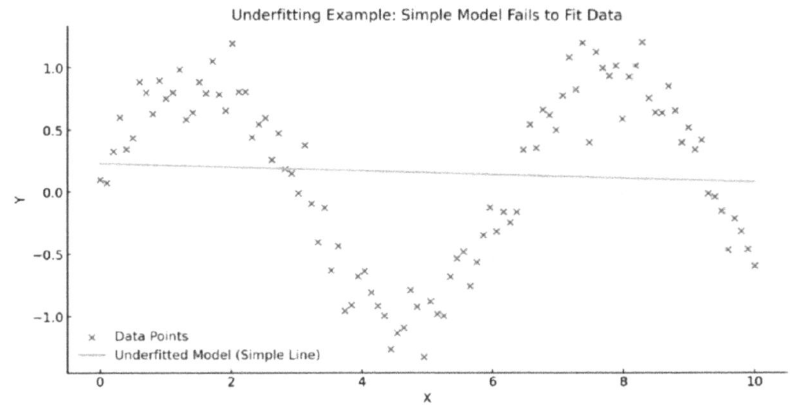

Figure 5.8: *Underfitting Example*

To mitigate overfitting, techniques such as **regularization**, **data augmentation**, and **early stopping** can be used. To avoid underfitting, it is necessary to increase the model's complexity either by increasing the number of parameters or adjusting the training duration, so that the model can better capture the data patterns.

Exam Tip: *Remember that overfitting means that the model memorizes training data, while underfitting means that it fails to learn enough. The key difference lies in the model's generalization ability.*

Detail Visual Examples and Images

- **Scatter Plot:** To visualize the relationship between a feature and a label, such as the square footage of a property and its price, scatter plots can be used. These plots help identify possible correlations and trends in the data. Below is an example scatter plot illustrating the relationship between square footage and the price of the property: In this example, we can see a positive correlation between the property's square footage and its price; as square footage increases, the price tends to increase. This visualization helps us identify how an important feature directly affects the label, while allowing the model to learn these relationships.

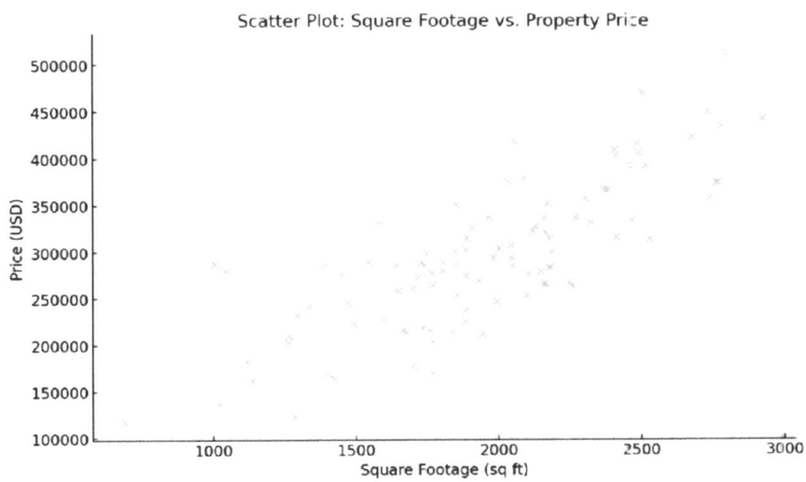

Figure 5.9: *Scatter Plot Example*

- **Histogram:** Histograms are useful to understand the distribution of a particular feature, such as the age of properties. They show how values are distributed, which can provide insights into data variability. For example, a histogram of property ages might show that most available properties are relatively new or that there is a high concentration of properties in a specific age range.

  This type of visualization helps identify whether data balancing or transformation is needed to improve model effectiveness.

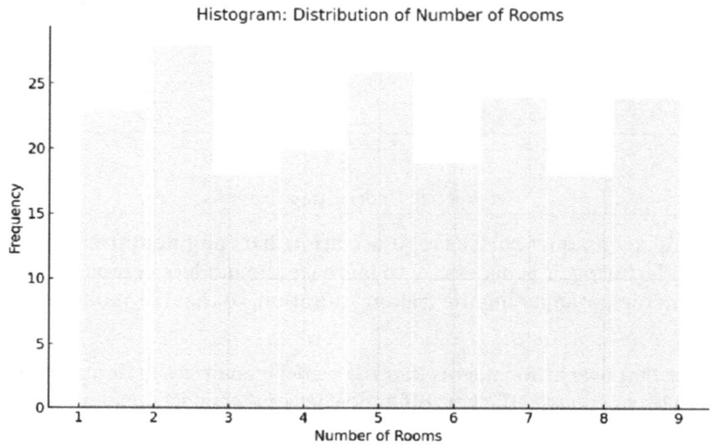

Figure 5.10: *Histogram Example*

- **Line Graph for Predictions:** A line graph comparing the model's predictions with the actual values can be used to evaluate prediction accuracy. The closer the lines are, the better the model performs. This type of graph is especially useful for time series problems, where we can observe how a given model behaves over time.

  This graph clearly shows where predictions align with actual values and where discrepancies occur, helping identify possible model improvements.

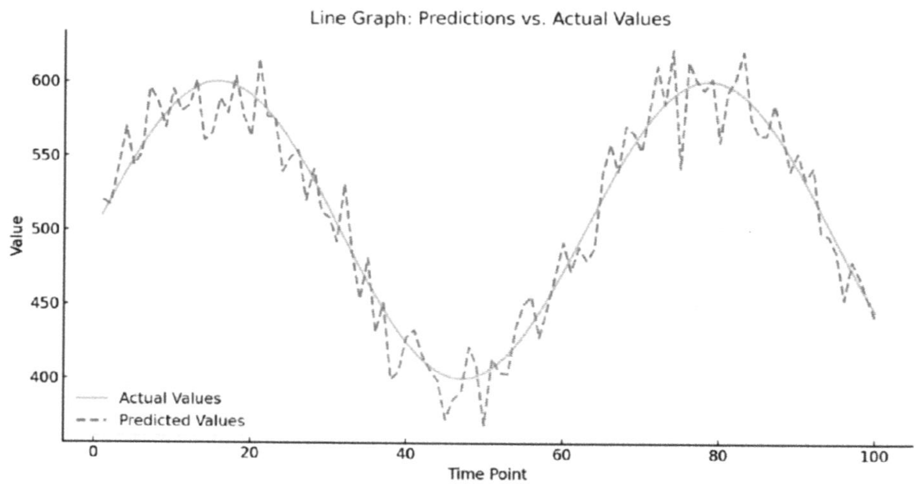

Figure 5.11: *Line Graph for Predictions Example*

- **Loss Graph:** During model training, the loss graph shows how the model's error changes over epochs. A consistent decline in error indicates that the model is learning properly.

  This graph allows us to visualize whether the model is converging or if there are problems, such as an extremely high learning rate, which might be hindering convergence.

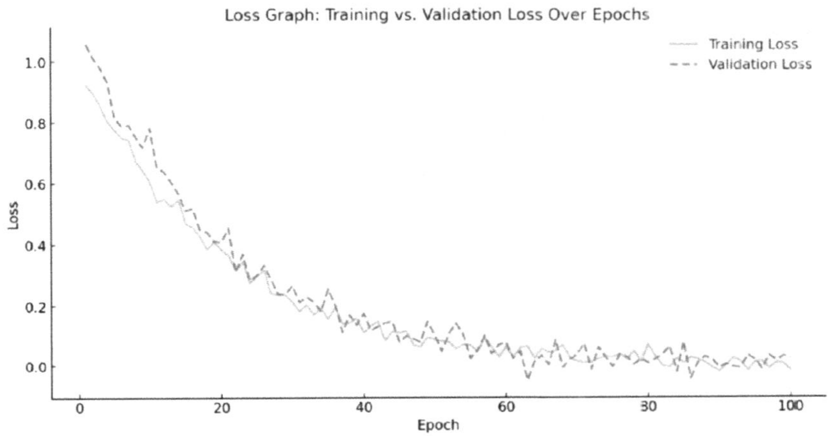

***Figure* 5.12:** *Loss Graph Example*

- **Training vs. Validation Error Graph:** This graph is used to verify the model's performance over time. A divergence between training and validation error may indicate overfitting.

  If the validation error starts increasing while the training error continues decreasing, it is a clear sign that the model is overfitting to the training data, which impairs its ability to generalize to new data.

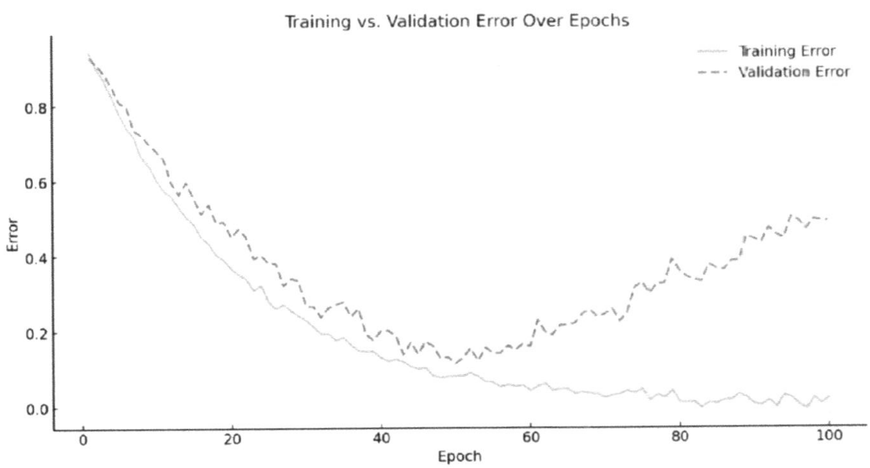

***Figure* 5.13:** *Training vs. Validation Error Graph Example*

These visual examples help illustrate the behavior of models and are fundamental for interpreting machine learning results clearly and objectively.

Conclusion

In this chapter, we explored the **core concepts of machine learning**, focusing on the essential components that enable systems to learn from data and make informed decisions. We discussed the importance of features and labels, the role of training and validation workflows, and key metrics for evaluating performance. Visual examples, such as scatter plots, learning curves, and confusion matrices, illustrated these concepts in action.

Thus, by mastering these principles, you are now equipped to:

- Identify and structure features and labels effectively
- Design robust workflows for training and validating machine learning models
- Evaluate and refine models to improve performance and address overfitting or underfitting

These foundational skills are vital for building reliable and impactful machine learning solutions in diverse real-world scenarios.

In the next chapter, we will explore how to apply these concepts using **Azure Machine Learning**, which is a powerful cloud-based service for building, training, and deploying machine learning models. This will introduce you to the tools and workflows Azure provides to streamline and enhance your machine learning projects.

Points to Remember

- **Features:** Independent variables that serve as input to the model (for example, house size, product category)
- **Labels:** Dependent variables or targets that the model aims to predict (for example, house price, spam classification)
- **Training Dataset:** Used to train the model by learning patterns between features and labels
- **Validation Dataset:** Used to test the model's performance on unseen data and prevent overfitting
- **Overfitting:** When the model memorizes training data instead of generalizing, resulting in poor performance on new data. Solutions include regularization and dropout.
- **Underfitting:** When the model is too simple to capture data patterns, leading to poor performance on both training and validation data. Solutions include using a more complex model or improving the training process.

Key Terms

- **Features:** Inputs to the machine learning model that help predict outcomes. Examples include numerical values like house size or categorical values like product type.
- **Labels:** The target outcome that the model aims to predict, such as house prices or email categories (spam or not spam)
- **Training Dataset:** A dataset used to help the model learn patterns by providing known features and labels
- **Validation Dataset:** A separate set of data used to evaluate how well the model generalizes to new data; helps in avoiding overfitting
- **Overfitting:** A situation where the model learns the training data too well, including noise; performs poorly on unseen data
- **Underfitting:** A situation where the model is too simple and fails to learn significant patterns in the data, leading to poor predictions

- **Hyperparameters:** Settings that control the training process of a model, such as learning rate, batch size, and number of epochs, that need to be tuned for optimal performance
- **Regularization:** Techniques used to prevent overfitting by adding a penalty to the model complexity, such as L1 or L2 regularization
- **Cross-Validation:** A method used to evaluate the performance of a model by splitting the dataset into multiple subsets, training on some, and validating on others
- **Learning Rate:** A hyperparameter that controls how much the model's weights are adjusted with respect to the loss gradient during training
- **Batch Size:** The number of training examples used in one iteration of training, which influence the stability and speed of the training process
- **Epoch:** One complete pass through the entire training dataset. Multiple epochs are often used to train a model until the desired performance is achieved.

Multiple Choice Questions

1. What are features in a machine learning model?
   a. The target outcomes the model aims to predict
   b. The independent variables or inputs to the model
   c. The process of splitting datasets into training and validation
   d. The metrics used to evaluate model performance
2. What is the purpose of a training dataset?
   a. To evaluate the model's ability to generalize
   b. To test the model after deployment
   c. To teach the model by identifying patterns between features and labels
   d. To visualize model performance
3. Which of the following is an example of a categorical feature?
   a. Square footage of a house
   b. Product category (for example, Electronics, Furniture)
   c. Temperature in degrees
   d. Subscription status as True/False
4. What is the main benefit of splitting data into training and validation sets?
   a. To maximize the model's accuracy on training data
   b. To identify and resolve data quality issues
   c. To evaluate the model's ability to generalize to unseen data
   d. To increase the size of the training dataset

Answers

1. b
2. c
3. b
4. c

CHAPTER 6
Describe Azure Machine Learning Capabilities

Introduction

In this chapter, we will explore the capabilities of **Azure Machine Learning**, Microsoft's cloud-based platform designed to support the complete machine learning lifecycle. Azure ML provides a unified environment for building, training, deploying, and managing machine learning models at scale, which makes it a powerful solution for both beginners and experienced practitioners.

We will begin by introducing the Azure Machine Learning platform and its core architecture, including the concept of workspaces, assets, and how experiments and models are tracked and reused. Next, we will explore how to automate ML workflows using pipelines and track experiments in a structured, reproducible manner.

We will then examine **Automated Machine Learning (AutoML)**, a feature that automates the model selection and training process. You will see how AutoML enables users to build high-performing models with minimal manual intervention through both visual tools and Python SDK.

Next, we will look into the data and compute resources available in Azure Machine Learning, such as datastores, datasets, compute clusters, and real-time inference endpoints. These resources provide scalability, flexibility, and integration with the broader Azure ecosystem.

We will also discuss model deployment capabilities, including model registration, version control, real-time and batch inference endpoints, and performance monitoring.

Finally, we will examine the governance, security, and responsible AI tools built into Azure ML that ensure the maintenance compliance, transparency, and accountability when building and managing AI solutions.

By the end of this chapter, you will understand how Azure Machine Learning enables teams to build, scale, and maintain enterprise-ready ML solutions with flexibility, control, and confidence.

Structure

In this chapter, we will discuss the following topics:

- Overview of Azure Machine Learning and Its Key Components
- Managing Experiments and Automating Pipelines
- Using Automated ML (AutoML) to Train and Evaluate Models
- Deploying and Testing Models with Real-Time Endpoints

Overview of Azure Machine Learning Platform

Azure Machine Learning (Azure ML) is an end-to-end cloud platform designed to **build, train, deploy, and manage machine learning models at scale**. It provides a unified and collaborative environment where data scientists, developers, and business teams can accelerate every stage of the machine learning lifecycle–from data preparation and experimentation to deployment and monitoring.

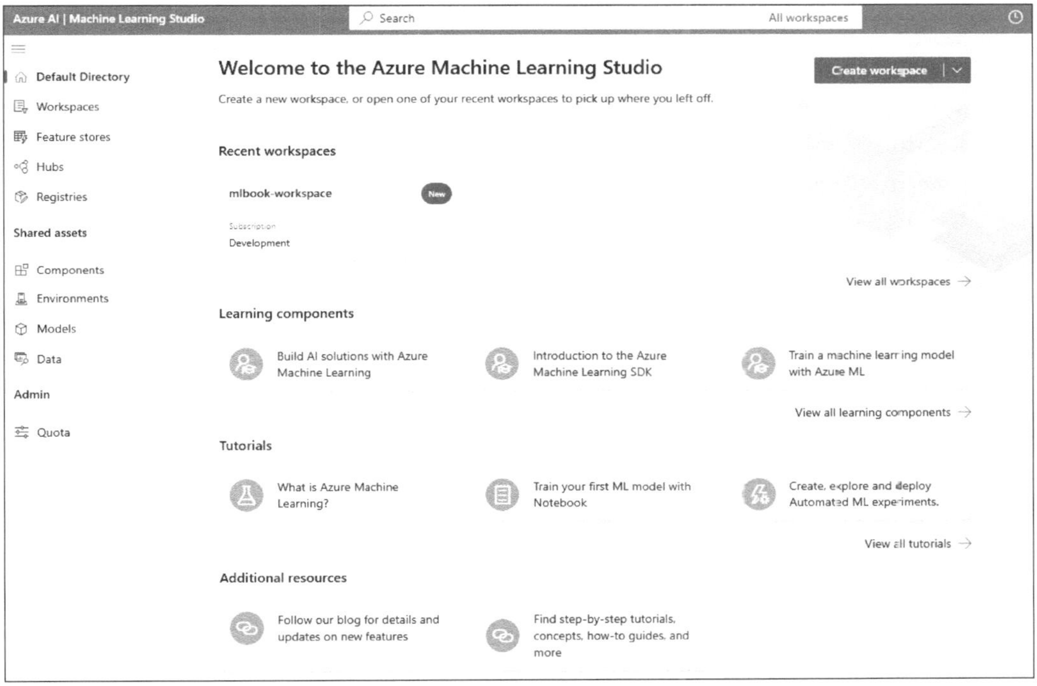

Figure 6.1: *Azure Machine Learning Studio*

Azure Machine Learning Studio serves as the main interface for working with the platform. From here, users can create and manage workspaces, access datasets, launch experiments, and monitor deployed models–all through a visual, browser-based experience.

Azure ML supports both **code-first** and **low-code** approaches, making it accessible to professionals with different levels of expertise. It integrates seamlessly with other Azure services, enabling organizations to operationalize AI in a secure, scalable, and efficient way.

Azure Machine Learning: Key Capabilities

Azure Machine Learning provides a comprehensive set of the following tools and services that simplify the creation and management of AI solutions:

- A centralized place to store, version, and reuse datasets across multiple experiments
- On-demand compute resources for training and running machine learning jobs efficiently
- AutoML capabilities to automatically identify the best algorithms and hyperparameters for your data
- Visual design tools, such as **Azure ML Designer** to build training and inference pipelines with minimal code

- Integration with tools like **MLflow** for advanced model tracking and lifecycle management
- **Responsible AI** features that help evaluate model behavior across fairness, bias, and interpretability metrics

Together, these capabilities make Azure Machine Learning a powerful and flexible platform for teams looking to scale their AI initiatives–from rapid prototyping to production-grade deployment.

Core Components of the Platform

At the heart of Azure Machine Learning are several essential components that work together to support the end-to-end ML process:

- **Workspaces:** Centralized environments that organize and manage all machine learning assets
- **Datasets:** Registered and versioned data used for model training and evaluation
- **Compute Targets:** Scalable cloud or on-prem resources used for training and inference
- **Experiments:** Logical groupings of training runs that track performance metrics and results
- **Models:** Trained artifacts ready for evaluation and deployment
- **Endpoints:** API interfaces that make trained models accessible for real-time predictions

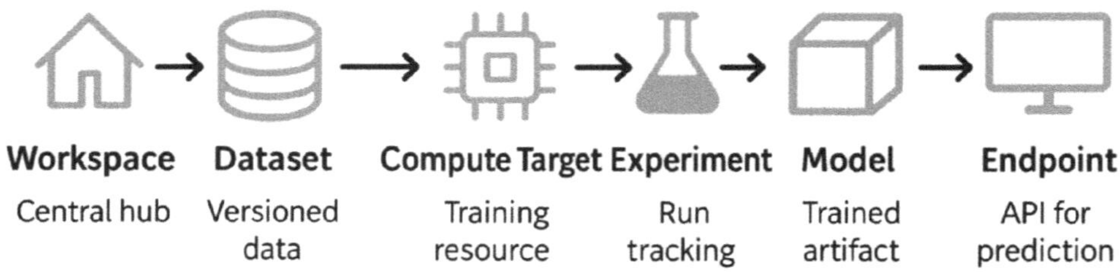

Figure 6.2: *Core Components Workflow in Azure Machine Learning*

These components form the foundation of Azure Machine Learning, which creates a structured ecosystem that supports both experimentation and production workflows.

Workspaces

A workspace is the central hub for all machine learning assets in Azure ML. It organizes and manages everything you use or create, such as datasets, models, environments, compute targets, and experiments.

Key Features of a Workspace:

- Acts as a boundary for collaboration, access control, and billing
- Enables versioning and tracking of machine learning assets
- Provides integration with Azure services like Key Vault and Application Insights

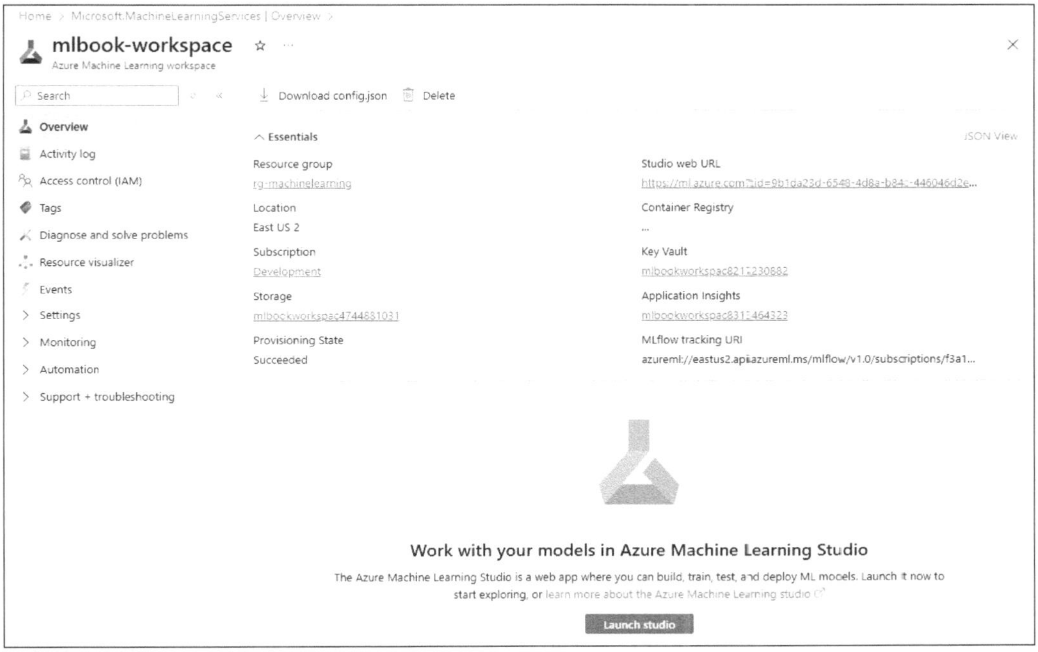

Figure 6.3: *Azure Machine Learning Workspace*

Datasets

Datasets are registered data assets used for training, validation, or inference. They can be tabular data (for example, CSV, SQL queries) or file-based (for example, images, documents).

Benefits of Using Datasets

- Version control and reuse across experiments
- Consistent access patterns, even across different compute environments
- Integration with data labeling and transformation pipelines

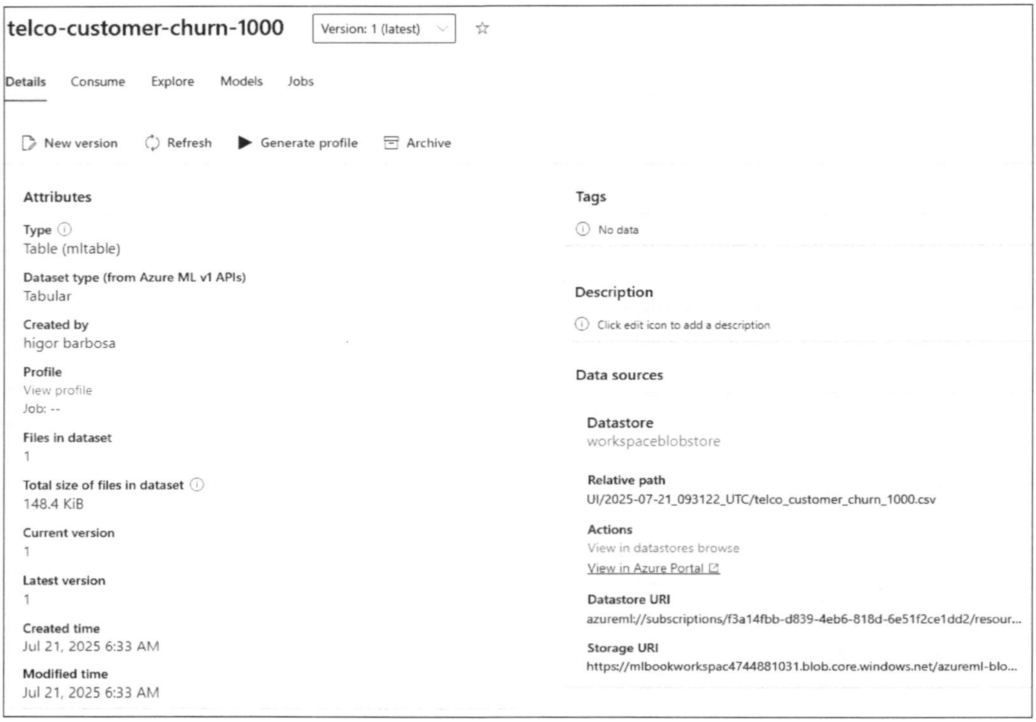

Figure 6.4: *Tabular-type Dataset in Azure Machine Learning Studio*

Environments

An environment defines the software configuration such as Python packages, Conda dependencies, or Docker images, which are required to run a training or inference job.

Why Environments Matter:

- To ensure reproducibility across machines and stages (such as development, testing, and production)
- To help isolate dependencies and avoid conflicts between packages
- As they can be shared and versioned like code

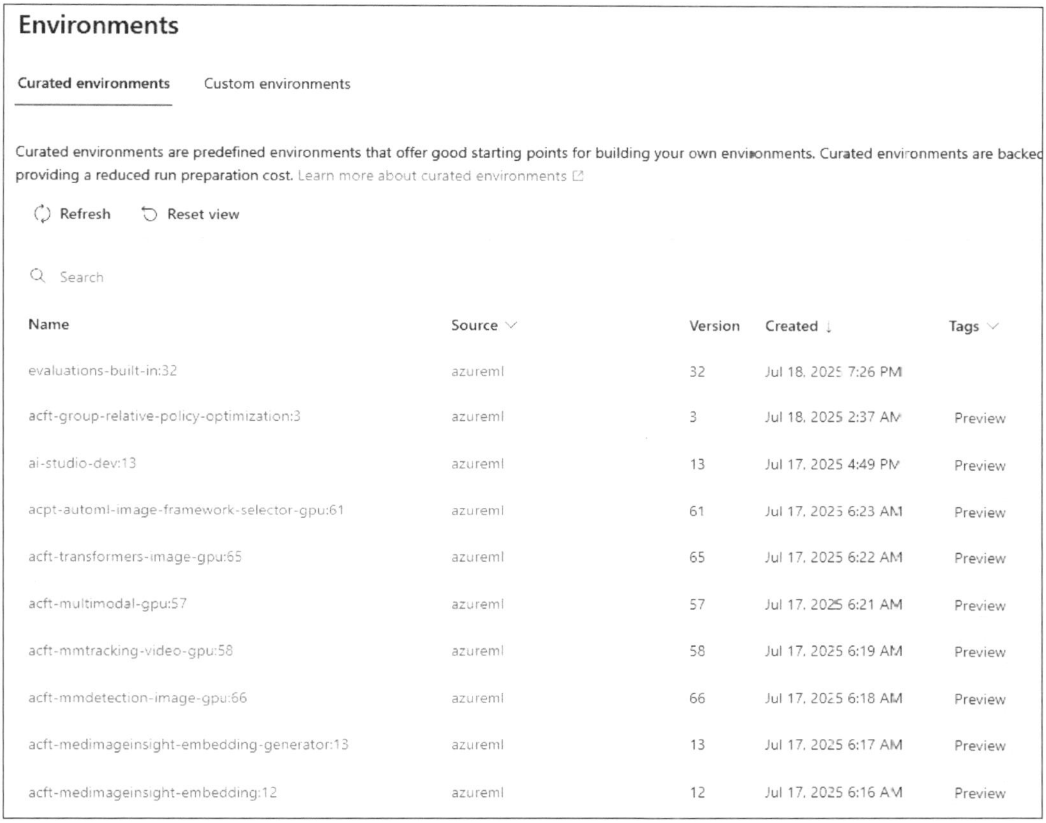

Figure 6.5: *List of Environments in Azure Machine Learning Studio*

Compute Targets

Azure ML supports multiple compute options to match different use cases such as:

- **Compute Instance:** A single VM used for interactive development with notebooks
- **Compute Cluster:** Scalable clusters used for training models in parallel
- **Inference Cluster (AKS or ACI):** For deploying models in real-time or batch modes
- **Attached Compute:** External resources like Azure Databricks and on-premises VMs

These resources are securely integrated into the workspace and can be configured with autoscaling and role-based access.

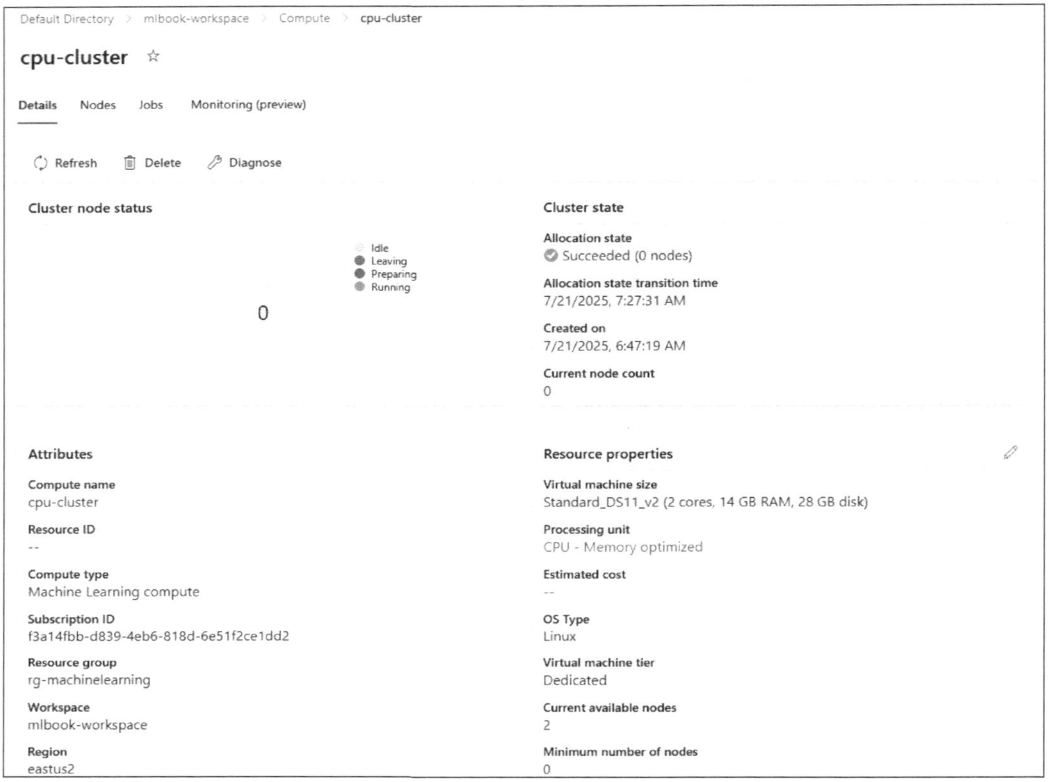

Figure 6.6: *Compute Cluster on Azure Machine Learning*

Models

Models are machine learning artifacts resulting from training processes. Azure ML allows you to register, track, and version models along with associated metrics and metadata.

Model Registry Features:

- Central place to compare versions and experiment outcomes
- Can be integrated with pipelines and endpoints for automated deployment
- Tags and properties to support governance and approval workflows

Figure 6.7: *Models on Azure Machine Learning*

Pipelines

Pipelines are reusable workflows that define each step in the ML process, right from data preparation to deployment. They enable automation, scalability, and consistency in model training and evaluation.

Key Capabilities:

- Modular design, where each step is independently defined and reusable
- Triggered manually or via schedule/integration (CI/CD)
- Built using Python SDK or visually in the Azure ML Designer

Endpoints

Endpoints expose trained models as REST APIs so that they can be consumed by applications. Azure ML supports both **real-time endpoints** for low-latency predictions and **batch endpoints** for large-scale, scheduled scoring tasks.

With endpoints, you can:

- Monitor request volume, latency, and prediction accuracy
- Perform blue/green deployments to reduce downtime
- Secure access with authentication tokens and virtual networks

Exam Tip: *When a question refers to exposing a trained model to external applications or obtaining predictions via an API, the correct Azure ML component to choose is* **Endpoints**.

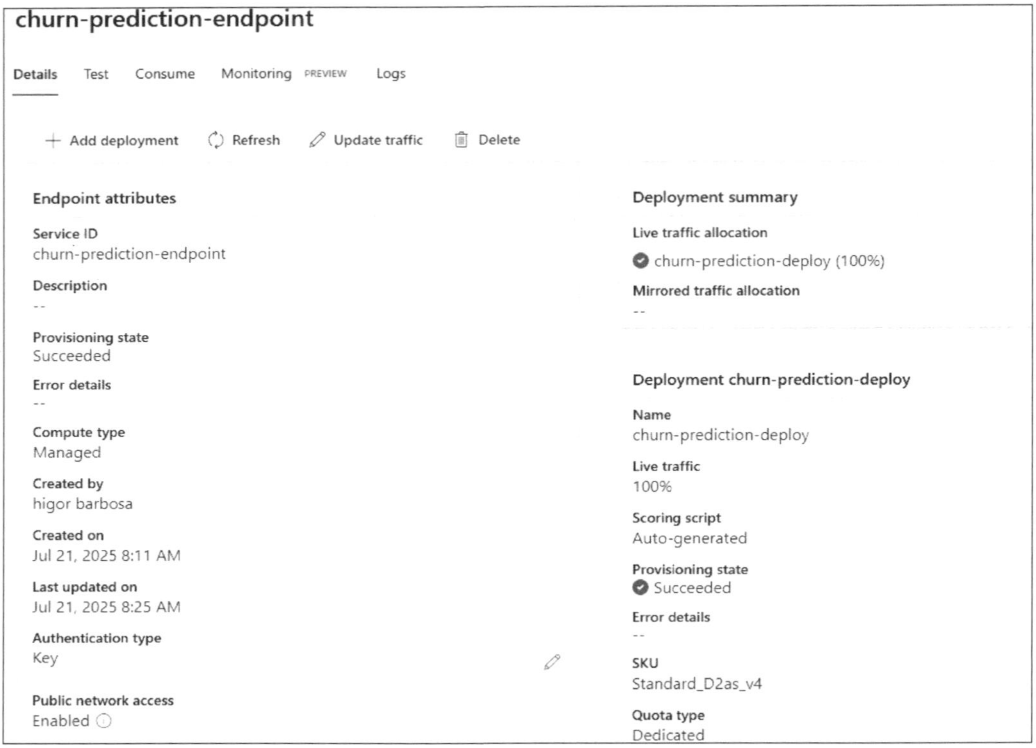

Figure 6.8: *Endpoint on Azure Machine Learning*

These components act as the foundation for scalable, secure, and collaborative machine learning in the cloud.

The following table summarizes the **core components of Azure Machine Learning**, outlining their purposes and typical examples in real-world environments:

Component	Purpose	Example
Workspace	Central hub for managing ML assets, compute targets, and collaboration	Azure ML workspace linked to a resource group
Dataset	Registered and versioned data used for training and testing	telco_customer_churn_1000.csv
Compute Cluster	Scalable resource for model training	cpu-cluster or gpu-cluster
Model	Trained and registered artifact ready for deployment	churn-prediction-model
Endpoint	API interface that serves predictions from deployed models	churn-prediction-endpoint

Table 6.1: *Core Components of Azure Machine Learning*

Together, these core components create an integrated environment where data scientists and engineers can collaborate efficiently on tasks like data preparation and model deployment.

They compose the **backbone of the Azure Machine Learning ecosystem**, while ensuring traceability, scalability, and operational consistency across the entire machine learning lifecycle.

With these building blocks in place, we can now explore how Azure Machine Learning connects them with **practical workflows** and initiates the process with **building and managing experiments and pipelines**.

Experiment Management and Pipeline Automation

A key aspect of building scalable and reliable machine learning solutions is their ability to manage experiments and automate workflows. Azure Machine Learning provides robust tools to track model development over time and streamline repetitive processes through reusable pipelines.

Experiment Tracking

An **experiment** in Azure Machine Learning represents a logical grouping of individual training runs. Each run logs inputs, outputs, metrics, configurations, and artifacts generated during model training or evaluation. This tracking allows data scientists and engineers to understand the relationship between different parameters and their impact on model performance.

Azure Machine Learning provides a **comprehensive tracking interface** in both the **Azure ML Studio** and the **Python SDK**. Every time you submit a run, the platform automatically records key information like:

- Dataset version and data splits that are used for training and validation
- Algorithm and hyperparameter configurations
- Compute target, runtime environment, and resource utilization
- Evaluation metrics like accuracy, precision, recall, or loss

You can view these details in the **Experiments** section of Azure ML Studio, where runs are visualized as interactive charts, tables, and logs. This allows users to easily compare multiple iterations and identify the best-performing model from amongst them.

Importance of Experiment Tracking

- It enables you to compare runs and identify the most accurate, efficient, and cost-effective models.
- It provides transparency into how data, code, and parameters evolve over time.
- It supports collaboration, auditability, and reproducibility, which is essential for enterprise-grade AI development.
- It simplifies debugging and model improvement and allows users to trace the lineage of every experiment.

Experiment tracking is the fundamental capability of Azure Machine Learning as it ensures that your machine learning workflows remain **organized, measurable, and reproducible** throughout the lifecycle.

Pipeline Automation

Machine learning pipelines allow you to define a sequence of steps–from data preparation to model training and deployment. Each step can be executed independently and reused across different workflows.

Typical Pipeline Steps:

1. Load and clean the data.

2. Engineer the features.
3. Train the model.
4. Evaluate the results.
5. Register the model.
6. Deploy it to a real-time or batch endpoint.

Azure ML pipelines support both code-first (Python SDK) and low-code (Designer UI) approaches. Pipelines can thus be versioned, parameterized, and triggered automatically, which allows the user to continuously train or retrain models as new data arrives.

Benefits of Using Pipelines

- **Modularity:** Each step is independent, which simplifies debugging and reuse.
- **Repeatability:** Workflows can be re-executed consistently with the same configurations.
- **Automation:** It facilitates integration with MLOps tools for CI/CD workflows.
- **Scalability:** Steps can run in parallel and scale across compute clusters.

Integration with MLOps

Azure ML pipelines can be integrated into broader MLOps practices. You can connect your pipelines to Git repositories, monitor them via Azure DevOps or GitHub Actions, and enforce approval workflows for promotion to production.

Once workflows are automated, you can accelerate model training using Azure's AutoML capabilities.

Automated Machine Learning (AutoML)

Automated Machine Learning (AutoML) is a powerful feature of Azure Machine Learning that simplifies the model development process by automatically selecting the best algorithm and tuning its hyperparameters.

Instead of manually coding and testing different models, AutoML allows you to define the objective (for example, classification or regression), provide the dataset, and let Azure handle the experimentation. It performs data preprocessing, algorithm selection, and model validation behind the scenes, while helping you build high-quality models with minimal effort and deep expertise.

Exam Tip: *When a question mentions automatic algorithm selection or hyperparameter tuning, the correct Azure Machine Learning feature is* ***Automated ML (AutoML)****.*

AutoML Capabilities

AutoML automates key tasks in the model-building process, including:

- **Algorithm Selection:** It chooses the best algorithm for your problem type (for example, classification, regression, time series forecasting).
- **Hyperparameter Tuning:** It automatically tests different configurations to optimize performance.
- **Data Preprocessing:** It applies necessary transformations, such as normalization, missing value imputation, and encoding categorical features.
- **Model Evaluation:** It compares multiple models using appropriate metrics and selects the top-performing one.

AutoML supports several ML tasks, including:

- Binary and multiclass classification
- Regression
- Time series forecasting

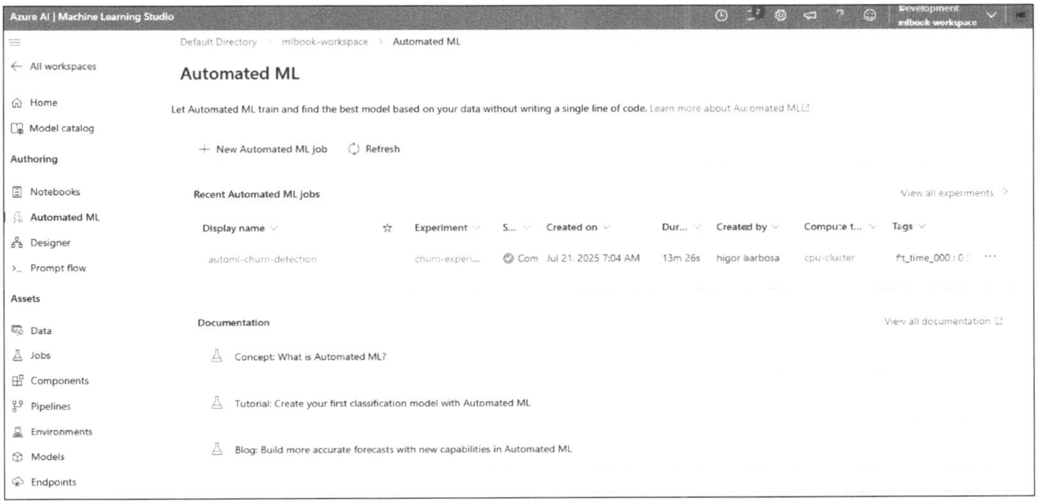

Figure 6.9: *Automated ML on Azure Machine Learning Studio*

Using AutoML

AutoML in Azure can be accessed in two main ways:

- **Azure ML Studio (GUI):** A no-code interface where you can upload your dataset, configure a few options, and let the system generate and evaluate models automatically
- **Python SDK:** A code-first approach where AutoML can be configured and launched as part of your ML workflow or pipeline, thus providing you greater flexibility and control

AutoML jobs can be run on scalable compute clusters. The platform logs each run's performance for ease of comparison and monitoring.

Benefits of AutoML

- **Accessibility:** No advanced knowledge of ML is required to build models.
- **Speed:** AutoML quickly evaluates dozens or hundreds of model variations.
- **Explainability:** Built-in tools like SHAP values and feature importance charts help a user interpret model predictions.
- **Integration:** AutoML seamlessly connects with other Azure ML services for dataset access, pipeline orchestration, model registration, and deployment.

Applications of AutoML

- When you need to get results fast without manually testing many models
- When you want to baseline model performance before diving into custom development
- In production pipelines that periodically retrain models with updated data

- In teaching environments or experimentation scenarios where accessibility matters

Hands-on Exercise: Train and Deploy a Classification Model with AutoML

In this hands-on exercise, we will use **Azure Machine Learning Studio** to train and deploy a machine learning model capable of predicting customer churn, which refers to whether a telecom customer is likely to cancel their subscription.

The dataset used for this project is a **fictional dataset** with **1,000 customer records**, with each containing demographic details, service subscription information, and a churn indicator (Yes/No). The file is publicly available and can be downloaded from: **https://github.com/higorbarbosa/AI900/blob/main/telco_customer_churn_1000.csv**

The main columns include:

- **`customerID`**, **`gender`**, **`SeniorCitizen`**, **`Partner`**, **`Dependents`**
- **`tenure`**, **`PhoneService`**, **`InternetService`**, **`OnlineSecurity`**
- **`Contract`**, **`PaymentMethod`**, **`MonthlyCharges`**, **`TotalCharges`**
- **`Churn`** (target variable)

In this exercise, you will:

- Create and configure a Machine Learning workspace in Azure.
- Upload and register the dataset.
- Create a compute cluster.
- Run an **AutoML classification experiment** to find the best churn prediction model.
- Deploy the best model as a **REST API endpoint.**
- Test predictions using JSON inputs.

By the end of this example, you will have a complete churn prediction solution running in the cloud, which is ready to be integrated into applications or decision-making workflows.

Create an Azure Machine Learning Workspace

1. Open the Azure portal and log in with your Microsoft account.
2. Create a **New Resource.**
   a. Click **`+ Create a resource`** in the left-hand menu.
   b. In the search bar, type **`Azure Machine Learning`** and select **`Azure Machine Learning`** from the results.
   c. Click **`Create`** > **`Azure Machine Learning`**.

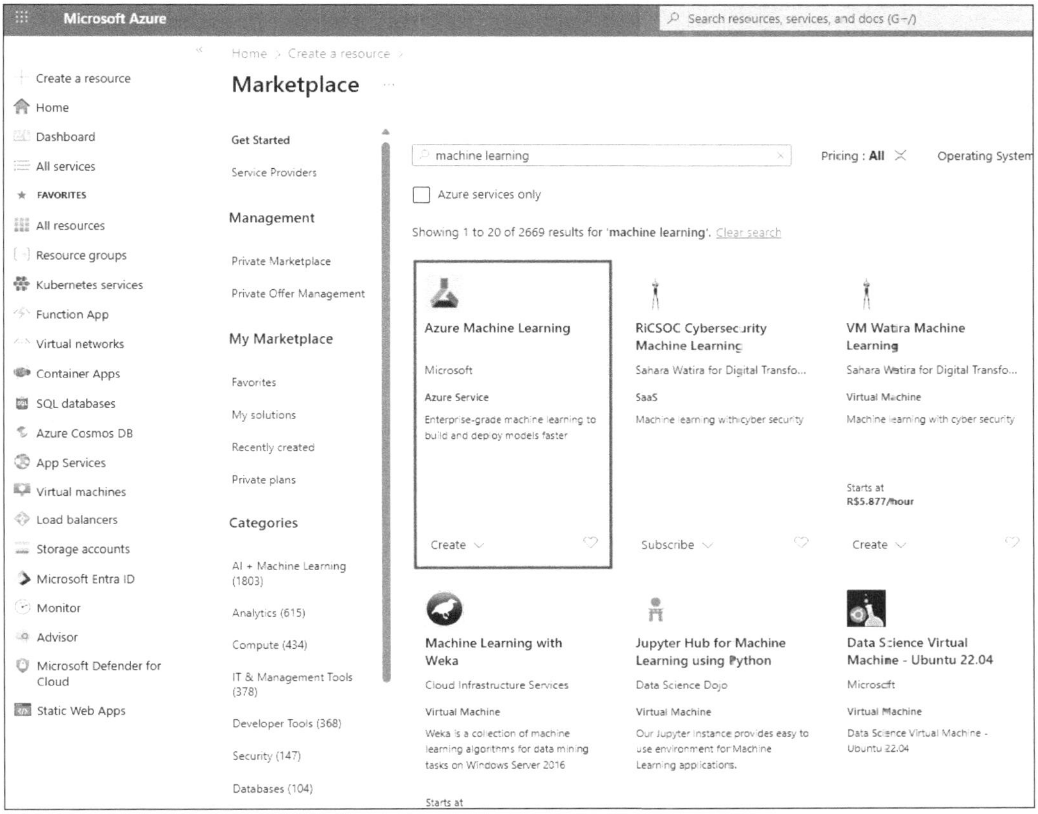

Figure 6.10: *Search for Azure Machine Learning*

3. Configure the **Resource Settings**
   a. In the Basics tab:
      i. Select your **Subscription** and **Resource group** (create one if needed).
      ii. Provide a **Workspace name** (for example, **ml-workspace**).
      iii. Choose the **Region** closest to your users.
      iv. For **Storage account**, **Key vault**, and **Application insights**, allow Azure to create new resources (default selections).
      v. Set **Container registry** to **None** (you can configure it later if needed).

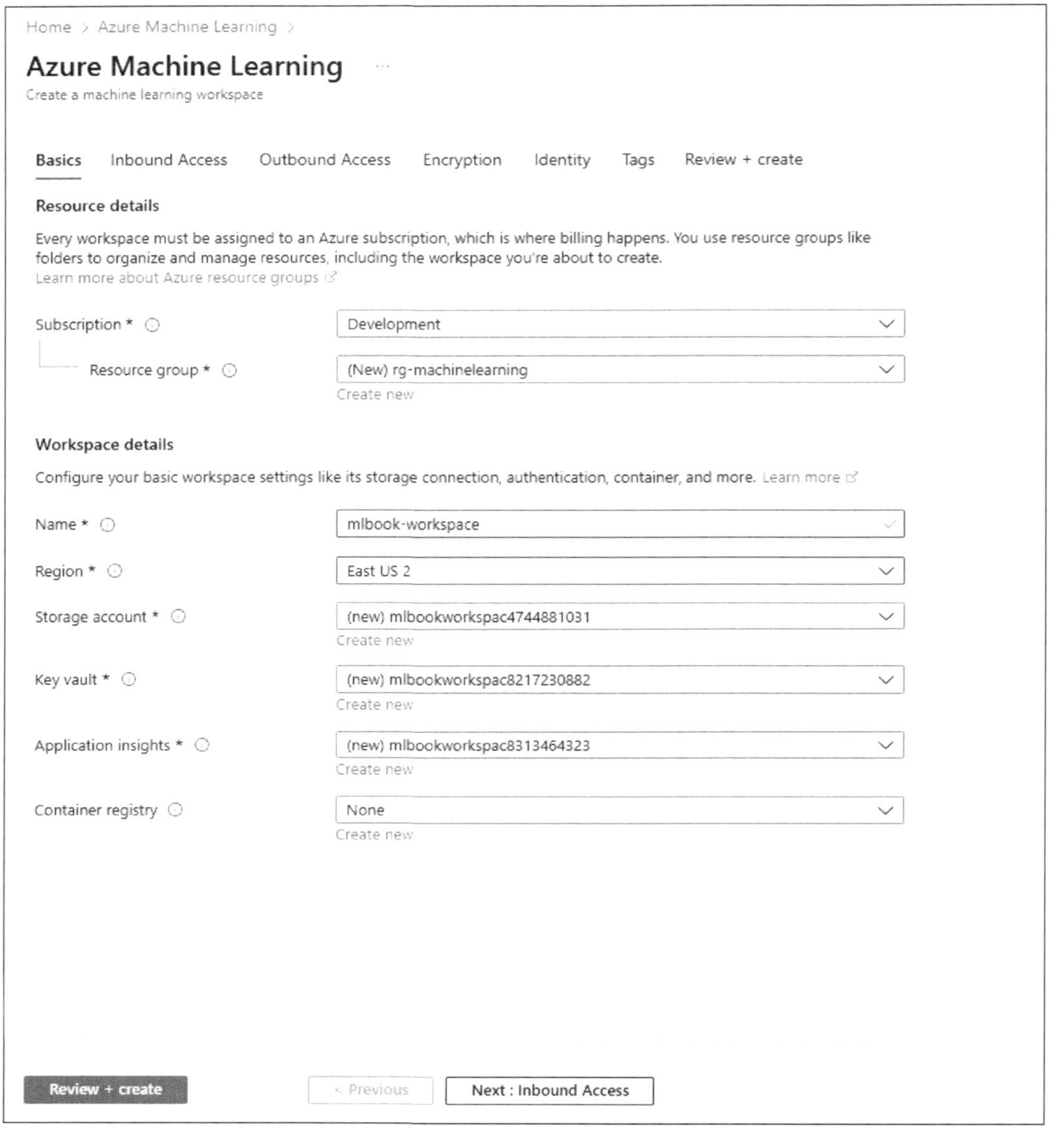

Figure 6.11: *Create Azure Machine Learning Service in Azure Portal*

4. On the **`Inbound Access`**, **`Outbound Access`**, **`Encryption`**, **`Identity`**, and **`Tags`** tabs, keep the default settings unless specific policies are required.
5. Click **`Review + Create`** and then **`Create`** to provision the workspace.

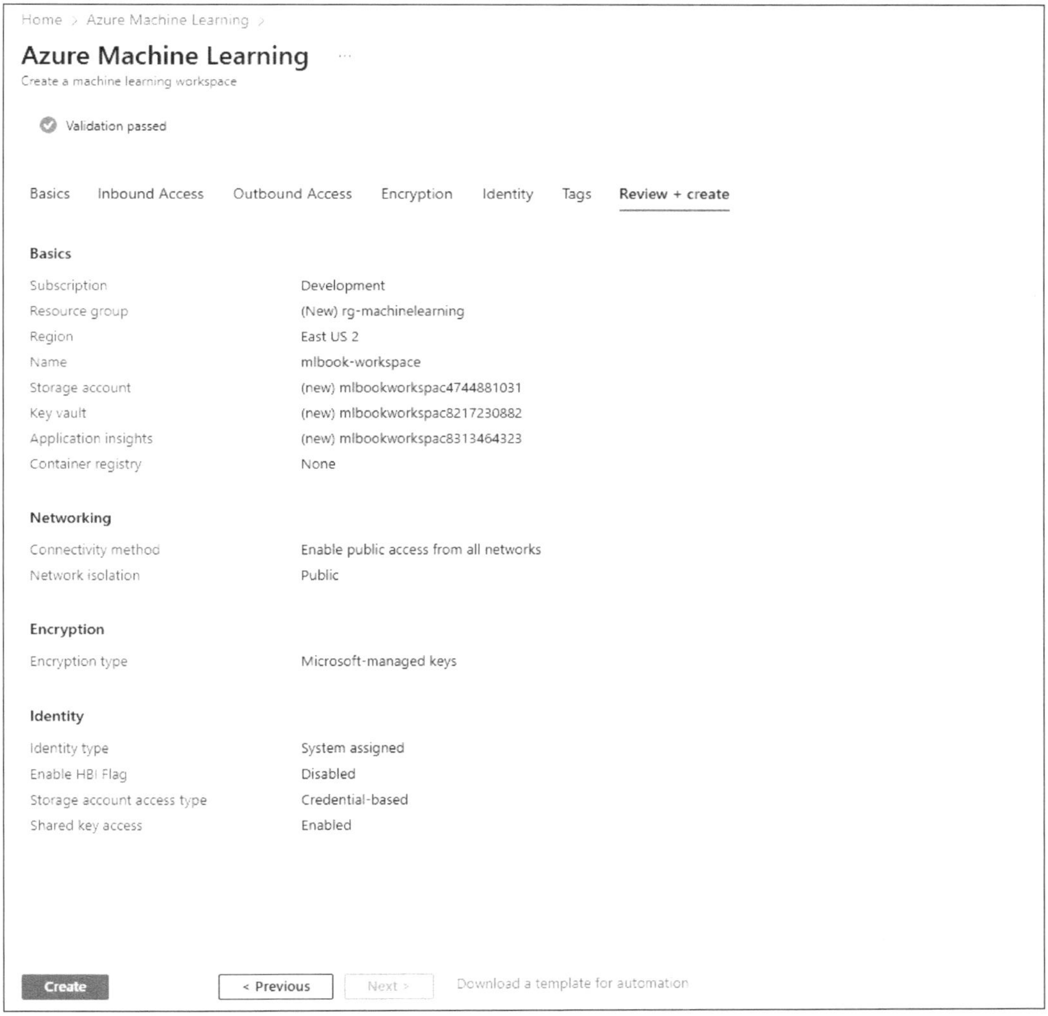

Figure 6.12: *Validating the Creation of Azure Machine Learning Service*

6. After deployment, go to https://ml.azure.com, select your subscription and the workspace you just created.

Access Azure Machine Learning Studio

1. After finishing creating the Azure Machine Learning service, access the resource.
2. On the screen of the created Azure Machine Learning workspace resource, access the **`Launch studio`** link.

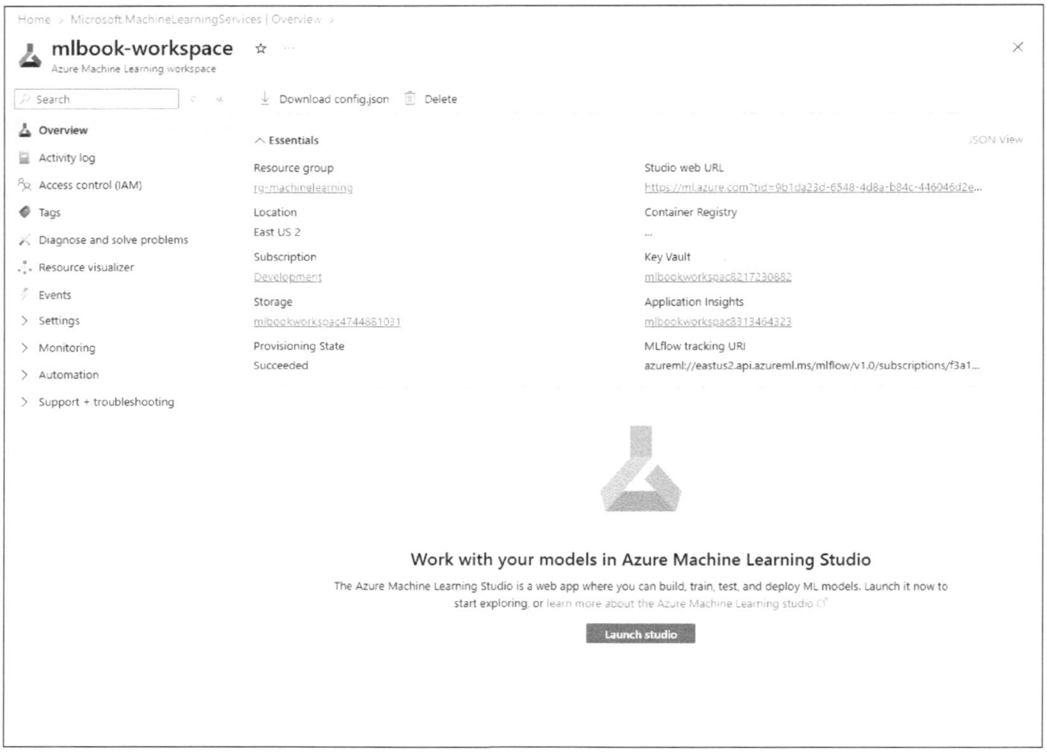

Figure 6.13: *Azure Machine Learning Workspace in Azure Portal*

3. A new tab will open in your browser with the **Azure Machine Learning portal**.
4. You will land on the home screen featuring several key tools and resources:
   - **Prompt flow** templates for Generative AI scenarios
   - **Notebook samples** to help you get started with ML training and deployment
   - **Model catalog** to browse and deploy prebuilt AI models
   - **The sidebar menu** with essential sections like **`Notebooks`**, **`Data`**, **`Jobs`**, **`Models`**, and **`Endpoints`**

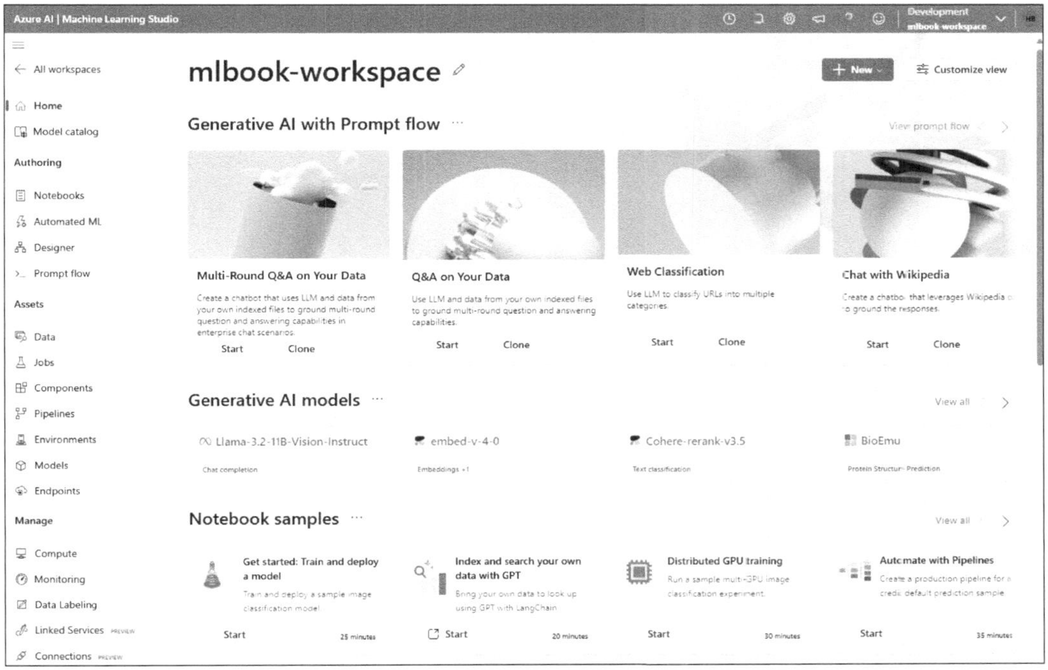

***Figure 6.14**: Azure Machine Learning Studio Portal*

Create a Compute Instance

To run notebooks and train your model, you will need a compute resource, which can be created by following the steps mentioned here:

1. In the left-hand menu, under **`Manage`**, select **`Compute`**.
2. Click the **`+ New`** button at the top.
3. In the **`Create compute instance`** form:
    - Set a name (for example, **`mlbook-compute`**).
    - Choose a virtual machine size (for example, **`Standard_DS11_v2`** or another suitable size).

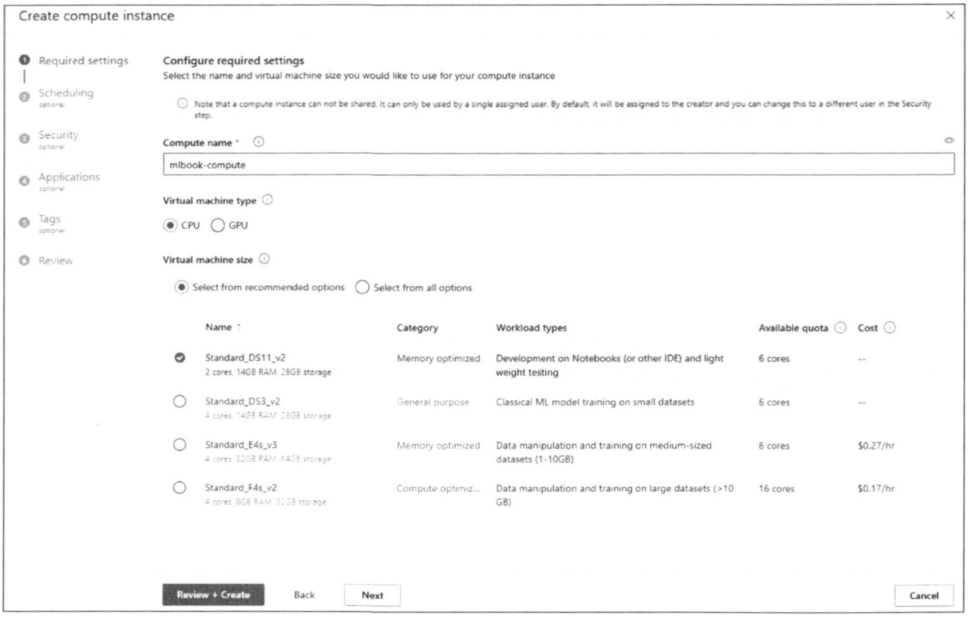

Figure 6.15: *Create a Compute Instance*

4. Keep the default values for the remaining fields.

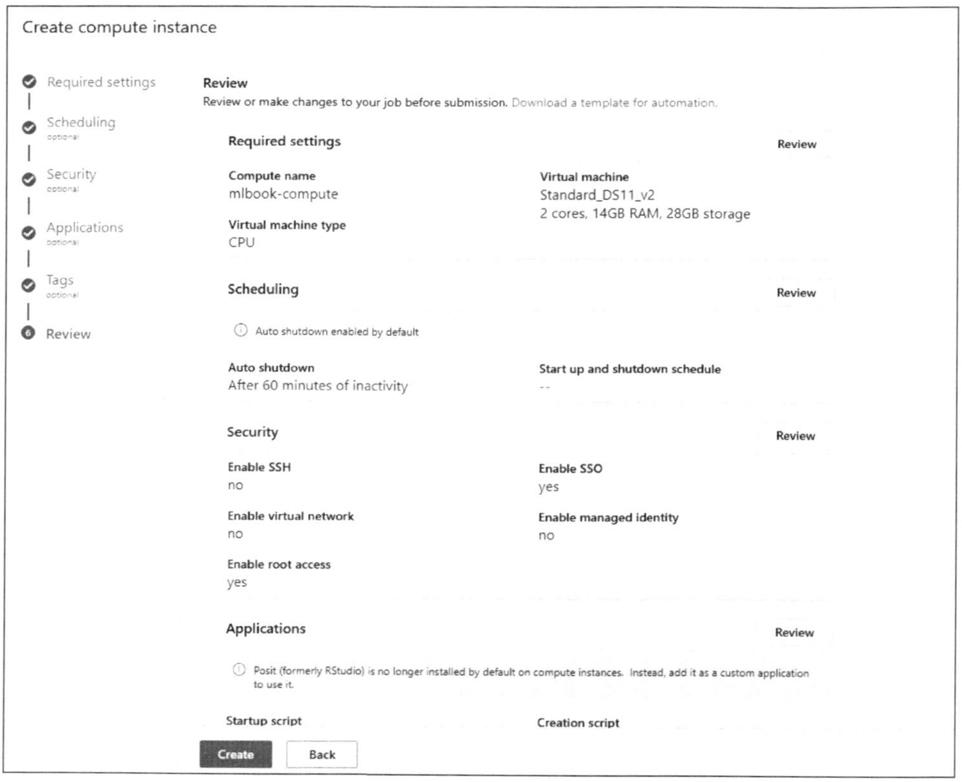

Figure 6.16: *Review a Compute Instance Creation*

5. Click **`Create`**
    - The creation process might take a few minutes. Once the compute status is Running, it will be ready to be used in notebooks and training jobs.

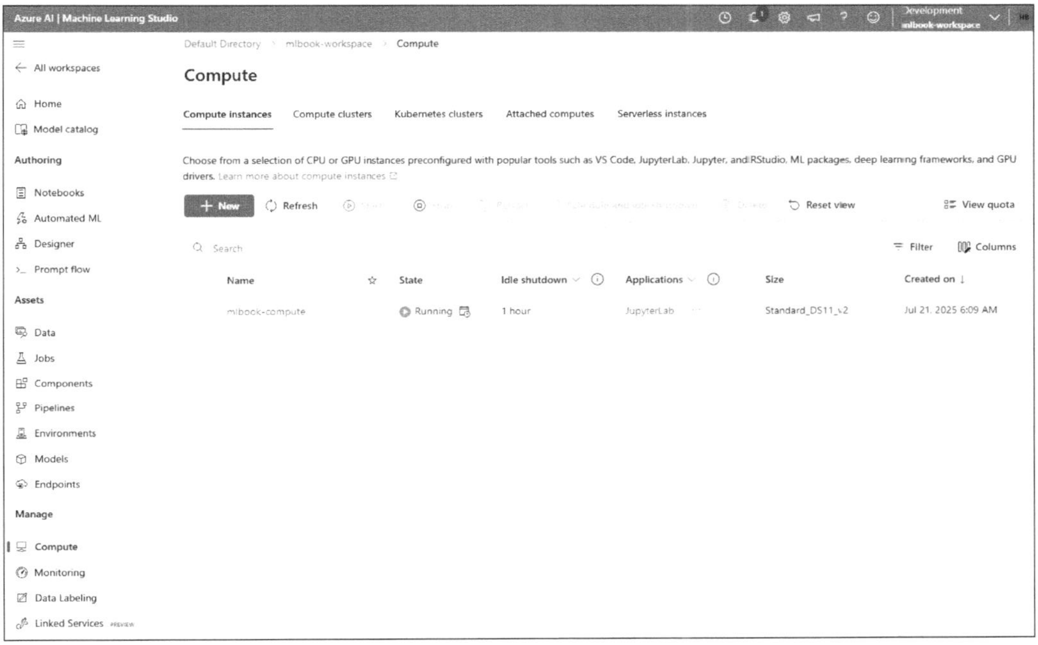

Figure 6.17: *Compute Instance Creation Completed*

Create Compute Clusters

To train machine learning models and run AutoML experiments in Azure Machine Learning, you will need a **compute cluster**. Unlike compute instances, which are used for development and testing, compute clusters are designed for scalable, on-demand workloads such as training jobs and batch inference.

1. In the left-hand menu, select **`Compute`**.
2. Click the **`Compute clusters`** tab.
3. Click **`+ New`** to create a new cluster.
4. In the **`Virtual Machine`** tab:
    - Select the **`Location`** closest to your data and users (for example, **`East US 2`**).
    - Choose **`Dedicated`** for the Virtual Machine Tier.
    - Select **`CPU`** as the Virtual Machine Type (unless your workload requires GPU).
    - Keep **`Select from recommended options`** checked.
    - Choose a size that suits your workload. (for example, **`Standard_DS11_v2`** for basic training and testing or select another option based on performance or cost.
5. Click **`Next`**.
6. In the **`Advanced Settings`** tab:
    - Name your cluster (for example, **`cpu-cluster`**).

- Set **Minimum number of nodes** to **0** (so it scales down when idle).
- Set **Maximum number of nodes** according to your needs (for example, **2** or **4**).
- Define **Idle seconds before scale down** (for example, **120** seconds).

7. Finally, click **Create**.

   Your compute cluster will be provisioned and appear under the **Compute clusters** tab once ready. It will scale up when running training jobs and scale down automatically when it is idle.

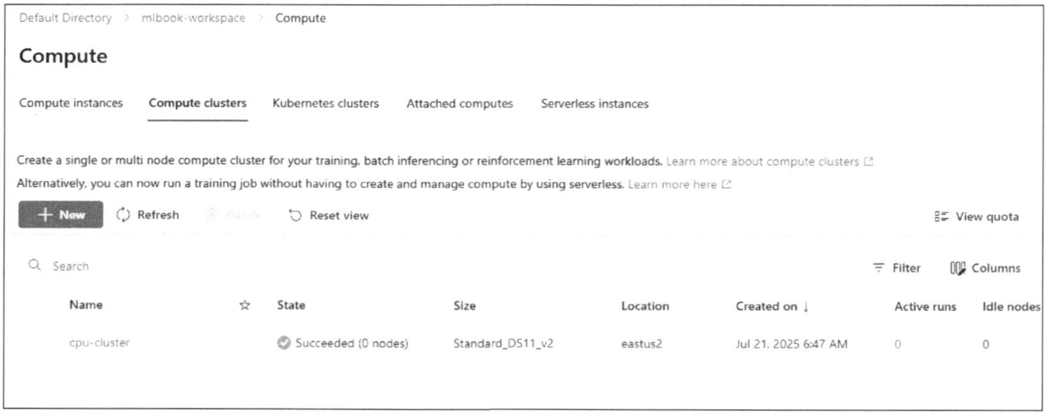

Figure 6.18: *Compute Cluster Creation Completed*

Upload the Dataset

As a starting point, we used a fictional dataset containing 1,000 records of customers from a telecom company. Each row represents an individual customer, with demographic attributes, subscribed services, and a column indicating whether the customer churned (**Churn = Yes**) or not (**Churn = No**).

The key columns in this dataset included fields like:

- **customerID**, **gender**, **SeniorCitizen**, **Partner**, **Dependents**
- **tenure**, **PhoneService**, **InternetService**, **OnlineSecurity**
- **Contract**, **PaymentMethod**, **MonthlyCharges**, **TotalCharges**
- **Churn** (target variable)

The dataset can be downloaded from the following GitHub repository: **https://github.com/higorbarbosa/AI900/blob/main/telco_customer_churn_1000.csv**

Now, you have to upload the dataset that will be used to train and test your machine learning model through the following steps:

1. In the left-hand menu, go to **Assets** > **Data**.
2. Click **+ Create**.
3. In the form that opens:
   a. **Name:** for example, **telco-customer-churn-1000**
   b. **Type:** Select **Tabular**
   c. Leave the **Description** empty or optionally fill it in.

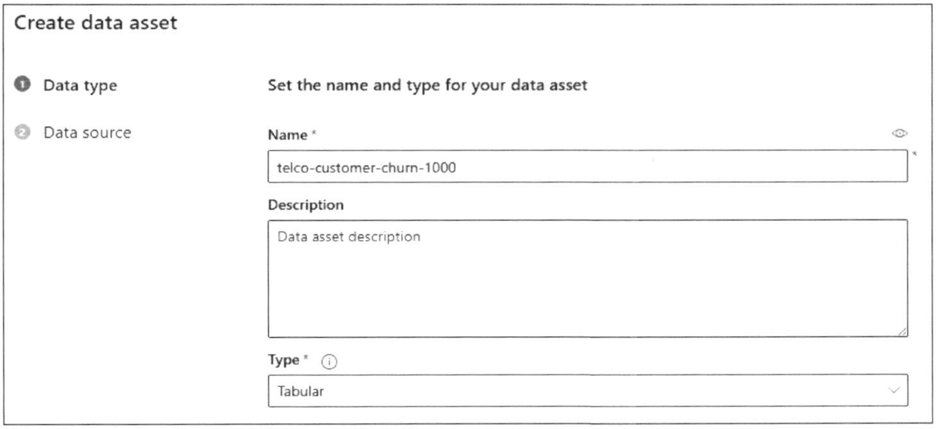

***Figure 6.19**: Set the Name and Type for Your Data Asset*

4. Click **`Next`**.
5. Select **`From local files`**, which allows you to upload a CSV file from your local computer.

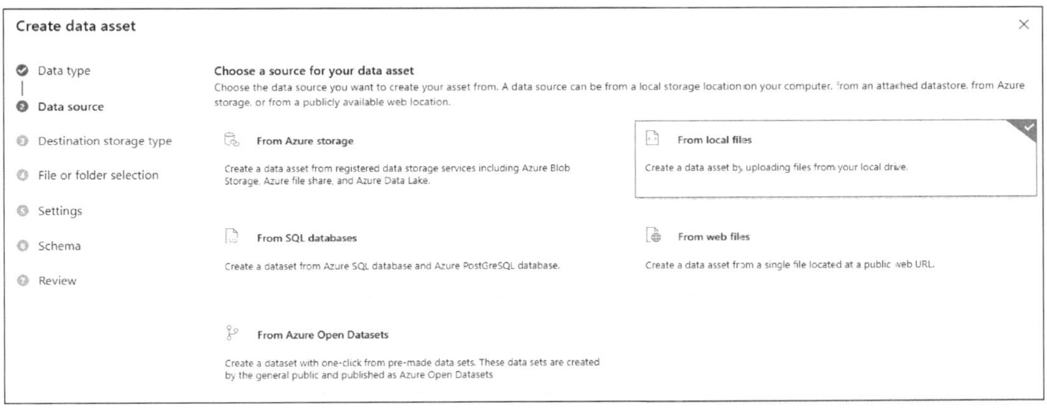

***Figure 6.20**: Choose a Source for Your Data Asset*

6. Click **`Next`**.
7. In this step, you define where the dataset will be stored:
   a. For **`Datastore type`**, select **`Azure Blob Storage`**.
   b. Choose an existing datastore (for example, **`workspaceblobstore`**). This is typically created by default with your workspace.
   c. Click **`Next`** to proceed.

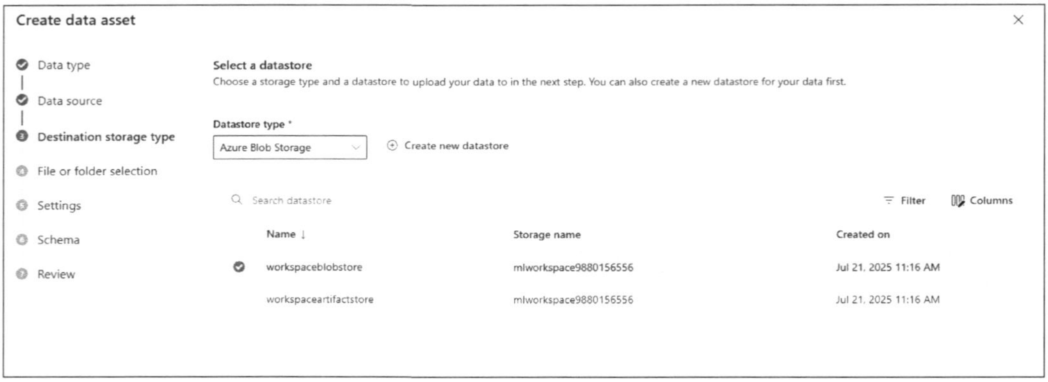

Figure 6.21: *Select a Datastore*

8. Now it is time to choose the file to upload from your local environment:

    a. In the **`Upload files or folder`** section, click **`Upload files or folder`** and select the dataset file (for example, **`telco-customer-churn-1000.csv`**).

    b. If a file with the same name already exists and you wish to replace it, check the box **`Overwrite if already exists`**.

    c. Once the file appears in the **`Upload list`**, click **`Next`**.

Figure 6.22: *Choose Your *.CSV File*

9. Configure **`File Parsing`** Settings. Now let us define how Azure should interpret your file content:

    a. **`File format`**: Select **`Delimited`**.

    b. **`Delimiter`**: Choose **`Comma`**.

    c. **`Encoding`**: Keep as **`UTF-8`**.

d. **`Column headers`:** Select **`All files have same headers`**.

e. **`Skip rows`:** Leave as **`None`**.

f. Leave **`Dataset contains multi-line data`** unchecked (for performance).

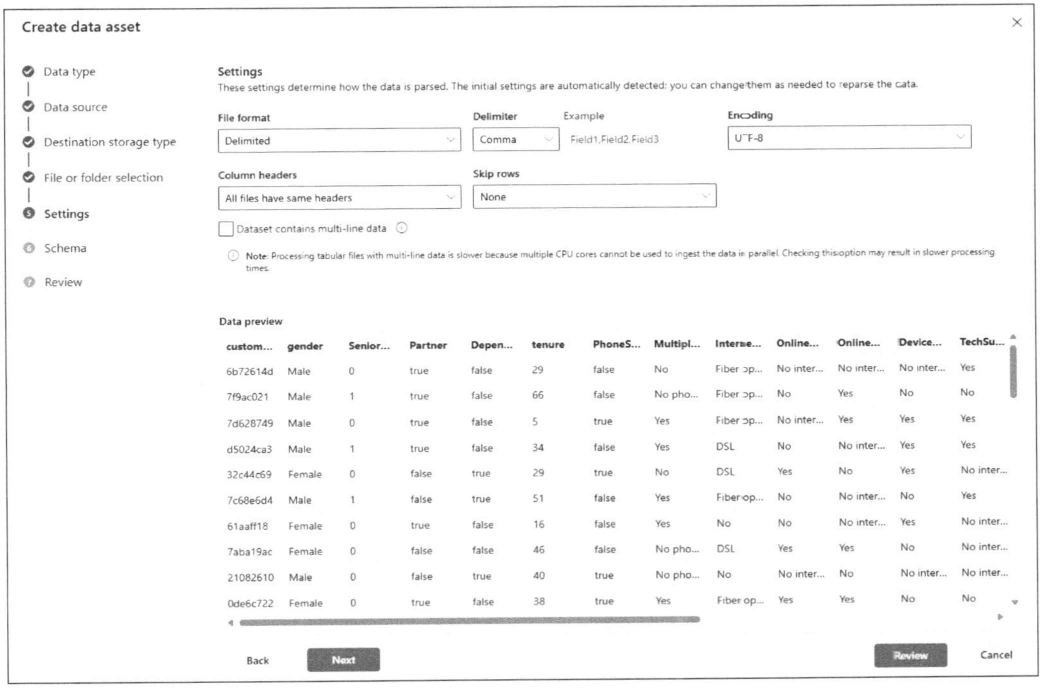

***Figure 6.23:** How the Data is Parsed*

10. A preview of the dataset will be shown at the bottom. Confirm if the structure looks correct and then click **`Next`**.

    Note: *Ensure your CSV file contains a header row, otherwise column names will be assigned as Field1, Field2, and so on.*

11. Confirm the **Dataset Schema**

    a. Azure automatically detects the column schema based on the uploaded file. You can review and adjust the column types if needed through the following actions:

       i. Ensure each **`Column name`** is included (toggle enabled).

       ii. Review the **`Type`** for each column (for example, **`String`**, **`Integer`**, **`Boolean`**) and adjust if detection was incorrect.

       iii. Check the **`Example values`** to verify data alignment.

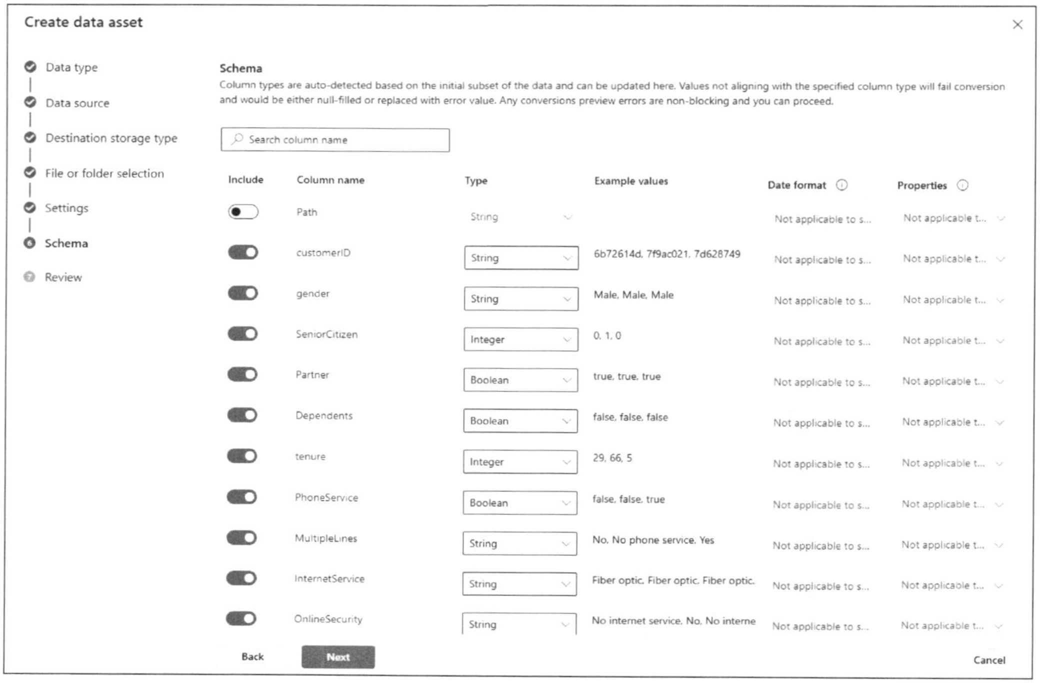

Figure 6.24: *Confirm the Dataset Schema*

12. Once the schema looks correct, click **`Next`**.

    Note: *Leave the **`Path`** column disabled unless your data structure requires it.*

13. Review all dataset settings before creation:

    a. **Name:** for example, **`telco-customer-churn-1000`**

    b. **Type:** Tabular

    c. **Source:** Local file

    d. **File:** Shows upload path and file name (for example, **`telco_customer_churn_1000.csv`**)

    e. **Storage:** Azure Blob (for example, **`workspaceblobstore`**)

    f. **Schema:** Auto-detected columns (for example, **`customerID`**, **`gender`**, **`SeniorCitizen`**, and so on.)

14. If everything is correct, click **`Create`** to finish uploading your dataset.

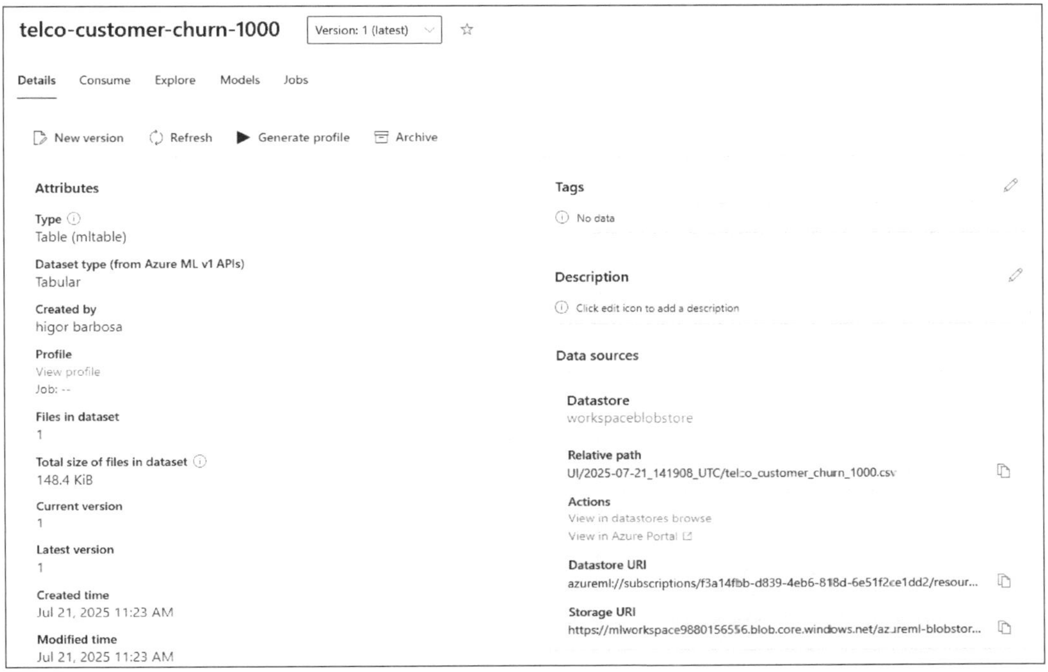

Figure 6.25: *Dataset was Successfully Created and is Now Available in Your Workspace*

After creation, the dataset will be available in your Azure ML workspace under the **Data** section.

Running AutoML Training

With your dataset and compute cluster ready, you are now prepared to launch an AutoML experiment to train a machine learning model. Make sure you go through the following steps to do so:

1. In **Azure Machine Learning Studio**, navigate to the **`Automated ML`** section from the left-hand menu.
2. Click **`+ New automated ML run`** to start a new job.
3. On the **`Training method`** screen:
    a. Select **`Train automatically`**, which allows Azure AutoML to explore algorithms and tune hyperparameters for you.
    b. Click **`Next`**.

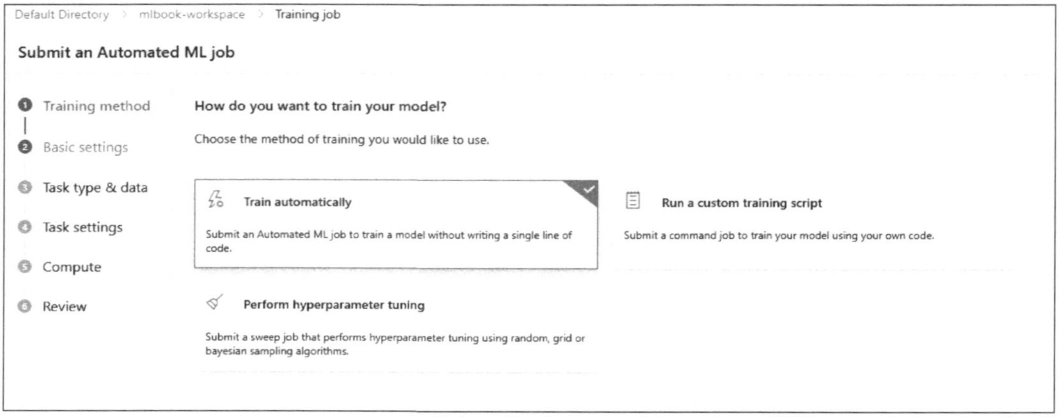

Figure 6.26: *Submit an Automated ML Job*

4. On the **Basic settings** screen:
   a. In **Job name**, enter a descriptive name such as **automl-churn-detection**.
   b. For **Experiment name**, select **Create new** and enter a name such as **churn-experiment**.
   c. Optionally, add a description and tags.
   d. Click **Next**.

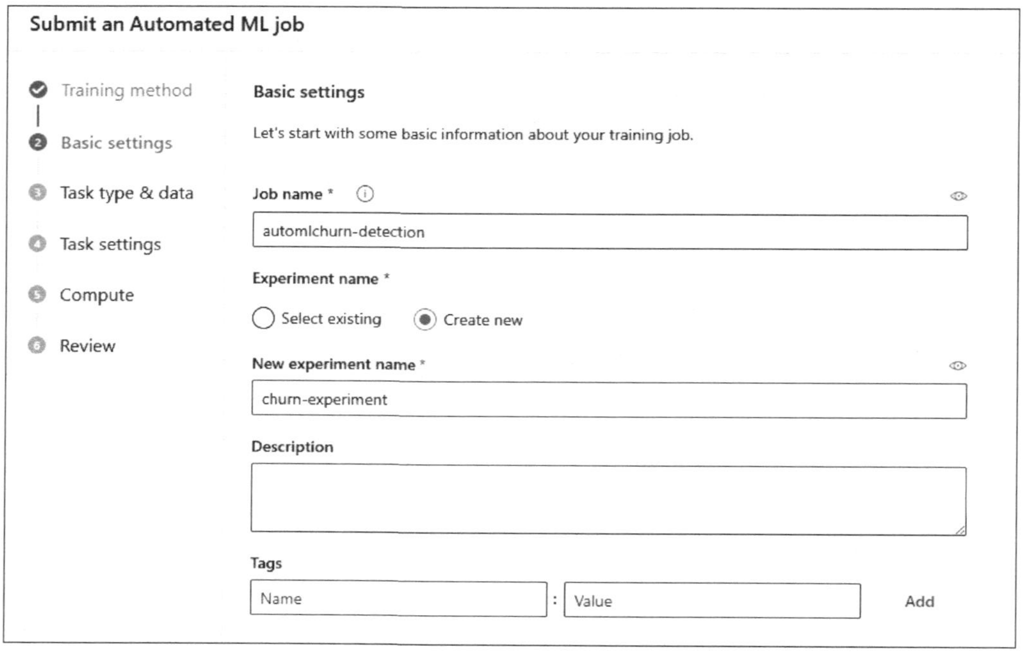

Figure 6.27: *Basic Settings for Automated ML job*

5. On the **Task type and data** screen:
   a. Choose **Classification** as the task type.
   b. Select your dataset, for example **telco-customer-churn-1000**.

c. Ensure the dataset is in table format and properly preprocessed.

d. Click **Next**.

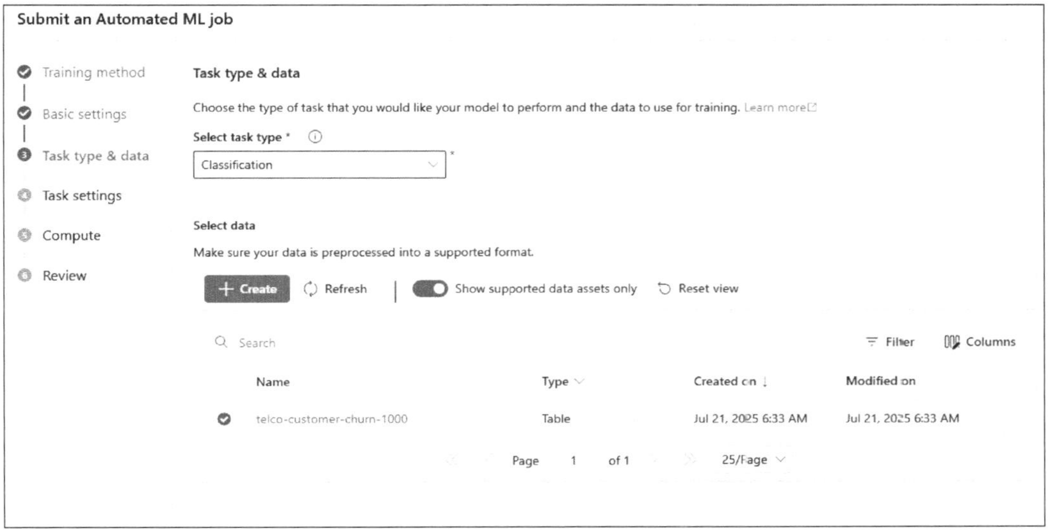

***Figure 6.28**: Choose the Type of Task*

6. On the **Task settings** screen:

   a. For **Target column**, select **Churn (Boolean)**–this is the column to be predicted.

   b. Leave **Enable deep learning** unchecked.

   c. Expand the **Limits** section to configure the runtime and resource constraints:

      i. **Max trials:** 4

      ii. **Max concurrent trials:** 2

      iii. **Max nodes:** Leave blank or set **2** to control parallelism.

      iv. **Metric score threshold:** Leave blank if not using early stopping based on performance.

      v. **Experiment timeout (minutes): 20**– this limits the total time of the AutoML run.

      vi. **Iteration timeout (minutes): 15**–this is the **minimum allowed**, so leave it as 15.

      vii. **Enable early termination:** Optional–this stops underperforming models early on.

   d. Under **Validate and test:**

      i. Set **Validation type** to **Automatic**.

      ii. Leave **Test data** as **None** if you do not have a separate dataset.

   e. Click **Next**.

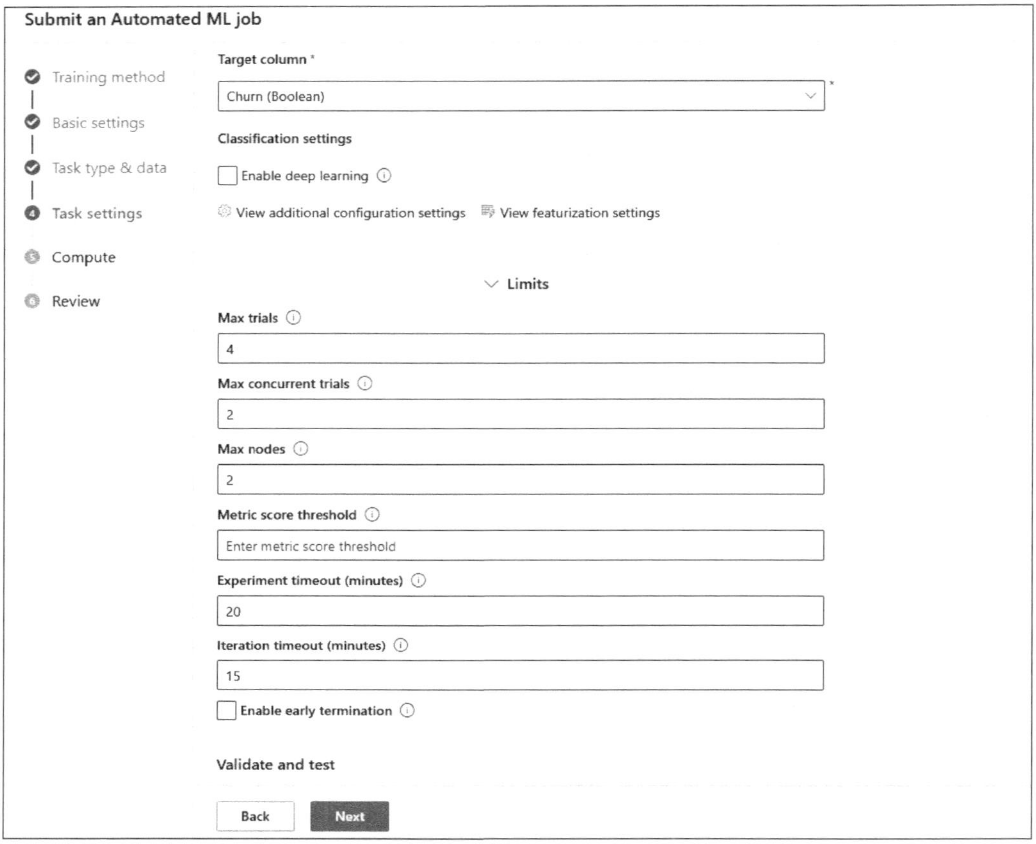

***Figure 6.29**: Task Settings for Automated ML job*

7. On the **`Compute`** screen:

   a. For **`Select compute type`**, choose **`Compute cluster`**.

   b. Under **`Select Azure ML compute cluster`**, pick the previously created compute target. For example, you can pick **`cpu-cluster`**, which uses the **`Standard_DS11_v2`** SKU with 2 vCPUs and 14 GB RAM.

   c. Click **`Next`** to proceed to the review step.

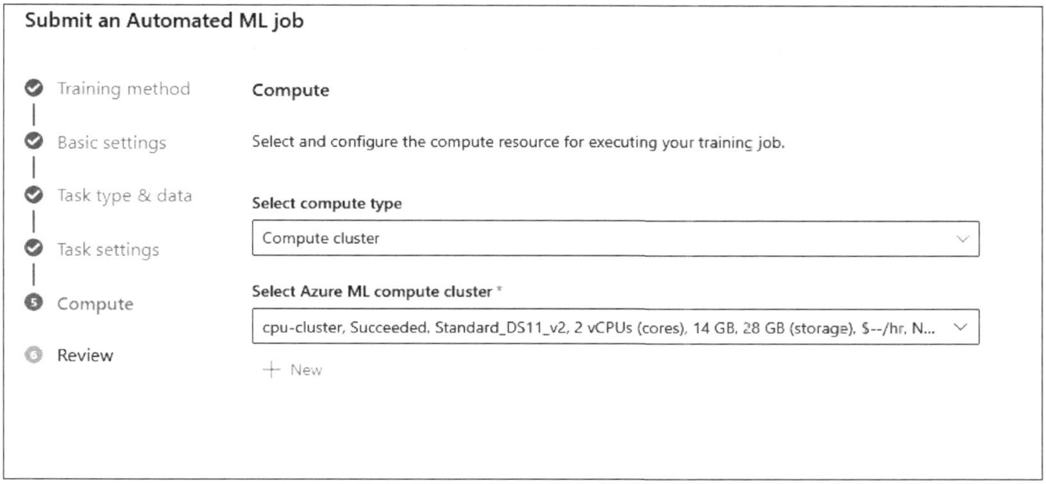

Figure 6.30: *Select and Configure the Compute Resource*

8. On the **`Review and submit`** screen:
   a. Review all configuration steps.
   b. Click **`Submit`** to begin the AutoML training job.

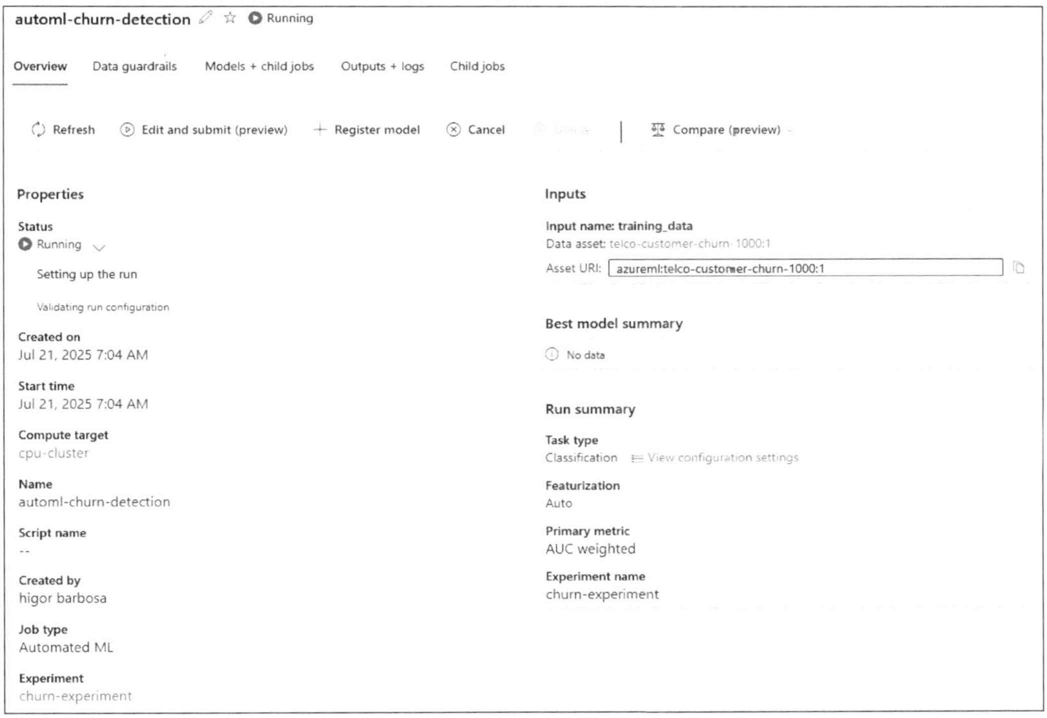

Figure 6.31: *AutoML Validating Run Configuration*

Azure will now run the AutoML experiment using the dataset and your **`cpu-cluster`**. It will evaluate multiple algorithms and hyperparameters to find the best-performing model automatically.

When the run is complete, you can view the metrics, download the model, and deploy it directly from the portal.

AutoML Run Completed

After submitting the AutoML training job, Azure Machine Learning automatically explored various algorithms and preprocessing techniques to find the most effective model for our dataset.

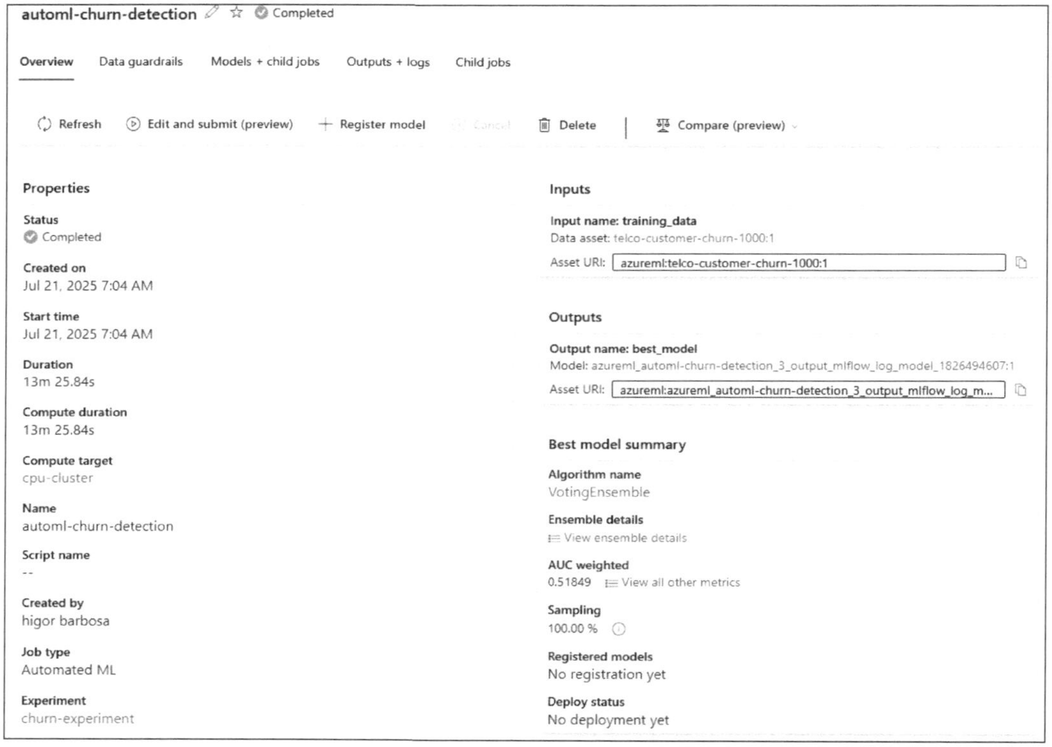

Figure 6.32: *AutoML Training Completed Successfully in Azure ML*

In this case, the run successfully completed in just over 13 minutes, while utilizing the configured compute cluster.

At the end of the process, Azure ML selected a **Voting Ensemble** model as the best performer based on the chosen primary metric (AUC). This model combines predictions from multiple algorithms to enhance accuracy and robustness.

The summary panel shows the following key results:

- **`Status: Completed`**
- **`Compute target: cpu-cluster`**
- **Best model:** Voting Ensemble
- **`AUC Weighted: 0.5185`**
- **Data used: `telco-customer-churn-1000`**
- **`Sampling: 100%`**

- **`Duration`:** ~13 minutes

At this point, the model is ready for registration and deployment, enabling you to operationalize your solution in just a few clicks—all without writing a single line of training code.

This marks the successful end of the AutoML training workflow.

Reviewing Results and Registering the Best Model

Once your AutoML job has completed, it is time to identify the best model and register it for deployment.

1. In Azure Machine Learning Studio, navigate to the **`Automated ML`** section and click your completed run, such as **`automl-churn-detection`**.
2. On the **`Overview`** tab of the run:
    a. Confirm the **`Status`** is marked as ✔ Completed.
    b. Under **`Best model summary`**, check the model selected as best:
        i. **`Algorithm name`: `VotingEnsemble`**—an ensemble approach that combines multiple models
        ii. **`AUC weighted`: `0.51849`**—the evaluation metric used to rank model performance

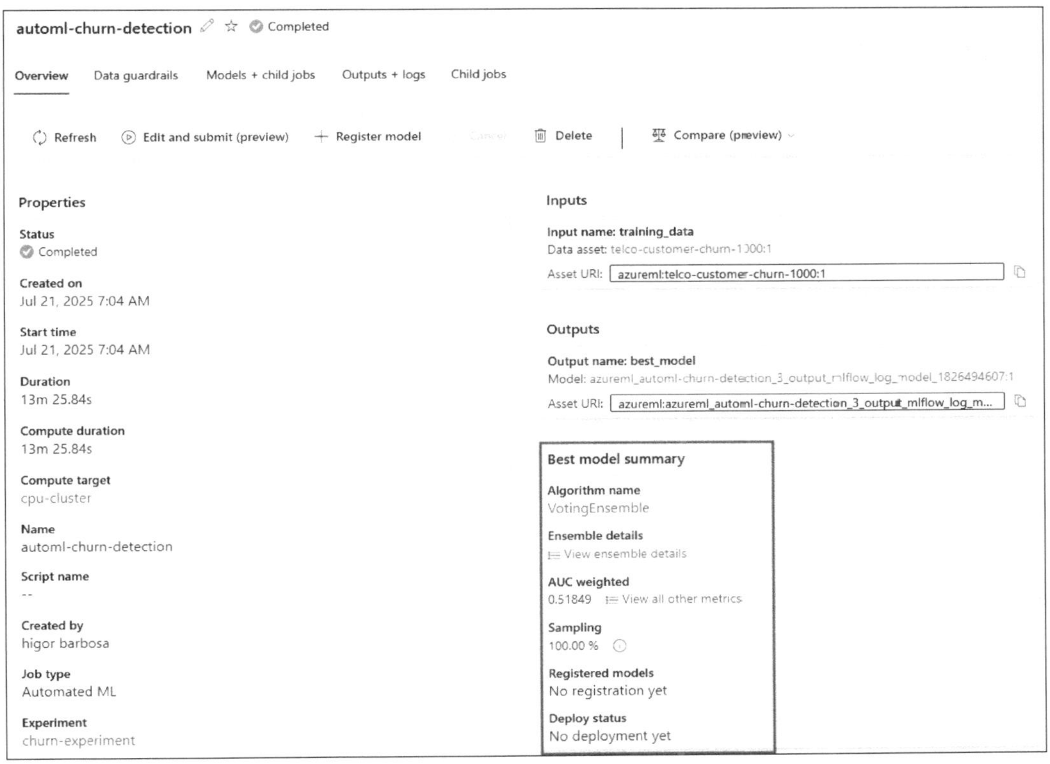

Figure 6.33: *Best Model Summary*

3. In the **Outputs** section, locate the link for the best model (for example, **`azureml_automl-churn-detection_3_output_mlflow_log_model...`**) and click it to view model details.

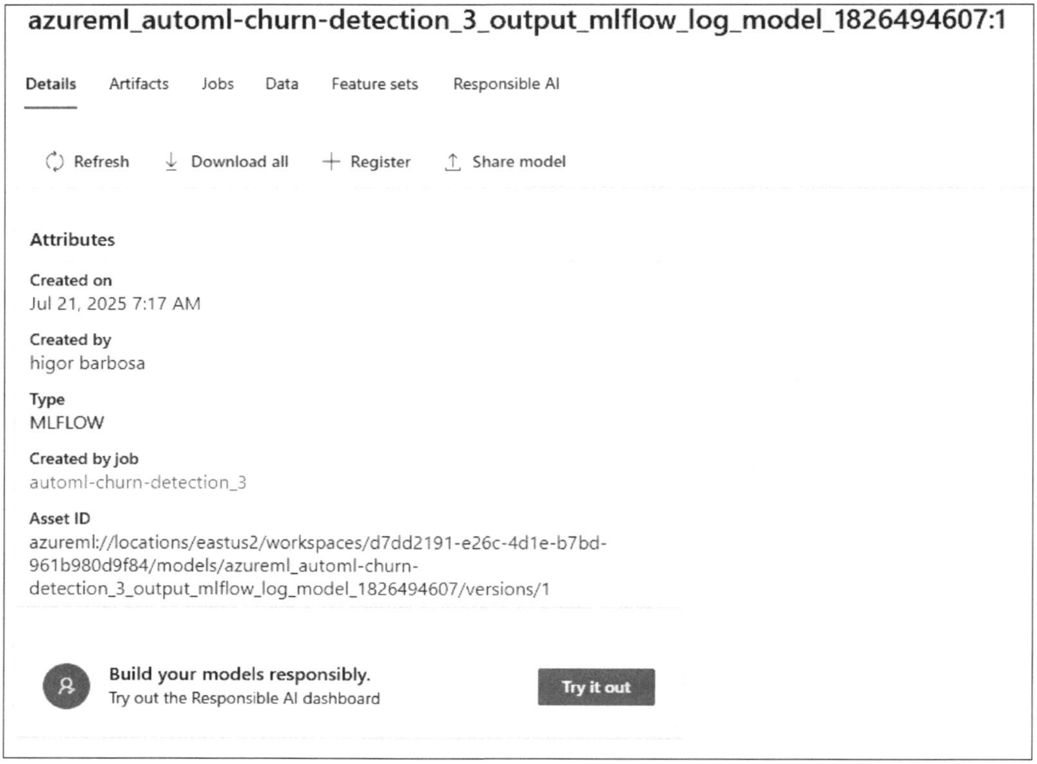

Figure 6.34: *Model Details Page Showing Metadata*

4. At the top of the **`model details page`**, click **`Register`** to begin the model registration process. In the **`Register model`** dialog:

    a. For **`Model name`**, enter a clear name such as `churn-prediction-ensemble`.

    b. Optionally add a version and description.

    c. Click **`Register`**.

5. Once registered, navigate to the **`Models`** section in Azure Machine Learning Studio to confirm that your model is listed and available for deployment.

Figure 6.35: *Registered Model*

You are now ready to deploy this model to an endpoint or use it for batch predictions.

Deploy the Model Using a Real-Time Endpoint

After registering the best model, the next step is to deploy it so it can receive predictions via a REST API in real time.

1. In the **`Registered Model`** view, click the **`Use this model`** dropdown.
2. Select **`Real-time endpoint`** from the options.

Figure 6.36: *Deployment Options*

3. The deployment wizard will open. Enter the following configuration:
    a. **`Instance count`**: Set to **`1`**—this indicates the number of virtual machines to run the model.
    b. **`Virtual machine`**: Choose **`Standard_D2as_v4`**, which provides 2 cores, 8 GB RAM, and costs approximately $0.10/hour.
    c. **`Endpoint`**:
        i. Select **`New`** to create a new endpoint.
        ii. In **`Endpoint name`**, enter: **`churn-prediction-endpoint`**.
    d. `Deployment name`:
        i. Suggest a meaningful name such as: **`churn-prediction-deploy`**.
    e. Leave **`Inferencing data collection`** and **`Package Model`** as **`Disabled`** (default options).
    f. Confirm that the **Endpoint URL** is previewed below, such as: `https://churn-prediction-endpoint.eastus2.inference.ml.azure.com/score`

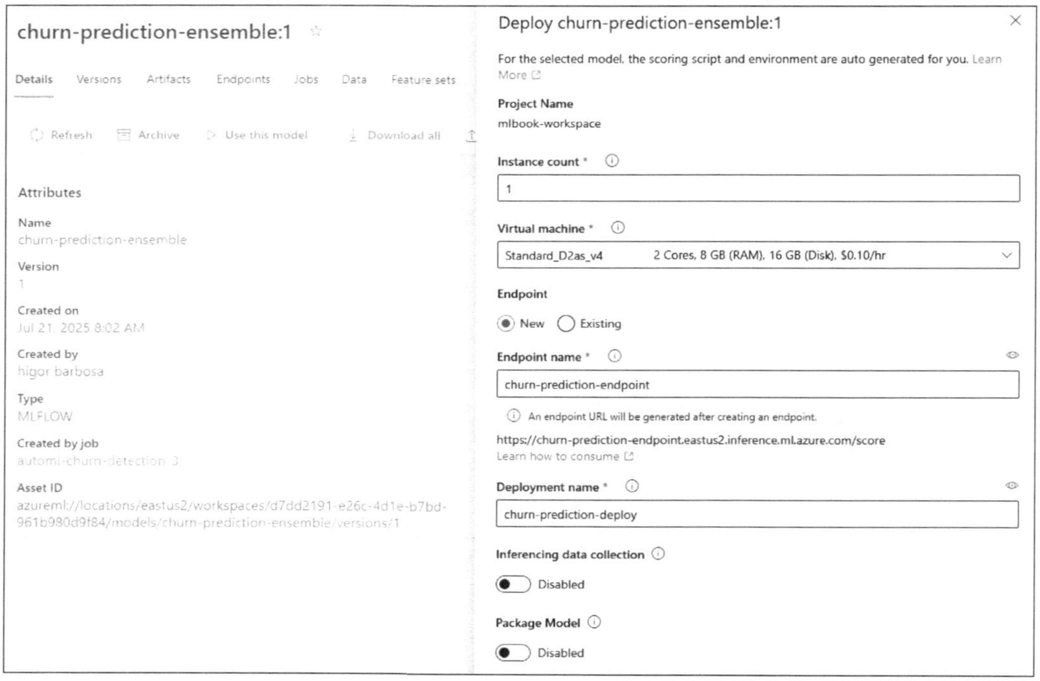

Figure 6.37: *Deploying the Model as a Real-time Endpoint*

4. Click **`Deploy`** to create the real-time inference endpoint.

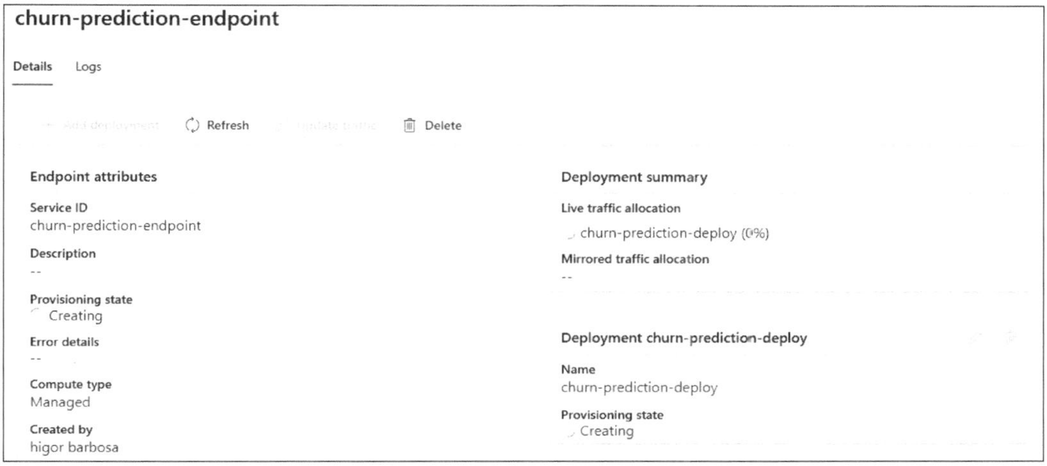

Figure 6.38: *Model is Being Created*

Once deployed, this endpoint will allow you to send JSON-formatted requests and receive predictions from your model in real time.

5. Once provisioning completes, the deployment state changes to **Succeeded**, and the REST endpoint becomes available for consumption. Key attributes to observe:

    a. **`Provisioning state`: `Succeeded`**

    b. **`Authentication type`: `Key`**

    c. **`Public network access`: `Enabled`**

    d. **`REST endpoint`:** This is the URL used to send scoring (inference) requests: `https://churn-prediction-endpoint.eastus2.inference.ml.azure.com/score`

    e. **`Swagger URI`:** Available for exploring the API schema and request format: `https://churn-prediction-endpoint.eastus2.inference.ml.azure.com/swagger.json`

    f. **Deployment name: `churn-prediction-deploy`**

    g. **Compute SKU: `Standard_D2as_v4`** with 1 instance

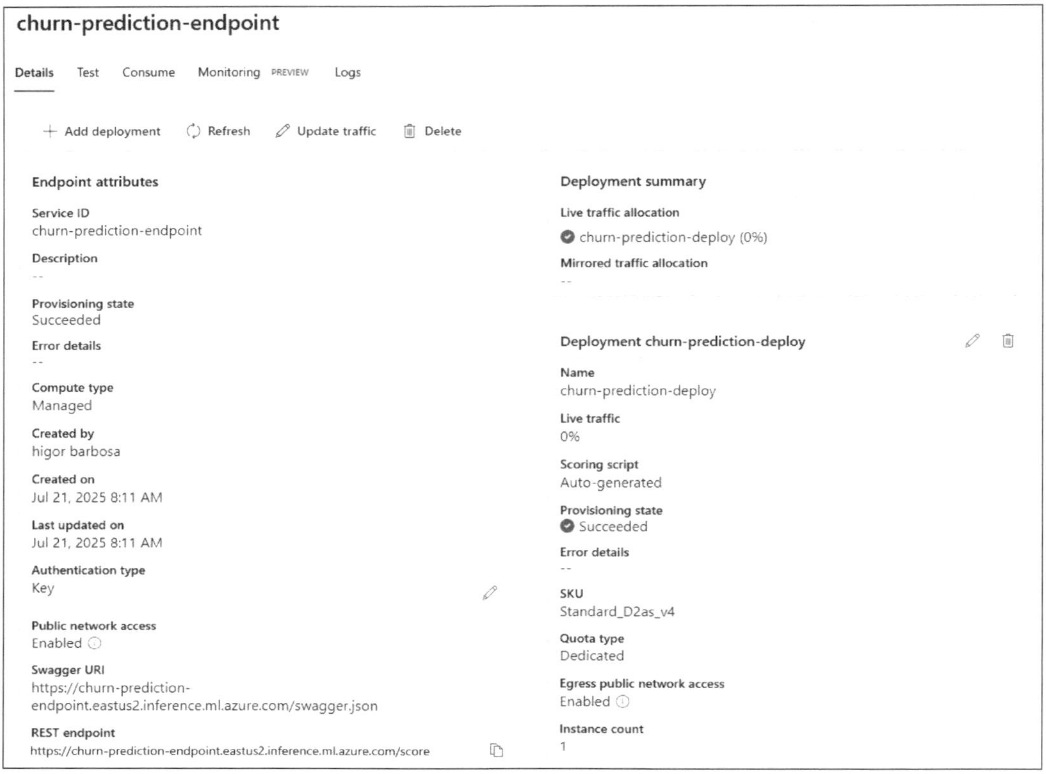

Figure 6.39: *Model Implemented*

At this point, the model is live and ready to receive requests via the REST API or through the integrated `Test` or `Consume` tabs in Azure ML Studio.

Testing the Model Using the Real-Time Endpoint (UI)

After deploying the model, you can use the `Test` tab in Azure Machine Learning Studio to send sample data and validate predictions. This is especially helpful to confirm whether the model is correctly identifying churn or not based on realistic customer profiles.

1. Go to the `Test` tab.
2. Select the deployment name: `churn-prediction-deploy`
3. In the `Input` box, a sample payload structure is shown in JSON format. This must include:
    a. `"input_data"`: Object that contains:
        i. `"columns"`: List of feature names used by the model.
        ii. `"data"`: A list of lists with sample values for prediction (you will add this in the next step).
4. Click `Examples` (optional) to load predefined examples, or manually paste a sample input using the correct format.
5. After filling in the required data, click `Test` to get prediction results.

6. **Example 1:** Customer Likely to Churn (Returns: **`True`**)

```
{
  "input_data": {
    "columns": [
      "customerID", "gender", "SeniorCitizen", "Partner", "Dependents",
      "tenure", "PhoneService", "MultipleLines", "InternetService",
"OnlineSecurity",
      "OnlineBackup", "DeviceProtection", "TechSupport", "StreamingTV",
"StreamingMovies",
      "Contract", "PaperlessBilling", "PaymentMethod", "MonthlyCharges",
"TotalCharges"
    ],
    "index": [0],
    "data": [
      ["6b72614d", "Male", 0, "Yes", "No", 29, "No", "No", "Fiber optic", "No
internet service",
       "No internet service", "No internet service", "Yes", "No", "No internet
service",
       "One year", "No", "Electronic check", 43.83, 2573.85]
    ]
  }
}
```

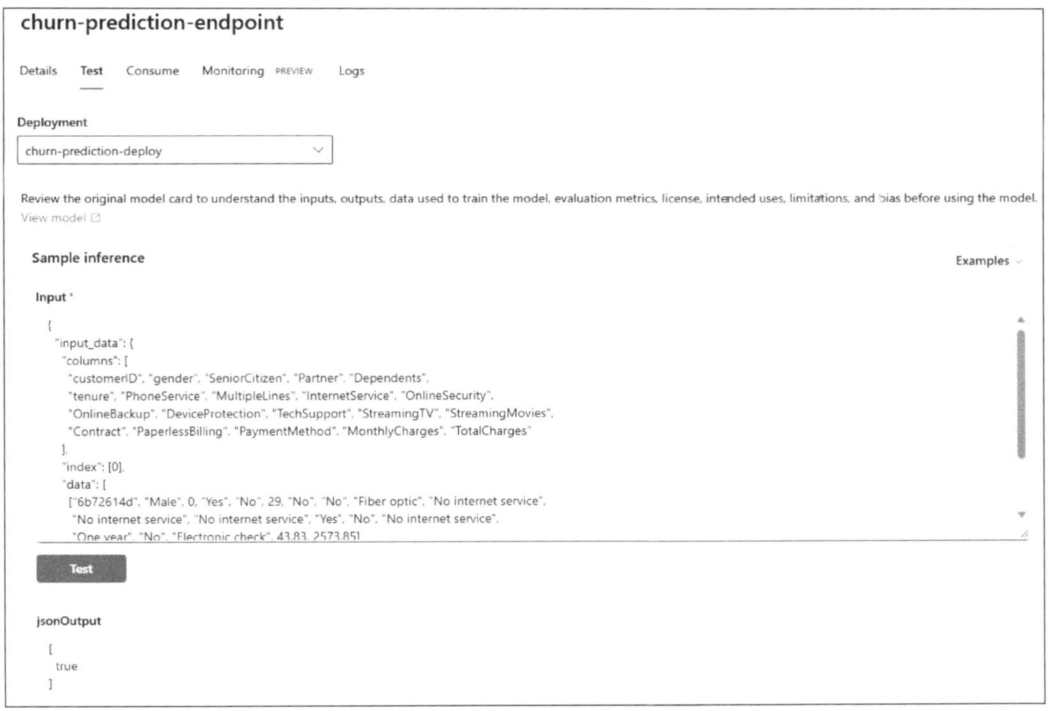

Figure 6.40: Customer Likely to Churn

7. **Example 2:** Customer Not Likely to Churn (Returns: **`False`**)

```
{
  "input_data": {
    "columns": [
```

```
      "customerID", "gender", "SeniorCitizen", "Partner", "Dependents",
      "tenure", "PhoneService", "MultipleLines", "InternetService",
"OnlineSecurity",
      "OnlineBackup", "DeviceProtection", "TechSupport", "StreamingTV",
"StreamingMovies",
      "Contract", "PaperlessBilling", "PaymentMethod", "MonthlyCharges",
"TotalCharges"
    ],
    "index": [1],
    "data": [
      ["7d628749", "Male", 0, "Yes", "No", 5, "Yes", "Yes", "Fiber optic", "No
internet service",
       "Yes", "Yes", "Yes", "No", "No", "Month-to-month", "Yes", "Bank
transfer (automatic)",
       21.85, 6256.76]
    ]
  }
}
```

Figure 6.41: *An Example of Customer Not Likely to Churn*

Congratulations! You've successfully built a full machine learning pipeline using Azure Machine Learning– right from creating a workspace and uploading data, to training a model with AutoML and deploying it via a real-time endpoint.

Conclusion

In this chapter, you explored how to build, train, and deploy machine learning models using **Azure Machine Learning**, which is a powerful platform that streamlines the entire ML lifecycle. From creating a workspace and compute resources to running experiments with **Automated ML** and deploying models as real-time endpoints, Azure ML empowers users of all skill levels to develop and operationalize AI solutions efficiently and responsibly.

Through hands-on experience, you also saw how **AutoML** intelligently selects and tunes models, thus simplifying the process of achieving accurate predictions with minimal effort. With its intuitive no-code interface, deep integration with other Azure services, and built-in support for **Responsible AI**, Azure Machine Learning serves as both a learning environment and a production-ready platform for scalable AI innovation.

With these foundational skills, you are now ready to move forward and explore another fascinating area of artificial intelligence. In the next chapter, we will dive into **computer vision** and discover how AI can analyze and interpret images and videos to unlock deeper insights from visual data.

Points to Remember

- **Azure Machine Learning** is a cloud-based service that helps data scientists and developers build, train, and deploy machine learning models at scale.
- You can use the **Azure ML Studio** graphical interface to manage datasets, experiments, compute clusters, models, and endpoints without writing code.
- **Automated ML (AutoML)** allows you to train machine learning models automatically by selecting algorithms and tuning hyperparameters based on your data and target metric.
- A **compute cluster** (for example, Standard_DS11_v2) is required to run training jobs. You can create and scale this resource directly in Azure ML.
- In AutoML, you need to specify the **task type** (for example, classification), the **target column**, and optionally configure settings such as trial limits and timeouts.
- After training, you can view the **model leaderboard** to identify the best-performing model based on a selected metric like Accuracy or AUC.
- Models can be **registered** and **deployed** to real-time endpoints, allowing you to test and consume them via REST API requests.
- JSON payloads must match the model's expected input schema for successful real-time inference.
- Always consider **resource management** to avoid unnecessary costs; delete unused compute clusters and resource groups when your experiments are done.

Key Terms

- **Azure Machine Learning:** A cloud-based platform from Microsoft for training, deploying, and managing machine learning models at scale
- **Automated ML (AutoML):** A feature in Azure ML that automates the process of selecting models and tuning hyperparameters, thereby enabling users to build high-quality ML models without extensive coding
- **Workspace:** A centralized environment in Azure Machine Learning that contains datasets, compute targets, experiments, and models

- **Compute Cluster:** A scalable set of virtual machines used to train ML models in Azure Machine Learning
- **Dataset:** A structured collection of data used for training and evaluating machine learning models
- **Experiment:** A named process in Azure ML that tracks the training of models and their associated metrics
- **Target Column:** The variable the model is trained to predict (also known as the label or output)
- **Primary Metric:** The main evaluation metric used to determine the best-performing model (for example, accuracy, AUC)
- **Leaderboard:** A ranked list of models generated by AutoML, ordered by their performance on the primary metric
- **Model Deployment:** The process of publishing a trained machine learning model as a real-time endpoint or a batch inference pipeline
- **Real-Time Endpoint:** A deployed model that can be accessed via a REST API to return predictions immediately upon request

Multiple Choice Questions

1. What is the main purpose of Azure Machine Learning?
    a. To store large datasets for analytics
    b. To manage compute and networking for virtual machines
    c. To build, train, and deploy machine learning models at scale
    d. To perform real-time monitoring of applications
2. What is Automated ML (AutoML) in Azure Machine Learning?
    a. A tool used for manually tuning models
    b. A feature that allows users to deploy pre-built models
    c. A no-code/low-code solution that automates model selection and hyperparameter tuning
    d. A visual designer used to build pipelines
3. Which option must be defined so Azure AutoML knows what to predict?
    a. The compute target
    b. The training timeout
    c. The primary metric
    d. The target column
4. What is the function of the leaderboard in AutoML runs?
    a. To compare compute cluster costs
    b. To rank the best performing models based on the selected metric
    c. To show dataset statistics
    d. To monitor pipeline execution

5. What should you do to avoid incurring unnecessary charges after completing your AutoML project?
    a. Change the compute type to serverless
    b. Register more models
    c. Delete the resource group
    d. Increase the maximum trial limit

Answers

1. c
2. c
3. d
4. b
5. c

CHAPTER 7

Identify Common Types of Computer Vision Solution

Introduction

In this chapter, we will explore fundamental concepts of computer vision solutions and their practical applications. As organizations and individuals increasingly rely on visual data such as images captured by smartphones and security camera feeds, understanding how to extract meaningful information efficiently thus becomes critical. Computer vision solutions enable us to interpret, classify, and analyze images and videos, thereby unlocking value across countless industries.

We will begin by examining image classification techniques that assign images to predefined categories. Whether categorizing products in an online catalog or organizing large image repositories, classification solutions help streamline workflows and improve decision-making. Next, we will explore object detection solutions that identify the presence of various objects and also determine their precise locations within an image, which is an invaluable capability for tasks such as quality control in manufacturing or autonomous vehicle navigation.

Furthermore, we will explore Optical Character Recognition (OCR) solutions that convert text embedded in images into editable, searchable data. OCR allows businesses to automate the processing of documents, extract meaningful insights from receipts or invoices, and enhance accessibility by making textual information more readily available.

Lastly, we will discuss facial detection and facial analysis solutions that identify human faces and evaluate attributes such as emotion, age approximation, and other characteristics. These insights support applications in customer experience enhancement, security, and user authentication, while also introducing important considerations around privacy, ethics, and responsible usage.

By the end of this chapter, you will gain a comprehensive understanding of these four common computer vision solution types. You will also learn about the key features, ideal usage scenarios, and potential challenges associated with each, equipping you with the knowledge needed to choose the most suitable solution for a variety of real-world applications.

Structure

In this chapter, we will discuss the following topics:

- Introduction to Computer Vision
- Identifying Features of Image Classification Solutions
- Identifying Features of Object Detection Solutions
- Identifying Features of Optical Character Recognition (OCR) Solutions
- Identifying Features of Facial Detection and Facial Analysis Solutions

Introduction to Computer Vision

Computer vision is a branch of Artificial Intelligence (AI) that enables software systems to perceive the world visually by analyzing still images and video sequences. While it seemed nearly impossible for computers to perform complex vision-related tasks just a few decades ago, recent advances in computational power, specialized hardware, and machine learning algorithms have opened up a remarkable range of possibilities. Today, it is feasible to automate tasks that once required significant human effort, thus saving time, reducing errors, and increasing overall efficiency.

The significance of computer vision for human understanding cannot be overstated; it is estimated that up to 80% of our perception of the world is derived from what we see. Until recently, computers did not possess this ability. Although implementing computer vision still demands substantial data, computational resources, and specialized AI expertise, the underlying concept remains relatively straightforward. The process begins with capturing images, usually through a camera, which can be considered as the computer's "eyes." This device converts the visible world into two-dimensional images composed of pixels. These tiny colored dots form recognizable patterns which, when processed by a computer vision model, which is the system's "artificial brain", enable the machine to detect distinctive features that interpret the content. For instance, the presence of wings is indicative of an airplane, while wheels might make you think of a car or a bicycle almost immediately.

Humans learn visual recognition naturally and unconsciously from early childhood. For instance, showing a young child numerous images of dogs over time will allow them to recognize a dog effortlessly. This learning process consumes a great deal of energy in a developing human brain. In the computational realm, the principle is similar: training a computer vision model requires processing power, a vast amount of quality data, and a deep understanding of data science and machine learning.

Hierarchy of Concepts

As you explore this domain, you will encounter a hierarchy of concepts that help clarify how computer vision fits within the broader field of AI:

- **Artificial Intelligence (AI):** The broad field focused on enabling machines to perform tasks that typically require human intelligence such as perception, reasoning, and learning
- **Machine Learning (ML):** A subset of AI where models are trained on data to learn patterns and make predictions or decisions without explicit instruction. For instance, if you provide many images of cats and dogs, a machine learning model can learn to distinguish between them.
- **Deep Learning (DL):** A subset of ML that leverages deep neural networks with multiple layers (hence "deep") to handle complex tasks, especially those involving unstructured data such as images and speech
- **Convolutional Neural Networks (CNNs):** A type of deep neural network particularly adept at analyzing visual data. CNNs process images in layers, first identifying edges and textures, then detecting object parts, and finally recognizing entire objects.
- **Recurrent Neural Networks (RNNs):** Neural network architectures designed for sequential data such as video, where context over time is important. RNNs can recognize actions or predict future events based on sequences of frames.

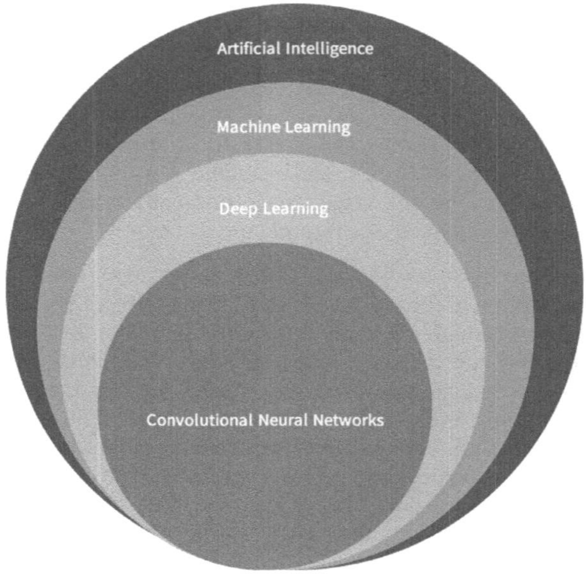

Figure 7.1: *Hierarchy of Concepts*

This layered structure illustrates how computer vision builds upon increasingly specialized levels of AI capability–from general intelligence principles, down to the neural networks that process pixels and patterns.

Foundations of Computer Vision Models

Building effective AI models, especially those related to computer vision, depends on the following fundamental elements:

- **High-Quality, Abundant Data:** The more diverse, accurate, and well-labeled the training images are, the more reliable the model will be. While open-source datasets such as Microsoft COCO or ImageNet provide a good starting point, having access to unique, domain-specific data can offer a competitive edge.
- **Substantial Computational Power:** Training and running sophisticated models require immense computational capacity. Industries increasingly rely on specialized hardware such as GPUs (Graphics Processing Units) or VPUs (Vision Processing Units) designed to handle the heavy workloads of AI and process large volumes of visual data efficiently.
- **Expertise in Data Science and Machine Learning:** Although frameworks like TensorFlow, PyTorch, Keras, and Caffe simplify aspects of development, professionals must still understand the full pipeline that is composed of stages such as data preprocessing, network architecture selection, hyperparameter tuning, and validation methods to build effective and efficient solutions.

From Concepts to Applications

Thanks to advances in technology, cloud computing platforms like Microsoft Azure now offer pre-built computer vision services. These services abstract away much of the complexity associated with building and training models from scratch. Developers and businesses can thus integrate vision capabilities into their applications such as image tagging, object recognition, and text extraction without requiring deep AI expertise.

By transforming raw visual data into actionable insights, computer vision is revolutionizing how machines interpret our world. From managing inventory in retail settings and detecting production defects in manufacturing plants to analyzing medical images in healthcare and monitoring security footage, the potential applications are vast and continually expanding.

Common Types of Computer Vision Solutions

Computer vision encompasses a diverse set of techniques and solutions designed to help machines interpret and understand the visual world. As this field has matured, distinct workloads have emerged, each targeting specific questions about the content of images and videos. The following figure represents some of the most common computer vision tasks like illustrating the progression from simply recognizing what is in an image, determining where objects are located, and comprehensively describing a scene in detail

- **Image Classification (What):** Image classification solutions focus on categorizing an entire image into one or more predefined classes. Rather than pinpointing specific items within the image, these models produce a label that best describes the primary content. For example, presented with a photograph of a car, the model might return the label "taxi" if it recognizes the vehicle as such. This approach is widely used in applications where simply knowing the dominant object or setting in an image is sufficient, such as when organizing large image libraries or tagging products in e-commerce catalogs.
- **Object Detection (Where):** While image classification identifies what is present, object detection takes this a step further by locating specific objects within an image. Instead of providing just a single label, these solutions draw bounding boxes around each detected item to highlight its position. For instance, an aerial image containing cars, buses, and cyclists might feature colored boxes around each object, labeling them accordingly. Object detection is crucial in scenarios like autonomous vehicles, warehouse inventory management, and security systems, where the precise location of an object influences decision-making.
- **Semantic Segmentation (Where):** Semantic segmentation goes beyond object detection by classifying every pixel of an image into a particular category. Instead of bounding boxes, the scene is represented as a detailed map where each region corresponds to a semantic class (for example, "car," "road," "pedestrian"). This level of granularity is vital for applications such as autonomous driving (where understanding the exact boundaries between roads, sidewalks, and obstacles is critical) and medical imaging (where accurately identifying tissue types can help in diagnosing serious illnesses).
- **Image Analysis (Describe):** Image analysis solutions aim to offer a more descriptive and holistic understanding of a scene. Rather than simply stating, "There is a car," the system might generate a caption like, "A person walking a dog on a street." Such solutions blend object recognition with contextual understanding, helping users quickly comprehend complex imagery. This approach proves useful in accessibility tools (for example, providing verbal descriptions of images for the visually impaired), content moderation systems, and any scenario where a narrative description of the scene is more valuable than a mere list of objects.
- **Facial Detection and Analysis (Who):** Facial detection and analysis solutions identify human faces in images and may infer attributes such as facial expressions, estimated age, and the presence of accessories (like glasses). Unlike facial recognition (which specifically identifies known individuals), facial analysis focuses on understanding general facial characteristics and emotions. This type of analysis is valuable in security and access control, retail analytics (for example, gauging customer sentiment), and user interface enhancements (like adapting content based on user emotion).
- **Optical Character Recognition (OCR) (Read):** OCR solutions extract textual information from images and convert it into searchable, editable text. For example, a snapshot of a street sign "Oxford Street W1 City of Westminster" can be transformed into usable text data. This

capability supports a wide range of applications such as automated document processing, data entry in business environments, and making visual information more accessible and easily retrievable in digital systems.

Solution Type	***Description***	***Primary Use Case***	***Example***
Image Classification	Assigns one or more labels to the entire image.	Product tagging, medical imaging.	Detecting "cat" in a photo.
Object Detection	Identifies and locates multiple objects within an image.	Autonomous driving, retail shelf monitoring.	Bounding boxes around people and vehicles.
Facial Detection & Analysis	Detects faces and infers attributes like age or emotion.	Access control, marketing, sentiment analysis.	Detecting emotion or presence of a mask.
Optical Character Recognition (OCR)	Extracts text from images and converts it into editable, searchable data.	Document digitization, accessibility.	Reading text from a receipt.

Table 7.1: *Comparison of Common Computer Vision Solutions*

These six tasks represent key building blocks in the computer vision domain. They can be integrated or combined to address more complex challenges. For instance, a sophisticated security system might employ object detection to identify people or vehicles, facial detection to understand who is present, and OCR to read license plates or signage. By harnessing multiple computer vision workloads, developers and organizations can create comprehensive, multi-faceted solutions that navigate and interpret the visual world with growing sophistication.

Figure 7.2: *Example of Using Image Analysis in Video*

As we move forward, the following sections will delve deeper into these four common computer vision solution types. You will gain insights into how each method works, the ideal application scenarios, potential challenges, and the best practices for implementation. Armed with this understanding, you will be able to choose the most suitable techniques to meet your specific needs.

Identifying Features of Image Classification Solutions

Image classification is one of the most fundamental tasks in the realm of computer vision. Rather than pinpointing the exact location of objects within an image, classification focuses on identifying the overall content by assigning one or more labels to the entire image. This could mean determining if an image contains a "cat," a "car," or a "forest," without specifying the location where these elements appear in the image.

Since it provides a straightforward way to categorize visual data, image classification is a foundational technique that supports a range of applications. From enhancing search capabilities in large photo libraries to guiding automated quality control checks in manufacturing, image classification underpins many intelligent systems that rely on fast and accurate recognition of visual patterns.

Modern image classification solutions typically utilize deep learning models, particularly Convolutional Neural Networks (CNNs), which learn to identify meaningful features such as edges, textures, and shapes directly from raw pixel data. Once trained on sufficiently diverse and well-labeled datasets, these models can apply their learned representations to new, unseen images, while correctly predicting their categories even when faced with variations in lighting, background, or perspective.

For example, consider a model classifying an image as follows:

Figure 7.3: *An Example of an Image Analyzed via Image Classification*

The following JSON snippet shows an example of how a classification model might return its output after analyzing an image:

```
{
  "categories": [
    {
      "label": "cat",
      "confidence": 0.98
    }
  ]
}
```

In this hypothetical JSON output, the classification model has determined that the image most likely contains a cat and assigned a confidence score (0.98) reflecting its certainty in this prediction. Unlike object detection, there are no bounding boxes or coordinates; just a label and a measure of how confident the model is in its judgment.

This simplicity makes image classification a practical starting point for various use cases. E-commerce platforms use it to categorize products, news agencies to tag images for faster content retrieval, and social media networks to sort user photos by topic or theme. By converting raw pixels into semantic labels, image classification streamlines data organization, speeds up content filtering, and enables automated decision-making based on visual information.

Exam Tip: *If an exam question describes labeling entire images without mentioning bounding boxes or coordinates, it refers to* ***image classification****, not* ***object detection****.*

Key Characteristics of Image Classification Solutions

Image classification solutions share several defining characteristics that make them both powerful and adaptable across a wide range of applications. The following points summarize their most important principles and practical considerations:

- **Purpose:** Image classification solutions determine what an image represents as a whole, assigning one or more categories that best describe its central content rather than analyzing individual components within the frame.
- **Model Training:** These solutions typically use **Convolutional Neural Networks (CNNs)** trained on large, labeled datasets to learn general visual features such as edges, textures, and shapes.
- **Transfer Learning: Pre-trained models** and **transfer learning techniques** simplify implementation, allowing organizations to fine-tune established architectures with smaller, domain-specific datasets—saving time and computational resources.
- **Integration and Deployment:** Since classification models generate a **label** and a **confidence score**, they can be easily integrated into various applications. They run efficiently across cloud platforms, smartphones, and edge devices, enabling scalable and accessible AI solutions.
- **Confidence Thresholds:** Developers can configure confidence thresholds to decide when to trust predictions automatically, request human validation, or trigger additional workflows, thereby simultaneously balancing accuracy, speed, and resource efficiency.
- **Responsible and Ethical Use:** Ensuring diverse, representative, and unbiased training data promotes fairness and accuracy. Compliance with **privacy and data protection laws** builds trust, particularly when images include sensitive or personal information.
- **Practical Applications:** Image classification supports diverse use cases such as analyzing **medical images**, monitoring **wildlife**, and managing **media content**, transforming visual data into actionable insights that drive smarter decision-making.
- **Continued Evolution:** As models advance and training techniques improve, image classification offers a **fundamental entry point** into computer vision as it allows systems to understand and leverage the growing volume of visual information in today's world.

Taken together, these characteristics form the foundation of image classification as a key capability within computer vision. Next, we will explore **object detection**, a complementary approach that extends beyond recognizing what is in an image to also determine **where** each object is located.

Identifying Features of Object Detection Solutions

Object detection enhances a computer vision system's ability to not only identify objects within an image, but also determine their exact positions. Unlike image classification, which assigns a single label to an entire scene, object detection locates multiple objects by drawing bounding boxes around them and assigning confidence scores to each detected item. This spatial awareness enables more informed interactions with the visual world by counting objects, tracking their motion, or understanding how they relate to one another in a scene.

Such capabilities prove invaluable in numerous fields. In autonomous driving, object detection highlights pedestrians, vehicles, and traffic signs, helping self-driving cars navigate safely. In retail, it can identify products on shelves to streamline inventory management. Security systems benefit by detecting suspicious items or intruders, alerting authorities in real time. Object detection's ability to focus on the "where" as well as the "what" makes it a cornerstone technology in many intelligent systems.

Deep learning models, which are often variants of Convolutional Neural Networks (CNNs), power these solutions. Since they are trained on large, annotated datasets, they learn to recognize visual patterns that correspond to specific object categories. Once trained, they can apply this knowledge to new images, outputting bounding boxes, class labels, and confidence scores. This structured output supports complex applications like guiding robots through a warehouse and aiding visually impaired individuals by describing the environment around them.

For example, consider a model analyzing the following image:

Figure 7.4: *Example of Object Detection in a Scene with Multiple People and a Laptop*

The following JSON example shows how an object detection model might return its output after analyzing an image:

```
{
  "objects": [
    {
      "object": "person",
      "confidence": 0.76,
      "boundingBox": {
```

```
          "left": 220,
          "top": 150,
          "width": 100,
          "height": 200
        }
      },
      {
        "object": "person",
        "confidence": 0.85,
        "boundingBox": {
          "left": 360,
          "top": 140,
          "width": 110,
          "height": 210
        }
      },
      {
        "object": "laptop",
        "confidence": 0.52,
        "boundingBox": {
          "left": 280,
          "top": 180,
          "width": 80,
          "height": 60
        }
      }
    ]
  }
```

In this hypothetical output, the model has identified two people and a laptop, assigning each a confidence score and specifying their locations by pixel coordinates. Armed with such detailed information, developers can create systems capable of more nuanced and effective decision-making in real-world environments, which proves that object detection significantly enriches the way machines understand and interact with visual data.

Key Characteristics of Object Detection Solutions

Object detection solutions share several key attributes that distinguish them from simpler image classification systems. The following points summarize their main principles and considerations:

- **Purpose:** Object detection goes beyond classification by identifying and locating multiple objects within a scene. Instead of assigning one label to an entire image, these models mark each object with a **bounding box** and a **confidence score**, providing valuable spatial context for decision-making.
- **Practical Applications:** This capability enables use cases such as **autonomous vehicles** recognizing pedestrians and traffic signs, and **factory systems** detecting defective parts on assembly lines.
- **Dual Challenge – What and Where:** Object detection must handle both **classification** ("what") and **localization** ("where"). Techniques such as **Faster R-CNN**, **SSD**, and **YOLO** achieve this balance between accuracy and speed, which is crucial for real-time scenarios.
- **Training and Data Requirements:** To perform reliably under varying conditions like lighting, angles, occlusions—models must be trained on **diverse, well-annotated datasets**. Techniques like **data augmentation** (for example, altering image brightness or scale) strengthen model robustness.

- **Transfer Learning and Deployment:** Using **pre-trained models** reduces training cost and time. Cloud APIs from major providers simplify integration, while optimized models can run on **edge devices** (such as smartphones and drones) for low-latency analysis.
- **Ethical and Privacy Considerations:** As object detection often involves sensitive data (like people, vehicles, or personal belongings), adhering to **privacy laws** and using **unbiased datasets** are essential to build trust and prevent misuse.
- **Impact Across Industries:** From **autonomous navigation** to **security**, **retail inventory**, and **manufacturing quality control**, object detection enhances efficiency, safety, and innovation across multiple sectors.
- **Continuous Improvement:** As datasets expand and architectures evolve, object detection continues to advance, thus enabling more accurate, real-time understanding of complex visual environments.

Together, these characteristics demonstrate how object detection bridges the gap between identifying **what** is present in an image and understanding **where** each element is located, which paves the way for more sophisticated computer vision solutions.

Identifying Features of Optical Character Recognition Solutions

Optical Character Recognition (OCR) solutions enable machines to extract textual information from images and convert it into editable, searchable, and analyzable content. Instead of treating the entire image as a collection of pixels, OCR focuses on identifying individual letters, words, and numbers and then reconstructs them into meaningful text. This technology transforms static visual data—such as scanned documents, receipts, product labels, or signage—into dynamic, machine-readable formats, unlocking a multitude of possibilities.

By digitizing text, OCR supports a wide range of use cases that benefit businesses, researchers, and everyday users. Physical documents like invoices, forms, or contracts can be rapidly scanned and indexed, making them easier to search, store, and retrieve. Historical archives and handwritten notes become accessible and researchable, while retailers and manufacturers can automatically analyze product information captured by camera-equipped devices. More importantly, OCR also enhances accessibility: text extracted from images can be read aloud by screen readers, making visual information available to individuals with visual impairments.

Modern OCR solutions often rely on advanced machine learning models—particularly deep learning approaches—that have been trained on diverse datasets containing various fonts, languages, and image qualities. Preprocessing techniques, such as adjusting brightness, contrast, or orientation, help these systems interpret even low-quality or skewed documents. As a result, OCR engines can accurately handle a wide spectrum of conditions, from pristine, printed documents to faded receipts and stylized signage.

For example, consider the output of an OCR model analyzing a product's nutritional label:

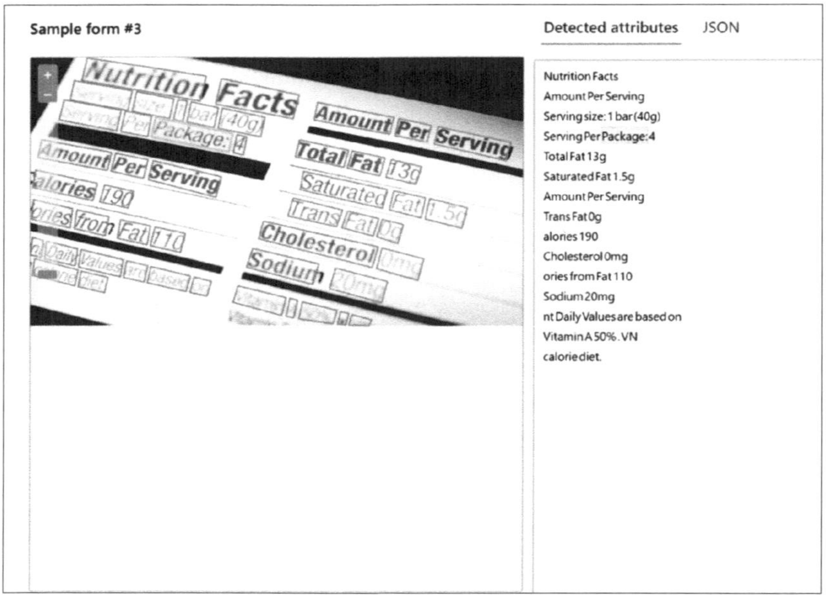

Figure 7.5: *Example of an Image to be Analyzed by Object Detection*

In this hypothetical scenario, the OCR solution has recognized and extracted the text from the product label. Rather than identifying objects or bounding boxes, the output provides a direct textual representation with line breaks that reflect the layout of the original label.

Key Characteristics of OCR

Optical Character Recognition (OCR) solutions possess several defining characteristics that make them indispensable for converting images of text into machine-readable information. The following points summarize their core features and responsible implementation practices:

- **Purpose:** OCR solutions transform images of text, whether it is from scanned documents, photographs, or video frames, into editable, searchable data and unlocks the potential for automation and analysis.
- **Adaptability:** Modern OCR systems can recognize **multiple languages**, a wide variety of **font types**, and even **handwritten text**, while ensuring flexibility across diverse input sources.
- **Preserving Structure:** Advanced models retain the **layout and formatting** of documents by detecting inherent tables, columns, and spacing. This seamlessly converts complex documents into digital formats while maintaining their original organizational structure.
- **Customization:** Through **transfer learning** and **fine-tuning**, OCR models can be adapted to specialized domains such as interpreting legal contracts, reading product labels with industry-specific terminology, or deciphering historical manuscripts.
- **Responsible Implementation:** Handling sensitive information such as **medical records**, **financial statements**, or **identification documents** demands strict **data protection** and **privacy compliance**.
- **Security and Compliance Measures:** Implementing **encryption**, **access controls**, and **internal privacy policies** ensures that extracted text is stored and managed securely, while maintaining system integrity and user trust.
- **Transparency:** Clearly communicating how data is stored, shared, or analyzed helps build confidence and aligns with ethical AI principles.

- **Operational Value:** OCR automates **labor-intensive workflows** such as processing invoices, validating identity documents, or indexing archival newspapers. This improves efficiency, accessibility, and speed in data processing.
- **Business Impact:** Organizations can leverage OCR to reduce manual effort, minimize errors, and unlock valuable insights from unstructured data sources.

Together, these characteristics illustrate how OCR serves as a vital bridge between **visual information** and **textual data**, enabling automation, accessibility, and digital transformation across industries.

Exam Tip: *When a question mentions text extraction or converting images into searchable or editable text, the correct Azure AI workload is* **Optical Character Recognition (OCR)**.

Identifying Features of Facial Detection and Facial Analysis Solutions

Facial detection and facial analysis solutions enable computer vision systems to not only locate human faces in images, but also derive meaningful insights about the individuals within those images. While basic face detection involves drawing bounding boxes to indicate where faces appear, facial analysis delves deeper, examining attributes like the person's apparent age, emotion, or whether they are wearing accessories like glasses or a face mask.

At the core of these solutions are deep learning models trained on extensive, varied datasets. These models learn to handle differing perspectives, lighting conditions, facial expressions, and obstructions. As a result, they can reliably detect faces, even when partially concealed by objects, facial coverings, or variable backgrounds. The insights gained can support numerous applications, from personalized marketing (adapting displayed content based on a viewer's detected mood) and security systems (verifying identity or restricting access) to enhancing user interfaces that respond to real-time emotions.

For instance, consider the following scenario: A facial detection and analysis model analyzes an image where a person's face is partially covered by a mask. The system locates the face and notes specific attributes just like shown in the following figure:

Figure 7.6: *Example of an Image to be Analyzed by Facial Detection*

The following JSON example shows how a facial detection and analysis model might return its output after processing an image:


```
{
  "faces": [
    {
      "boundingBox": {
        "left": 250,
        "top": 100,
        "width": 150,
        "height": 200
      },
      "attributes": {
        "facemask": "yes",
        "facemaskCoveringNoseAndMouth": "yes"
      },
      "confidence": 0.95
    }
  ]
}
```


In this example, the model identifies the presence of a single face and detects that the individual is wearing a mask, covering both nose and mouth. Although identifying more detailed attributes such as emotional state or approximate age is also possible, the important point is that the model has analyzed the face beyond simple detection, while extracting useful context.

Key Characteristics of Facial Detection and Facial Analysis Solutions

Facial detection and facial analysis solutions share a set of defining characteristics that enable machines to interpret and respond to human features effectively. The following points summarize their essential principles and applications:

- **Purpose:** These solutions allow computer vision systems not only to detect the presence of human faces in images or videos but also to analyze a variety of facial attributes and expressions.
- **Depth of Analysis:** Unlike basic object recognition, facial analysis goes further by **estimating age**, **detecting emotions**, and identifying **accessories** such as glasses, masks, or hats. Some models can even recognize facial hair or hairstyles.
- **Technology Foundation:** Modern **deep learning models**, trained on **diverse and representative datasets**, ensure robust performance across different lighting conditions, camera angles, and partial obstructions.
- **Fairness and Accuracy:** Diversity in training data—addressing various **skin tones, genders, and facial features**—is crucial to prevent bias and maintain consistent accuracy across populations.
- **Applications Across Industries:**
    - In **marketing**, facial analysis measures audience reactions to advertisements and helps tailor content dynamically.
    - In **security and access control**, it verifies identity or detects the presence of masks.
    - In **education** or **healthcare**, it monitors engagement or emotional well-being.
- **Ethical and Privacy Considerations:** Since facial data is closely tied to personal identity, developers must adhere to **data protection laws** and adopt transparent, responsible data handling practices.

- **Continuous Improvement:** As model architectures evolve and datasets grow, facial detection and analysis are becoming more accurate, inclusive, and responsive to real-world human diversity.

Together, these characteristics highlight how facial detection and analysis bridge the gap between **technical perception** and **human understanding**, thereby driving applications that are increasingly adaptive, ethical, and user-centered.

Conclusion

By understanding these concepts, you are now equipped to select the appropriate computer vision workload for your specific use case, recognize the importance of diverse and high-quality training data, computational resources, and suitable model architectures such as CNNs, and carefully consider ethical and privacy-related implications to ensure that computer vision is implemented in a responsible and trustworthy manner. You are also prepared to refine and scale your solutions using techniques like transfer learning and cloud-based services, enabling you to build more efficient, adaptable, and production-ready models.

These foundational skills will help you build, evaluate, and deploy computer vision models that transform raw visual data into actionable intelligence, driving innovation and improving decision-making across industries.

In the next chapter, we will explore how to leverage Azure Cognitive Services and Azure Machine Learning to streamline the process of developing, training, and deploying computer vision models. By tapping into Azure's rich ecosystem, you will gain the tools and workflows needed to confidently bring your computer vision projects to life at scale.

Points to Remember

- **Image Classification (What):** It assigns labels to entire images and focuses on identifying the overall content rather than specific object positions.
- **Object Detection (Where):** It locates and classifies individual objects within an image, while providing bounding boxes and confidence scores for each detected item.
- **Facial Detection and Analysis (Who):** This technology identifies human faces and infers attributes like expressions, approximate age, or accessories to facilitate more human-centric interactions.
- **Optical Character Recognition (OCR) (Read):** This transforms textual content found in images into machine-readable text, thus enhancing searchability, automation, and accessibility of content.
- **Data Quality and Quantity:** High-quality, well-annotated training data improves model accuracy and generalization in all computer vision tasks.
- **Deep Learning Models (for example, CNNs):** Automatically learns features from raw pixel data, thereby reducing reliance on manual feature engineering and improving adaptability to new scenarios
- **Ethical and Responsible Use:** Ensuring fairness, privacy, and compliance with data protection laws builds trust and prevents misuse of sensitive visual information.
- **Transfer Learning and Pre-Trained Models:** A user can accelerate development by adapting existing models to new domains to reduce training time and resource requirements.
- **Continuous Improvement:** Regular updates, retraining with fresh data, and feedback loops maintain model accuracy and relevance as conditions evolve.

Key Terms

- **Computer Vision:** A branch of artificial intelligence that enables software systems to perceive the world visually by analyzing still images and video sequences
- **Deep Learning:** A subset of ML that leverages deep neural networks with multiple layers to handle complex tasks, especially those involving unstructured data like images and speech
- **Convolutional Neural Networks (CNNs):** A type of deep neural network particularly adept at analyzing visual data by processing images in layers to identify edges, textures, and complete objects
- **Recurrent Neural Networks (RNNs):** Neural network architectures applicable to video sequences where context over time is important to recognize actions or predict future events
- **High-Quality, Abundant Data:** Diverse, accurate, and well-labeled training images that increase the reliability of computer vision models
- **Computational Power:** The processing capacity required to train and run sophisticated computer vision models efficiently
- **Graphics Processing Units (GPUs):** Specialized hardware designed to handle the heavy computational loads of AI and process large volumes of visual data
- **Vision Processing Units (VPUs):** Specialized hardware focused on processing visual data in AI applications
- **Image Classification:** A computer vision task that categorizes an entire image into predefined classes, while assigning labels without specifying the location of objects
- **Object Detection:** A computer vision task that identifies and locates specific objects within an image by drawing bounding boxes around them
- **Semantic Segmentation:** A computer vision task that classifies each pixel in an image into a specific category, thereby creating a detailed map of the scene
- **Image Analysis:** A computer vision task that offers a descriptive, holistic understanding of a scene to generate captions that describe the content contextually
- **Facial Detection and Analysis:** A computer vision task that locates human faces in images and infers attributes like expressions, estimated age, and presence of accessories
- **Optical Character Recognition (OCR):** A computer vision technology that extracts textual information from images and converts it into editable and searchable text
- **YOLO (You Only Look Once):** An object detection algorithm that allows for the rapid and accurate identification of multiple objects in real-time
- **Faster R-CNN:** A neural network architecture for object detection that combines speed and accuracy, suitable for high-performance applications
- **SSD (Single Shot MultiBox Detector):** An object detection model that performs identification and localization in a single pass through the network, thus ensuring efficiency
- **Open-Source Datasets:** Publicly available datasets such as Microsoft COCO and ImageNet used for training and developing models

Multiple Choice Questions

1. Which of these options best describes image classification?
    a. Assigning one or more labels to the entire image without identifying object locations
    b. Identifying the exact positions of objects within an image
    c. Extracting text from images into machine-readable formats
    d. Detecting facial expressions and attributes in an image
2. Which technique is primarily used to locate and categorize multiple objects within an image?
    a. Image Classification
    b. Object Detection
    c. Semantic Segmentation
    d. Optical Character Recognition (OCR)
3. What is the main purpose of facial detection and analysis?
    a. To identify every pixel's category in an image
    b. To locate human faces and infer attributes like emotion or age
    c. To convert images of text into searchable data
    d. To classify entire scenes without focusing on individuals
4. Which of the following describes OCR (Optical Character Recognition)?
    a. Assigning labels to an entire image
    b. Identifying objects and their positions within an image
    c. Detecting human faces and their attributes
    d. Converting images of text into editable, machine-readable text
5. What is a key consideration while implementing computer vision solutions involving personal data (such as faces)?
    a. Ignoring privacy and ethical guidelines since the data is visual
    b. Using only small datasets to ensure efficiency
    c. Adhering to privacy laws, ensuring fairness, and maintaining transparency
    d. Always storing all data indefinitely for future use

Answers

1. a
2. b
3. b
4. d
5. c

Chapter 8
Identify Azure Tools and Services for Computer Vision Tasks

Introduction

In this chapter, we will explore the fundamental concepts behind Azure tools and services for computer vision tasks. As organizations increasingly rely on visual data such as surveillance footage, digital asset management, and user-generated content, the ability to extract meaningful insights from images becomes essential. Azure provides a comprehensive suite of services that enable developers to harness advanced computer vision capabilities to transform raw visuals into actionable intelligence.

We will begin by examining the Azure AI Vision service, which offers robust features like image classification, object detection, and optical character recognition (OCR). These functionalities are vital for converting unstructured images into structured data, enhancing analytics and decision-making processes. Next, we will learn about Azure AI Face service, focusing on its facial detection and analysis capabilities. This service is critical for applications ranging from biometric authentication and secure access to personalized customer experiences and beyond.

After understanding these tools and their capabilities, you will be able to integrate computer vision into your solutions, driving innovation and operational efficiency across various industries.

By the end of this chapter, you will have a comprehensive understanding of these essential Azure computer vision tools. You will learn about their key features, ideal usage scenarios, and the potential challenges associated with their implementation. With this knowledge, you will be able effectively to select and deploy the most appropriate computer vision solutions for a variety of real-world applications.

Structure

In this chapter, we will discuss the following topics:

- Capabilities of the Azure AI Vision Service
  - Key Features of Azure AI Vision Service
  - Use Cases of Azure AI Vision Services
  - Hands-on Experience: Practical Guide to Image Analysis with Azure Vision AI
- Capabilities of the Azure AI Face Detection Service
  - Key Features of Azure AI Face Detection Service
  - Use Cases of Azure AI Face Detection Service
  - Hands-on Experience: Practical Guide to Face Detection with Azure AI Face

Capabilities of the Azure AI Vision Service

The Azure AI Vision service is a comprehensive suite of tools that enables businesses and developers to analyze and process visual data efficiently. It provides powerful computer vision capabilities to extract insights, classify images, detect objects, and even read text from images via OCR. By leveraging advanced deep learning models, Azure AI Vision empowers organizations to build intelligent applications that can understand and interpret visual content at scale.

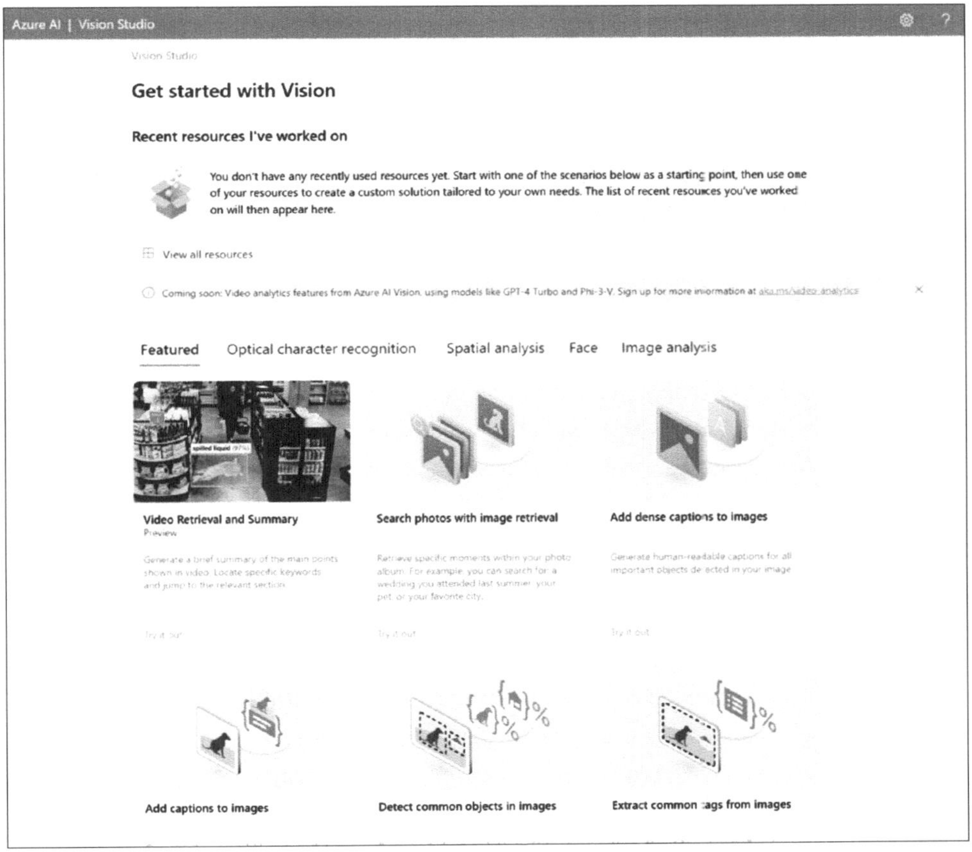

Figure 8.1: *Azure AI Vision Studio*

Key Features of Azure AI Vision Service

Azure AI Vision Service offers a comprehensive set of functionalities designed to extract valuable insights from visual data, automate image processing tasks, and enhance decision-making. These features help organizations manage large volumes of unstructured visual content efficiently and are an asset in applications such as automated surveillance, inventory management, and quality control.

Image Analysis

Azure AI Vision provides advanced image analysis capabilities to interpret and understand the content of images. This includes:

- **Image Classification:** Automatically categorizes images by identifying key objects and scenes, while summarizing the primary content effectively

- **Object Detection:** Locates and identifies objects within an image by drawing bounding boxes around them, thereby facilitating detailed analysis of scene composition
- **Image Captioning:** Generates descriptive captions for images using deep learning models, which helps in quickly summarizing visual content

Optical Character Recognition (OCR)

The OCR functionality extracts both printed and handwritten text from images and documents. This feature enables organizations to:

- Digitize paper-based documents for improved accessibility and searchability.
- Automate data entry by converting visual text into machine-readable formats.
- Streamline document processing workflows in sectors such as finance, logistics, and administration.

Exam Tip: *When a question refers to* ***extracting text*** *from images or scanned documents, it most probably relates to* ***Optical Character Recognition (OCR)*** *in the* ***Azure AI Vision service****. Remember that OCR can process both* ***printed*** *and* ***handwritten text****, while converting it into machine-readable data.*

Custom Vision

For domain-specific needs, Custom Vision allows organizations to build and train their own models tailored to unique visual tasks. This enables users to:

- Fine-tune models to achieve higher accuracy on specialized imagery.
- Identify objects or features that are not covered by pre-built models.
- Rapidly prototype and iteratively improve solutions using an intuitive training interface.

Exam Tip: *If an exam scenario involves* ***training a custom model*** *for image recognition or classification, the correct choice to go for is* ***Azure AI Custom Vision*** *and not* ***Azure AI Vision****.*

Spatial and Scene Analysis

Beyond simple object recognition, Azure AI Vision can analyze spatial relationships and overall scene composition. This capability is essential for:

- Understanding the interactions and placements of objects within a scene
- Enhancing applications in security, urban planning, and automated monitoring systems
- Integrating visual data with other modalities for a holistic analysis of environments

Capability	**Azure AI Vision Service**	**Azure AI Face Detection Service**
Primary Purpose	Analyze and extract insights from general images	Detect, analyze, and verify human faces
Key Features	Image Classification, Object Detection, OCR, Custom Vision	Face Detection, Attribute Analysis, Face Verification
Data Type Processed	Images and documents	Images and videos with human faces
Output Examples	Labels, bounding boxes, and text extraction results	Bounding boxes, facial attributes, and confidence scores
Typical Use Cases	Document automation, visual search, inventory management	Identity verification, attendance tracking, personalized experiences

Table 8.1: *Comparison of Azure AI Vision and Azure AI Face Detection Capabilities*

Use Cases of Azure AI Vision Services

Azure AI Vision supports a wide range of real-world applications across industries, while helping organizations automate image analysis, enhance security, and optimize document management through intelligent visual insights. Here are a few use cases where Azure AI Vision is employed:

- **Enhancing Security and Surveillance:** By leveraging object detection and facial recognition capabilities, organizations can automate real-time monitoring of premises, detect suspicious activities, and trigger alerts for enhanced security.
- **Streamlining Visual Document Processing:** Businesses in sectors such as logistics and finance can utilize OCR to digitize and automate the processing of invoices, receipts, and forms, thus reducing manual data entry and improving operational efficiency.
- **Improving Digital Asset Management:** Media and e-commerce platforms can use image classification and custom vision models to automatically tag, organize, and retrieve visual content, thereby enhancing search accuracy and content discoverability.

By applying these capabilities, organizations can transform visual data into actionable insights, driving automation, accuracy, and innovation across their operations.

Hands-on Experience: Practical Guide to Image Analysis with Azure Vision AI

In this exercise, you will explore the capabilities of Azure AI Vision by analyzing images and extracting useful information, such as object detection, text recognition (OCR), and facial detection. You will also use Azure Vision Studio to test these features in a hands-on manner.

1. **Create a Language Resource**
    a. Open the Azure portal and log in with your Microsoft account
    b. Search for `Computer Vision`.

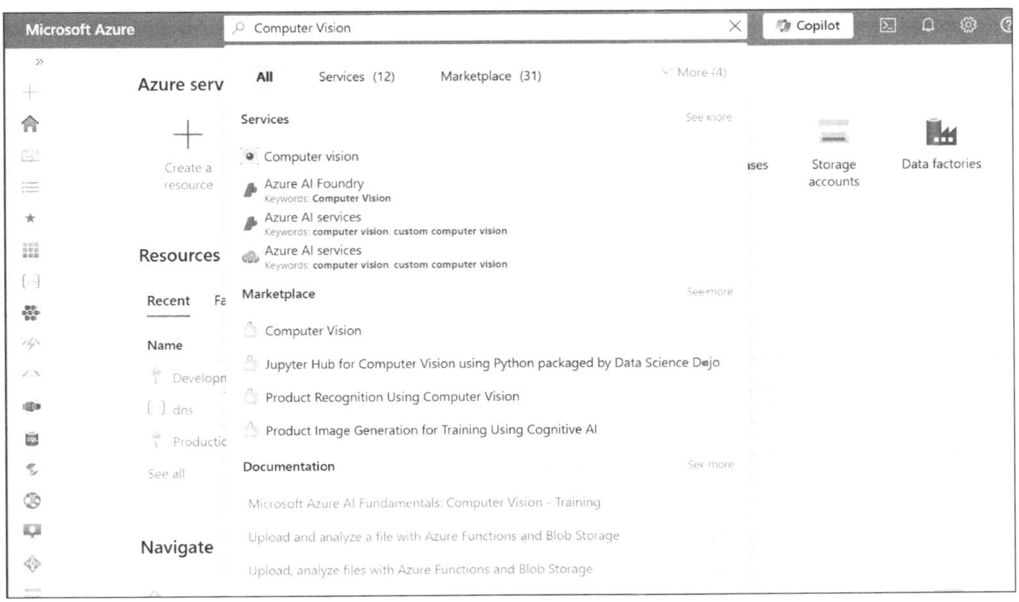

Figure 8.2: *Search for Computer Vision Service*

c. Select **Create Computer Vision**, configure the service, and deploy it with the following settings:

   i. **Subscription:** Choose your Azure subscription.

   ii. **Resource group:** Select or create one.

   iii. **Region:** Choose the nearest data center.

   iv. **Name:** Provide a unique name.

   v. **Pricing tier:** Free F0 or a standard tier.

d. Click **Review + create**, then **Create** and wait for deployment.

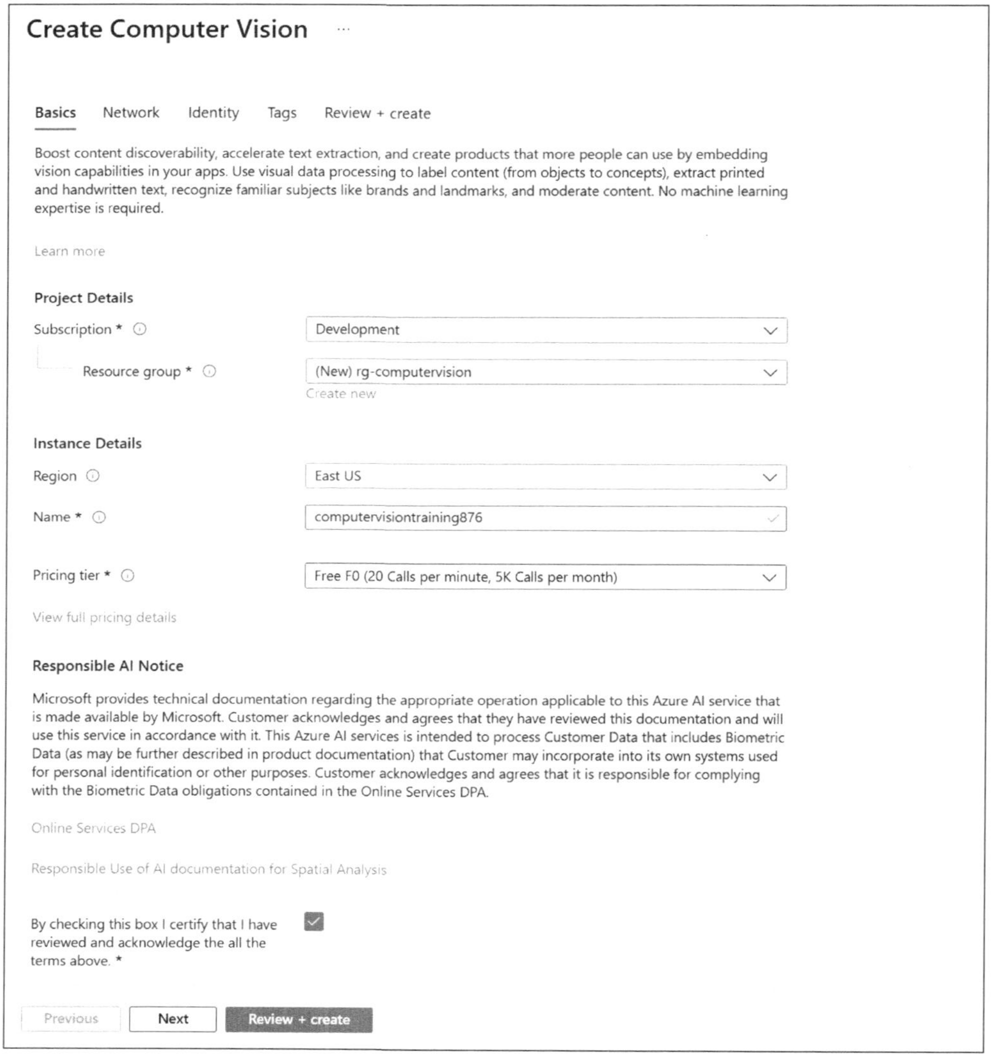

Figure 8.3: *Create Computer Vision Service in the Azure Portal*

2. **Configure Azure Vision Studio**
   a. Open Azure Vision Studio (https://portal.vision.cognitive.azure.com/) and sign in.
   b. When prompted, configure:
      i. Azure Directory: Set it to **`Default`**.
      ii. Azure Subscription: Select your active subscription.
      iii. Resource Type: Select **`Computer Vision`**.
      iv. Resource Name: Select the Language service you created.
   c. Click **`Done`**.
3. **Detect Common Objects in Image**
   a. In **`Azure Vision Studio`**, select the **`Image Analysis`** tab.
   b. Select **`Detect common objects in images`**.

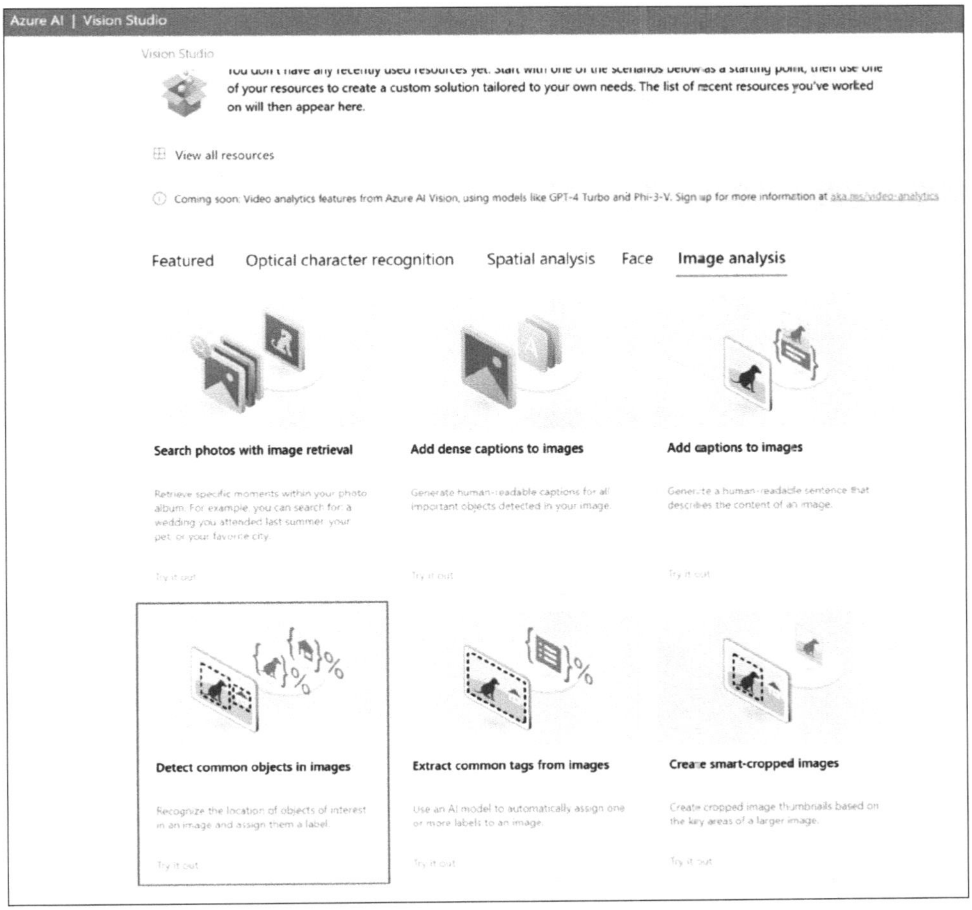

Figure 8.4: *Options for Image Analysis in Azure AI Vision Studio*

   c. First, acknowledge the resource usage policy at the top of the page to try out, and detect common objects in images.

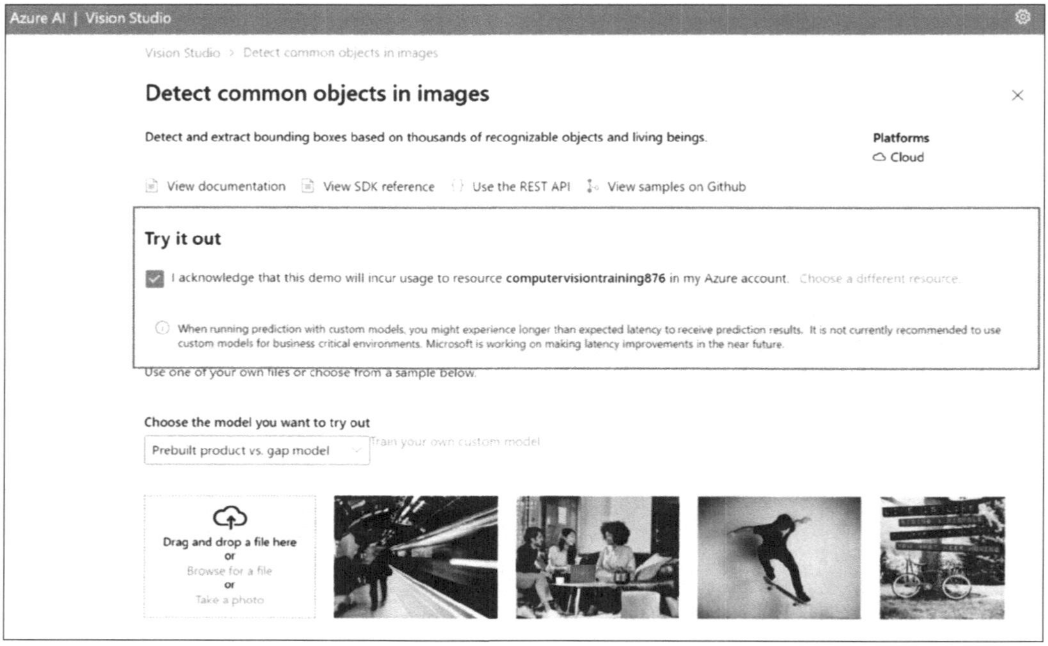

Figure 8.5: *Recognize the Resource Usage Policy*

d. Select one of the sample images or upload your own.

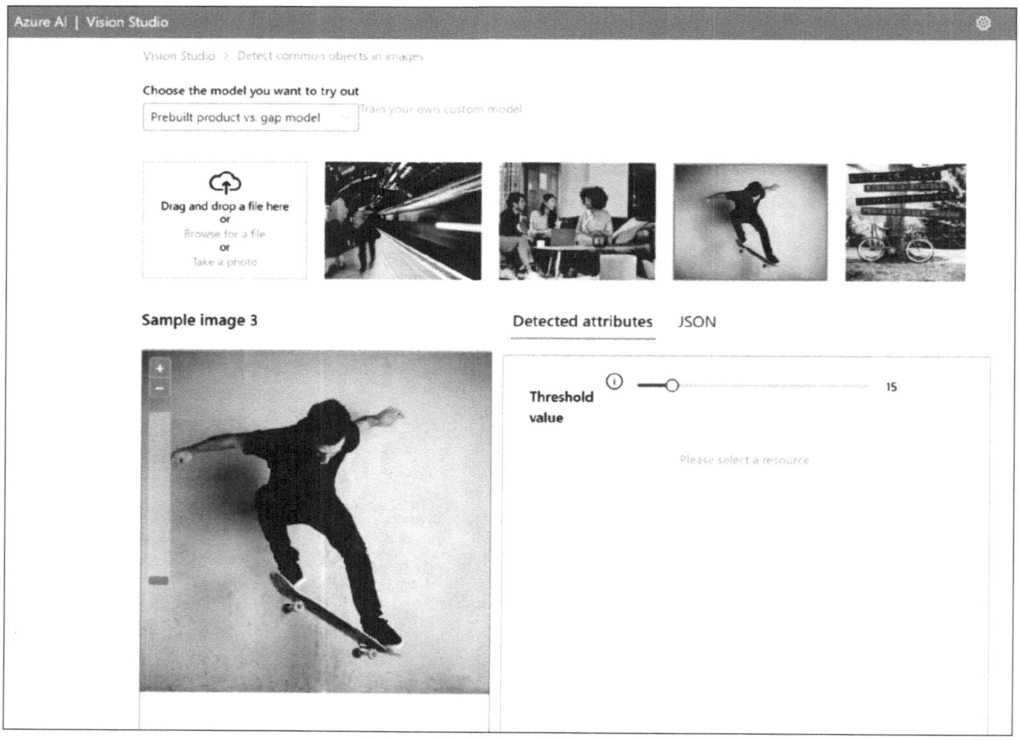

Figure 8.6: *Options for Image Analysis in Azure AI Vision Studio*

e. Before analyzing the image, you will need to select a resource. Click **`Please select a resource`**.

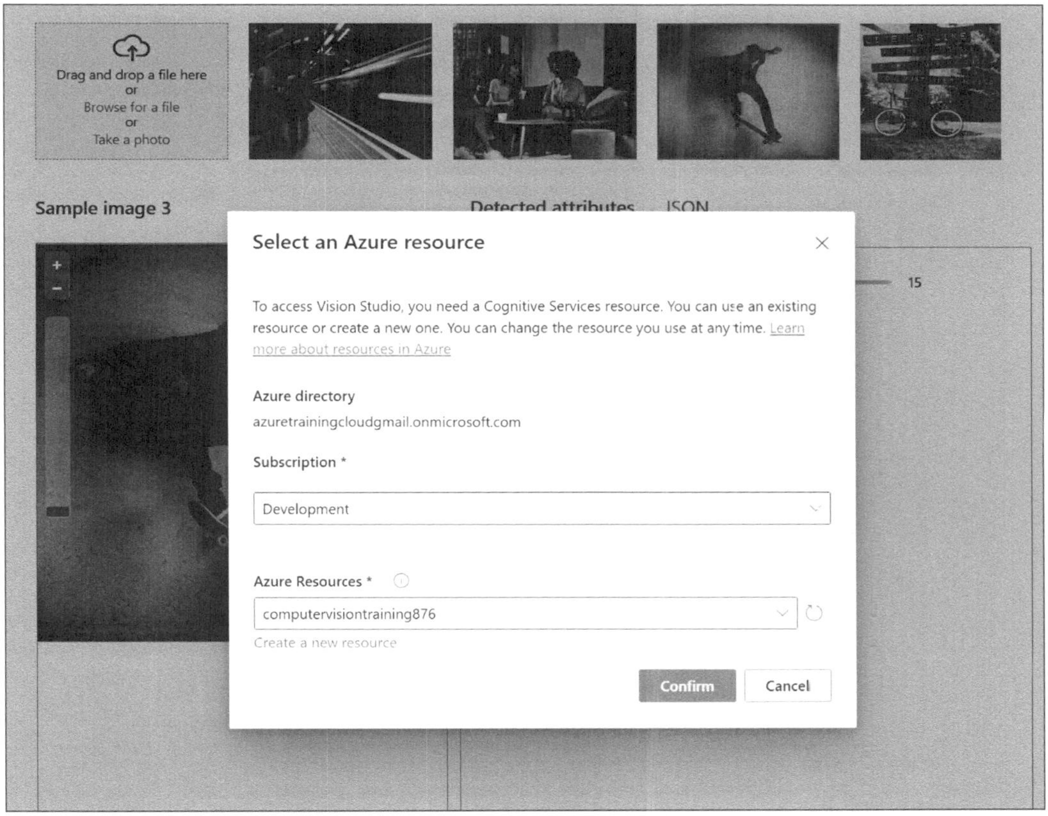

Figure 8.7: *Select the Computer Vision Resource*

f. Confirm the Azure resource created earlier.

g. When we select the skateboarder image shown in the example, we will see the following – Threshold values: Skateboard (90.40%) and person (95.50%).

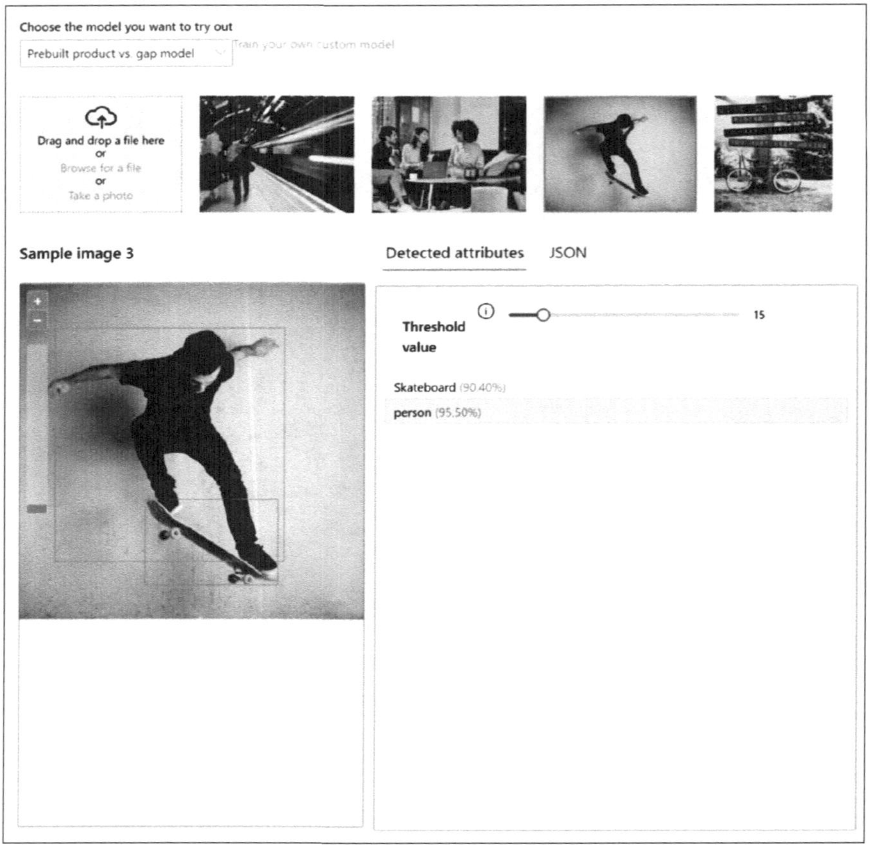

Figure 8.8: *Result of the Skateboarder's Image Analysis*

The **Threshold Value** in this context represents the minimum confidence level required for an object to be detected and displayed in the results.

In the **Azure Vision AI detection model**, objects in the image are assigned a confidence score, which indicates how certain the model is about identifying them correctly. The threshold slider allows you to filter out detections that fall below a certain confidence level.

For example: If the Threshold Value is set to **15**, it means all objects detected with a confidence score above 15% will be displayed.

In this case, the model has detected:

- A person with 95.50% confidence
- A skateboard with 90.40% confidence

Since both confidence scores are above 15%, they are displayed. If the threshold was increased (say, to 95%), the skateboard might not be displayed unless its confidence score also increased.

- Let us now change the Threshold value to **95** in the following illustration:

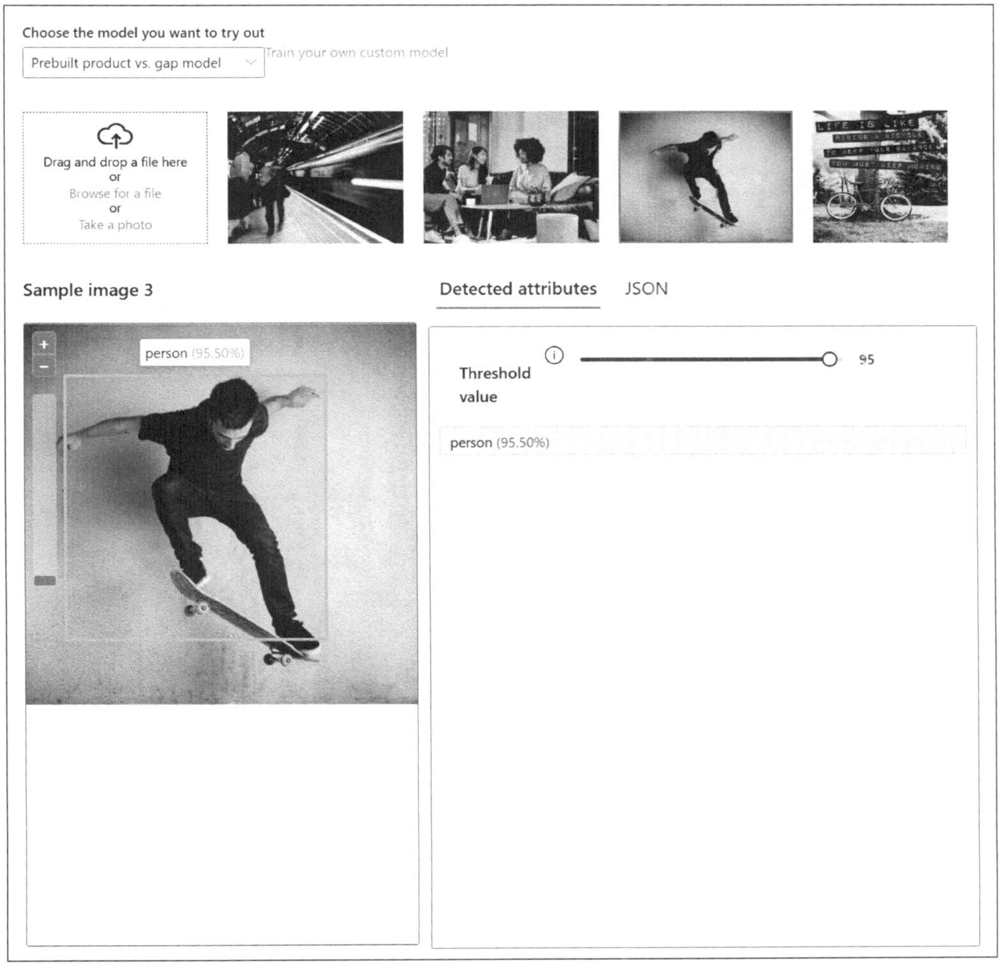

Figure 8.9: *Result of the Skater Image Analysis*

The **person** is still detected (albeit with **95.50% confidence**) because it now meets the threshold.

- The **skateboard** (which was previously detected at **90.40% confidence**) is now missing because its confidence score is falling **below** the new threshold.

By adjusting the threshold, you can filter out lower-confidence detections. A **higher threshold** ensures that only highly confident predictions appear, while a **lower threshold** includes more detected objects, while also introducing less accurate results.

- Go to the **JSON** tab to view the detailed results.

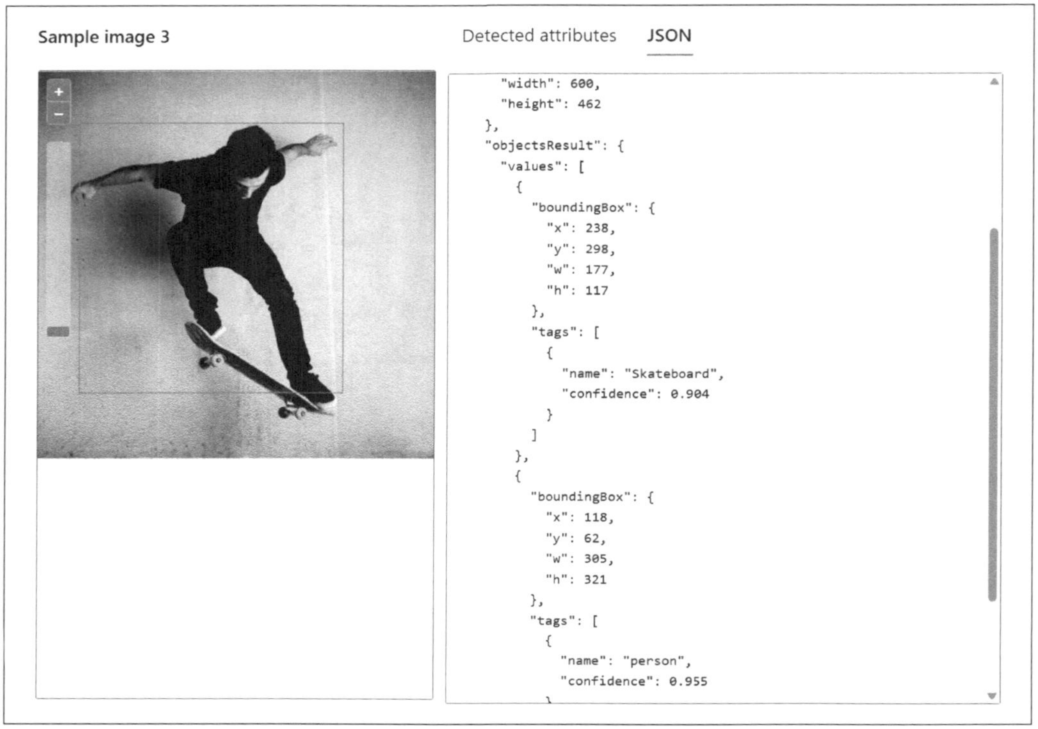

Figure 8.10: *Detects Common Objects in Image*

Key Details from the JSON Output

- **Image Size:** 600x462 pixels
- **Detected Objects:**
  - **`Skateboard`**
    - **`Bounding Box:`** (x: 238, y: 298, width: 177, height: 117)
    - **`Confidence Score:`** 90.4%
  - **`Person`**
    - **`Bounding Box:`** (x: 118, y: 62, width: 305, height: 321)
    - **`Confidence Score:`** 95.5%

This Information is Used:

- The **bounding box coordinates** specify the location and size of each detected object in the image.
- The **confidence scores** indicate how certain the model is about each detection.
- If the **threshold value** is set above **95.5%**, only the **person** will be detected.
- If the **threshold is set below 90.4%**, both objects will be detected.

4. **Detect common objects in image**

   a. Go back to Azure **Vision Studio**, select the **`Optical character recognition`** tab.

   b. Select **`Extract text from images`**.

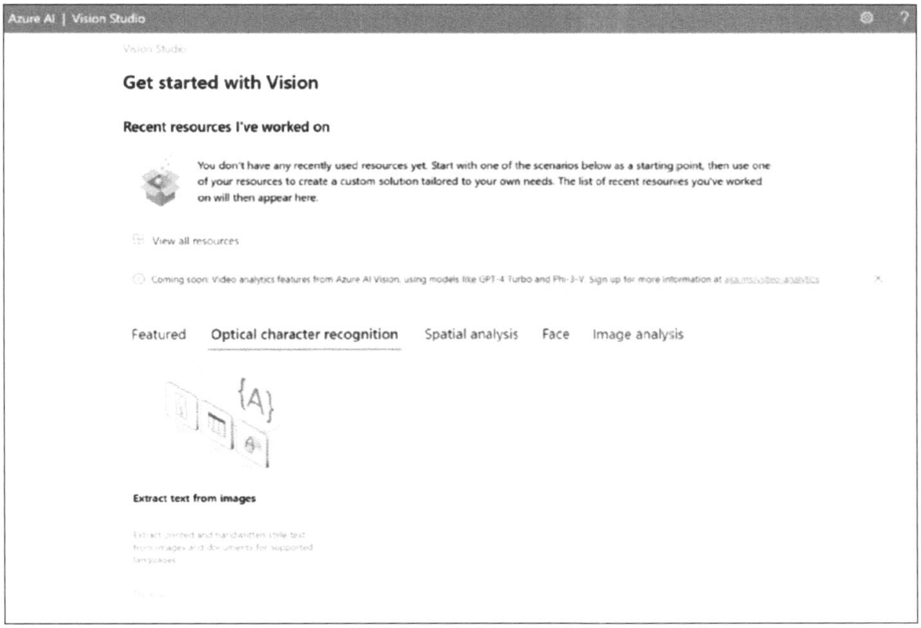

Figure 8.11: *Extract Text from Images Option in Azure AI Vision Studio*

c. Select one of the sample images or upload your own.

Figure 8.12: *Extract Text from Credit Card*

Key Observations

- The **OCR model** successfully extracted text from the credit card, including:
  - **Card Type:** `CreditCard`
  - **Bank Name:** `BANK`
  - **Card Number:** `1234 5678 9012 3456`
  - **Security Code:** `0123`
  - **Validity Information:** `VALID THRU 06/15`
  - Cardholder Name: `Name Surname`

Azure Vision AI Processes this as follows:

- The **OCR model** detects and extracts text from structured and semi-structured documents.
- The extracted text can be used for:
  - Automating **document processing**
  - **Identity verification** in banking applications
  - Extracting and storing **key information** for compliance purposes

Possible Use Cases:

- **Financial Institutions:** Automating customer onboarding by extracting data from credit cards
- **Retail and Ecommerce:** Streamlining card-based transactions for online payments
- **Security Applications:** Detecting and masking sensitive credit card details
- Go to the `JSON` tab to view the detailed results.

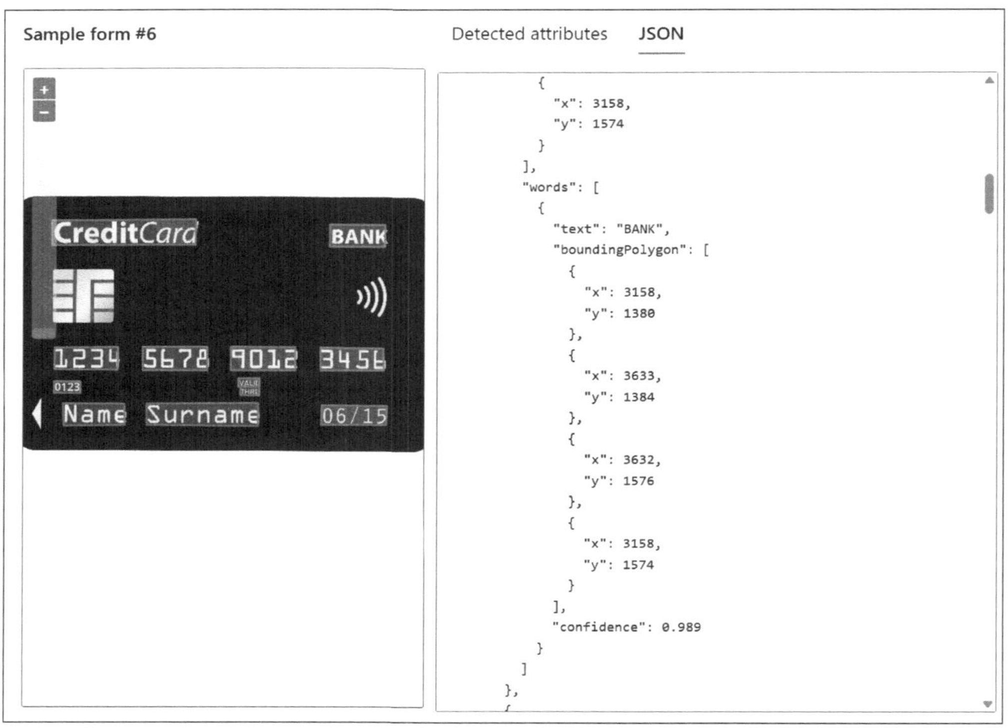

__Figure 8.13:__ JSON Output of the Credit Card Used in the Text Extraction

Key Extracted Information:

- **Card Type**: `CreditCard` (**Confidence: 99.3%**)
- **Bank Name**: `BANK` (**Confidence: 98.9%**)
- **Card Number**: `1234 5678 9012 3456` (**Confidence: ~99%** for each block)
- **Security Code**: `0123` (**Confidence: 98.9%**)
- **Validity**: `VALID THRU (06/15)` (**Confidence: 99.4%**)
- **Cardholder Name**: `Name Surname` (**Confidence: 99.2%** for "Name" and 99.4% for "Surname")

Bounding Box Information:

- Each detected text entry has **bounding box coordinates** (x, y, width, height), which specify the exact position of the text in the image.
- The **confidence score** for each word indicates the model's certainty in recognizing the text.

5. **Clean Up Resources**
   - If you no longer need the Language resource, delete it in the Azure portal to avoid extra costs.
   - Navigate to the resource group, select the Language service, and click **`Delete`**.

This hands-on exercise demonstrated how Azure AI Vision can be used to analyze images, recognize text, and detect faces. These tools allows businesses to automate tasks such as identity verification, image categorization, and document processing.

Exam Tip: *You may expect questions that ask you to describe* ***practical business scenarios*** *such as automating* ***document processing*** *or analyzing* ***images for inventory management****. Identify the corresponding* **Azure AI Vision capability** *(***Object Detection**, **OCR**, *or* **Custom Vision***) that best fits the described use case.*

Capabilities of the Azure AI Face Detection Service

The ***Azure AI Face Detection Service*** is a cloud-based solution that enables applications to detect and analyze human faces in images and videos. It has capabilities such as face detection, facial landmark recognition, emotion analysis, and face similarity matching, which make it a powerful tool for identity verification, security, and user experience personalization. As it leverages advanced machine learning models, the service ensures high accuracy and adaptability across various industries like retail, healthcare, and financial services.

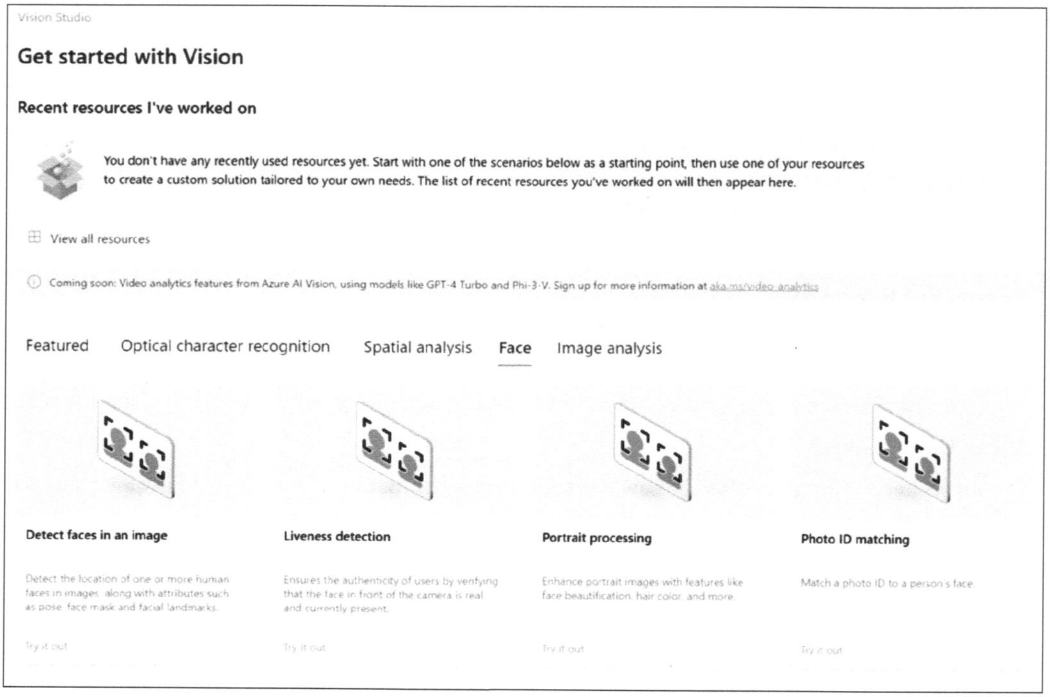

Figure 8.14: *Face Tab in Azure AI Vision Studio*

Key Features of Azure AI Face Detection Service

Azure AI Face Detection Service provides powerful facial recognition capabilities that enable applications to detect, analyze, and interpret human faces in images and videos. These features support a wide range of use cases, including identity verification, security, personalized user experiences, and sentiment analysis across industries such as retail, healthcare, and finance.

Face Detection

The Face Detection feature identifies human faces within an image or video and provides precise location data and facial landmarks. It allows applications to recognize multiple faces in a single image and detect key attributes. Its benefits include:

- Accurate detection of faces in real-time and batch processing
- Bounding box coordinates to locate and track detected faces
- Integration with security and attendance systems for facial recognition

Facial Attribute Analysis

Azure AI Facial Attribute Analysis extracts detailed attributes from detected faces, such as age, gender, hair color, and emotions. This capability enhances customer insights, personalizes interactions, and automates identity verification. Its key capabilities include:

- Emotion detection, that is identifying expressions like happiness, sadness, surprise, and anger
- Estimation of age range and gender classification for demographic analysis
- Identification of facial hair, glasses, and head pose for better recognition accuracy

Face Similarity Matching

This feature allows applications to compare faces across different images to determine similarity. It is useful for user authentication, duplicate detection, and security applications. Its key advantages include:

- Matching and grouping similar faces for identity verification
- High-accuracy similarity scoring to distinguish individuals
- Secure authentication for login systems using facial recognition

Face Identification

Face Identification allows applications to recognize known individuals from a database of faces. This is particularly valuable for access control, customer personalization, and automated check-ins. Its key benefits include:

- Enrollment of faces in a secure database for repeated recognition
- Fast and accurate identification of individuals from an existing dataset
- Use in smart security systems, automated retail, and employee attendance tracking

Exam Tip: *When a question involves* ***identifying, verifying, or analyzing human faces****, the appropriate service is the* ***Azure AI Face Detection service****. It covers* ***face detection****,* ***facial attributes****, and* ***identity verification****, while* ***Azure AI Vision*** *focuses on general image analysis.*

Face Mask Detection (Optional with Custom Models)

The service can be customized to detect whether a person is wearing a mask, thus making it useful in public safety, healthcare, and compliance scenarios. Its key benefits include:

- Detection of mask usage in crowded areas and workplaces
- Integration with access control systems to enforce mask policies
- AI-powered insights for compliance monitoring and reporting

Use Cases of Azure AI Face Detection Service

Azure AI Face Detection Service supports a wide range of practical applications across industries, enabling more secure, personalized, and efficient user experiences.

- **Enhancing Security with Facial Recognition:** Organizations can integrate face detection into security systems to improve authentication and access control. By using facial recognition instead of traditional passwords or keycards, businesses can strengthen security while offering a seamless user experience. This is particularly useful for corporate offices, data centers, and smart buildings.
- **Personalizing Customer Experiences:** Retailers and service providers can use face detection to recognize returning customers and deliver personalized experiences. For example, digital signage can display targeted promotions based on customer demographics, and hotel check-in kiosks can offer personalized greetings.
- **Automating Attendance Tracking:** Schools, universities, and workplaces can streamline attendance tracking with facial recognition. Instead of relying on manual check-ins or badge scanning, face detection can automatically log attendance, reducing administrative workload and minimizing fraudulent check-ins.
- **Improving Public Safety and Law Enforcement:** Government agencies and security organizations can utilize face detection to enhance surveillance and public safety efforts. By analyzing live camera feeds, authorities can identify persons of interest, detect suspicious activity, and improve emergency response times.

- **Enhancing Healthcare and Patient Monitoring:** Hospitals and healthcare providers can implement face detection to monitor patients' conditions and ensure personalized care. The said technology can help track patient emotions, detect distress, and assist in non-contact authentication for medical records.
- **Optimizing User Authentication in Banking and Finance:** Financial institutions can improve identity verification processes using facial recognition for secure logins, fraud prevention, and transaction approvals. This technology enhances security, while reducing the need for passwords and multi-factor authentication.

Hands-on Experience: Practical Guide to Face Detection with Azure AI Face

In this exercise, you will explore the capabilities of Azure AI Face Detection by analyzing facial attributes in images. You will use Azure Face Studio to detect faces, analyze emotions, and match facial similarities.

1. **Create a Face Resource**
   a. Open the Azure portal (https://portal.azure.com) and log in with your Microsoft account.
   b. Search for **`Face APIs service`**.

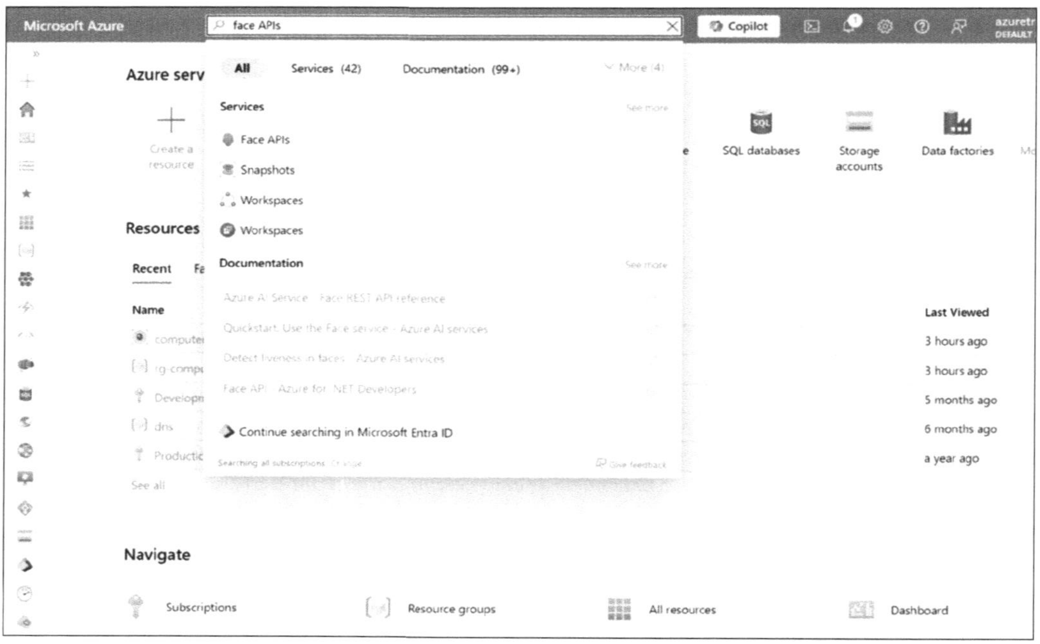

Figure 8.15: *Search for Speech Service*

   c. Select **`Create Face API`**, configure the service, and deploy it with the following settings:
      i. **`Subscription`:** Choose your Azure subscription.
      ii. **`Resource group`:** Select or create one.
      iii. **`Region`:** Choose the nearest data center.
      iv. **`Name`:** Provide a unique name.

v. **`Pricing tier`:** Free F0 or a standard tier.

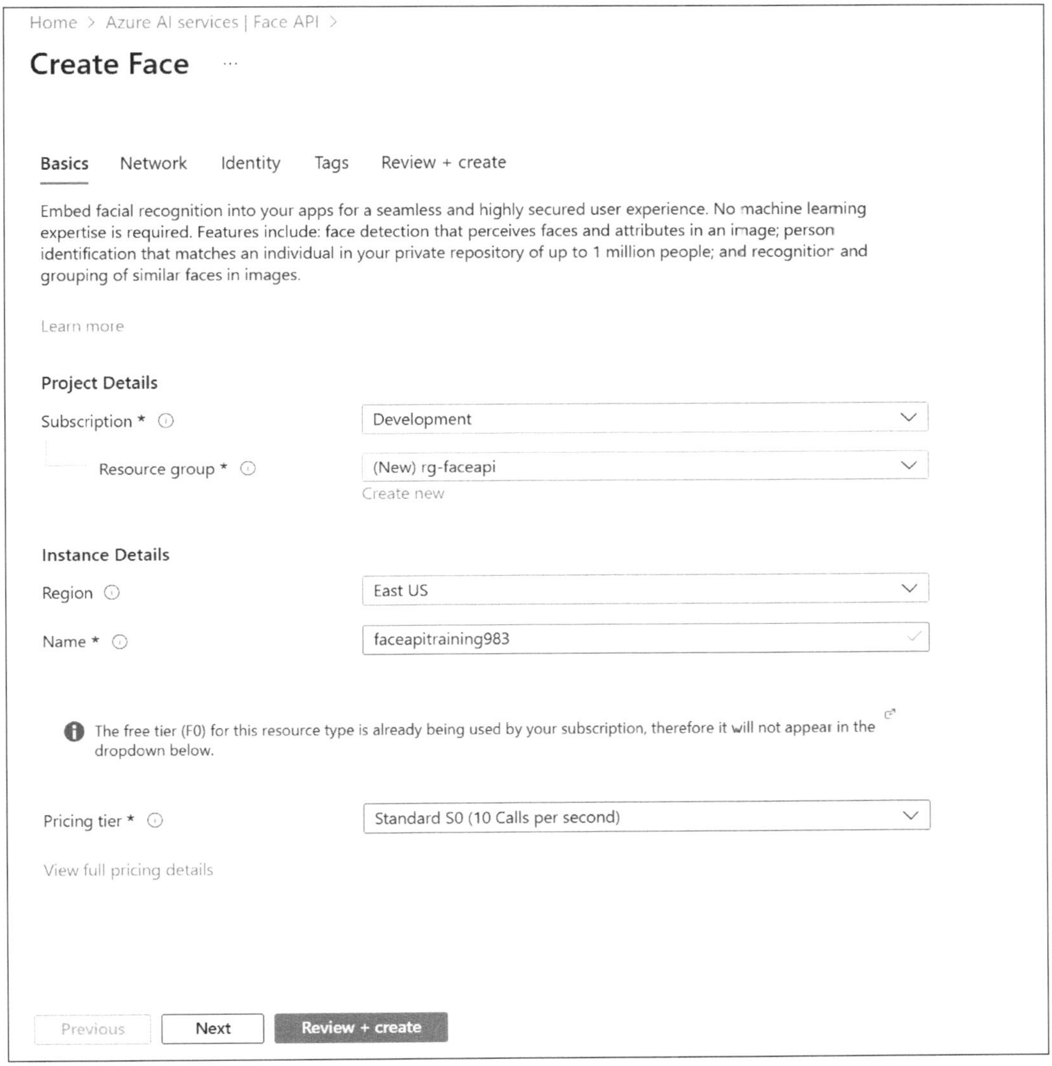

Figure 8.16: *Create Face AI API Service in Azure Portal*

d. Click **`Review + create`**, then **`Create`** and wait for deployment.

2. **Configure Vision Studio**

   a. Open Azure Vision Studio (https://portal.vision.cognitive.azure.com/) and sign in.

   b. When prompted, configure:

      i. **Azure Directory:** Set to **`Default`**

      ii. **Azure Subscription:** Select your active subscription.

      iii. **Resource Type:** Select **`Computer Vision`**.

      iv. **Resource Name:** Select the Language service you created.

   c. Click **Done**.

3. **Detect Common Objects in Image**

   a. In **Azure Vision Studio**, select the **`Face`** tab.

   b. Select **`Detect faces in images`**.

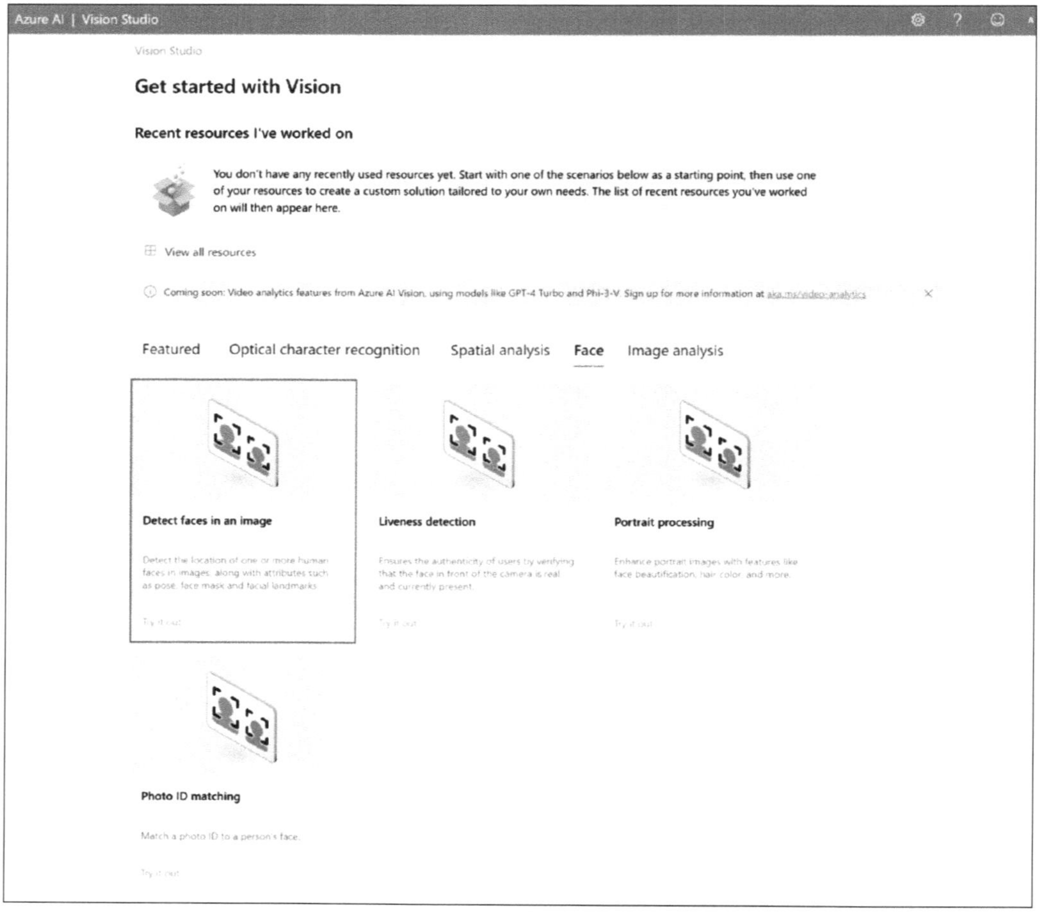

Figure 8.17: *Detect Faces in an Image in Azure AI Vision Studio*

   c. Upload or select an example of an image with a woman without a mask.

Figure 8.18: *Attribute Detector Using Face API in Visual Studio*

d. Now, upload or select an image of a person wearing a mask.

Figure 8.19: *Attribute Detector Using Face API in Visual Studio*

The Azure Face API effectively detects facial attributes, including whether a person is wearing a mask. This capability is particularly valuable for public safety, healthcare compliance, and access control systems, which enables organizations to monitor and enforce mask-wearing policies automatically.

In this example, the Face API successfully identified:

- A face without a mask, confirming unrestricted facial visibility
- A face with a mask, distinguishing that the nose and mouth are covered

By leveraging Azure's AI-powered facial recognition technology, businesses and institutions can integrate automated mask detection into security checkpoints, workplaces, and public spaces, while ensuring compliance with health guidelines and maintaining seamless user interactions.

4. **Clean up Resources**

   If you no longer need the **Face API** resource, delete it in the **Azure Portal** to avoid extra costs.

   a. Navigate to the **`Resource Group`**.

   b. Select the **`Face API`** service.

   c. Click **`Delete`** to remove the resource.

The **Azure AI Face API** provides advanced facial recognition capabilities, including face detection, attribute analysis, emotion recognition, and identity verification. By integrating these features, businesses can enhance security, personalize user experiences, and automate identity-related processes across various industries like retail, healthcare, and finance.

This hands-on exercise demonstrates how easily developers can use Azure's pre-built AI capabilities to implement visual intelligence without extensive machine learning expertise.

Conclusion

In this chapter, we explored the capabilities, applications, and use cases of **Azure AI Vision** and **Azure AI Face Detection Service**. These AI-powered solutions enable businesses to analyze visual content, detect objects, extract text, and recognize faces with high accuracy, thereby enhancing automation, security, and personalized experiences across various industries.

We started with **Azure AI Vision**, which provides robust image analysis capabilities, including object detection, image classification, and Optical Character Recognition (OCR). These features allow organizations to process and analyze large volumes of visual data, enabling applications like automated document processing, inventory management, and digital asset organization.

Next, we explored **Azure AI Face Detection**, highlighting its ability to detect faces, analyze facial attributes, recognize emotions, and verify identities. These features are critical for applications such as identity verification, security monitoring, and customer engagement as they allow businesses to implement biometric authentication, smart surveillance, and contactless access control.

Additionally, we covered practical implementations of these services, including mask detection for compliance monitoring, real-time security enhancements, and AI-driven customer experience optimization.

In the next chapter, we will shift our focus from **visual data** to **language data** and explore how **Natural Language Processing (NLP)** enables machines to understand, interpret, and generate human language. You will also learn how to identify **common NLP workload scenarios** and the **Azure tools** that make these capabilities possible.

Points to Remember

- **Azure AI Vision Service** provides advanced image analysis capabilities, including object detection, image classification, and OCR, thus enabling businesses to extract insights from visual data and automate processes.
- **Image Analysis** includes object detection, image captioning, and spatial analysis, thus helping organizations enhance security, streamline workflows, and improve customer experiences.
- **Optical Character Recognition (OCR)** extracts text from printed and handwritten documents, thereby enabling automated document processing, identity verification, and data extraction.
- **Custom Vision** allows businesses to train and fine-tune AI models for domain-specific image recognition tasks, thus improving accuracy and adaptability for unique use cases.

- **Azure AI Face API** enables face detection, facial attribute analysis, and identity verification, thereby enhancing security, authentication, and personalization.
- **Face Detection** provides bounding box coordinates, facial landmarks, and multiple face recognition, while supporting applications in access control, surveillance, and smart retail.
- **Facial Attribute Analysis** detects age, gender, emotions, and accessories (glasses, masks, and so on), thus helping businesses understand customer sentiments and enhance user engagement.
- **Face Similarity Matching** allows comparison of facial features across images, supporting identity verification, fraud detection, and automated check-in processes.
- **Face Identification** recognizes and verifies individuals from a database, thereby improving biometric authentication and personalized user experiences.
- **Mask Detection** (customizable with AI models) helps enforce compliance regulations in healthcare, workplaces, and public spaces.

Thus, mastering these Azure AI Vision and Face API capabilities helps organizations in creating intelligent, scalable solutions that enhance decision-making, improve efficiency, and deliver superior user experiences.

Key Terms

- **Azure AI Vision:** A cloud-based service that provides advanced computer vision capabilities like image analysis, object detection, optical character recognition (OCR), and spatial analysis to extract insights from visual data
- **Image Analysis:** A feature of Azure AI Vision that interprets images by detecting objects, identifying key attributes, and generating descriptive captions using AI models
- **Optical Character Recognition (OCR):** Extracts text from images, including printed and handwritten documents, enabling applications such as document digitization, identity verification, and automated data entry
- **Custom Vision:** Allows users to train and deploy their own AI models for specific image recognition tasks, improving accuracy in domain-specific applications such as product classification and medical imaging
- **Object Detection:** Identifies and locates objects within an image by drawing bounding boxes, useful for applications like inventory management, surveillance, and automated quality control
- **Image Captioning:** Automatically generates natural language descriptions for images using deep learning models, improving accessibility and digital content management
- **Spatial Analysis:** Analyzes the spatial relationships between objects in an image or video feed, enabling applications such as crowd monitoring and smart surveillance
- **Azure AI Face API:** A cloud-based facial recognition service that detects, analyzes, and verifies faces in images and videos for identity verification, security, and customer engagement
- **Face Detection:** Identifies human faces in an image or video, providing bounding box coordinates and facial landmarks such as eyes, nose, and mouth positions
- **Facial Attribute Analysis:** Extracts attributes from detected faces, including age, gender, emotions, hair color, facial hair, glasses, and head pose, enabling sentiment analysis and personalized interactions
- **Face Verification:** Compares two faces to determine if they belong to the same person, supporting biometric authentication and identity verification
- **Face Similarity Matching:** Measures the similarity between faces across different images, used for applications like duplicate detection and fraud prevention

- **Face Identification:** Recognizes individuals by comparing detected faces against a pre-registered database, commonly used in access control and customer personalization
- **Emotion Detection:** Analyzes facial expressions to determine emotions such as happiness, sadness, anger, surprise, and neutrality, enhancing customer sentiment analysis and AI-driven user interactions
- **Mask Detection:** Identifies whether a person is wearing a mask and whether it covers the nose and mouth, useful for public safety, healthcare compliance, and workplace monitoring
- **Bounding Box:** A set of coordinates defining the area in an image where an object or face is detected, which enable tracking and analysis of visual elements
- **Confidence Score:** A numerical value indicating the model's certainty in detecting objects, faces, or text in an image, helping businesses fine-tune AI-powered decisions

Multiple Choice Questions

1. Which feature of Azure AI Vision enables the extraction of text from images?
   a. Optical Character Recognition (OCR)
   b. Object Detection
   c. Image Captioning
   d. Spatial Analysis
2. What is the primary function of the Face Detection feature in Azure AI Face API?
   a. Identifying emotions in a detected face
   b. Detecting human faces and providing bounding box coordinates
   c. Recognizing individuals from a database
   d. Predicting the age and gender of a person
3. Which capability of Azure AI Vision allows businesses to train their own AI models for specific visual tasks?
   a. Image Analysis
   b. Face Verification
   c. Object Detection
   d. Custom Vision
4. How does Azure AI Face API support biometric authentication?
   a. By detecting objects in an image
   b. By identifying and verifying individuals using facial recognition
   c. By converting text into speech
   d. By extracting text from scanned documents

Answers

1. a
2. b
3. d
4. b

CHAPTER 9
Identifying Common NLP Workloads

Introduction

In this chapter, we will explore the key principles and practical applications of **Natural Language Processing (NLP)**–a field that allows computers to understand, interpret, and generate human language. As text and speech data continue to grow exponentially in the form of emails, chats, and voice assistants, NLP has become essential for automating communication, improving customer interactions, and deriving insights from unstructured information. By leveraging these capabilities, organizations can efficiently **analyze text and speech, extract meaning, and uncover business value** across industries.

We will examine core NLP workloads that power today's intelligent solutions, including **Key Phrase Extraction** (to identify the most relevant terms in text), **Entity Recognition** (to detect and categorize information such as names or locations), and **Sentiment Analysis** (to interpret emotions and opinions). We will also explore **Language Modeling**, **Speech Recognition and Synthesis**, and **Machine Translation**, which enable predictive text, chatbots, voice-driven systems, and multilingual communication. Together, these workloads form the foundation of Azure AI's NLP capabilities and transform how organizations process and understand language.

Structure

In this chapter, we will discuss the following topics:

- Identify Features and Uses for Key Phrase Extraction
- Identify Features and Uses for Entity Recognition
- Identify Features and Uses for Sentiment Analysis
- Identify Features and Uses for Language Modeling
- Identify Features and Uses for Speech Recognition and Synthesis
- Identify Features and Uses for Machine Translation

Introduction to Natural Language Processing (NLP)

Natural Language Processing (NLP) is a multidisciplinary field at the intersection of Artificial Intelligence (AI), computer science, and human language. It enables software systems to understand, interpret, and generate human language in meaningful ways. While machines struggled with language-related tasks just a few decades ago, recent advancements in computational power, sophisticated algorithms, and large-scale datasets have revolutionized NLP, thereby making it a cornerstone of AI-driven innovation.

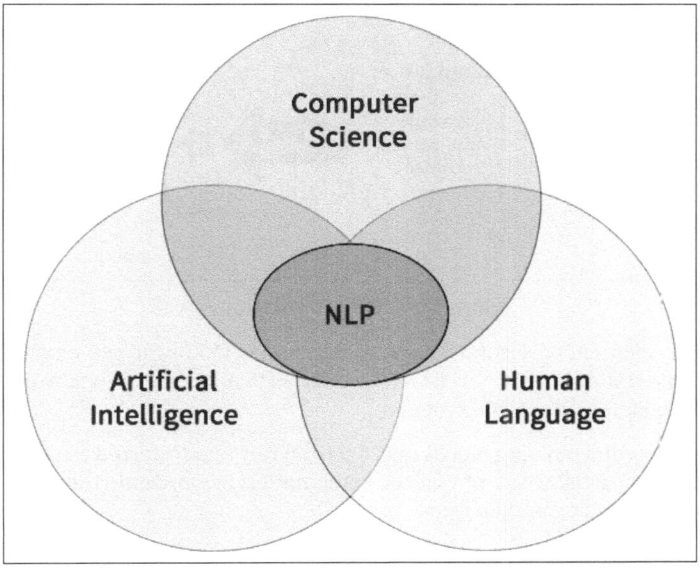

Figure 9.1: *NLP at the Intersection of AI, Computer Science, and Human Language*

The importance of language in human communication cannot be overstated. Language is the primary medium through which individuals and organizations exchange information, express ideas, and collaborate with each other. However, until recent technological breakthroughs, computers lacked the ability to process and analyze text or speech effectively. Today, with the advent of NLP, tasks such as sentiment analysis, speech recognition, translation, and automated text summarization are not only possible but are also becoming increasingly accurate and scalable.

At its core, NLP involves transforming unstructured linguistic data such as text and speech, into structured formats that AI models can process. This transformation allows systems to extract insights, perform categorization, and even generate responses autonomously. For example, chatbots use NLP to understand customer queries and provide appropriate answers, while translation engines enable seamless cross-language communication.

NLP (Natural Language Processing) Concepts

One of the earliest methods for text analysis involves using statistical techniques to derive semantic meaning from a collection of texts (commonly referred to as a *corpus*). This process combines classification and summarization to analyze the words within the text, while identifying patterns and extracting insights about the central topic. The initial stage of this process, which is known as *tokenization*, involves breaking the text into smaller units called *tokens*, which represent words, phrases, or other components. This step is critical for processing and analyzing textual data effectively.

To interpret written or spoken language, NLP solutions follow a structured workflow. This typically begins with ingesting raw text, followed by processing, tokenization, and model training. These stages enable advanced tasks, such as sentiment analysis, machine translation, summarization, and conversational AI, to be performed with high precision and accuracy.

The following diagram illustrates how different NLP applications are interconnected, from the initial processing steps to the utilization of language models for various purposes, including text analysis and conversational AI:

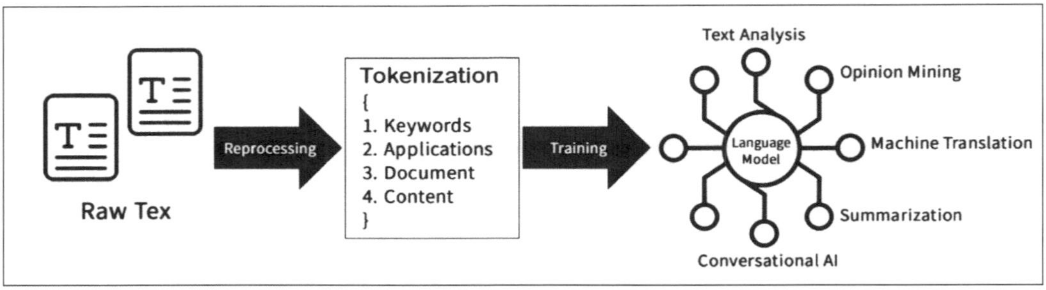

Figure 9.2: *Flow of NLP Applications*

Tokenization is a key element of Natural Language Processing (NLP) and serves as a critical foundation for building your understanding as you develop AI expertise. It plays a vital role in breaking down complex text into smaller, manageable units.

Tokens are the fundamental building blocks derived from raw text (referred to as a *corpus*). Each token represents a distinct or partial word, phrase, or combination of words, further providing structure to the data for further processing and analysis.

Understanding Tokenization

Imagine you are breaking a large puzzle into smaller pieces to make it easier to work with. Tokenization does something similar with text: it breaks a sentence or paragraph into smaller, manageable parts called *tokens*. These tokens are typically individual words, but they can also be phrases or even characters, depending on the context.

Let us look at this sentence as an example:

"She sells seashells by the seashore."

When it is tokenized, the sentence becomes:

- She
- sells
- seashells
- by
- the
- seashore

Each word is treated as a separate unit. Notice that every occurrence of a word is counted. For instance, if "*she*" appeared twice in the sentence, it would still have the same token but would be reused in processing.

Why is this useful?

- **Simplifies Analysis:** By breaking text into tokens, systems can focus on understanding smaller parts like counting how many times a word appears or analyzing the meaning of specific terms.
- **Efficient Processing:** Instead of dealing with entire sentences or paragraphs, computers can work with these smaller, standardized pieces of text and will be able to process them efficiently.
- **Foundational Step:** Tokenization is the first step in many advanced tasks like sentiment analysis, language translation, or even chatbots.

Think of tokens as the building blocks for teaching machines how to understand and work with human language. Without this step, processing language would be much harder!

Foundations of NLP Models

Building effective NLP models depends on three fundamental components that are explained as follows:

- **High-Quality, Diverse Data:** The more varied, accurately labeled, and contextually rich the training data is, the more reliable and adaptable the NLP model will be. Open-source datasets such as Common Crawl, Wikipedia corpora, and specialized linguistic databases provide a strong foundation for NLP development. However, custom domain-specific datasets can give organizations a competitive advantage in specialized applications.
- **Computational Resources:** Training and deploying NLP models require significant computational power. Industries increasingly rely on specialized hardware like GPUs (Graphics Processing Units) and TPUs (Tensor Processing Units) to process large volumes of text and speech data efficiently. Cloud-based AI services like **Microsoft Azure's NLP offerings** further streamline model development by providing scalable infrastructure.
- **Expertise in Data Science and Linguistics:** Although frameworks like TensorFlow, PyTorch, and spaCy simplify NLP development, designing highly effective models still demands expertise in machine learning, linguistic theory, and data preprocessing techniques. Professionals working in NLP must have a firm grasp of tokenization, syntactic parsing, embedding techniques, and model fine-tuning to build robust and efficient solutions.

As you continue exploring NLP, it is important to understand how this field builds upon concepts introduced earlier in the book. NLP operates at the intersection of Artificial Intelligence (AI), Machine Learning (ML), and Deep Learning (DL), using specialized architectures such as Transformers and Recurrent Neural Networks (RNNs) to process and generate human language efficiently.

These advanced models enable NLP systems to learn patterns in text and speech and are useful in applications such as machine translation, sentiment analysis, and conversational AI, when it comes to delivering accurate and context-aware results.

From Theory to Practical Applications

The evolution of NLP has unlocked countless applications across industries. With services like Azure AI Services for Language, organizations can automate workflows, enhance customer experiences, and gain actionable insights from large datasets. Some key applications include:

- **Sentiment Analysis:** Identifying emotional tone in customer feedback or social media posts
- **Key Phrase Extraction:** Highlighting the most relevant information from large text bodies
- **Speech Recognition and Synthesis:** Converting speech to text and vice versa, thus enabling voice-driven interfaces
- **Language Translation:** Facilitating seamless communication across linguistic barriers

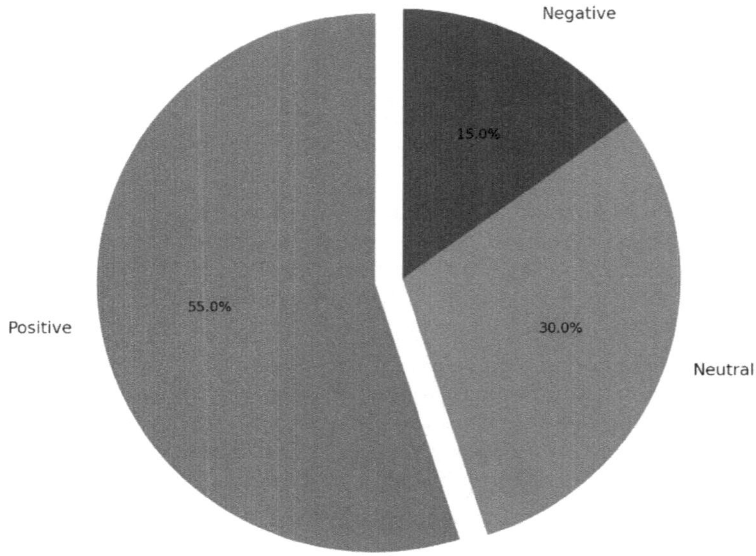

***Figure 9.3**: Example of NLP Model Output Distribution*

NLP Technique	Primary Function	Common Applications
Key Phrase Extraction	Identifies important terms or topics	Summarization, SEO, Document tagging
Entity Recognition (NER)	Extracts structured data (names, dates, places)	Compliance, Search indexing, CRM
Sentiment Analysis	Determines emotional tone	Customer feedback, Brand monitoring
Language Modeling	Predicts or generates text	Chatbots, Autocomplete, Text generation
Speech Recognition / Synthesis	Converts speech to text and vice versa	Voice assistants, Accessibility
Machine Translation	Converts text between languages	Localization, Multilingual communication

***Table 9.1**: Comparison of NLP Techniques and Their Primary Applications*

By leveraging the principles and methodologies behind NLP, businesses and individuals can implement powerful, scalable solutions tailored to tackle diverse real-world challenges.

Identifying Features and Uses for Key Phrase Extraction

Key phrase extraction is a Natural Language Processing (NLP) technique designed to identify and extract the most relevant and meaningful phrases from a given text. Rather than focusing on individual words, it identifies combinations of terms that capture the main ideas within a document.

This capability enhances content summarization, improves search functionality, and supports information retrieval, thereby making it an essential tool for modern data-driven applications.

Whether analyzing customer feedback, research papers, or financial reports, key phrase extraction allows systems to quickly determine core topics and themes, while improving efficiency and decision-making across various industries. This chapter explores the key features, applications, and underlying mechanisms of key phrase extraction.

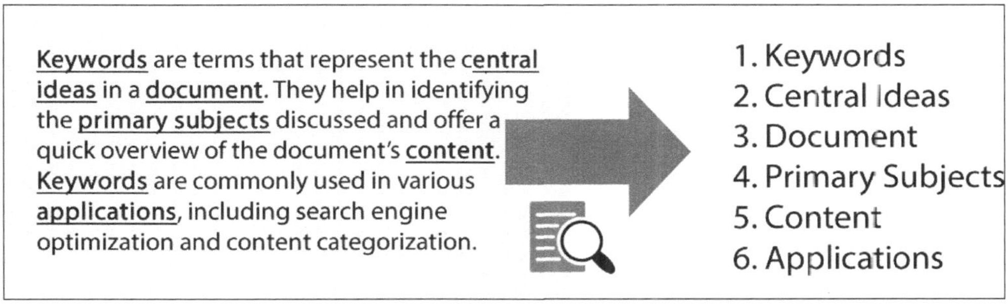

Figure 9.4: *Key Phrase Extraction Summarizing Main Topics from a Document*

Features of Key Phrase Extraction

Key phrase extraction leverages linguistic analysis and machine learning algorithms to identify phrases that provide meaningful insight into a document's content. Unlike basic keyword detection, that highlights frequently used but contextually insignificant words, this technique ensures that extracted phrases are semantically relevant and useful for downstream applications like text classification, search indexing, and sentiment analysis.

Identifying Key Concepts

A fundamental capability of key phrase extraction is its ability to detect and extract phrases that encapsulate the main topics of a document. Instead of merely selecting common words, it focuses on contextually significant terms that carry deeper meaning.

Example:

Input Text: "*Natural language processing is a subset of artificial intelligence that focuses on understanding human language.*"

Extracted Key Phrases:

- "Natural language processing"
- "artificial intelligence"
- "human language"

These extracted phrases provide a concise representation of the text's core ideas, thereby enabling systems to categorize and retrieve documents more effectively.

Language-Agnostic Capability

Key phrase extraction is not limited to a single language; modern NLP models can analyze multilingual text, making them invaluable for global applications. This capability supports:

- **International Content Analysis:** Allows business operating across different markets to extract and compare key topics from multilingual documents
- **Real-Time Translation Support:** Helps bridge language gaps by identifying equivalent phrases across languages
- **Global Market Research:** Enables businesses to track emerging trends, customer opinions, and industry insights in different regions

Hence, by leveraging language models trained on diverse datasets, organizations can apply key phrase extraction across various linguistic and cultural contexts without compromising on accuracy.

Scalability for Large Datasets

A crucial advantage of key phrase extraction is its ability to process vast amounts of text data efficiently. From thousands of customer reviews to millions of business reports, modern NLP algorithms are designed to handle large-scale processing in real-time.

Some practical applications of large-scale key phrase extraction include:

- **Customer Feedback Analysis:** Identifies recurring themes in product reviews and user surveys
- **Automated Reporting:** Extracts critical insights from financial, legal, and operational reports
- **Sentiment Analysis:** Detects public perception and brand reputation by extracting the most discussed topics

Thus, by ensuring high-speed and accurate extraction, businesses can automate and streamline text analysis, allowing for better decision-making and faster response times.

Customizability for Industry-Specific Needs

Different industries rely on specialized terminology, which general-purpose NLP models might not recognize. Key phrase extraction algorithms can be customized and trained to identify domain-specific vocabulary, while ensuring more accurate results in specialized fields.

- **Healthcare:** Extracts medical terms, drug names, and symptoms from clinical records and research papers
- **Finance:** Identifies key financial indicators, stock trends, and legal terms from market reports and financial statements
- **Legal Services:** Recognizes important clauses, case law references, and compliance terms in contracts and regulatory documents

This level of customization ensures that businesses in highly technical domains can **leverage NLP-driven insights** tailored to their needs.

Applications of Key Phrase Extraction

Key phrase extraction has diverse applications across industries, enhancing both automated systems and human decision-making processes.

Summarization

By extracting key phrases, lengthy documents can be condensed into concise summaries, which makes it easier to grasp the main topics. This is especially useful in:

- Generating executive summaries for business reports
- Highlighting critical points in news articles
- Creating research abstracts from academic papers

Search Engine Optimization (SEO)

Key phrase extraction plays a crucial role in improving content visibility on search engines by:

- Identifying high-value keywords for better ranking
- Generating metadata and tags for web content
- Enhancing topic relevance for search queries

Customer Feedback Analysis

By analyzing customer reviews, surveys, and support tickets, businesses can quickly undertake actions such as:

- Identifying common concerns among customers
- Tracking emerging trends in product or service feedback
- Prioritizing improvements based on customer needs

Information Retrieval

Key phrase extraction enhances search functionality by:

- Indexing key phrases instead of entire documents, thereby making searches more efficient
- Improving document ranking by highlighting relevant content
- Facilitating quick retrieval of important business or legal records

Knowledge Management

Organizations that manage large volumes of documents use key phrase extraction for:

- Automatically tagging and categorizing content in internal databases or wikis
- Improving search and navigation within corporate knowledge bases
- Enhancing document retrieval for employees and decision-makers

Process of Key Phrase Extraction

The process of key phrase extraction follows a structured pipeline to ensure **accuracy and efficiency** as demonstrated in the following figure:

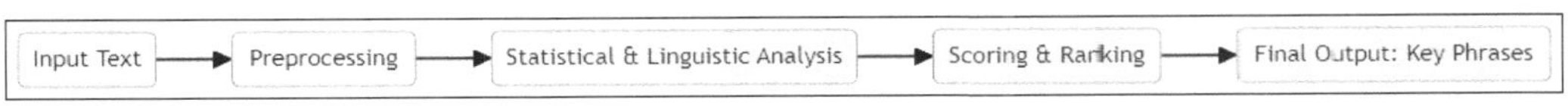

Figure 9.5: *Process of Key Phrase Extraction*

1. **Preprocessing the Text**

Preprocessing is the foundation of key phrase extraction. It involves **cleaning and structuring the text** to remove noise, and ensure consistency.

Here is a list of the key tasks undertaken in this step:

a. **Tokenization:** Breaks the text into smaller units, such as words, phrases, or subwords. This helps structure the text into a format suitable for further analysis.

   Example:

   Input: "*Key phrase extraction simplifies content analysis.*"

   Output: ["Key", "phrase", "extraction", "simplifies", "content", "analysis"]

b. **Stop Word Removal:** Filters out frequently used but contextually insignificant words (for example, "the," "and," "is").

   Example:

   Input: "*The process of extracting phrases is efficient.*"

   Output: ["process", "extracting", "phrases", "efficient"]

c. **Normalization:** Standardizes the text by converting it to lowercase and removing special characters or punctuation.

   Example:

   Input: "AI-*Driven Analytics!*"

   Output: "ai-driven analytics"

By the end of this step, the text is clean, tokenized, and ready for analysis.

2. **Statistical and Linguistic Analysis**

Once the text is preprocessed, this step identifies **key candidates for extraction** using a combination of **statistical metrics** and **linguistic insights**. These techniques are further categorized as:

a. **Statistical Techniques:** Statistical methods prioritize phrases based on their frequency and uniqueness within the document. Algorithms like **TF-IDF** determine how relevant a term is in relation to the overall corpus.

   Example: A phrase like "*natural language processing*" might score highly in a technical document, but not in a general corpus of unrelated topics.

b. **Linguistic Techniques:** Linguistic analysis focuses on the grammatical structure of sentences to extract meaningful phrases. For example, **noun phrases** like "*customer satisfaction survey*" are often more informative than isolated words.

   Example:

   Input: "*The company conducted a customer satisfaction survey.*"

   Output: "customer satisfaction survey"

These techniques ensure that the extracted phrases are both **statistically significant** and **contextually meaningful**.

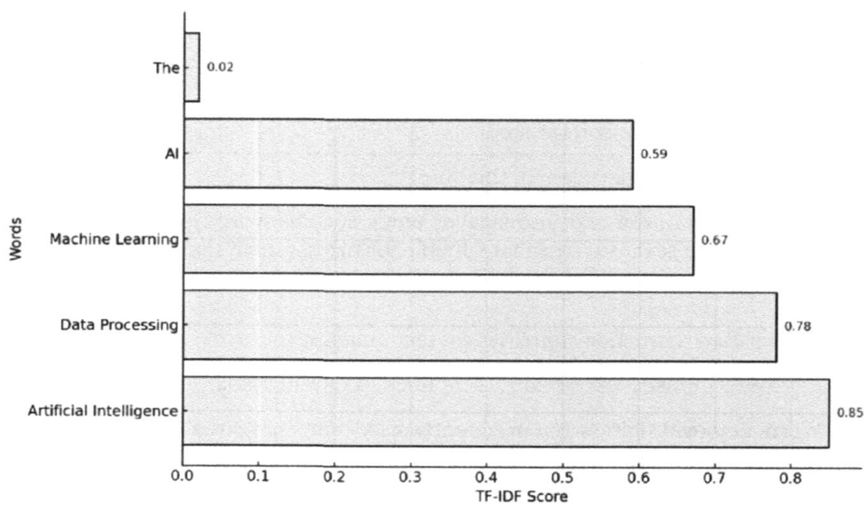

Figure 9.6: *Bar Chart Illustrating TF-IDF Scores for Words in a Document*

3. **Weighting and Scoring**

The third step involves assigning a **score** to each candidate phrase based on its **importance and relevance**. This ranking helps prioritize the most meaningful phrases for the specific context.

a. **TF-IDF (Term Frequency-Inverse Document Frequency):** Assigns higher scores to terms that are frequent in the document but rare across a larger corpus.

   Example: In a medical report, "*radiological imaging*" might have a high score due to its domain-specific relevance.

b. **Neural Embeddings:** Advanced AI models, such as **BERT** or **Word2Vec**, capture the **semantic relationships** between words for more nuanced scoring.

   Example: Words like "AI" and "*machine learning*" might receive similar scores due to their contextual similarity, even if they appear separately in the text.

The combination of statistical metrics and deep learning models enables the system to rank phrases with greater precision.

4. **Extracting the Key Phrases**

The final step involves **filtering and selecting** the most relevant phrases based on the scores assigned in the previous step. This stage ensures that only the most meaningful and contextually appropriate phrases are retained.

Key refinements at this stage include:

a. **Semantic Understanding:** Machine learning models incorporate **contextual awareness** to ensure that the extracted phrases are aligning with the document's overall theme. *Example*: In a dataset about software development, "*agile methodologies*" and "*scrum framework*" are recognized as key phrases due to their relevance to the topic.

b. **Topic Modeling:** It groups related phrases under broader categories to improve organization and comprehension.

   Example: For a business report, key phrases like "*profit margins*," "*revenue growth*," *and* "*market trends*" might be grouped under the broader topic of "*financial performance*."

By the end of this step, the **final list of key phrases** is ready for downstream tasks like **summarization, indexing, or sentiment analysis.**

5. **Optional Post-Processing**

In some cases, additional steps are applied to fine-tune the results, depending on the use case:

a. **Removing Redundant Phrases:** Ensures that the final output does not contain repeated or overly similar phrases

b. **Formatting for Output:** Converts the extracted phrases into the desired format, such as lists, tags, or tables

Exam Tip: *When a question refers to identifying the* ***most relevant phrases or terms*** *in a text, it usually relates to* ***Key Phrase Extraction*** *and not* ***Entity Recognition****. Key Phrase Extraction focuses on summarizing content, while Entity Recognition classifies specific data points like names or dates.*

Challenges in Key Phrase Extraction

Key phrase extraction is a crucial Natural Language Processing (NLP) task that identifies the most important terms in a text. While it enhances searchability, summarization, and information retrieval, there are several challenges that affect its accuracy and effectiveness. These challenges are mentioned as follows:

- **Contextual Ambiguity:** Words and phrases may have different meanings depending on the context, thereby making accurate extraction difficult.
- **Handling Multi-Word Phrases:** Identifying meaningful multi-word key phrases is complex as splitting them incorrectly can alter their meaning.
- **Domain-Specific Terminology:** General models struggle with specialized fields (for example, medicine, finance) that require domain adaptation.
- **Lack of Standardized Evaluation Metrics:** Different algorithms prioritize various factors, thus making quality assessment inconsistent.
- **Data Sparsity in Low-Resource Languages:** Many languages lack annotated datasets, which reduces model accuracy in non-dominant languages.
- **Noise and Redundancy:** Extracted phrases may be repetitive, irrelevant, or too generic without proper filtering.
- **Sensitivity to Text Length and Structure:** Long texts add complexity, while short texts may lack enough context for accurate extraction.

Addressing these challenges requires continuous advancements in NLP techniques, including transformer-based models, contextual embeddings, and adaptive learning approaches to improve the precision and relevance of extracted key phrases.

Identifying Features and Uses for Entity Recognition

Entity recognition, also known as **Named Entity Recognition (NER)**, is a key Natural Language Processing (NLP) technique that identifies and classifies specific entities within a text. These entities can include names of people, organizations, locations, dates, monetary values, and more. By converting unstructured text into structured data, entity recognition supports a wide range of applications like enhancing search functionality and improving decision-making processes.

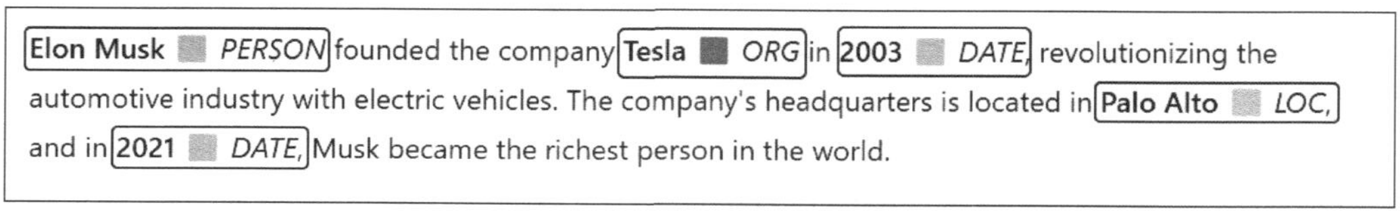

Figure 9.7: *Example of Named Entity Recognition in a Sentence*

Features of Entity Recognition

Entity recognition is a fundamental task in Natural Language Processing (NLP) that allows systems to automatically identify and classify key elements in text. By leveraging sophisticated algorithms, entity recognition extracts meaningful data from unstructured content, thereby improving searchability, automation, and analytics.

The core strength of entity recognition lies in its ability to detect and categorize entities with high accuracy and adapt to different contexts and languages. The following are some essential aspects of how entity recognition functions:

Entity Detection

The system identifies and extracts predefined entities such as names, dates, and locations directly from text. It can recognize both single-word entities (for example, "Microsoft") and multi-word entities (for example, "San Francisco Bay Area"), ensuring that relevant information is captured correctly.

Example:

- **Input:** *"John Smith works at Microsoft and lives in Seattle."*
- **Extracted Entities:**
    - "John Smith" → **PERSON**
    - "Microsoft" → **ORGANIZATION**
    - "Seattle" → **LOCATION**

Categorization

Once an entity is detected, it is classified into predefined categories such as **PERSON**, **ORGANIZATION**, or **LOCATION**. This categorization helps structure data for applications like knowledge graphs, search engines, and chatbots. Additionally, custom entity types can be defined based on domain-specific requirements, such as recognizing chemical compounds in scientific texts or product names in e-commerce.

Language Support

Modern entity recognition models handle multilingual content effectively, while adapting to various linguistic structures and nuances. By incorporating language-specific models, these systems ensure that entities are recognized even in complex grammatical constructions, which makes them highly adaptable for global applications.

Context Awareness

A critical challenge in entity recognition is resolving ambiguity. The same word can refer to different things depending on context. For instance, "*Apple*" might refer to its namesake tech company or a fruit. Advanced models consider surrounding words to improve classification accuracy to reduce misinterpretations and enhance precision in extracting relevant information.

Entity recognition continues to evolve and have become an indispensable tool for industries such as finance, healthcare, and customer support, where automated data processing plays a crucial role in efficiency and decision-making.

Applications of Entity Recognition

Entity recognition is widely used across industries to automate processes and extract actionable insights. Its applications span diverse fields, while streamlining operations and facilitating efficient decision-making.

Information Extraction

Thus, by automating the identification of key data points, entity recognition simplifies the process of retrieving critical information from unstructured sources like emails, contracts, and reports. This is especially useful in:

- Extracting company names and transaction amounts from financial reports
- Identifying dates, locations, and organizations in legal documents
- Highlighting key metrics in business contracts for faster reviews

Search Optimization

By enhancing indexing with recognized entities, search engines can deliver more accurate and targeted results. This is especially useful in:

- Refining search results for specific queries, such as "hospitals in New York"
- Improving content relevance by tagging entities in web pages
- Enabling faster discovery of related topics and entities in large datasets

Sentiment Analysis

By linking entities with sentiment data, entity recognition helps analyze public perception and understand opinions more effectively. This is especially useful in:

- Monitoring brand reputation through social media mentions
- Identifying customer sentiment in product reviews
- Measuring public opinion about organizations or events

Knowledge Graph Construction

By identifying relationships between entities, entity recognition facilitates the creation of interconnected data structures for research and analytics. This is especially useful in:

- Building knowledge graphs to connect researchers, institutions, and publications
- Organizing domain-specific knowledge for machine learning models
- Structuring relationships in datasets for advanced analytics

Entity Recognition Process Steps

Entity recognition involves a structured pipeline of steps to process and classify entities effectively. Each step is explained in detail, as follows:

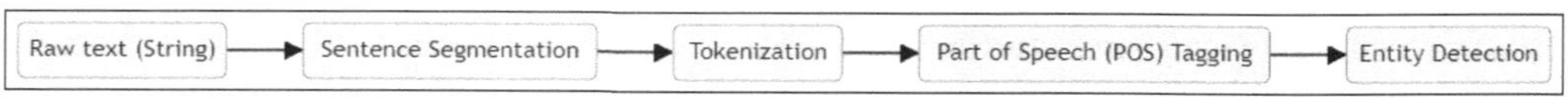

Figure 9.8: *Entity Recognition Process Steps*

1. **Raw Text Input**

The process begins with raw text, which can be a document, a sentence, or any string of unstructured data. This serves as the primary input for analysis.

   a. **Purpose:** Establishes the foundation for subsequent processing
   b. *Example*: Input text like "*Alice visited Paris last summer.*"

2. **Sentence Segmentation**

The raw text is divided into smaller units, such as sentences, to simplify processing and maintain contextual coherence.

   a. **Purpose:** Breaks down large text into manageable parts for easier analysis
   b. *Example*: Text like "*Alice visited Paris. She loved the Eiffel Tower.*" is split into two distinct sentences.

3. **Tokenization**

Each sentence is further divided into smaller components called tokens, typically words or phrases, enabling granular analysis.

a. **Purpose:** Prepares text for fine-grained processing by isolating words or phrases

b. *Example*: The sentence "*Alice visited Paris.*" is tokenized into ["Alice", "visited", "Paris"].

4. **Part-of-Speech (POS) Tagging**

Each token is analyzed for its grammatical role, such as noun, verb, or adjective, to identify patterns and relationships in the text.

a. **Purpose:** Provides linguistic context by tagging words with their grammatical roles

b. *Example*: For the sentence "*Alice visited Paris,*" the tags might be:

i. Alice → **NOUN**

ii. visited → **VERB**

iii. Paris → **PROPER NOUN**

5. **Entity Detection**

In the final step, entities are extracted and classified into predefined categories like **PERSON**, **ORGANIZATION**, or **LOCATION**.

a. **Purpose:** Identifies meaningful elements within the text and categorizes them

b. *Example*: For the text "*Alice visited Paris,*" the detected entities would be:

i. Alice → **PERSON**

ii. Paris → **LOCATION**

These steps combine **linguistic techniques** and **machine learning models** to ensure accurate and efficient identification of entities in text. Each phase builds on the previous one, thus allowing for precise and context-aware classification of key information.

Exam Tip: *If an exam question mentions identifying names, locations, organizations, or dates, it refers to Entity Recognition (NER). Remember that NER converts unstructured text into structured data for analytics and automation.*

Challenges in Entity Recognition

Entity recognition is a fundamental task in natural language processing that involves identifying names, locations, organizations, and other key entities within text. Despite its wide applications, entity recognition faces several challenges that affect accuracy, adaptability, and scalability.

- **Ambiguity in Named Entities:** Same names can refer to different things (for example, "Apple" as a company or fruit), thus requiring deep contextual understanding.
- **Variability in Entity Representation:** Entities appear in multiple forms (for example, "United States," "U.S.," "USA"), thereby making normalization difficult.
- **Lack of Standardized Entity Labels:** Different industries use varied entity categories, requiring domain-specific adaptations.
- **Low-Resource Language Limitations:** Models perform well in high-resource languages but struggle with underrepresented languages due to data scarcity.
- **Handling Unstructured and Noisy Text:** Informal text, social media, and OCR errors introduce inconsistencies that models must manage.
- **Scalability across Domains:** General-purpose models need retraining for specialized fields like healthcare, finance, or law.

- **Ethical and Privacy Concerns:** Processing sensitive data requires compliance with regulations and bias mitigation in entity recognition.

Overcoming these challenges requires advancements in contextual embeddings, transfer learning, and the development of more diverse and representative training datasets to improve the accuracy and adaptability of entity recognition models.

Identify Features and Uses for Sentiment Analysis in NLP

Sentiment Analysis, also known as Opinion Mining, is an NLP technique that determines the emotional tone expressed in text. It is widely used in industries such as marketing, customer service, and finance to analyze opinions, reviews, and feedback. By classifying text as positive, negative, or neutral, sentiment analysis helps organizations understand public perception and make data-driven decisions.

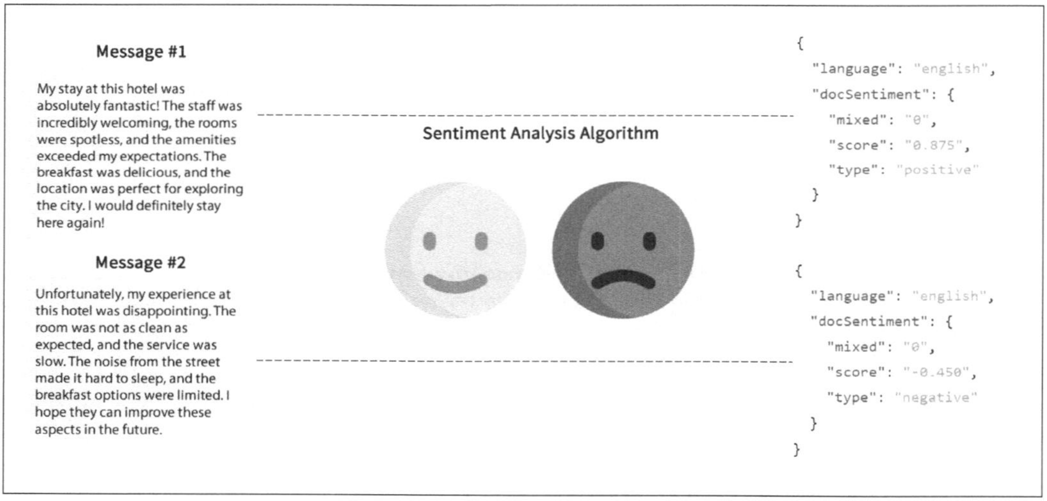

Figure 9.9: *Sentiment Analysis Algorithm*

Features of Sentiment Analysis

The features of sentiment analysis enable systems to detect and interpret emotions in text with high accuracy. These features provide the foundation for effective text classification and contextual understanding. The following are the core elements that define sentiment analysis:

- **Lexical Features**
  - Uses predefined **sentiment lexicons** (word lists) to identify sentiment
  - *Example: "happy"* → Positive, *"hate"* → Negative
- **Syntactic Features**
  - **Part-of-Speech (POS) tagging** helps understand context
  - *Example: "not good"* (Negation detection) should be classified as **negative**.

- **Word Embeddings**
  - Converts words into **vector representations** using models like:
    - **Word2Vec**
    - **GloVe**
    - **BERT**
  - *Example*: The model understands that *"fantastic"* and *"great"* have similar meanings.
- **Sentiment Score Calculation**
  - Assigns a **numerical sentiment score** (for example, -1 for negative, 0 for neutral, 1 for positive)
  - *Example*: *"This is an amazing product!"* → Sentiment score = **0.9** (Positive)

Sentiment Analysis Process

Sentiment analysis follows a structured workflow to extract and classify emotions expressed in text. This process involves multiple stages, from data preparation to emotion classification, with each contributing to the overall accuracy of the analysis.

Types of Sentiment Analysis

Sentiment analysis can be performed at different levels:

Document-Level Sentiment Analysis: Classifies the overall sentiment of a *full document*

Example: A restaurant review – "The food was delicious, and the staff was friendly." → **Positive Sentiment**

Sentence-Level Sentiment Analysis: Analyzes individual sentences to determine sentiment

Example: "The laptop is fast, but the battery life is terrible."

- Sentence 1: Positive (fast laptop)
- Sentence 2: Negative (poor battery life)

Aspect-Based Sentiment Analysis (ABSA): Identifies specific aspects being reviewed

Example: "The camera quality is excellent, but the battery drains too quickly."

- Camera Quality → Positive
- Battery Life → Negative

Emotion Detection: Detects specific emotions such as joy, anger, sadness, or surprise

Example: A comment like "*I'm so frustrated with this app!*" would be classified as **anger**.

Workflow of Sentiment Analysis

Sentiment analysis uses **Machine Learning (ML)** models and **lexicon-based** approaches to classify emotions expressed in text. The process generally involves four main steps:

Step 1: Data Collection

a. **Gathering text data** from sources like social media, product reviews, customer feedback, news articles, and emails

b. *Example*: Collecting tweets about a product launch

Step 2: Text Preprocessing

a. **Cleaning the text** by removing special characters, stop words, and irrelevant data

b. **Tokenizing and normalizing words** (for example, stemming or lemmatization)

c. *Example*: Converting "*amazing, Amazed!!*" to "*amaze*" for better analysis

Step 3: Feature Extraction

a. **Extracting important linguistic features**, such as:

   i. **Word frequency:** How often words like "*happy*" or "*sad*" appear

   ii. **Polarity detection:** Judging that words like "*great*" are positive, while "*terrible*" are negative

   iii. **Contextual embeddings:** Using deep learning models like **BERT** or **GPT**

b. *Example*: Identifying words like "*awesome*" and "*love*" to indicate positive sentiment

Step 4: Sentiment Classification

a. **Using a machine learning model** to categorize text as positive, negative, or neutral

b. **Advanced models** can detect emotions like happiness, anger, or sadness.

c. *Example*: A review saying, "*The service was slow, but the food was great!*" may be classified as neutral due to mixed sentiments.

Features Used in Sentiment Analysis

For sentiment classification, NLP models use different types of **features** such as:

- **Lexical Features**
  - Uses predefined **sentiment lexicons** (word lists) to identify sentiment
  - *Example*: "*happy*" → positive, "*hate*" → negative
- **Syntactic Features**
  - Part-of-Speech (POS) tagging helps understand context
  - *Example*: "*not good*" (Negation detection) should be negative.
- **Word Embeddings**
  - Converts words into vector representations using models like:
    - **Word2Vec**
    - **GloVe**
    - **BERT**
  - *Example*: The model understands that "*fantastic*" and "*great*" have similar meanings.
- **Sentiment Score Calculation**
  - Assigns a numerical sentiment score (for example, -1 for negative, 0 for neutral, 1 for positive)
  - *Example*: "*This is an amazing product!*" → Sentiment score = 0.9 (Positive)

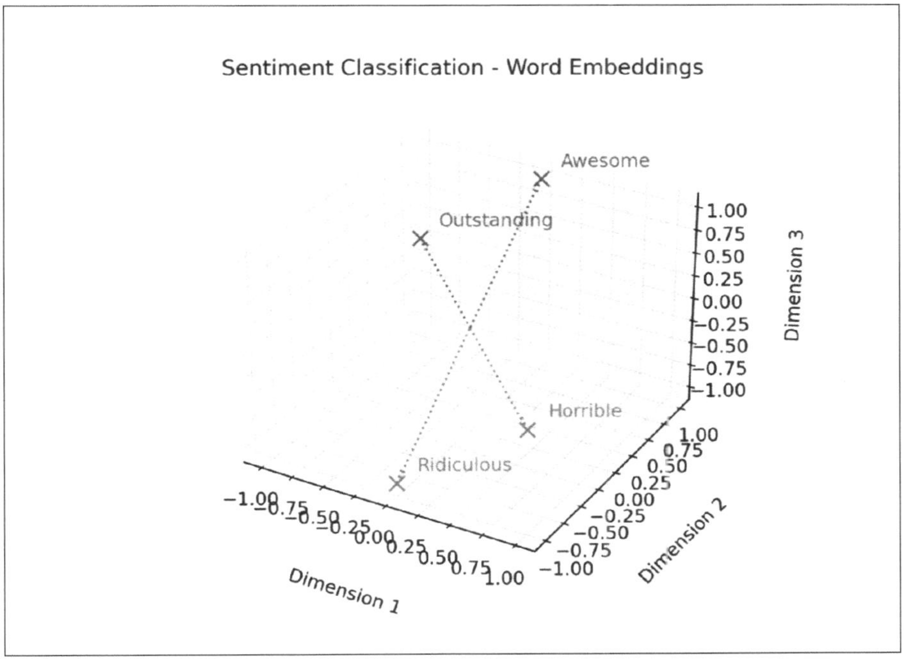

***Figure 9.10:** Word Vectors Mapped into Space for Few Words*

Exam Tip: *When a question asks about analyzing **customer opinions, emotions, or tone**, the correct answer will be **Sentiment Analysis**. It classifies text as **positive**, **negative**, or **neutral**, helping organizations understand public perception.*

Applications of Sentiment Analysis

Sentiment analysis has diverse applications across industries, enabling organizations to derive actionable insights from textual data. These applications enhance decision-making, streamline processes, and improve customer satisfaction.

Customer Feedback Analysis: By analyzing customer reviews, surveys, and support tickets, businesses can quickly:

- Identify common concerns among customers.
- Track emerging trends in product or service feedback.
- Prioritize improvements based on customer needs.

Social Media Monitoring: Sentiment analysis helps brands monitor mentions on social media platforms to:

- Gauge public perception of products or campaigns.
- Identify potential crises early by tracking spikes in negative sentiment.
- Engage proactively with customers to resolve issues.

Financial Market Prediction: Sentiment analysis of news and online discussions can assist investors by:

- Identifying stock sentiment trends to anticipate market behavior
- Analyzing public reactions to economic or business developments

- Providing data-driven insights for investment strategies

Political and Public Opinion Analysis: Governments and organizations use sentiment analysis to:

- Understand public sentiment on policies or social issues.
- Evaluate election campaign responses in real-time.
- Inform decision-making in public administration.

Healthcare and Mental Health Analysis: In the healthcare sector, sentiment analysis can:

- Detect signs of mental health issues such as depression or anxiety.
- Analyze patient feedback to improve care quality.
- Personalize therapeutic approaches based on emotional patterns.

Challenges in Sentiment Analysis

Sentiment analysis in NLP determines the emotional tone of text, but several challenges impact its accuracy and reliability. These challenges arise due to the complexity of human language, context interpretation, and the limitations of machine learning models. Some of them are mentioned as follows:

- **Understanding Sarcasm and Irony:** Models struggle to detect sarcasm when positive-sounding words carry negative intent.
- **Contextual Ambiguity:** Sentiment depends on context, and isolated word analysis can lead to misinterpretations.
- **Handling Mixed Sentiment:** Texts often contain both positive and negative sentiments, which makes classification difficult.
- **Cultural and Linguistic Differences:** Sentiment expressions vary across cultures and languages, requiring adaptation.
- **Identifying Emotion Beyond Polarity:** Basic models classify sentiment as positive, negative, or neutral, while missing nuanced emotions.
- **Domain-Specific Sentiment Variations:** General models may not perform well in specialized fields like healthcare or finance.
- **Handling Negations and Intensifiers:** Words like "not" or "barely" alter sentiment, requiring advanced linguistic processing.

Addressing these challenges requires making improvements in deep learning models, contextual embeddings, and cultural adaptability. Enhancing sentiment analysis with more sophisticated language understanding will lead to more accurate and meaningful insights.

Identify Features and Uses for Language Modeling

Language modeling is a fundamental aspect of **Natural Language Processing (NLP)** that enables machines to understand, generate, and predict human language. At its core, a language model (LM) assigns probabilities to sequences of words, thus helping machines interpret linguistic patterns and generate text that closely resembles natural human communication.

Language models are essential in various AI applications, from autocorrect and chatbots to machine translation and text summarization. With the advancement of deep learning and transformer-based architectures, modern language models, such as GPT (Generative Pre-Trained Transformer) and BERT

(Bidirectional Encoder Representations from Transformers), have significantly improved the ability of computers to understand and generate human-like text.

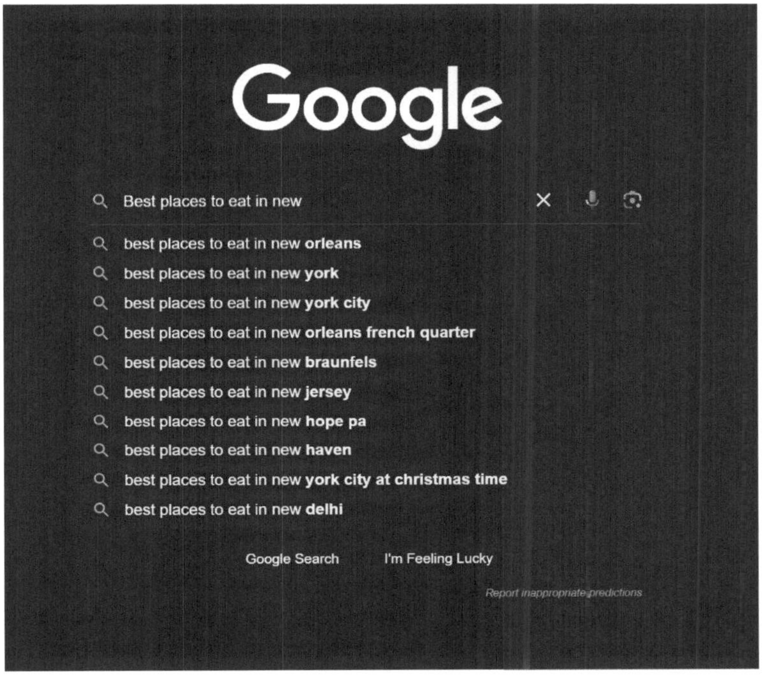

Figure 9.11: *Sentence Completion and Generation for Google Search*

Features of Language Modeling

Language models are designed with several key features that allow them to process and generate human-like text effectively. These features include:

- **Context Awareness**
  - Advanced models understand the broader meaning of sentences and their context.
  - Example:
    - "He went to the bank to withdraw money."
    - "She sat by the bank of the river."
    - The model distinguishes the meaning of "*bank*" based on context.
- **Bidirectional Understanding**
  - Traditional models predict words in a forward order only.
  - Models like **BERT** process text bidirectionally, improving comprehension.
  - *Example:*
    - Masked input: "*The _ dog ran across the yard.*"
    - Prediction: "*black*," "*small*," "*friendly*" based on context.
- **Sentence Completion and Generation**
  - Language models power auto completion systems in search engines and other applications.

- Example:
  - Google Search: "*Best places to eat in...*" → Model suggests: "*New York*"
- **Handling Ambiguity**
  - Some words have multiple meanings (**polysemy**), and language models disambiguate them based on context.
  - Example:
    - "*The crane flew across the sky.*" (Bird)
    - "*The crane lifted the heavy load.*" (Machine)

Understanding Language Modeling

Language models **predict the next word** (or phrase) in a sequence, based on the previous context. They analyze massive amounts of **text data** to learn linguistic structures, grammar, semantics, and contextual meanings.

A **probabilistic approach** is used where a model computes the probability of a word sequence. It is demonstrated in the following example:

$$P(W_1, W_2, W_3, \ldots, W_n)$$

Figure 9.12: *Probability of Word Sequence*

Here, P represents the probability of a sequence of words, and $W_1, W_2, \ldots, W_n$ represent the individual words (tokens) in that sequence. The model assigns higher probabilities to word sequences that are more likely to occur naturally in a language.

For example, given the input phrase "*I am going to the*", a trained language model might predict:

- "*store*" (high probability)
- "*moon*" (lower probability)
- "*abstract*" (very low probability)

The model learns from data and can **adjust predictions** based on context.

Types of Language Models

Language modeling techniques vary in complexity and application. The common types include:

N-Gram Language Models

- Use fixed-length sequences of words to predict the next word
- Example (Bigram Model - n=2):
  - Input: "*I am*" → Prediction: "*going*"
  - Input: "*going to*" → Prediction: "*the*"

Limitations:

- Suffers from sparse data issues
- Cannot capture long-range dependencies
- Requires large datasets for better performance

Statistical Language Models

- Incorporate probabilistic methods, such as:
  - **Hidden Markov Models (HMMs):** Predict words using states and probabilities
  - **Bayesian Models:** Use probability distributions to enhance predictions

Challenges: Struggles with complex language structures and requires extensive feature engineering.

Neural Language Models (NLMs)

Leverage deep learning to improve language understanding

Types of Neural Models:

- **Recurrent Neural Networks (RNNs):** Capture sequential patterns but struggle with long-range dependencies
- **Long Short-Term Memory (LSTMs):** Improve memory capabilities but are computationally expensive
- **Transformer-Based Models:** (State-of-the-Art)
  - Examples: **BERT, GPT, T5, RoBERTa**
  - Capture long-term dependencies and contextual meanings effectively

Example (GPT-4 Predicting the Next Word):

- Input: "*The weather today is*"
- Prediction: "*sunny and warm*" (high probability)

Exam Tip: *If a question involves **predicting the next word** or **generating text automatically**, it refers to **Language Modeling**. Models like* **GPT** *and* **BERT** *use context to understand and complete sentences.*

Applications of Language Models

Language models power various NLP applications across industries, enhancing automation, improving user experience, and streamlining tasks.

Chatbots and Virtual Assistants

Language models enable AI assistants to engage in human-like conversations, while improving interaction quality and providing helpful responses.

- *Example:*
  - User: "*Hey Siri, what's the weather today?*"
  - Siri: "*The weather is sunny with a high of 25°C.*"

Machine Translation

Language models facilitate translation between languages, thus breaking communication barriers and supporting global interaction.

- *Example:*
  - English: "*Hello, how are you?*"
  - Spanish: "*Hola, ¿cómo estás?*"

Text Summarization

Language models condense lengthy text into concise summaries while retaining the core information.

- *Example:*
  - Original: "*Artificial Intelligence is transforming industries, revolutionizing automation and improving decision-making.*"
  - Summary: "AI *transforms industries and enhances automation.*"

Speech Recognition

Language models convert spoken words into text, enabling applications like voice typing and transcription services.

- *Example:*
  - YouTube's auto-captioning system transcribes speech into subtitles for videos.

Challenges in Language Modeling

While language modeling has achieved remarkable advancements, it still faces significant challenges that impact its development and application. These challenges are mentioned as follows:

- **Computational Power and Cost:** Training and deploying large-scale models require an immense number of computational resources, which makes it difficult for smaller organizations to access them.
- **Bias in Language Models:** Models inherit biases from training data, which can potentially reinforce stereotypes and prejudices.
- **Understanding Sarcasm and Humor:** Models can often struggle with interpreting nuanced expressions that rely on tone, context, or cultural knowledge.
- **Handling Low-Resource Languages:** Most advancements focus on widely spoken languages, which leaves underrepresented languages with limited support.

These challenges highlight the complexities of language modeling and the importance of ongoing efforts that can make these technologies more effective, inclusive, and accessible.

Identify Features and Uses for Speech Recognition and Synthesis

Speech recognition and speech synthesis are two key components of Natural Language Processing (NLP) that enable machines to interpret and generate human speech. These technologies form the foundation of voice assistants, transcription services, accessibility tools, and automated customer support systems.

- **Speech recognition** (also known as **Automatic Speech Recognition, ASR**) converts spoken language into **text**, thereby allowing machines to understand verbal communication.
- **Speech synthesis** (commonly referred to as **Text-to-Speech, TTS**) generates **artificial speech from text**, thereby enabling human-like voice output.

These technologies power applications such as voice-activated assistants (Alexa, Siri), live transcription, accessibility tools for the visually impaired, and real-time translation services.

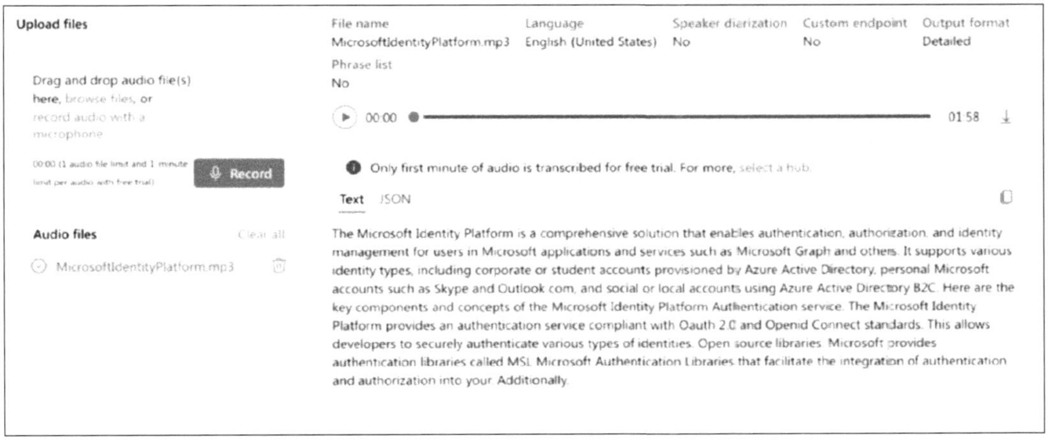

Figure 9.13: *Speech to Text Using Azure AI Speech Services*

Features of Speech Recognition

Speech recognition systems offer advanced capabilities that enable machines to interpret and transcribe spoken language with high accuracy. These features include:

- **Speaker Adaptation:** Learns from a user's voice for improved accuracy
  - *Example*: A transcription tool becomes more accurate as it adapts to an individual's accent and speech patterns.
- **Noise Cancellation:** Filters out background noise for clearer recognition
  - *Example*: A voice assistant accurately understands commands in a noisy kitchen.
- **Multilingual Support:** Recognizes and transcribes speech in multiple languages
  - *Example*: A meeting transcription service that supports English, Spanish, and Mandarin inputs
- **Real-Time Processing:** Converts speech to text instantaneously
  - *Example*: Live captioning during a video conference
- **Context Awareness:** Improves accuracy by interpreting the context of words and phrases
  - *Example*: Differentiates between "bank" (financial institution) and "bank" (riverbank) based on sentence context

Features of Speech Synthesis

Speech synthesis systems provide the following five primary features that make text-to-speech technology highly effective:

- **Natural-Sounding Voices:** Generates lifelike and expressive speech using neural AI models
  - *Example*: Virtual assistants like Alexa that provide human-like responses
- **Custom Voice Generation:** Allows users to create unique voice personas tailored to specific needs
  - *Example*: A brand that develops a signature voice for its advertisements
- **Emotion-Based Speech:** Modulates tone and emotion (for example, happy, sad, neutral) to match content
  - *Example*: An e-learning app that uses varied tones to emphasize key concepts

- **Multilingual Speech Output:** Produces speech in multiple languages to serve global audiences
    - *Example:* A navigation app that provides directions in English, Mandarin, and Hindi
- **Speech Speed and Pitch Control:** Allows users to adjust the speed and pitch of speech output for better comprehension
    - *Example:* A language learning app that lets users slow down speech when practicing pronunciation

Understanding Speech Recognition

Speech recognition involves converting spoken words into text using a combination of acoustic modeling, linguistic processing, and deep learning models. The process follows these steps:

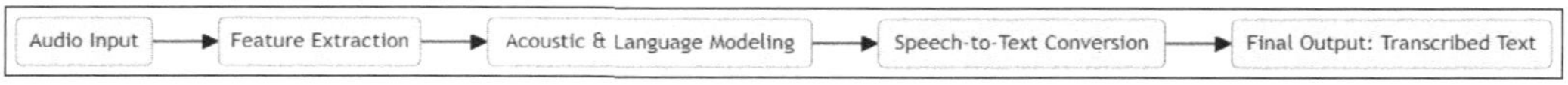

Figure 9.14: *Steps in Speech Recognition*

Step 1: Audio Input

a. The system receives **audio input** through a microphone or pre-recorded file.

b. *Example:* Speaking to **Siri** or dictating a message on a smartphone

Step 2: Feature Extraction

a. The speech waveform is broken down into **smaller acoustic features** (for example, phonemes).

b. Spectral analysis is used to analyze **pitch, frequency, and tone**.

Step 3: Acoustic and Language Modeling

a. Acoustic models map speech sounds to phonemes (smallest sound units).

b. Language models use probability-based word predictions to improve recognition.

Example:

- Spoken input: "*What is the weather like today?*"
- Transcribed text: "*What is the weather like today?*" (ASR output)

Step 4: Speech-to-Text Conversion

- The system uses deep learning models (for example, Hidden Markov Models, Transformer-based models) to convert phonemes into words and sentences.
- The final text is formatted for punctuation and grammar corrections.

Understanding Speech Synthesis

Speech synthesis, or Text-to-Speech (TTS), converts written text into spoken words using linguistic analysis and voice modeling.

Figure 9.15: *Process Steps in Speech Synthesis*

Step 1: Text Processing

a. The input text is analyzed, and **words are broken down into phonemes**.

b. Example: The system **converts "Dr." into "Doctor"** when spoken.

Step 2: Prosody Modeling

a. The system adds **intonation, pitch, and rhythm** to simulate natural speech. This step ensures that synthesized voices sound expressive and human-like, rather than robotic.

b. **Prosody modeling** refers to the process of analyzing and reproducing the **melodic and rhythmic patterns of speech**. In other words, it is about how tone, speed, and emphasis vary throughout an utterance. It helps convey emotions, intentions, and distinguish sentence types, **for example, questions versus statements**.

c. *Example*: Rising intonation for questions ("*What time is it?*")

Step 3: Speech Generation

a. The text is synthesized using concatenative or parametric speech models.

Types of Speech Synthesis

- **Concatenative TTS**
  - Uses pre-recorded human speech segments
  - Produces **high-quality**, but **less flexible** speech
  - *Example*: **GPS voice navigation**
- **Parametric TTS**
  - Uses AI-generated voices
  - More flexible and customizable
  - *Example*: **Google Assistant's speech output**
- **Neural TTS (NTTS)**
  - Uses deep learning models (for example, Tacotron, WaveNet) to create human-like speech
  - *Example*: Amazon Polly or Azure AI Speech

Applications of Speech Recognition and Synthesis

Speech recognition and synthesis have transformed industries by enabling voice-driven AI interactions, improving accessibility, and enhancing user experiences.

Virtual Assistants and Smart Speakers: Speech recognition powers AI systems like Siri, Alexa, and Google Assistant, which enables seamless interaction through voice commands.

Example:

User: "*Set an alarm for* 7 AM."

Assistant: "*Alarm set for* 7 AM."

Automated Transcription Services: Speech-to-text technology converts spoken content into written text, which simplifies documentation for meetings, interviews, and lectures.

Example: Platforms like **Otter.ai**, **Rev**, and **Azure Speech-to-Text** transcribe audio into editable text.

Accessibility for Visually and Hearing Impaired Users: Speech recognition and synthesis make technology more inclusive for individuals with disabilities.

- **Speech-to-Text:** Converts spoken dialogue into captions for hearing-impaired users
- **Text-to-Speech (TTS):** Reads written content aloud for visually impaired individuals

Example: Screen readers like **JAWS**, **NVDA**, and **VoiceOver** enhance accessibility by converting text into speech.

Call Center Automation: AI-driven interactive voice response (IVR) systems streamline customer service by automating queries and routing calls.

Example: When you come across directions like "Press 1 for account balance," the system transcribes responses and directs your calls to the appropriate department.

Language Learning and Pronunciation Training: Speech synthesis and recognition aid in language education by offering real-time feedback on pronunciation and listening exercises.

Example: Apps like **Duolingo** use Text-to-Speech (TTS) to provide instructions and practice.

Real-Time Translation: Speech recognition enables instant translation of spoken languages, breaking communication barriers across the globe.

Example: **Google Translate Live Speech Translation** provides instant spoken translations during conversations conducted in foreign languages.

Exam Tip: *When a question describes **voice-based systems** such as **virtual assistants**, **speech-to-text**, or **text-to-speech**, it refers to **Speech Recognition and Synthesis**, both of which are key NLP workloads in Azure AI Services.*

Challenges in Speech Recognition and Synthesis

Despite significant advancements, speech recognition and synthesis still face challenges that impact their accuracy, usability, and inclusivity across different applications. Some of them are mentioned as follows:

- **Accents, Dialects, and Pronunciation Variability:** It struggles with accurately transcribing diverse accents and non-standard pronunciations, thus limiting accessibility.
- **Background Noise and Audio Quality:** Environmental noise, overlapping speech, and poor audio quality reduce recognition accuracy, especially in real-world scenarios.
- **Homophones and Context Ambiguity:** It encounters difficulty in distinguishing words with identical pronunciation but different meanings (for example, "two" vs. "too" vs. "to").
- **Ethical and Privacy Concerns:** It faces persistent issues around voice data collection, storage, and concerns about surveillance and regulatory compliance.
- **Expressiveness in Speech Synthesis:** AI-generated voices often lack emotional variation and natural intonation, which can make interactions feel robotic.
- **Limited Support for Low-Resource Languages:** Less widely spoken languages receive inadequate support due to a lack of high-quality training data.

These challenges highlight the ongoing efforts needed to refine speech recognition and synthesis as they ensure that these advents become more inclusive, accurate, and ethically responsible.

Identify Features and Uses for Translation in NLP

Translation is a fundamental NLP capability that enables machines to **convert text or speech from one language to another**. With advancements in **machine learning and deep learning**, modern translation systems have now evolved from simple word-to-word conversions to **context-aware and grammatically accurate** translations.

Machine Translation (MT) is widely used in global communication, business localization, customer support, and cross-language content accessibility. Technologies like Neural Machine Translation (NMT), transformer-based models (for example, Google Translate, Microsoft Translator, OpenAI's GPT), and multilingual NLP models have dramatically improved the accuracy and fluency of translation efforts.

Figure 9.16: *Translating Text or Speech Using Google Translate*

Features of Translation Technology

Translation models are designed to provide high-quality, contextually accurate translations across multiple languages and use cases. Here are few of their features:

- **Context-Aware Translations:** Analyzes sentence structure and surrounding context to determine the most appropriate translation, thus improving fluency and reducing ambiguity
- **Multilingual Support:** Supports translation across dozens to hundreds of languages, enabling global communication and accessibility
- **Voice and Speech Translation:** Converts spoken words into another language, thereby facilitating real-time multilingual conversations
- **Real-Time Translation:** Processes and delivers translations instantaneously for live interactions like virtual meetings and chat applications
- **Customization:** Allows businesses to train domain-specific translation models, ensuring accuracy for industry-specific terminology in fields like healthcare, finance, and law

Understanding Machine Translation

Machine translation uses AI and NLP to process and translate text while preserving the meaning, grammar, and context.

Key Steps in Translation:

1. **Text Input:** The user enters text in one language.
2. **Tokenization and Parsing:** The text is split into **words or phrases** and analyzed for **grammar and structure**.
3. **Semantic Analysis:** The system determines the **meaning** of the input text

4. **Translation Model:** The model maps the input language to the target language.
5. **Post-Processing:** Grammar corrections and refinements improve fluency.

Example:

- **English:** "*How are you today?*"
- **Spanish:** "*¿Cómo estás hoy?*"
- **French:** "*Comment ça va aujourd'hui?*"

The translation model ensures that the context, tone, and grammar remain intact.

Applications of Machine Translation

MT technology is widely used across industries to facilitate global communication, enhance accessibility, and streamline cross-language interactions.

Real-Time Language Translation: Machine translation enables live translation during meetings and conferences, while facilitating seamless communication between participants speaking different languages. This is especially useful in:

- Translating conversations in multilingual meetings
- Facilitating global collaboration during international conferences
- Providing real-time subtitles in online events

Example: Microsoft Teams provides real-time translation for multilingual conference calls.

Cross-Language Customer Support: Businesses leverage machine translation to deliver instant support in multiple languages, improving customer satisfaction. This is especially useful in:

- Translating customer queries in real-time
- Assisting global customers in understanding product documentation
- Resolving issues across diverse regions without language barriers

Example: Zendesk, Freshdesk, and Microsoft Translator provide instant translations for customer interactions.

Localization for Global Businesses: Machine translation helps companies adapt their websites, applications, and documents to cater to different regions. This is especially useful in:

- Translating e-commerce websites for international customers
- Localizing mobile apps and digital tools
- Making product manuals available in regional languages

Example: Netflix and Amazon localize their content and platforms for various regions.

Travel and Tourism: Machine translation assists travelers in communicating effectively, making navigation and interaction in foreign countries easier. This is especially useful in:

- Translating signs and menus in real-time
- Enabling conversations between tourists and locals
- Providing language support during guided tours

Example: Google Translate's camera feature instantly translates signs and menus for tourists.

Exam Tip: *If a question mentions **converting text or speech from one language to another**, the correct answer is **Machine Translation**. Translation enables **cross-language communication** and **global accessibility** in NLP workloads.*

Challenges in Machine Translation

While machine translation has improved significantly with the help of deep learning and neural networks, several challenges remain unaddressed when it comes to ensuring accuracy, cultural relevance, and inclusivity across different languages. These challenges are mentioned as follows:

- **Accuracy and Contextual Understanding:** Struggles with preserving meaning in complex sentences, idioms, slang, and domain-specific terms. Literal translations often lead to awkward or incorrect interpretations.
- **Low-Resource Language Support:** Most advancements focus on major languages, leaving lesser-known ones with limited or inaccurate translations due to a lack of bilingual datasets.
- **Cultural Sensitivity and Localization:** Direct translations may miss cultural nuances, humor, and formalities, requiring proper adaptation for context and audience.
- **Grammar and Syntax Differences:** Structural variations between languages create challenges in maintaining grammatical accuracy and natural phrasing.
- **Ambiguity and Polysemy:** Words with multiple meanings (for example, "bank" as a financial institution vs. riverbank) can cause misinterpretations without enough context.
- **Real-Time and Low-Latency Processing:** Instant translation for live conversations and subtitles requires balancing speed and accuracy while maintaining fluency.

These challenges highlight the complexities of translation in NLP and the ongoing advancements that are required to make it more accurate, inclusive, and context-aware across all languages.

Tools for Natural Language Processing (NLP)

NLP requires robust tools and platforms to handle diverse tasks, ranging from text preprocessing to advanced applications like sentiment analysis and language modeling. The following is an overview of some widely used tools and platforms for NLP:

Cloud-Based Services

Cloud-based AI services have revolutionized the way organizations build and deploy NLP solutions. Instead of developing models from scratch, developers can now leverage pre-trained models and APIs offered by major cloud providers. These services provide scalability, flexibility, and seamless integration with existing applications, while enabling businesses to perform tasks like sentiment analysis, translation, and entity recognition at scale with due efficiency.

Azure AI Services for Language

- Offers pre-trained models for key NLP tasks such as sentiment analysis, key phrase extraction, entity recognition, and translation
- Provides scalable APIs for easy integration into applications
- Supports multilingual data and customizable solutions for domain-specific needs

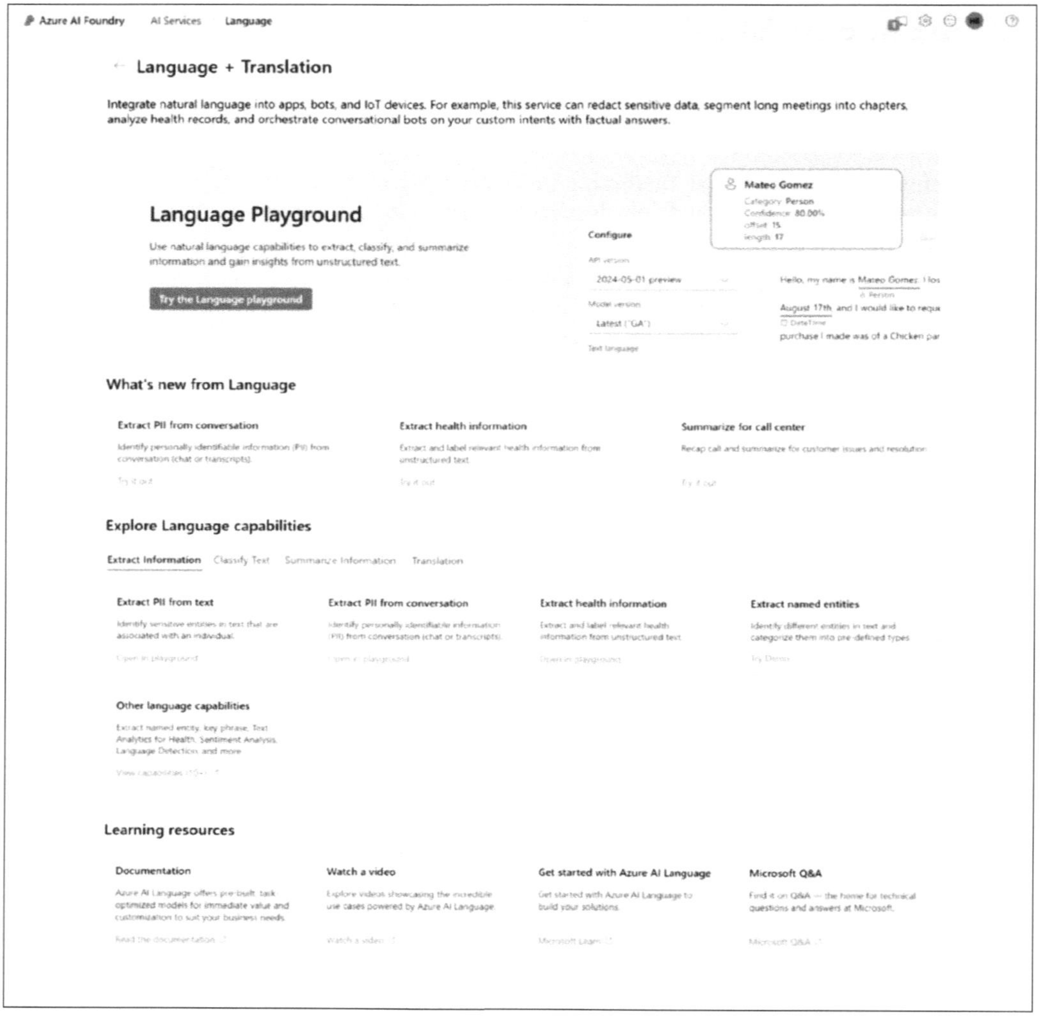

Figure 9.17: *Azure AI Services for Language in Azure AI Foundry Portal*

Google Cloud Natural Language

- Supports entity analysis, syntax analysis, and text classification
- Includes pre-trained models optimized for scalability and integration

Python Libraries

Python is the go-to language for NLP due to its rich ecosystem of libraries and frameworks.

spaCy

- Provides pipelines for text preprocessing, entity recognition, and dependency parsing
- Known for its speed and efficiency, with pre-trained models for various languages
- Can be customized for domain-specific NLP tasks

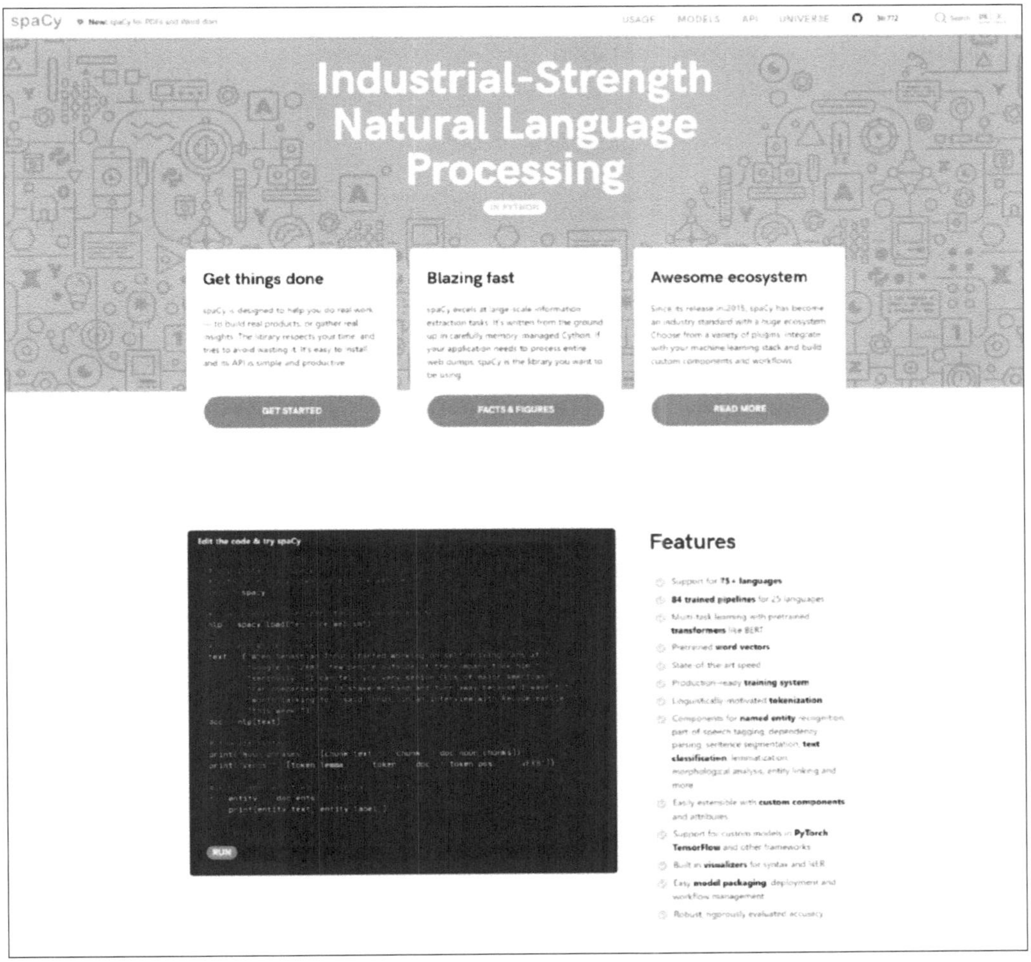

Figure 9.18: *The spaCy Official Website*

NLTK (Natural Language Toolkit)

- Offers tools for tokenization, stemming, lemmatization, and more
- Is suitable for educational and research purposes due to its comprehensive documentation and ease of use

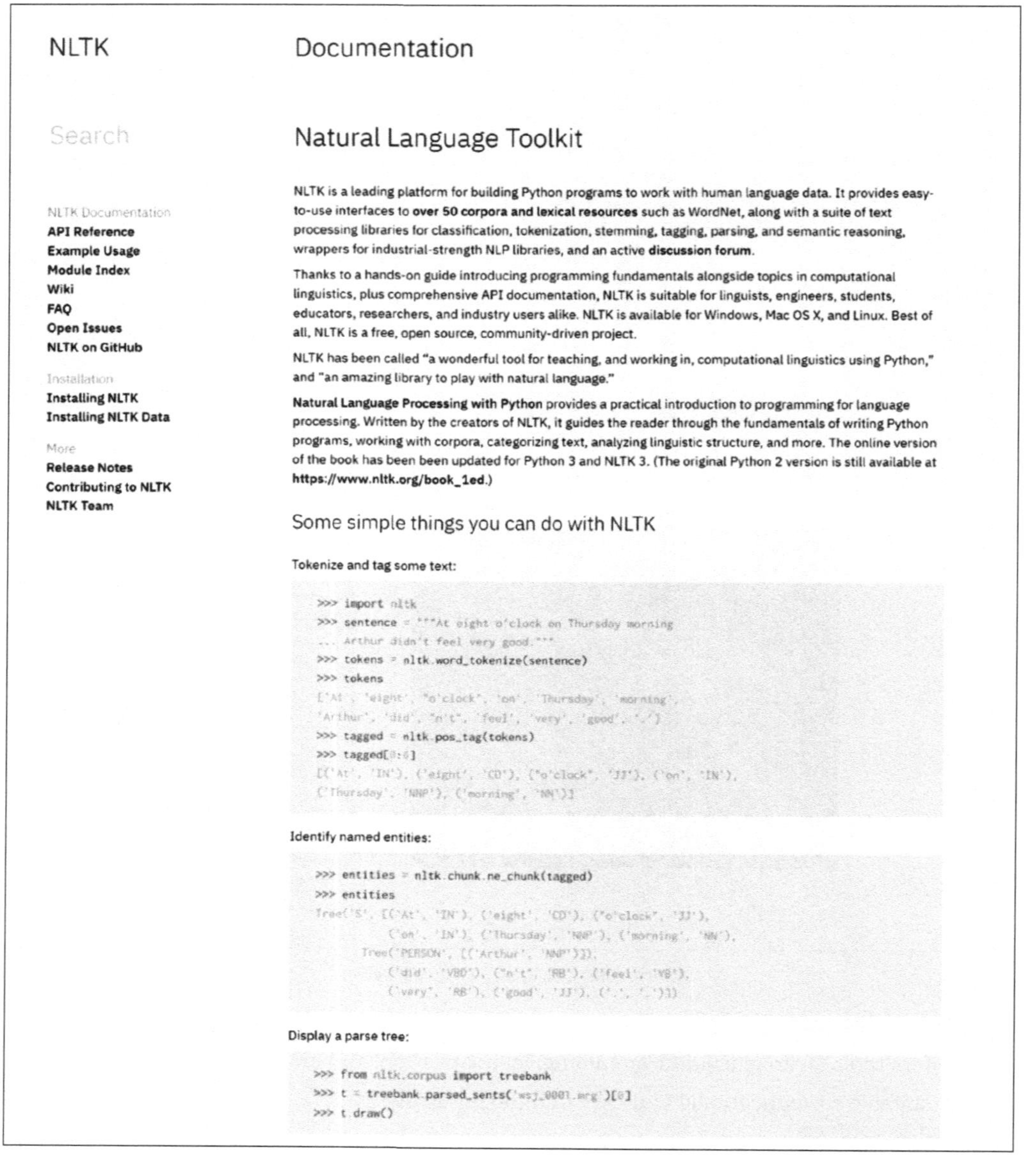

Figure 9.19: *The NLTK Official Website*

Transformers (Hugging Face)

- Facilitates access to state-of-the-art transformer-based models such as BERT, GPT, and T5
- Provides pre-trained models and tools for fine-tuning on specific datasets

Figure 9.20: *Hugging Face Official Website*

Custom Models

Organizations can develop custom NLP models tailored to their specific requirements using the following machine learning frameworks:

TensorFlow

- Supports the creation and training of custom NLP models for tasks such as sentiment analysis or language generation
- Offers TensorFlow Text, a library for preprocessing text data

Example Use Case:

- Building a domain-specific model for analyzing legal documents

PyTorch

- Provides a flexible and dynamic environment for developing NLP models
- Popular for research and production due to its ease of experimentation

Example Use Case:

- Creating a language translation model optimized for rare dialects

Visualization and Annotation Tools

Annotation and visualization are crucial for preparing training data and understanding NLP model outputs. Some tools used for this purpose are:

Prodigy

- A data annotation tool that streamlines the labeling process for NLP tasks such as entity recognition and text classification.

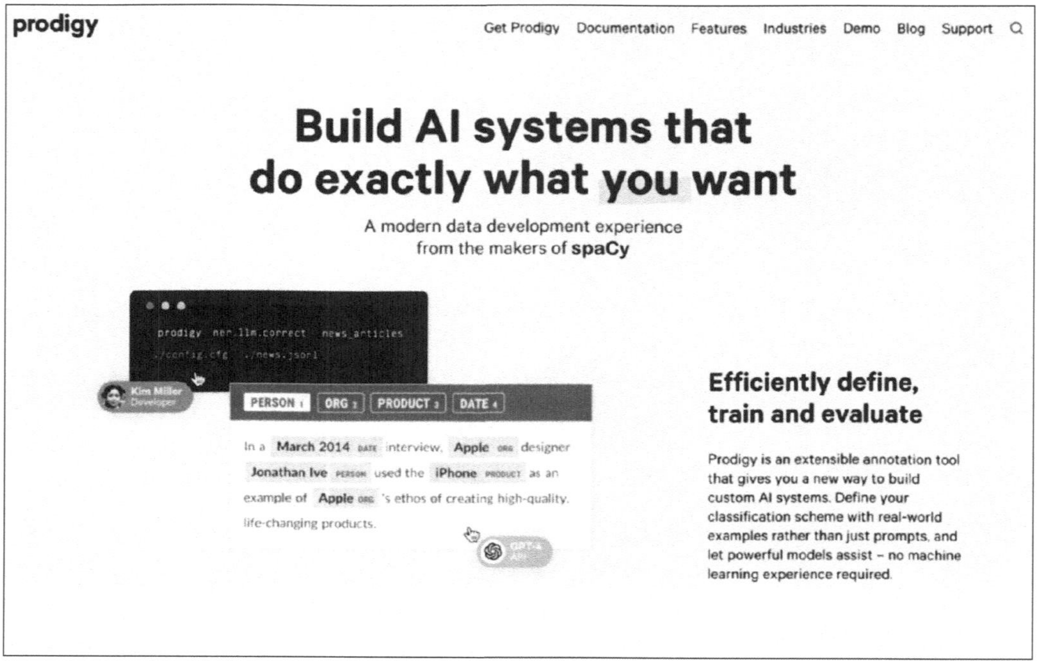

Figure 9.21: *Prodigy Official Website*

WordCloud

- Visualizes the frequency of words in text data using intuitive word clouds.

Integrated Development Environments (IDEs) and Platforms

Integrated Development Environments (IDEs) and cloud-based platforms play a crucial role in modern NLP development. They provide interactive interfaces that allow developers and data scientists to write, execute, and visualize code efficiently. These tools streamline experimentation with machine learning models, simplify data processing workflows, and enable seamless integration with popular AI libraries such as TensorFlow, PyTorch, and Hugging Face. By combining accessibility and computational power, IDEs and platforms accelerate the end-to-end development of NLP solutions.

Jupyter Notebooks

- Provides an interactive environment for developing, visualizing, and experimenting with NLP models
- Ideal for integrating libraries such as spaCy, Hugging Face, and TensorFlow

Google Colab

- Cloud-based platform for running Python code, offering free GPU and TPU access for NLP model training

Conclusion

In this chapter, we explored the core concepts and practical applications of Natural Language Processing (NLP), focusing on how machines can understand, interpret, and generate human language. We examined key workloads such as key phrase extraction, entity recognition, sentiment analysis, language modeling, speech recognition and synthesis, and machine translation, which address unique challenges in processing and analyzing text and speech data.

By understanding these concepts, you are now equipped to:

- Identify and select the most suitable NLP workload for your specific use case.
- Recognize how data quality, linguistic diversity, and model architectures influence NLP performance and reliability.
- Implement effective strategies to enhance model accuracy, scalability, and ethical compliance.
- Integrate NLP capabilities into broader AI workflows using modern tools and services.

These foundational skills will enable you to design and deploy intelligent solutions that transform unstructured language data into actionable insights, empowering automation, accessibility, and innovation across industries.

In the next chapter, we will explore how to leverage **Azure tools and services for NLP workloads**, while learning how to build, deploy, and scale language-based applications efficiently using Azure's robust ecosystem of AI capabilities.

Points to Remember

- **Key Phrase Extraction** identifies the most relevant terms in a text, improving summarization, searchability, and content categorization.
- **Entity Recognition** extracts structured data from unstructured text by identifying names, organizations, dates, and locations. It is instrumental in applications like document indexing and compliance monitoring.
- **Sentiment Analysis** determines the emotional tone of a text, while helping businesses analyze customer feedback, monitor brand perception, and enhance decision-making.
- **Language Modeling** enables predictive text, chatbots, and text generation by recognizing linguistic patterns and context, thus improving human-computer interactions.
- **Speech Recognition** converts spoken words into text, enabling voice-driven applications such as virtual assistants, automated transcription, and accessibility tools.
- **Speech Synthesis (Text-to-Speech)** transforms written text into natural-sounding speech, thus enhancing accessibility and improving voice-based applications.
- **Machine Translation** facilitates communication across languages, while supporting multilingual customer service, content localization, and global collaboration.
- **Challenges in NLP** include handling ambiguous language, thereby ensuring contextual accuracy, mitigating bias, and improving support for low-resource languages.

Understanding these key NLP concepts and their applications will help in selecting the right solutions for different use cases, improving efficiency and user experiences in various domains.

Key Terms

- **Natural Language Processing (NLP):** The field of AI that enables computers to understand, interpret, and generate human language
- **Tokenization:** The process of breaking text into words, phrases, or sentences for analysis
- **Part-of-Speech Tagging (POS Tagging):** Assigns grammatical categories (noun, verb, adjective) to words in a sentence
- **Stop Words:** Common words (for example, "the", "and", "is") that are often removed in text processing to improve analysis
- **Lemmatization:** Reduces words to their base form (for example, "running" → "run") to improve text standardization
- **Stemming:** A simpler approach to lemmatization which consists of cutting words to their root (for example, "playing" → "play")
- **Key Phrase Extraction:** Identifies the most relevant terms in a text to improve search, summarization, and content categorization
- **Entity Recognition:** Detects and classifies entities such as names, locations, and dates within unstructured text
- **Sentiment Analysis:** Determines the emotional tone of a text, categorizing it as positive, negative, or neutral
- **Language Modeling:** Predicts the next word or phrase in a sentence using deep learning techniques for text generation and completion
- **Speech Recognition:** Converts spoken language into written text for applications like virtual assistants and automated transcription
- **Speech Synthesis (Text-to-Speech, TTS):** Transforms written text into natural-sounding speech, improving accessibility and voice interfaces
- **Machine Translation:** Automatically translates text between different languages using neural networks or statistical models
- **Contextual Embeddings:** Uses models like BERT and GPT to understand word meanings based on surrounding text for better language processing
- **Aspect-Based Sentiment Analysis (ABSA):** Analyzes sentiment related to specific aspects of a product, service, or topic rather than an entire text
- **Named Entity Recognition (NER):** A subset of entity recognition focused on identifying proper names in text, such as brands, companies, and people
- **Prosody Modeling:** In speech synthesis, adds natural variations in tone, pitch, and rhythm to make AI-generated speech more human-like
- **Low-Resource Languages:** Languages with limited NLP datasets that make translation, speech recognition, and other language tasks more challenging
- **Ambiguity in NLP:** Occurs when words or phrases have multiple meanings and requires additional contextual understanding to resolve the issues
- **Transformer Models:** Deep learning architectures like GPT and BERT that improve accuracy in NLP tasks such as translation, summarization, and chatbots

Multiple Choice Questions

1. What is the primary purpose of key phrase extraction in NLP?
    a. Translating text between different languages
    b. Identifying the most relevant terms in a document
    c. Converting speech to text
    d. Detecting emotions in customer feedback
2. Which of the following best describes entity recognition?
    a. Identifying and classifying key elements such as names, dates, and locations in text
    b. Analyzing customer emotions from reviews and social media posts
    c. Predicting the next word in a sentence using deep learning
    d. Translating spoken words into text
3. What is a major challenge in sentiment analysis?
    a. Recognizing numerical data in a document
    b. Understanding sarcasm and contextual ambiguity
    c. Translating low-resource languages accurately
    d. Extracting key phrases from structured data
4. Which NLP technique is used to generate human-like text and predict words in a sentence?
    a. Speech synthesis
    b. Machine translation
    c. Language modeling
    d. Sentiment analysis
5. Which of the following is an example of speech synthesis (Text-to-Speech)?
    a. Converting audio recordings into text
    b. Translating a document into another language
    c. Reading written content aloud using AI-generated speech
    d. Extracting key phrases from a news article
6. What is the primary benefit of machine translation in NLP?
    a. Extracting entities such as names and locations from text
    b. Converting spoken words into text
    c. Enabling communication between people who speak different languages
    d. Identifying sentiment in social media posts

7. Which of the following is a common challenge in speech recognition?
    a. Handling multiple translations in a single document
    b. Distinguishing between homophones in spoken language
    c. Identifying images within a text document
    d. Extracting structured data from an unstructured dataset
8. What role does contextual embeddings (for example, BERT, GPT) play in NLP?
    a. Improve the accuracy of language models by understanding word meanings based on surrounding text
    b. Generate synthetic speech from text input
    c. Detect and remove bias in AI-generated translations
    d. Extract numerical values from financial documents

Answers

1. b
2. a
3. b
4. c
5. c
6. c
7. b
8. a

Chapter 10
Identify Azure Tools and Services for NLP Workloads

Introduction

In this chapter, we will explore fundamental concepts of Natural Language Processing (NLP) solutions and their practical applications. As organizations and individuals increasingly rely on textual and spoken data for a variety of operations and integrate new innovations like voice assistants and chatbots, understanding how to extract meaningful information efficiently becomes critical. NLP solutions enable us to interpret, categorize, and analyze text and speech, thus unlocking value across countless industries.

We will begin by examining the Azure AI Language service, which has capabilities like text analysis, sentiment detection, and named entity recognition. These features are essential for extracting insights from unstructured text and improving decision-making processes. Next, we will delve into the Azure AI Speech service, which supports speech-to-text, text-to-speech, and real-time translation. This service plays an important role in enhancing accessibility and enabling seamless cross-lingual communication.

Thus, by the end of this chapter, you will gain a comprehensive understanding of these essential Azure NLP tools. You will learn about their key features, ideal usage scenarios, and the potential challenges associated with their implementation. With this knowledge, you will be equipped to select and deploy the most appropriate NLP solutions for a variety of real-world applications.

Structure

In this chapter, we will discuss the following topics:

- Capabilities of the Azure AI Language Service
- Capabilities of the Azure AI Speech Service

Capabilities of the Azure AI Language Service

The Azure AI Language Service is a comprehensive suite of tools that enables businesses and developers to analyze and process textual data efficiently. It has powerful Natural Language Processing (NLP) capabilities to extract insights, understand sentiments, classify content, and enhance search functionality. By leveraging machine learning models, Azure AI Language enables organizations to build intelligent applications that can comprehend human language at scale.

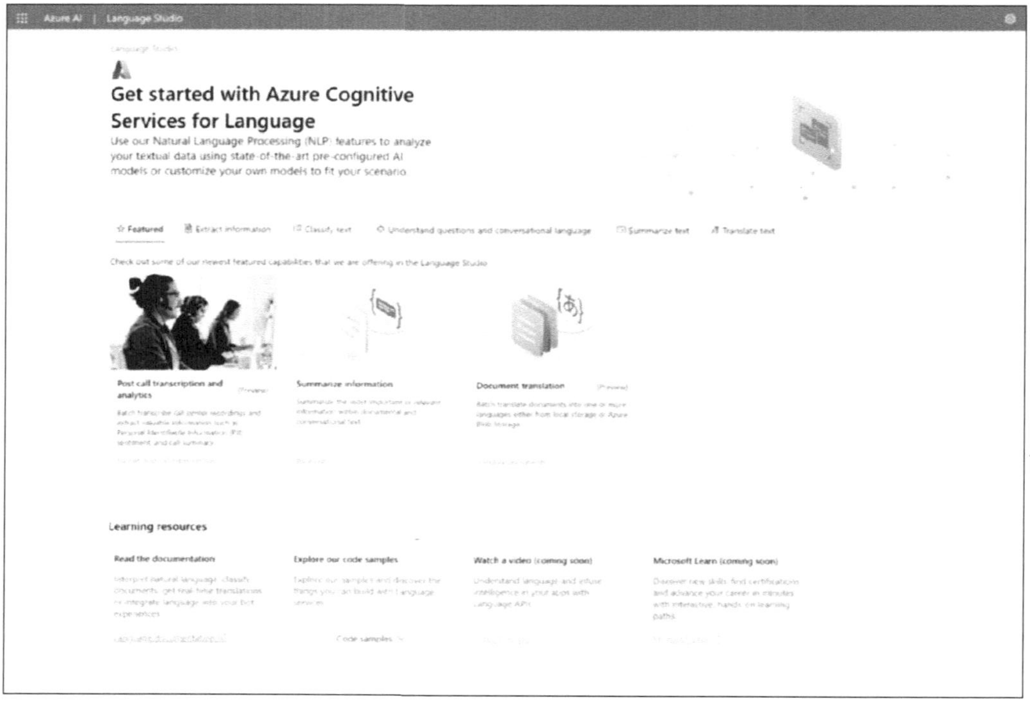

Figure 10.1: *Azure AI Language Portal*

Key Features of Azure AI Language Service

Azure AI Language Service provides a range of functionalities designed to extract meaningful insights from text, automate data processing, and enhance business intelligence. These features help organizations handle large volumes of unstructured text efficiently and are also useful in automated customer support, document classification, and real-time content analysis.

Text Analytics

Azure AI Language offers text analytics that provides deep insights into textual content. This feature includes:

- **Key Phrase Extraction:** Identifies the most important phrases in a document to summarize key points efficiently
- **Sentiment Analysis:** Evaluates the emotional tone of a piece of text, classifying it as positive, neutral, or negative
- **Opinion Mining:** Extracts subjective information from text, helping businesses understand customer opinions at a granular level
- **Language Detection:** Automatically detects the language of a given text, supporting multilingual applications

Named Entity Recognition (NER)

NER identifies specific entities such as names, dates, locations, and product names within unstructured text. This allows businesses to:

- Improve content categorization and tagging
- Extract relevant details from legal and financial documents

- Enhance search engine indexing by understanding contextual meaning

Question Answering (Q and A)

This feature extracts answers from structured and unstructured content, allowing organizations to create smart FAQ systems and virtual assistants. It can:

- Find precise answers from a body of documents
- Enable conversational AI applications to deliver accurate responses
- Improve customer support by automating question-answer interactions

Custom Text Classification and Custom Named Entity Recognition

Organizations with domain-specific needs can create and train their own models to:

- Categorize text based on business requirements
- Identify unique entity types that are not covered in the pre-built NER models
- Improve workflow automation by recognizing specialized content types

Use Cases of Azure AI Language Service

- **Enhancing Customer Support:** By integrating sentiment analysis and question-answering capabilities, businesses can automate customer interactions, providing instant and relevant responses based on user queries.
- **Streamlining Document Processing:** Legal firms and financial institutions can use NER and text analytics to extract critical information from contracts, reports, and regulatory documents, reducing manual processing time.
- **Improving Search and Content Management:** Search engines and knowledge management systems can leverage key phrase extraction and text classification to deliver more relevant search results and improve content discoverability.

Exam Tip: *Azure AI Language includes multiple prebuilt features such as Sentiment Analysis and Named Entity Recognition. Custom models are only needed when domain-specific entities or categories are required.*

Hands-on Exercise - A Practical Guide to Text Analysis with Language Studio

In this exercise, you will explore the capabilities of Azure AI Language by analyzing example hotel reviews. You will use Language Studio to determine whether reviews are mostly positive or negative, while applying key NLP concepts.

Step 1: Create a Language Resource

1. Open the Azure portal, and log in with your Microsoft account.
2. Click `+Create a resource` and search for `Language service`.

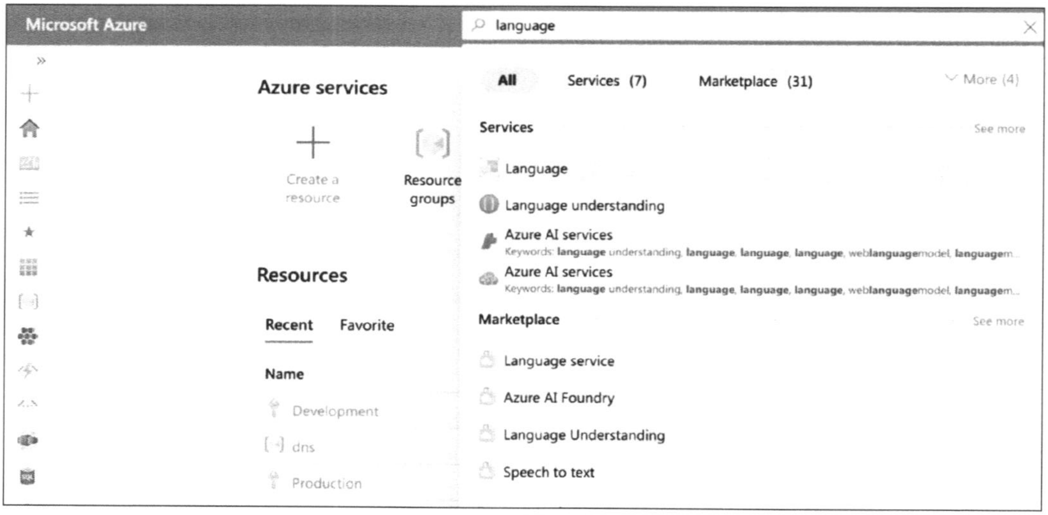

Figure 10.2: Search for Language Service

3. Select **`Create`**, configure the service, and deploy it with the following settings:
   a. **`Subscription`:** Your Azure subscription
   b. **`Resource Group`:** Select or create one
   c. **`Region`:** Choose the nearest data center
   d. **`Name`:** Provide a unique name
   e. **`Pricing Tier`:** Free F0 or a standard tier
4. Click **`Review + create`**, then **`Create`** and wait for deployment.

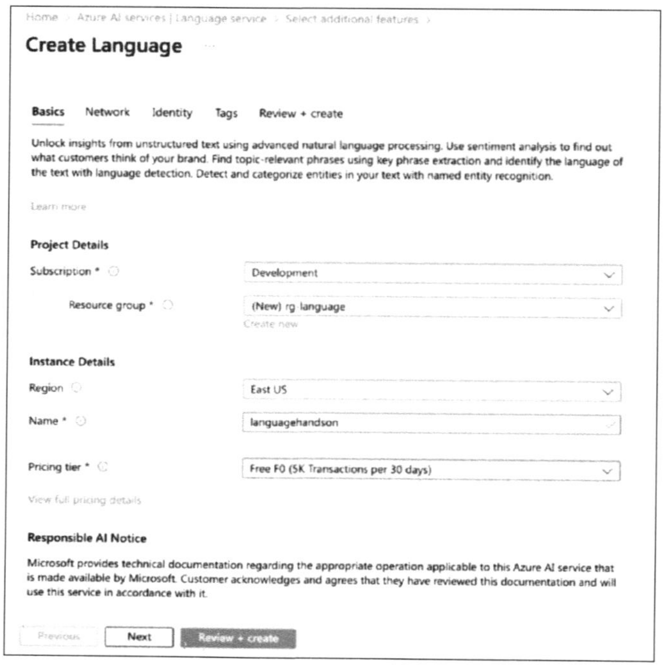

Figure 10.3: Create Language Service in Azure Portal

Step 2: Configure Language Studio

1. Open Language Studio (https://language.cognitive.azure.com/) in a new tab.
2. When prompted, configure:
    - `Azure Directory`: Default
    - `Azure Subscription`: Select your active subscription
    - `Resource Type`: `Language`
    - `Resource Name`: Select the Language service you created
3. Click **Done**.

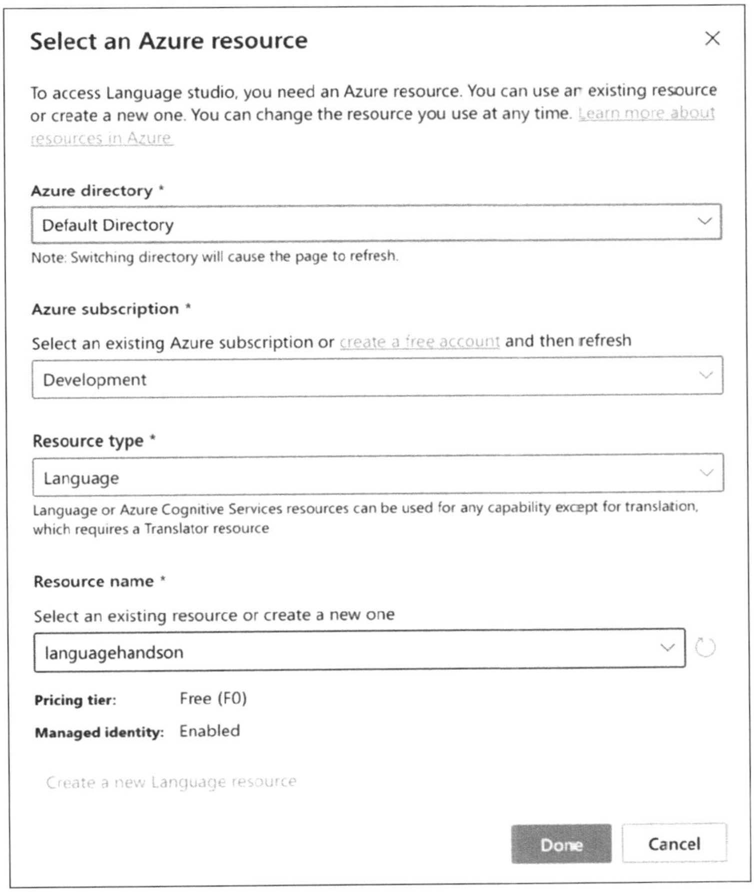

***Figure 10.4**: Select Your Azure Source in Language Studio*

Step 3: Analyze Sentiment and Opinions

1. In Language Studio, select `Classify text`, then `Analyze sentiment and mine opinions`.

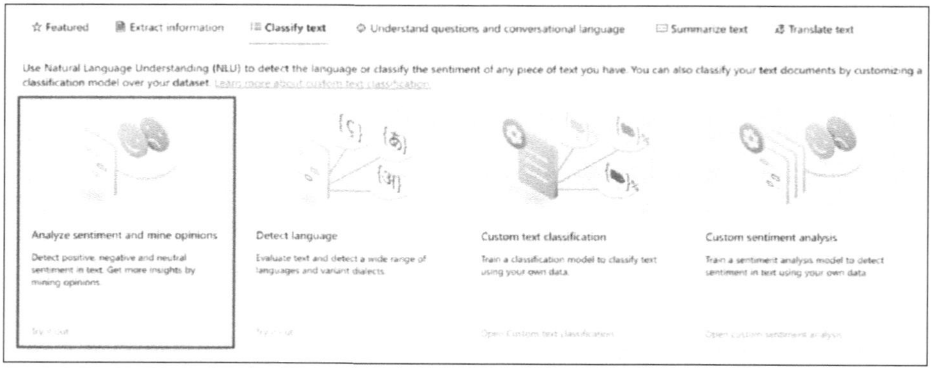

Figure 10.5: *Select Analyse Sentiment and Mine Opinions Option*

2. Select **`English`** under **`Select text language`**.
3. Select your Azure resource and paste the following review into the text box:

```
"Disappointing Service and Food
The Gourmet Haven, Los Angeles, USA
02/02/2025
I had high hopes for The Gourmet Haven, but unfortunately, it didn't live up
to the expectations. Despite having a reservation, we waited nearly 40
minutes to be seated. The service was slow and inattentive, making the
experience frustrating.
The food was underwhelming. The seafood pasta was bland, and the chicken dish
was dry and lacking seasoning. Given the high prices, I expected much better
quality.
While the ambiance was nice, the poor service and mediocre food left much to
be desired. I won't be returning."
```

Figure 10.6: *Enter Some Text to Sentiment and Opinion Mining*

4. Acknowledge the costs and click **Run** to analyze the text.
5. Review the output, including:
    a. Overall sentiment analysis
    b. Sentence-by-sentence sentiment classification
    c. Confidence scores for positive, neutral, and negative sentiments

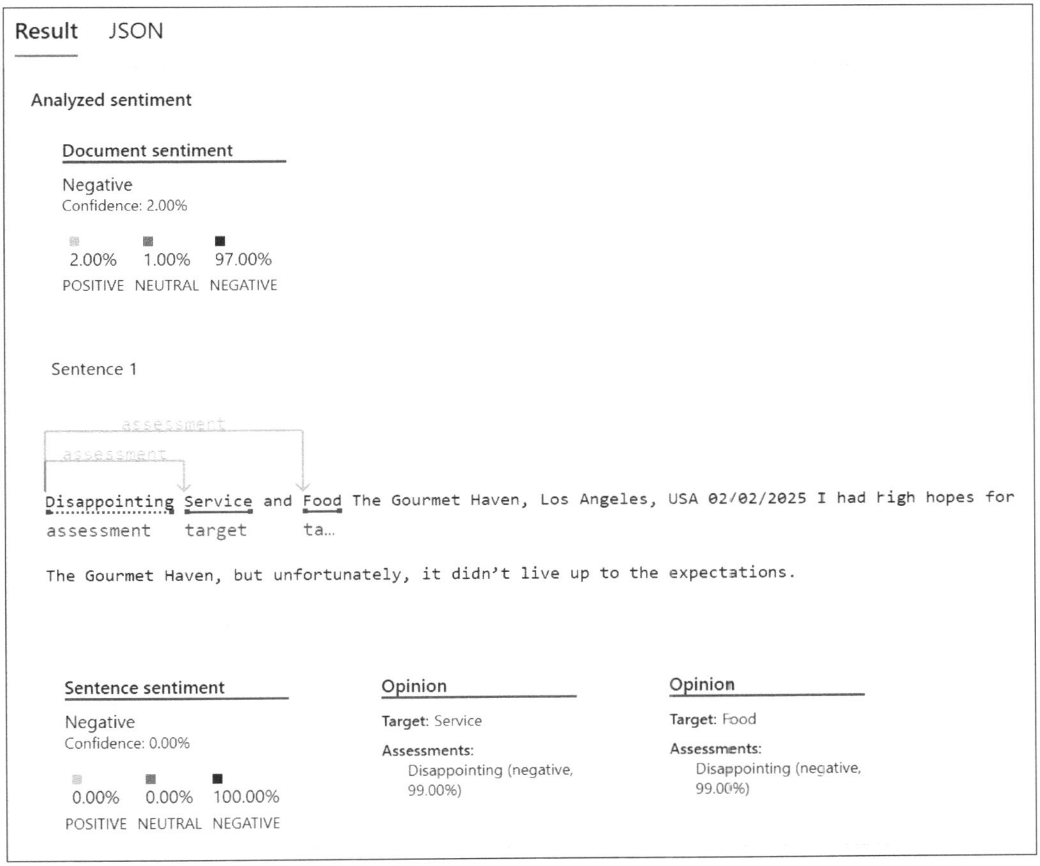

Figure 10.7: *Sentiment and Opinion Mining Result*

6. Go to **JSON** tab to view the detailed results.

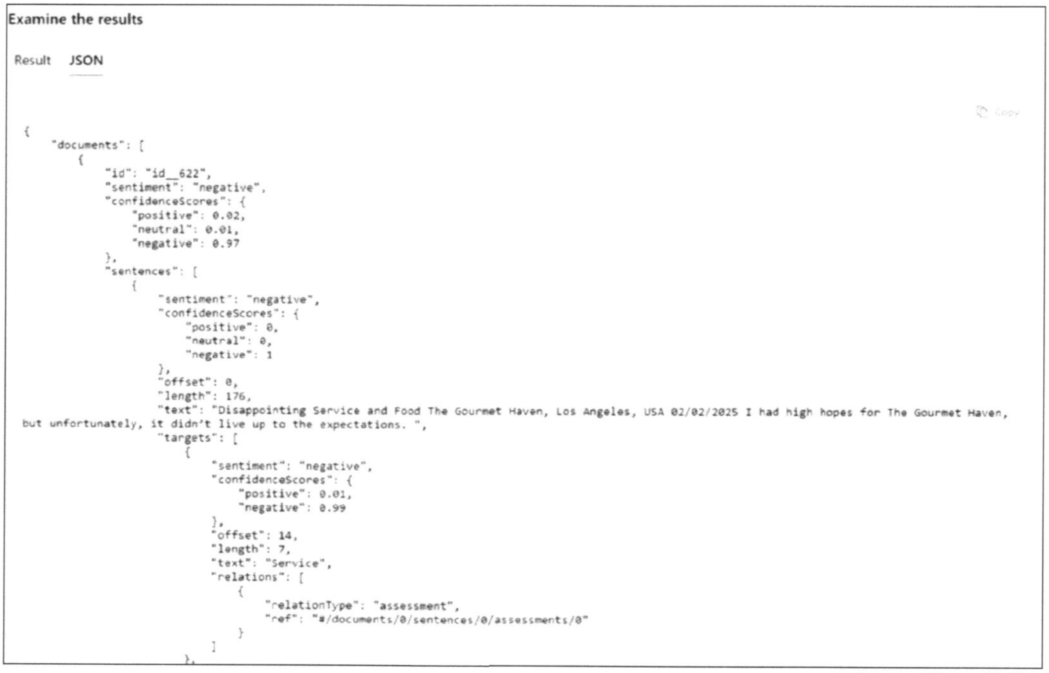

Figure 10.8: *Sentiment and Opinion Mining JSON Result*

Example Analysis for Review 1

- **Document Sentiment:** Negative
    - Positive: 2.00%
    - Neutral: 1.00%
    - Negative: 97.00%
- Sentence-Level Analysis:
    - **Sentence:** "`Disappointing Service and Food The Gourmet Haven, Los Angeles, USA 02/02/2025 I had high hopes for The Gourmet Haven, but unfortunately, it didn't live up to the expectations.`"
        - **Sentiment:** Negative
        - **Confidence:** 100.00%
- **Opinion Mining:**
    - **Target:** Service
        - **Assessment:** Disappointing
        - **Sentiment:** Negative
        - **Confidence:** 99.00%
    - **Target:** Food
        - **Assessment:** Disappointing
        - **Sentiment:** Negative
        - **Confidence:** 99.00%

Step 4: Compare Sentiment Results with Different Reviews

1. Clear the text box and paste the following review:

```
"Fantastic Dining Experience
The Gourmet Haven, Los Angeles, USA
02/02/2025
From the moment I walked in, The Gourmet Haven exceeded my expectations. The
ambiance was warm and elegant, perfect for a relaxing evening. The service was
exceptional—attentive but never intrusive.
The highlight was the food. The ribeye steak was perfectly cooked, and the
truffle risotto was bursting with flavor. The dessert, a rich chocolate soufflé,
was the perfect way to end the meal. Every detail was thoughtfully executed.
Highly recommended for anyone looking for a top-tier dining experience. I'll
definitely be back!"
```

2. Acknowledge the costs and click **Run**.
3. Review and compare the sentiment analysis results to the previous review:

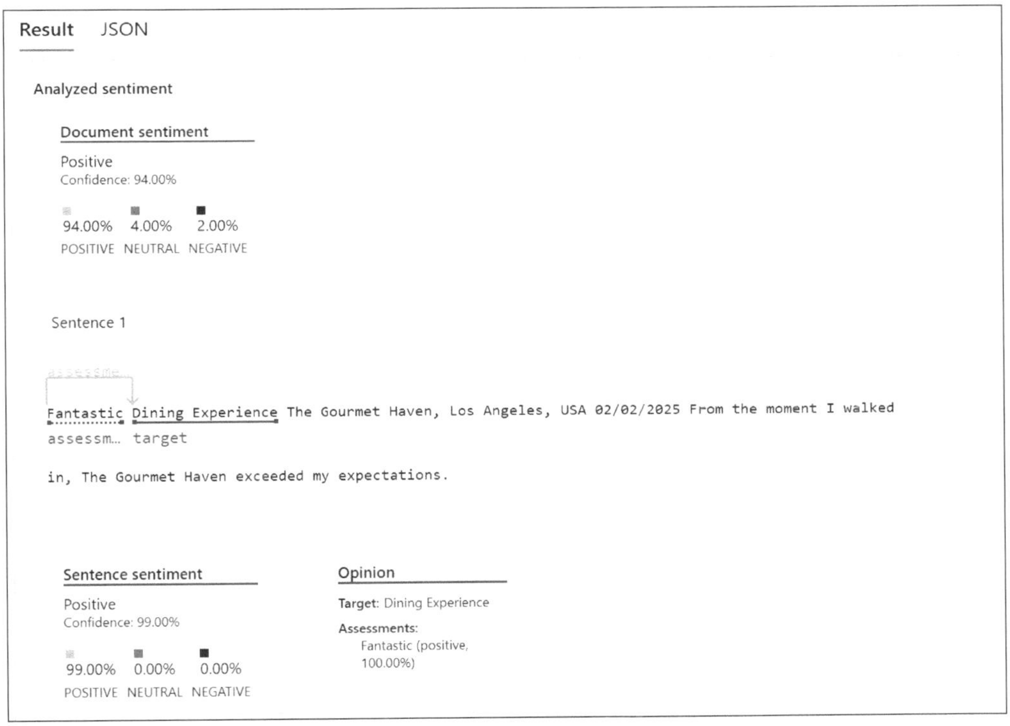

***Figure 10.9**: Sentiment and Opinion Mining Result*

Example Analysis for Review 2

- **Document Sentiment:** Positive

  Confidence Levels:

  - Positive: 94.00%
  - Neutral: 4.00%
  - Negative: 2.00%

- **Sentence-Level Analysis**
  - **Sentence:** "`Fantastic Dining Experience The Gourmet Haven, Los Angeles, USA 02/02/2025 From the moment I walked in, The Gourmet Haven exceeded my expectations.`"
    - **Sentiment:** Positive
    - **Confidence:** 99.00%
- **Opinion Mining**
  1. **Target:** Dining Experience
  - **Assessment:** Fantastic
  - **Sentiment:** Positive
  - **Confidence:** 100.00%

Observation:

- The negative review had a document sentiment of **97% negative** and identified specific issues with service and food.
- The positive review showed a **94% positive sentiment**, highlighting outstanding aspects such as ambiance, service, and food quality.

Step 5: Clean Up Resources

1. If you no longer need the Language resource, delete it in the Azure portal to avoid extra costs.
2. Navigate to the resource group, select the Language service, and click **Delete**.

This hands-on activity demonstrated the Azure AI Language Service's ability to accurately analyze text, detect sentiment, and identify key opinion targets within a document. By using the tools provided in Language Studio, businesses can gain actionable insights from unstructured text data to improve decision-making and customer interactions.

Capabilities of the Azure AI Speech Service

The Azure AI Speech Service is a cloud-based offering that enables applications to process and understand human speech. It provides capabilities for speech-to-text, text-to-speech, speech translation, and speaker recognition, making it an essential tool for businesses looking to build voice-enabled applications, enhance accessibility, and improve communication efficiency. By leveraging cutting-edge machine learning models, the service ensures high accuracy and adaptability across multiple use cases.

Figure 10.10: *Speech Studio Portal*

Key Features of Azure AI Speech Service

Azure AI Speech Service delivers a comprehensive set of features designed to enhance voice interactions, transcribe audio content, and provide natural-sounding synthesized speech. These capabilities support various industries, including customer service, healthcare, finance, and accessibility applications.

Speech-to-Text (STT)

This feature converts spoken language into written text with high accuracy. The Speech-to-Text API supports multiple languages and can be customized to recognize domain-specific vocabulary, improving transcription quality. The key benefits include:

- Automatic transcription of meetings, interviews, and customer interactions
- Real-time voice input for applications such as virtual assistants and automated support systems
- Custom speech models that enhance recognition for industry-specific terminology

Text-to-Speech (TTS)

Text-to-Speech technology converts written text into natural-sounding spoken audio. It supports various voices and languages, making it ideal for accessibility tools, audiobooks, and automated phone systems. Key capabilities include:

- Neural voice synthesis for human-like speech quality
- Custom voice models that allow businesses to create branded voice experiences
- Support for multiple languages and regional accents

Speech Translation

Azure AI Speech Translation enables real-time spoken language translation, making cross-lingual communication seamless. This feature is particularly useful for global enterprises, multilingual customer support, and accessibility solutions. Benefits include:

- Instant translation of spoken content into multiple target languages
- Customizable translation models for industry-specific terminology
- Support for transcription and subtitle generation in multimedia applications

Speaker Recognition

This capability allows applications to identify and authenticate users based on their unique voice patterns. Speaker recognition can enhance security and enable personalized interactions in voice-driven applications. Key advantages include:

- Voice authentication for secure access to applications and services
- Speaker diarization to distinguish multiple speakers in a conversation
- Adaptive models that improve recognition over time with continued use

Exam Tip: *Azure AI Speech offers real-time speech-to-text and text-to-speech. Remember that you can build custom neural voices for branded experiences.*

Use Cases of Azure AI Speech Service

- **Enhancing Customer Support:** Businesses can implement speech-to-text and text-to-speech capabilities in their customer service workflows to automate responses, transcribe support calls, and improve chatbot interactions, thereby enhancing customer satisfaction and operational efficiency.
- **Improving Accessibility:** Organizations can leverage Azure AI Speech Service to create solutions for individuals with disabilities. Text-to-speech technology enables screen readers, while speech recognition allows users with limited mobility to interact with applications using voice commands.
- **Enabling Real-Time Translation:** Multinational companies and event organizers can deploy speech translation features to break down language barriers, providing real-time translation for meetings, conferences, and customer interactions.
- **Strengthening Security with Voice Authentication:** Financial institutions, healthcare providers, and enterprise security systems can utilize speaker recognition to implement secure voice authentication, ensuring that only authorized individuals can access sensitive information and services.

Hands-on Exercise - Practical Guide to Speech Analysis with Azure AI Speech

In this exercise, you will explore the capabilities of Azure AI Speech by analyzing recorded speech samples. You will use Speech Studio to transcribe, synthesize, and translate spoken content.

Step 1: Create a Speech Resource

1. Open the Azure portal (https://portal.azure.com) and log in with your Microsoft account.
2. Click `+Create a resource` and search for `Speech service`.

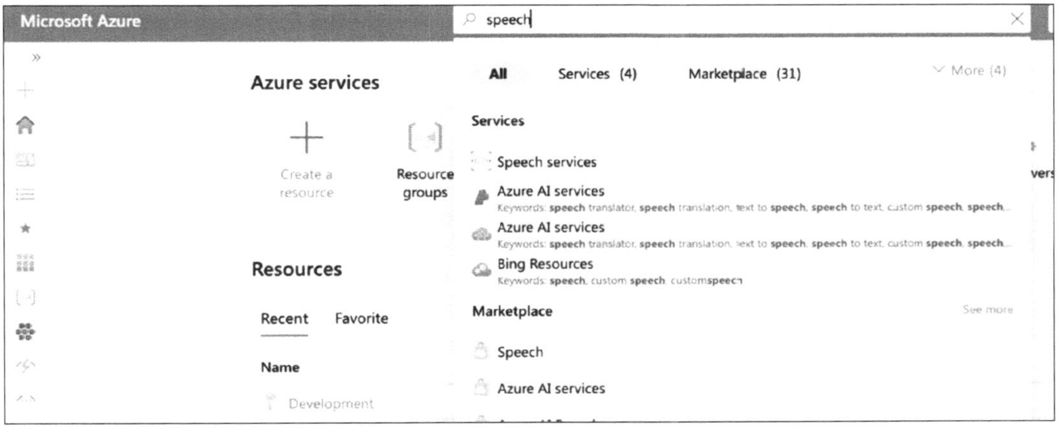

Figure 10.11: *Search for Speech Service*

3. Select **`Create`**, configure the service, and deploy it with the following settings:
   a. **`Subscription`:** Your Azure subscription
   b. **`Resource group`:** Select or create one
   c. **`Region`:** Choose the nearest data center
   d. **`Name`:** Provide a unique name
   e. **`Pricing tier`:** Free F0 or a standard tier

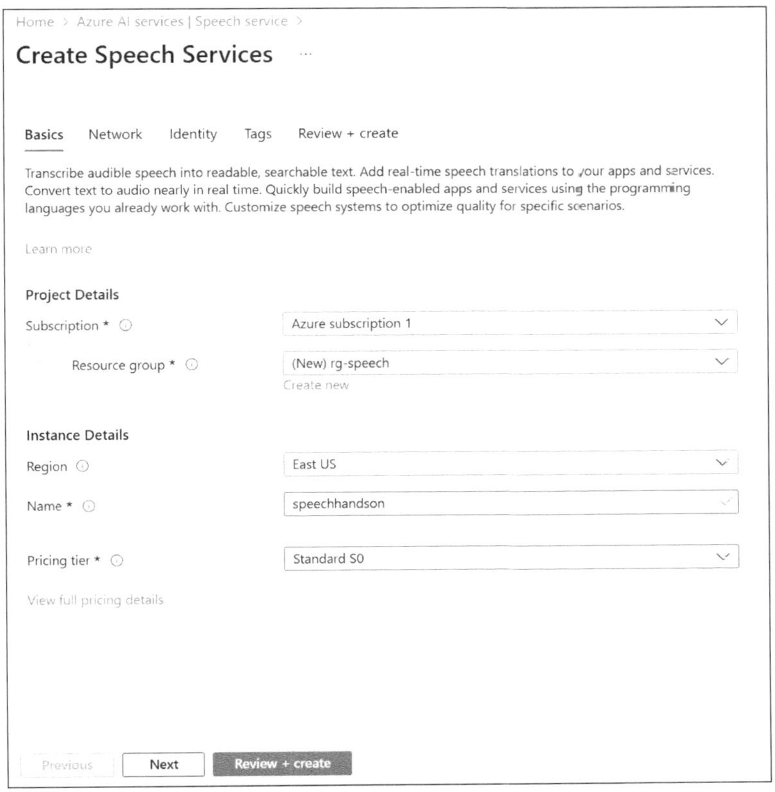

Figure 10.12: *Create Speech Service in Azure Portal*

4. Click **`Review + create`**, then **`Create`** and wait for deployment.

Step 2: Configure Speech Studio

1. Open Speech Studio (https://speech.microsoft.com/) in a new tab.
2. When prompted, configure:
    a. **Azure Directory:** Default
    b. **Azure Subscription:** Select your active subscription
    c. **Resource Type: Speech**
    d. **Resource Name:** Select the Speech service you created
3. Click **`Done`**.

Step 3: Perform Speech-to-Text Transcription

1. In Speech Studio (https://speech.microsoft.com/), select **`Real-time speech to text`**.
2. Choose your Azure resource and language (for example, English).
3. Upload an audio file or use the microphone for live speech input.
4. Click **`Run`** to transcribe the audio.
5. Review the output, including recognized text and confidence scores.

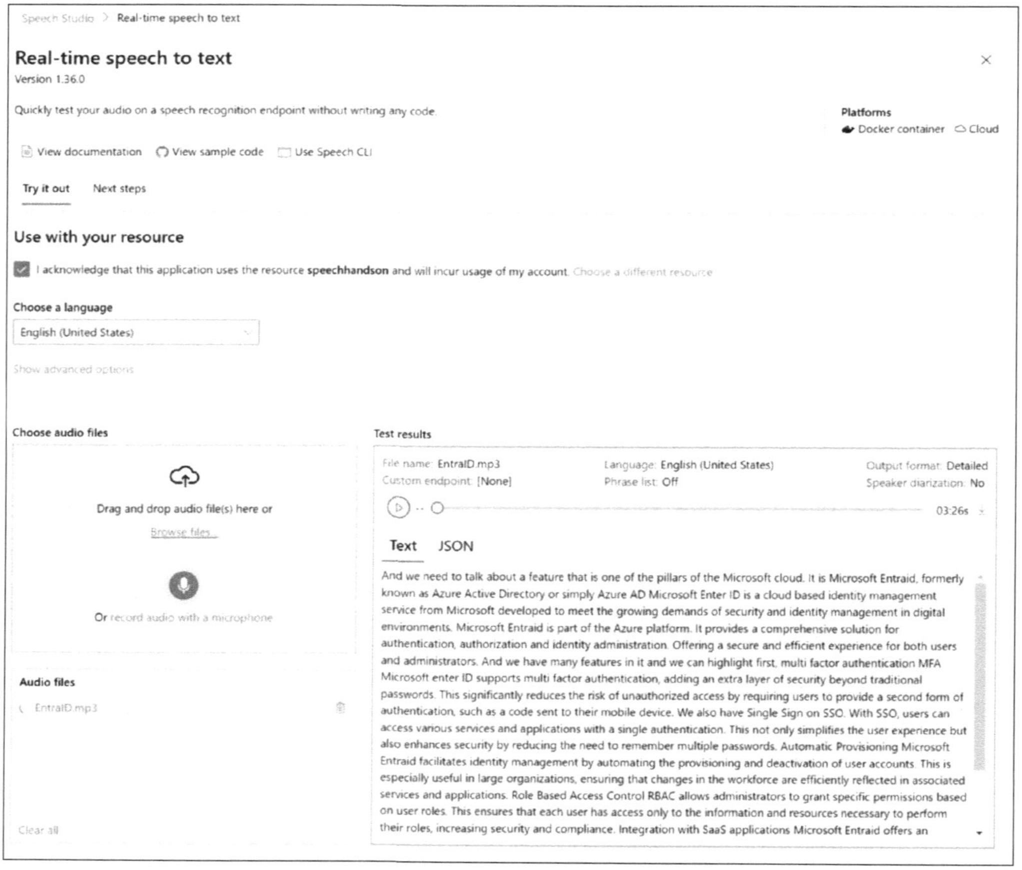

Figure 10.13: *Real-Time Speech to Text Result*

Step 4: Generate Speech from Text

a. Navigate to the **`Text to Speech`** session in Speech Studio,

b. Select **`Voice Gallery`**.

c. Select a neural voice and adjust parameters such as speed and pitch.

d. Enter a sample text, such as: `Welcome to Azure AI Speech! This powerful service allows applications to convert speech to text, text to speech, and even translate spoken language, enabling seamless integration of natural-sounding speech capabilities into your solutions.`

e. Click **`Play`** to generate speech and listen to the output.

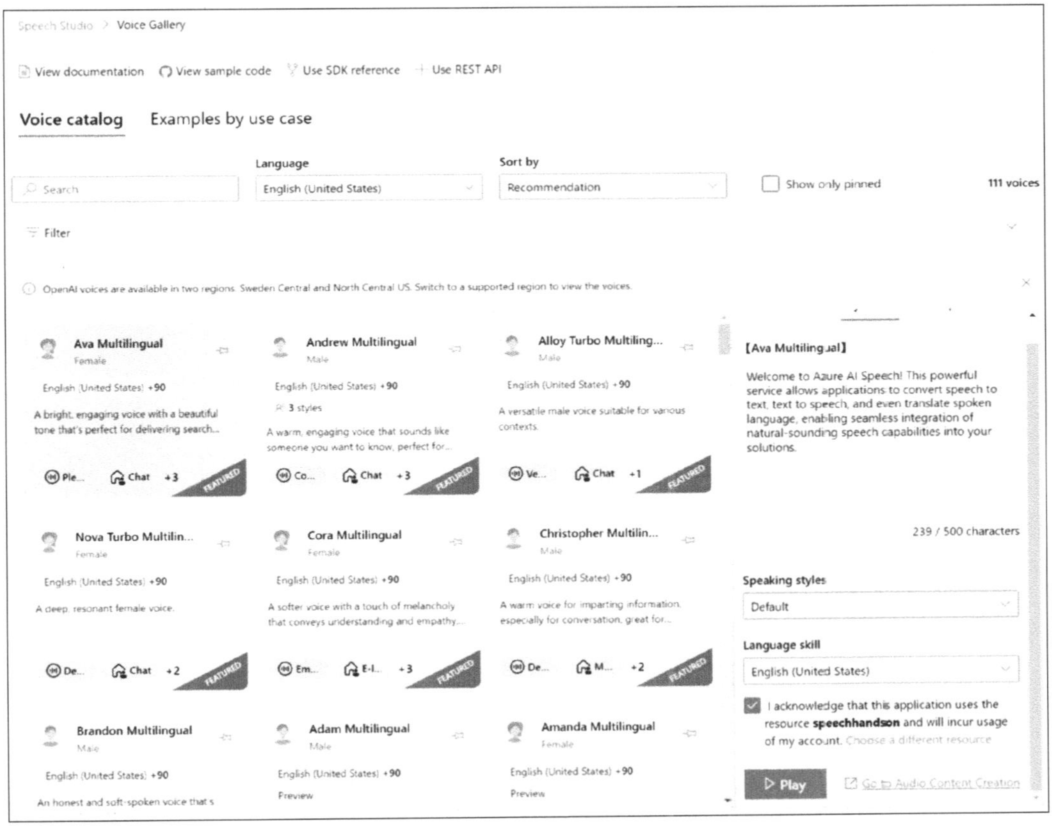

Figure 10.14: *Generate Speech Result*

Step 5: Translate Speech in Real-Time

1. Open the **`Speech Translation`** tool in Speech Studio.
2. Select input and output languages (for example, English to Spanish).
3. Upload an audio file or use live speech input.
4. The audio will be automatically transcribed and played in the Spanish language with the selected voice.
5. Review the translated text and synthesized speech output.

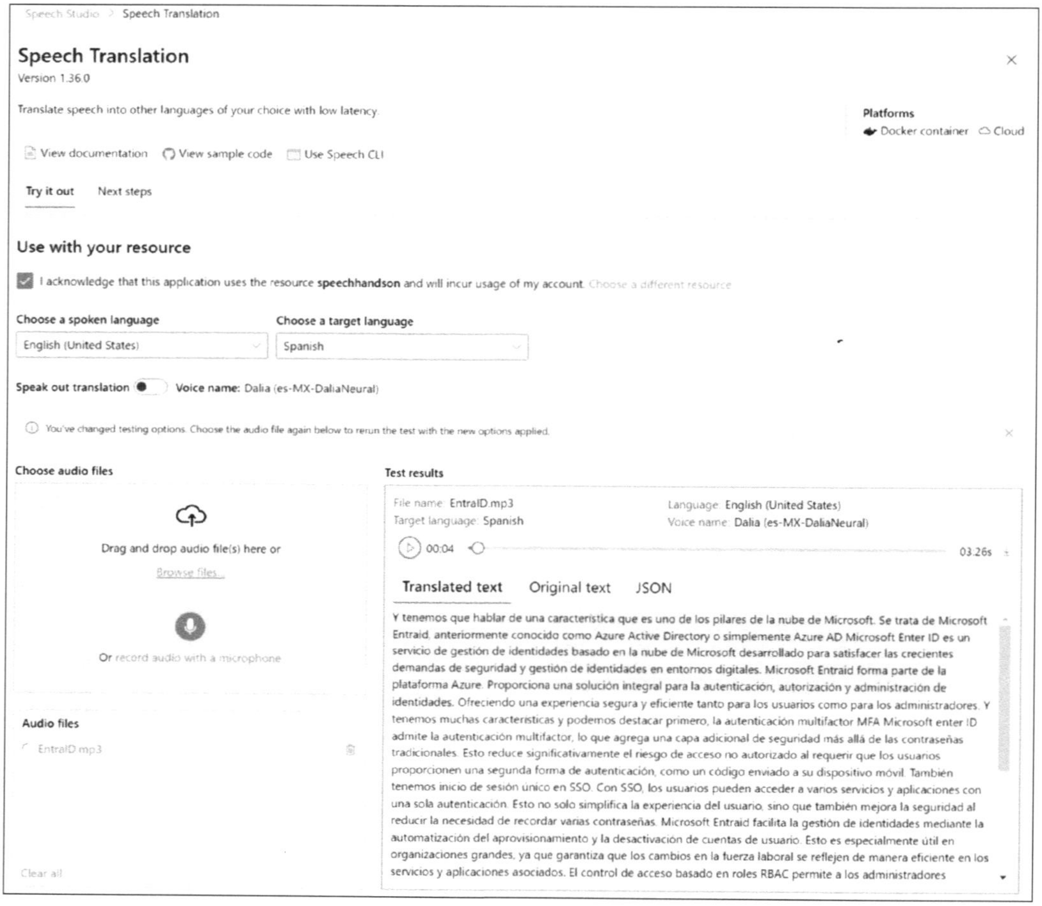

Figure 10.15: *Speech Translation Result*

Step 6: Clean up Resources

1. If you no longer need the Speech resource, delete it in the Azure portal to avoid extra costs.
2. Navigate to the resource group, select the Speech service, and click **`Delete`**.

Azure AI Speech Service provides powerful capabilities for converting, generating, and translating speech. By integrating these features, businesses can improve accessibility, automate interactions, and enhance communication experiences across various industries.

The following table summarizes the main differences and use cases between Azure AI Language and Azure AI Speech services:

Feature / Capability	**Azure AI Language Service**	**Azure AI Speech Service**
Primary Function	Analyzes and interprets written text to extract insights and meaning.	Processes and understands spoken language for transcription, synthesis, and translation.
Key Features	Text Analytics, Sentiment Analysis, Key Phrase Extraction, Named Entity Recognition, Custom Text Classification.	Speech-to-Text (STT), Text-to-Speech (TTS), Speech Translation, Speaker Recognition.

Input Type	Textual data (documents, reviews, messages).	Audio input (microphone, recordings).
Output Type	Structured text insights, categorized entities, sentiment results.	Transcribed text, synthesized speech, translated audio.
Customization Options	Custom Text Classification and Custom NER models.	Custom Speech and Neural Voice models.
Common Use Cases	Customer feedback analysis, document classification, knowledge mining.	Virtual assistants, accessibility solutions, real-time translation, call transcription.
Integration Tools	Azure Language Studio, SDKs, REST APIs.	Azure Speech Studio, SDKs, REST APIs.

***Table 10.1:** Comparison of Azure AI Language and Azure AI Speech Services*

Thus, by comparing the Azure AI Language and Azure AI Speech services, it becomes clear that both play complementary roles in enabling Natural Language Processing solutions. While the Language service focuses on understanding and interpreting written text, the Speech service bridges the gap between spoken and written communication. Together, they form the foundation for building intelligent, multilingual, and accessible applications that can process and respond to human language in all its forms.

Conclusion

In this chapter, we explored how Azure AI Language and Speech services help machines understand and process human language. From text analytics and sentiment analysis to speech recognition and translation, these tools enable businesses to create intelligent, accessible, and multilingual solutions.

We began with the **Azure AI Language Service**, which offers capabilities such as text analytics, sentiment analysis, named entity recognition, and custom text classification. These features enable organizations to extract actionable insights from unstructured data, automate repetitive tasks, and improve content management. Next, we delved into the **Azure AI Speech Service**, highlighting features such as speech-to-text, text-to-speech, speech translation, and speaker recognition. These tools provide robust solutions for creating voice-enabled applications, improving multilingual communication, and enhancing user accessibility.

Additionally, we learned about the practical applications of these services, including customer support automation, accessibility enhancements, and real-time translation. By adopting these technologies, organizations can optimize operations, improve customer experiences, and unlock new avenues for innovation.

By understanding these tools, you are now equipped to:

- Choose and implement the right Azure AI solutions for specific business needs.
- Leverage the strengths of NLP and speech technologies to enhance productivity.
- Optimize AI-driven solutions for accuracy, scalability, and efficiency.

As advancements in NLP and AI-powered speech continue to evolve, their role in shaping automation, communication, and data analysis will only grow. Staying informed about these innovations will ensure that businesses can effectively leverage them to remain competitive and achieve sustainable success.

In the next chapter, we will explore the core features of Generative AI solutions and understand how they enable machines to create original content–from text and images to code and audio–thus, transforming the way humans and AI collaborate.

Points to Remember

- **Azure AI Language Service** offers robust natural language processing capabilities, including text analytics, sentiment analysis, named entity recognition, and custom text classification. It enables businesses to derive insights from unstructured data and streamline workflows.
- **Text Analytics** provides features like key phrase extraction, sentiment analysis, language detection, and opinion mining to help businesses understand and act on customer feedback, classify documents, and enhance search relevance.
- **Named Entity Recognition (NER)** identifies and categorizes entities like names, dates, locations, and more within text, aiding in applications like automated data structuring and compliance monitoring.
- **Sentiment Analysis** helps organizations classify text as positive, negative, or neutral, offering valuable insights for decision-making, brand monitoring, and customer feedback management.
- **Azure AI Speech Service** delivers cutting-edge speech capabilities, including speech-to-text, text-to-speech, and real-time translation, enhancing multilingual communication and accessibility.
- **Speech-to-Text (STT)** accurately transcribes spoken words into text, improving efficiency in tasks such as call center automation, meeting transcriptions, and voice-command applications.
- **Text-to-Speech (TTS)** converts written text into natural-sounding spoken audio, ideal for accessibility tools, voice assistants, audiobooks, and automated customer service.
- **Speech Translation** facilitates real-time spoken language translation, enabling seamless multilingual communication for businesses, global events, and customer interactions.
- **Speaker Recognition** provides voice authentication and speaker diarization, enhancing security and personalization in voice-enabled applications.
- **Use Cases of Azure AI Services** include automating customer support, processing legal and financial documents, improving search functionality, and enabling real-time multilingual communication.
- **Challenges in NLP and Speech Solutions** include achieving high accuracy across languages, reducing AI bias in text and speech analysis, and ensuring scalability for real-time applications.

Therefore, by mastering these Azure AI Language and Speech capabilities, organizations can create intelligent, scalable solutions that enhance decision-making, improve efficiency, and deliver superior user experiences.

Key Terms

- **Azure AI Language Service:** A cloud-based platform that provides NLP capabilities, including sentiment analysis, named entity recognition, and custom text classification
- **Text Analytics:** A feature of Azure AI Language Service that extracts key phrases, detects language, performs sentiment analysis, and identifies topics in unstructured text data
- **Sentiment Analysis:** Analyzes the emotional tone of text, classifying it as positive, neutral, or negative to provide insights into customer feedback and opinions
- **Custom Text Classification:** Enables users to build and train machine learning models to categorize text based on custom business needs
- **Azure AI Speech Service:** A cloud-based service offering capabilities like speech-to-text, text-to-speech, speech translation, and speaker recognition for voice-driven applications
- **Speech-to-Text (STT):** Converts spoken language into written text with high accuracy, supporting transcription, virtual assistants, and voice commands

- **Text-to-Speech (TTS):** Converts text into natural-sounding speech, widely used for voice assistants, audiobooks, and accessibility tools
- **Speech Translation:** Provides real-time spoken language translation, allowing seamless multilingual communication for meetings, conferences, and customer support
- **Speaker Recognition:** Authenticates and identifies users based on their unique voice patterns, improving security and enabling personalized interactions
- **Real-Time Speech Processing:** Processes spoken input instantly, supporting applications like live captioning and conversational AI

Multiple Choice Questions

1. Which feature of Azure AI Language Service enables the extraction of key phrases from text?
    a. Speech-to-Text (STT)
    b. Sentiment Analysis
    c. Key Phrase Extraction
    d. Text-to-Speech (TTS)
2. What capability does Azure AI Speech Service provide for real-time communication?
    a. Text summarization
    b. Real-time speech translation
    c. Named Entity Recognition
    d. Sentiment analysis
3. What is the purpose of Speaker Recognition in Azure AI Speech Service?
    a. Authenticating users based on their unique voice patterns
    b. Synthesizing human-like speech for virtual assistants
    c. Translating speech in real-time
    d. Detecting key phrases in spoken content
4. Which Azure AI Language Service capability is best suited for analyzing customer opinions in reviews?
    a. Speech-to-Text (STT)
    b. Sentiment Analysis
    c. Speaker Recognition
    d. Text-to-Speech (TTS)

Answers

1. c
2. b
3. a
4. b

CHAPTER 11
Identify Features of Generative AI Solutions

Introduction

In this chapter, we will explore the foundational concepts of **Generative AI** and its wide-ranging applications. Unlike traditional AI models that analyze data and make predictions, generative AI is designed to create new and diverse outputs across multiple modalities, including text, images, audio, video, code, and music. This expanded capability is transforming industries by enabling multimodal experiences, intelligent copilots, and automation that blend creativity and reasoning.

We will begin by **identifying the key features of generative AI models**, such as how they work, their underlying architectures, and the types of tasks they can perform. Understanding the mechanics of these models, like Transformer-based architectures like GPT and diffusion models for image generation, will provide insights into their strengths and limitations.

Next, we will explore **common scenarios for generative AI**, covering real-world use cases such as automated content generation, conversational AI, image synthesis, code completion, and personalized recommendations. These applications are driving innovation in fields such as marketing, healthcare, finance, and entertainment, enabling businesses to improve efficiency and user engagement.

Additionally, we will examine the **responsible AI considerations** that come with deploying generative models. As these technologies become more advanced, ethical concerns such as bias, misinformation, intellectual property rights, and data privacy must be addressed to ensure fair and transparent AI usage.

By the end of this chapter, you will have a solid understanding of **how generative AI works, where it is most effectively applied, and the ethical implications surrounding its use**. This knowledge will help you evaluate and integrate generative AI solutions into various business and technological contexts.

Structure

In this chapter, we will discuss the following topics:

- Introduction to Generative AI
- Exploring Large Language Models (LLMs)
- Examining the Transformer Architecture
- Understanding Tokenization and Embeddings
- Identifying Features of Generative AI Models
- Identifying Common Scenarios for Generative AI
- Identifying Responsible AI Considerations for Generative AI

Introduction to Generative AI

Unless you have been completely disconnected in recent years, you must have heard of **Generative Artificial Intelligence (Generative AI)**. This technology powers services such as ChatGPT, enabling natural conversations and producing semi-original content. As **Generative AI continues to rise**, now is the perfect time to explore its applications and potential impact.

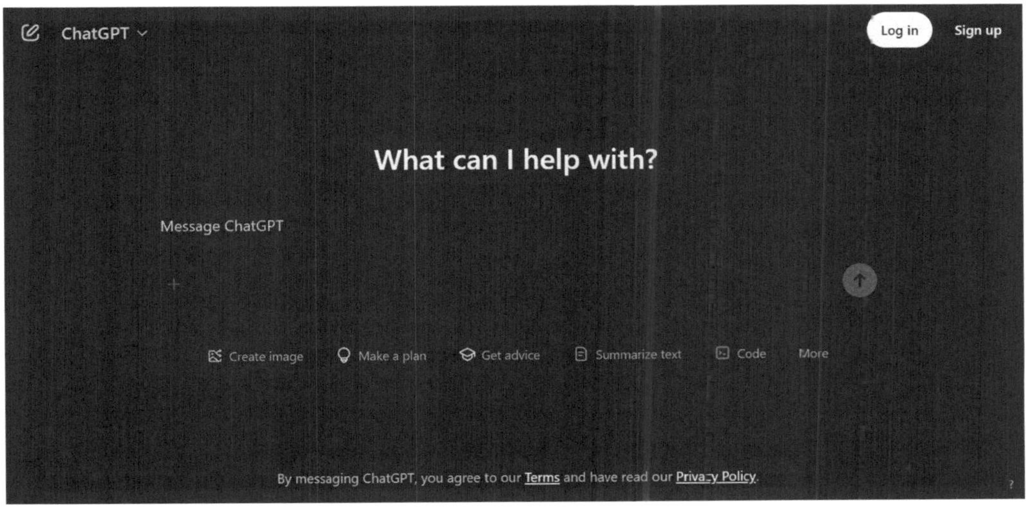

Figure 11.1: *Generative AI with ChatGPT*

Introduction to Generative AI

Generative AI is a branch of artificial intelligence that creates new content, such as text, images, music, and code. Unlike traditional AI models that primarily analyze and process existing data, generative AI learns patterns and generates new information based on that knowledge.

This technology has evolved significantly through deep neural networks, especially Transformer models, which power innovations such as OpenAI's GPT (Generative Pre-Trained Transformer) for text generation and DALL-E for image creation.

Key Features of Generative AI

Generative AI stands out due to several unique capabilities, including:

- **Content Creation:** Generates original text, images, videos, and code that did not exist before
- **Pattern Learning:** Processes large datasets to recognize structures and generate coherent outputs
- **Personalization:** Adapts to user preferences to create tailored content
- **Continuous Improvement:** Can be fine-tuned with new data for better accuracy and creativity
- **Interactivity:** Enables real-time user interaction through conversational agents and voice assistants

These features collectively enable Generative AI to transform data into creative, context-aware, and highly personalized outputs across multiple domains.

Working of Generative AI

Generative AI models leverage deep learning techniques to create new content by learning patterns from vast amounts of data. These models are widely used for generating text, images, music, and more. The most common types are as follows:

Generative Adversarial Networks

Generative Adversarial Networks (GANs) operate through two competing neural networks:

- **Generator:** Produces synthetic data that mimics real-world examples by refining patterns and structures
- **Discriminator:** Evaluates whether the generated content is real or artificially created, providing feedback to improve the generator's accuracy

This adversarial process continues iteratively and allow the generator to produce increasingly realistic and high-quality outputs over time.

GANs are widely applied in image synthesis, video generation, artistic style transfer, and deepfake creation. Additionally, they are used in medical imaging enhancements, super-resolution techniques, and data augmentation for training AI models.

Transformer-Based Models

Transformers are a breakthrough in natural language processing and content generation. They rely on self-attention mechanisms to understand and generate human-like text.

- **Examples:** GPT-4 and BERT, T5
- **Applications:**
  - **Text generation** (for example, chatbots, AI-powered writing assistants).
  - **Summarization** (for example, condensing long documents into key insights).
  - **Translation** (for example, real-time language translation tools).

Transformer architectures revolutionized Natural Language Processing (NLP) by leveraging self-attention mechanisms to efficiently process sequential data. Unlike traditional RNNs or LSTMs, transformers can analyze entire text inputs simultaneously, which enhances their ability to capture long-range dependencies.

- **Key Examples:** GPT-4 (text generation), BERT (contextual understanding), and T5 (multi-task learning)
- **Applications:**
  - **Conversational AI:** Enables chatbots and virtual assistants to generate coherent, human-like responses
  - **Text Summarization:** Condenses long-form content into concise, structured insights
  - **Machine Translation:** Enhances real-time multilingual communication with context-aware translation
  - **Question Answering Systems:** Empowers search engines and knowledge retrieval platforms

These models are the foundation of generative AI applications, optimizing search engines, voice assistants, and content generation tools.

Variational Autoencoders

Variational Autoencoders (VAEs) are deep learning models that learn efficient representations of data to generate new variations with similar characteristics.

- **How they work:** VAEs encode input data into a compressed representation, modify it, and decode it into a new output.
- **Applications:**
    - **Music composition** (generating melodies based on learned patterns)
    - **Image creation** (style transfer, artistic effects, and enhanced image generation)
    - **Data augmentation** (generating synthetic but realistic training data for AI models)

These generative AI models continue to evolve, expanding their capabilities and improving the realism and quality of generated content across various industries.

Applications of Generative AI

Generative AI is transforming multiple industries by automating creativity and streamlining processes.

Recently, the rise of *agentic* AI has enabled models to act as autonomous assistants capable of reasoning, executing tasks, and connecting to external tools. This evolution extends Generative AI beyond creative generation, empowering intelligent automation and real-world decision support. Some key applications include:

- **Text Generation and Chatbots**
    - AI models such as ChatGPT enable natural conversations.
    - Automates content creation, report generation, and scriptwriting
- **Image Generation and Digital Art**
    - Tools such as DALL-E and Stable Diffusion create images from text prompts.
    - Used for design, illustrations, and branding
- **Music Composition and Audio Production**
    - AI models such as Jukebox (OpenAI) generate music in different styles.
    - Text-to-speech (TTS) converts written text into realistic voice output.
- **Software Development and Code Generation**
    - AI models such as Codex assist in writing, completing, and debugging code.
    - Integrated into IDEs for faster development and error detection
- **Healthcare and Biotechnology**
    - AI-generated drug discovery models accelerate medical research.
    - Medical image analysis assists in diagnostics.
- **Marketing and Content Automation**
    - AI-driven product descriptions, ads, and social media posts.
    - Personalized marketing campaigns based on user behavior

Challenges of Generative AI

While generative AI unlocks new opportunities, it also introduces several ethical, technical, and regulatory challenges:

- **Bias in AI Models:** Generative AI can replicate and amplify societal biases if trained on unbalanced datasets. Therefore, strategies such as bias mitigation techniques and human-in-the-loop feedback are necessary.

- **Misinformation and Fake Content:** AI-generated text and deepfake technology raise concerns about trustworthiness and the spread of disinformation. Implementing watermarking, content verification, and regulatory frameworks can mitigate risks.
- **Intellectual Property and Copyright Issues:** AI-generated content blurs the lines of ownership, challenging traditional copyright laws and licensing rights. Legal frameworks for AI-generated media are currently evolving to address these concerns.
- **Computational and Environmental Costs:** Training large-scale models (for example, GPT-4, DALL-E) requires extensive energy consumption, impacting sustainability. Optimizing AI efficiency through model distillation and energy-efficient algorithms is crucial.
- **Malicious Use and Security Threats:** Generative AI can be exploited for deepfake fraud, phishing, and cyber-attacks. Advancements in AI detection and content **authentication** are essential to combat misuse.

Identifying Features of Generative AI Models

Generative AI models are designed to create new content, including text, images, music, and code, based on learned patterns from large datasets. These models utilize deep learning techniques to generate outputs that mimic human-created content, while maintaining coherence and context.

- **Learning from Large Datasets:** Generative AI models are trained on vast amounts of data, enabling them to identify complex patterns, relationships, and structures. This allows them to produce contextually relevant and coherent outputs.
- **Probabilistic Generation:** Unlike deterministic models, generative AI produces outputs based on probability distributions. The generated content is not an exact copy of the training data but rather a statistically likely new creation based on learned patterns.
- **Context Awareness:** Modern generative AI models, especially those based on Transformer architectures, utilize self-attention mechanisms to maintain context across long sequences of data. This enables them to generate responses that are coherent and contextually aligned with user input.
- **Adaptability and Fine-Tuning:** Generative models can be fine-tuned for specific applications, such as chatbot interactions, medical text generation, or artistic image creation. Fine-tuning involves retraining the model on domain-specific data to improve relevance and accuracy.
- **Multi-Modal Capabilities:** Advanced generative AI models can process and generate multiple types of content, including text, images, and audio. Examples include:
    - **GPT-4:** Text generation and natural language understanding
    - **DALL-E:** Image generation from textual descriptions
    - **Jukebox:** Music composition based on learned styles
- **Ability to Handle Unstructured Data:** Generative AI models can process unstructured data, such as natural language text, raw images, or audio recordings, and generate meaningful outputs without requiring structured input formats.
- **Token-Based Processing:** Text-based generative AI models utilize tokenization to break down input text into smaller units, allowing the model to analyze and generate content efficiently. Tokenization improves the model's ability to work with long-form text.
- **Model Scalability:** Generative AI models, particularly large-scale language models (LLMs), can scale up with increased data and computational power, leading to improved performance in generating diverse and high-quality outputs.

- **Ethical and Bias Considerations:** Generative AI models inherit biases from their training data. Developers implement techniques such as bias filtering, Reinforcement Learning with Human Feedback (RLHF), and responsible AI principles to mitigate unwanted outputs.
- **Creativity and Novelty:** Unlike rule-based systems, generative AI models can produce creative and novel content, making them useful for applications like content writing, designing, and creating personalized recommendations.

Generative AI models leverage deep learning, probabilistic techniques and contextual understanding to create human-like content across multiple domains. Their adaptability and ability to process unstructured data make them valuable for applications in text generation, image synthesis, and beyond. However, considerations about bias, ethics, and scalability remain critical for responsible deployment.

Role of Large Language Models in Generative AI

Generative AI applications leverage large language models (LLMs) for various natural language processing (NLP) tasks, such as:

- **Sentiment Analysis:** Understanding emotions and opinions in text
- **Text Summarization:** Condensing large amounts of text into concise summaries
- **Semantic Similarity:** Comparing meanings and relationships between different texts
- **Text Generation:** Producing human-like text based on context and prompts

Despite the mathematical complexity behind these models, understanding LLM architectures provides insight into how they operate and generate meaningful content. As generative AI continues to evolve, mastering these concepts will be essential for responsible and effective deployment in various industries.

Understanding Large Language Models

Large Language Models (**LLMs**) are advanced artificial intelligence models trained on vast amounts of text data to learn linguistic patterns and predict the next word in a sequence. They utilize **deep neural networks**, particularly **Transformer-based architectures**, to generate text that is coherent and contextually relevant.

LLMs are a specialized subset of Generative AI focused on understanding and producing human language.

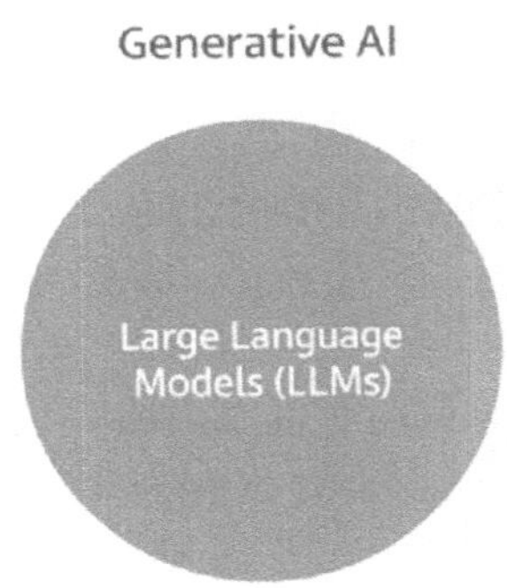

Figure 11.2: *Relationship between Generative AI and Large Language Models*

Key Features of LLMs

Large Language Models (LLMs) possess several defining capabilities that enable them to process, generate, and refine human-like text across various applications. We have mentioned some of their core features as follows:

- **Training on Large-Scale Data:** LLMs learn from billions of words sourced from books, articles, and internet content.
- **Natural Language Understanding and Generation:** These models process queries and generate structured responses.
- **Fine-Tuning for Specific Tasks:** LLMs can be adapted for specialized applications such as customer service and programming assistance.
- **Contextual Memory:** They maintain coherence over long interactions, improving response relevance.

The Architecture of LLMs: The Role of Transformers

Modern language models rely on Transformers, an architecture introduced in the 2017 paper "*Attention Is All You Need.*"

Transformers form the **backbone of Large Language Models (LLMs)** by organizing how text is processed, understood, and generated.

LLMs built on the Transformer architecture typically include **three core layers** that work together to produce coherent and contextually accurate text:

- **Embedding Layer:** Converts words or tokens into numerical vectors that capture their semantic meaning. This forms the input representation for the model.
- **Transformer Blocks:** These blocks contain multiple **self-attention** and **feed-forward** layers. The self-attention mechanism determines which words in a sentence are most relevant to each other, allowing the model to maintain context across long sequences.
- **Output Layer:** Generates predictions by decoding the processed representations into meaningful words or phrases. In auto-regressive LLMs like GPT, this layer predicts one token at a time, using previous outputs as context for the next prediction.

Modern LLMs often consist of dozens or even hundreds of Transformer layers, each refining the contextual understanding learned from earlier layers. This multi-layered approach enables models such as GPT-4, Claude, Gemini, and Mistral to produce coherent, human-like responses and perform complex reasoning tasks.

Recent innovations, such as FlashAttention, quantization, and Retrieval-Augmented Generation (RAG), have further optimized Transformer architectures, improving efficiency, scalability, and factual accuracy in real-world applications.

Core Components of Transformers

- **Self-Attention Mechanism:** Enables models to identify the most relevant words in a sentence
- **Encoders and Decoders:**
    - **Encoders:** Process input text and generate numerical representations of language
    - **Decoders:** Use these representations to generate responses or complete text sequences
- **Word Embeddings:** Convert words into numerical vectors, capturing semantic and syntactic relationships

Examples of LLMs and Their Use Cases:

- **GPT-4 (OpenAI):** Advanced text generation, used in conversational AI
- **BERT (Google):** Optimized for search engine queries and contextual understanding
- **T5 (Google):** Applied to translation, summarization, and question answering
- **LLaMA (Meta):** Designed for efficiency with reduced computational costs

Exam Tip: *Remember that transformer models rely on self-attention mechanisms rather than sequential processing. This makes them more efficient for handling long-range dependencies in text.*

Attention Mechanism in Transformer Models

The attention mechanism in Large Language Models (LLMs) and Generative AI (GenAI) has transformed how models process sequential data such as text. By selectively focusing on relevant parts of the input, attention mechanisms improve contextual understanding and enhance the accuracy of generated outputs.

Importance of Attention Mechanism

- Allows models to determine the contextual relevance of each token
- Ensures that significant input elements receive higher weights in prediction and text generation
- Plays a critical role in tasks such as machine translation, question answering, and text generation

Functioning of the Attention Mechanism

The attention mechanism assigns weights to input tokens, indicating their importance in a given task. The model calculates attention scores to determine which words contribute most to the final output.

Example

Sentence: "*Tokenization is essential for NLP.*"

- The model may assign higher attention weights to "*Tokenization*" and "NLP", as they define the context.
- "*essential*" may receive a moderate weight as it describes the relationship between the key terms.
- "*is*" and "*for*" may have lower attention since they serve grammatical functions.

Steps in the Attention Mechanism:

1. **Input Embeddings:**
    a. Each token is converted into a numerical vector representation.
2. **Attention Layer:**
    a. The model computes **attention scores** to determine token relevance.
3. **Prediction of the Next Token:**
    a. The decoder uses attention weights to generate the next most probable token.
4. **Computation of Attention Weights:**
    a. The model updates weight distributions for subsequent predictions.
    b. Multi-head attention allows different embeddings to be analyzed simultaneously.

4. **Feedback Mechanism:**
    a. Predicted tokens are added to the sequence for the next iteration.
5. **Weight Adjustment:**
    a. During training, model predictions are compared with actual values.
    b. Weights are updated to minimize loss and improve accuracy.

Attention Scores

Attention scores define the relative importance of each token in a sequence.

- **Higher scores** indicate greater relevance for the task.
- **Lower scores** indicate less significant tokens, such as function words and connectors.

In models utilizing multi-head attention, multiple attention scores are computed, capturing different contextual relationships.

Role of Attention in Transformers

The attention mechanism is a core component of Transformer models, including BERT and GPT, which have led to significant advancements in Natural Language Processing (NLP).

- **Self-Attention:** Evaluates the importance of each token relative to all other tokens in the sequence
- **Multi-Head Attention:** Captures multiple perspectives on token relationships, improving representation quality

Example of Attention in Action

Consider the sentence: "*The cat sat on the mat.*"

- When asked, "*Where is the cat?*", the model assigns higher attention to "*cat*" and "*mat*".
- It assigns lower attention to "*The*", "*sat*", and "*on*", as they contribute less meaning to the response.

Challenges of Attention Mechanisms

- **Computational Cost:** Calculating attention scores for long sequences requires high computational resources
- **Dependency on Training Data:** Bias in training data can impact model predictions, influencing the distribution of attention weights
- **Interpretability:** Understanding how attention weights are assigned in complex models remains a challenge

The attention mechanism is essential for the efficiency of Transformer-based models and modern Generative AI architectures. It enables models to process text effectively and accurately by emphasizing the most relevant elements.

Despite challenges like computational cost and interpretability, attention mechanisms continue to drive advancements in natural language processing and AI-driven text generation, thus supporting increasingly sophisticated applications.

Applications of LLMs in Generative AI

LLMs play a role in a variety of text generation and comprehension tasks across multiple industries.

- **Chatbots and Virtual Assistants:** LLMs enable structured, human-like interactions in applications such as ChatGPT, Alexa, and Google Assistant.

Example:

- **User:** *"What is the weather forecast for tomorrow?"*
- **Assistant:** *"Tomorrow's forecast predicts clear skies with temperatures between 25°C and 30°C."*

- **Automatic Translation:** LLMs enhance machine translation systems by improving context retention and fluency.

  Example:
  - **English:** *"Artificial Intelligence is transforming industries."*
  - **Portuguese:** "A *Inteligência Artificial está transformando indústrias.*"

- **Content Generation:** These models generate structured text for applications such as articles, scripts, summaries, and code generation.

  Example:
  - **Input:** "Summarize machine learning principles."
  - **Output:** "Machine learning is a field of artificial intelligence that enables systems to improve performance based on data without explicit programming."

- **Sentiment Analysis**: LLMs classify emotional tone in text for applications such as brand monitoring and customer service.

  Example:
  - **Text:** "The service was efficient and met expectations."
  - **Output**: Neutral

- **Information Retrieval and Search Optimization**: LLMs improve search engines by providing more relevant and contextualized results.

  Example:
  - **User Query:** *"Best practices for training a deep learning model."*
  - **LLM Response:** Returns technical articles and research papers related to the query.

Challenges of LLMs

Despite their capabilities, LLMs present several challenges that affect their reliability and efficiency.

- **Bias in Training Data:** Since LLMs learn from large-scale internet data, they can reflect social, cultural, or political biases present in their training sources
- **High Computational Cost:** Training and deploying LLMs require significant processing power, thus increasing operational costs.
- **Limitations in Logical Reasoning:** While LLMs generate structured responses, they may struggle with logical reasoning, problem-solving, and factual accuracy.
- **Security and Privacy Concerns:** Using LLMs for data processing and automated decision-making raises concerns regarding privacy, misinformation, and responsible AI use.

Transformer Models: Architecture and Applications

Over the past few years, Transformer models have become the foundation of modern artificial intelligence, driving breakthroughs not only in Natural Language Processing (NLP) but also in computer vision, audio processing, and multimodal AI. Originally introduced in the 2017 paper "*Attention Is All You Need*," the Transformer architecture revolutionized how models handle sequential data by relying entirely on **self-attention mechanisms** instead of recurrent or convolutional layers.

Modern Large Language Models (LLMs), such as GPT-4, Claude, Gemini, and LlaMA, build upon this architecture, integrating billions of parameters and optimized attention techniques to achieve greater contextual understanding, reasoning ability, and efficiency.

Transformers are trained on massive and diverse datasets, enabling them to **capture semantic relationships**, **generate coherent long-form content**, and **adapt across tasks** including language, vision, and code generation.

Today, transformer-based architectures form the backbone of Generative AI, powering applications like **chatbots, summarization, image synthesis, audio generation, and cross-modal understanding**, thereby solidifying their role as the most influential deep-learning architecture of the last decade.

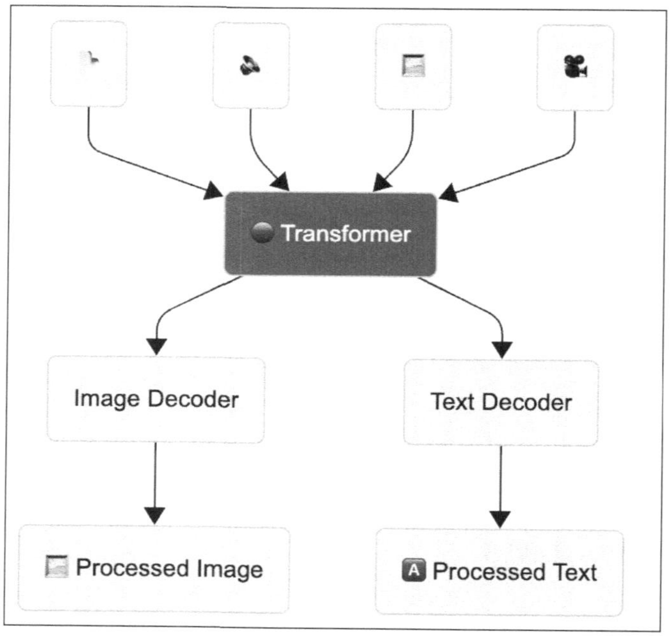

Figure 11.3: *Transformer's High Perspective Overview*

Structure of the Transformer Architecture

The Transformer architecture consists of two primary components:

- **Encoder Block:** Processes input text, generating **semantic representations** of words based on their context within a sequence
- **Decoder Block:** Generates new text sequences using the representations created by the encoder

Different implementations of the Transformer architecture emphasize the following distinct components:

- **BERT (Google):** Focuses on the **encoder block** to improve search engine results and contextual text comprehension
- **GPT (OpenAI):** Relies primarily on the **decoder block** to generate realistic, coherent text

Operation of Transformer Models

Transformers utilize a mechanism called self-attention, which allows the model to consider all words in a sentence simultaneously when generating an output. This mechanism ensures that the model accurately captures the full context and meaning of a phrase, enhancing coherence and precision in text generation.

Example: Self-Attention in Action

Consider the sentence: "*The dog runs fast because it is excited.*"

- A traditional model may struggle to correctly associate "*it is excited*" with "*the dog.*"
- With self-attention, the Transformer assigns contextual weights to each word, ensuring that "*it is excited*" is correctly linked to "*the dog.*"

Applications of Transformer Models

Transformers have become the foundation of many artificial intelligence applications, particularly in NLP.

Machine Translation

- Models such as **T5** and **mT5** are trained to translate text between multiple languages.
- Example: Converting "*Hello, how are you?*" to "*Olá, como você está?*" with high accuracy

Text Generation

- Models such as **GPT-4** generate structured, contextually relevant text.
- Example: Writing **articles, stories, or chatbot responses** with human-like fluency

Text Summarization

- Models such as **BART** condense long documents into concise summaries.
- Example: Summarizing **news articles or research papers** without losing key information

Question Answering (QA)

- **BERT-based models** extract answers from large text corpora.
- Example:
  - **Input:** "*Who discovered Brazil?*"
  - **Output:** "*Pedro Álvares Cabral.*"

Sentiment Analysis

- Transformers analyze **emotion and intent** in text data.
- Example: Classifying **customer reviews, tweets, or survey responses** as positive, negative, or neutral

Transformer models form the foundation of modern generative AI solutions and utilize advanced capabilities in text creation, language translation, and conversational AI. Their scalability and contextual understanding allow for highly sophisticated outputs that continue to improve as models are refined and trained on larger datasets.

Understanding the architecture and mechanisms of Transformer models provides valuable insight into how LLMs such as GPT and BERT generate context-aware responses, advancing AI-driven applications across industries.

Tokenization in Generative AI

Tokenization is a fundamental process in Large Language Models (LLMs) and Generative AI (GenAI), where text is converted into smaller units called tokens. These tokens can represent words, sub words, or individual characters. Tokenization enables AI models to process language efficiently and serves as the foundation for tasks, such as **text generation, machine translation, and sentiment analysis**.

Introduction to Tokenization

Tokenization divides text into smaller components, facilitating the recognition of linguistic patterns by AI models. Depending on the approach used, a token can represent:

- Individual words (*word-based tokenization*)
- Sub-words or word fragments (*sub word tokenization*)
- Individual characters (*character-based tokenization*)

This segmentation optimizes text processing, allowing models to manage vocabulary effectively, recognize relationships between words, and maintain grammatical structure.

Exam Tip: *In the AI-900 exam, questions about tokenization often focus on how text is broken into smaller units (tokens) to improve model performance in tasks such as translation and summarization.*

Importance of Tokenization in LLMs and GenAI

Generative AI models rely on tokenization to structure and interpret large-scale text data. The process contributes to:

- Reducing text complexity by breaking down sentences into manageable components
- Preserving semantic relationships by enabling models to recognize word associations
- Facilitating model training by improving the ability to process unknown words through decomposition into recognizable parts
- Enhancing text generation by improving prediction accuracy for the next token in a sequence

Types of Tokenization

Tokenization is a fundamental step in Natural Language Processing (NLP), breaking down text into smaller units for analysis. Different tokenization methods offer unique advantages and challenges, as outlined:

- **Word-Based Tokenization:** This method splits text into individual words.

  Example:

  Original sentence: "*Tokenization is essential for NLP.*"

  Generated tokens: ["*Tokenization*", "*is*", "*essential*", "*for*", "NLP", "."]

  Advantages: Simple and widely used in NLP

  Disadvantages: Requires large vocabulary storage and struggles with out-of-vocabulary words

- **Sub word Tokenization:** This approach divides words into smaller segments to improve vocabulary efficiency and manage unknown words.

Example:

Word: "*Tokenization*"

Generated tokens: ["*Token*", "*ization*"]

Advantages: Reduces vocabulary size and improves model performance for unseen words

Disadvantages: Increases the number of tokens per sentence, raising computational costs

Common sub word tokenization techniques include:

- Byte Pair Encoding (BPE)
- WordPiece (used in BERT)
- SentencePiece (used in T5 and GPT-3)

- **Character-Based Tokenization:** This method treats each character as a token.

  Example:

  Word: "AI"

  Generated tokens: ["A", "I"]

  Advantages: Useful for processing unknown words and languages with complex morphology

  Disadvantages: Generates a large number of tokens, increasing computational load

Embeddings in Language Models and Generative AI

Embeddings are numerical representations of tokens used in Large Language Models (LLMs) and Generative AI (GenAI). They play a fundamental role in capturing semantic and syntactic relationships between words, allowing AI models to process and interpret text more effectively.

This chapter examines how embeddings function, how they are generated, and how they impact tasks such as word prediction, sentence generation, and semantic analysis.

Introduction to Embeddings

Embeddings are **high-dimensional vectors** that represent tokens derived from the **tokenization** process. Each token is mapped to a point in a geometric space, where the **distance and direction** between points reflect linguistic and contextual relationships between words.

Words with similar meanings are positioned **closer** to each other in the vector space, while unrelated words are placed further apart.

Example: The words "*sun*" and "*moon*" would have embeddings that are closer compared to "*sun*" and "*computer*", as they share more semantic similarity.

Importance of Embeddings in LLMs

LLMs use embeddings to learn complex text patterns. Representing words as numerical vectors enables models to:

- Capture **semantic relationships**, ensuring that related words have similar representations.
- Understand **context variations**, allowing the same word to be interpreted differently based on sentence structure.

- Improve **prediction and response accuracy**, enhancing tasks such as text generation and machine translation.
- Reduce **dimensionality**, compressing meaningful information into an efficient format for processing.

Creating Embeddings in NLP

Embeddings are generated during the training phase of a language model. Each token is assigned numerical coordinates in a multi-dimensional space. Early approaches such as Word2Vec, GloVe, and FastText introduced word embeddings, while modern Transformer-based models (for example, BERT, GPT) have improved these representations.

Embedding Creation Process

1. **Tokenization:** The text is divided into smaller units (words, sub words, or characters).
2. **Vector Mapping:** Each token is assigned a set of numerical coordinates.
3. **Training on Large Datasets:** The model adjusts token placements based on contextual usage.
4. **Fine-Tuning:** Embeddings can be refined for domain-specific applications.

Example of Embeddings in a Language Model

Consider the sentence:

"Advancements in machine learning improve AI performance."

Each word is converted into a numerical vector with coordinates in a multi-dimensional space as illustrated in the following table:

Token ID	Token	X	Y	Z
1	Advancements	6	2	8
2	In	-3	5	1
3	Machine	4	3	7
4	Learning	-5	2	6
5	Improve	-2	-4	6
6	AI	9	4	11
7	Performance	7	8	12

Table 11.1: *Token Embeddings Representation*

Note: *The numerical coordinates shown here are illustrative and do not represent actual model outputs.*

Tokens "*AI*" and "*Machine*" have similar coordinates, indicating their **semantic proximity** within the language model.

Utilization of Embeddings in Models

Embeddings are applied in various Natural Language Processing (NLP) tasks, including:

- **Word Prediction:** Models use embeddings to predict the next word in a sequence.

Example:

- **Input:** "*The system was designed to*"
- **Predicted output:** "*optimize*", "*improve*", "*automate*"

- **Machine Translation:** Embeddings align similar meanings across languages.

  Example

  - **English:** "*sun*"→**Spanish:** "*sol*"
  - **French:** "*ordinateur*"→**Portuguese:** "*computador*"

- **Semantic Analysis and Text Similarity:** Embeddings allow models to compare sentences and determine their degree of similarity.

  Example

  - **Sentence 1:** "*Solar energy is a sustainable power source.*"
  - **Sentence 2:** "*Solar panels are used to generate clean electricity.*"
  - **Output:** High similarity score

Challenges of Embeddings

Despite their advantages, embeddings present several challenges in LLMs and Generative AI applications, which are mentioned as follows:

- **Bias in Training Data:** Embeddings are trained on large text corpora that may contain cultural, social, or political biases, which can influence model predictions.
- **Context Dependency:** Words can have different meanings depending on their context. Early models struggled with this, but newer approaches, such as **BERT and GPT**, incorporate contextual embeddings to improve accuracy.
- **Computational Cost:** Generating high-quality embeddings requires significant computational resources, increasing the cost and complexity of model training.

Embeddings are an essential component of modern language models, providing **numerical representations** that enable AI systems to process, generate, and interpret text effectively. They facilitate various NLP applications, including **text prediction, translation, and semantic analysis**. However, challenges such as bias, context dependency, and computational demands must be addressed for improved model performance and ethical AI development.

Identifying Common Scenarios for Generative AI

Generative Artificial Intelligence (Generative AI) is a key technological advancement that enables the creation of new content and solutions across multiple industries. From generating images and text to drug discovery and predictive maintenance, the applications of generative AI continue to expand.

This session explores the primary use cases of generative AI, highlighting its practical applications and industry impact.

Common Use Cases of Generative AI

Generative AI technologies enable a wide range of applications across industries, offering new ways to generate content, automate tasks, and enhance user experiences.

Text Generation and Automation

Generative AI models, such as **GPT-4**, create human-like text that can be used for multiple purposes, including content creation, summarization, and chatbots.

- **Use Cases**
    - Automating content writing for articles, blogs, and reports
    - Generating summaries of long documents
    - Enhancing chatbot responses in customer service

Image Generation and Enhancement

Models such as **DALL-E** generate high-quality images from textual descriptions, supporting creative and commercial applications.

- **Use Cases**
    - Designing marketing materials and visual assets
    - Generating concept art and digital illustrations
    - Enhancing low-resolution images using AI-based upscaling

Figure 11.4: *AI Generating Images*

Code Generation and Software Development

AI-powered tools, such as **GitHub Copilot**, assist developers by generating, optimizing, and debugging code.

- **Use Cases**
    - Writing code snippets based on natural language prompts
    - Auto-generating documentation for software projects
    - Assisting with bug detection and code refactoring

Audio and Speech Synthesis

Generative AI models, such as **WaveNet**, convert text into realistic speech, enhancing accessibility and automation.

- **Use Cases**
    - Creating voiceovers for audiobooks, videos, and podcasts
    - Generating synthetic voices for virtual assistants
    - Enabling real-time language translation in spoken communication

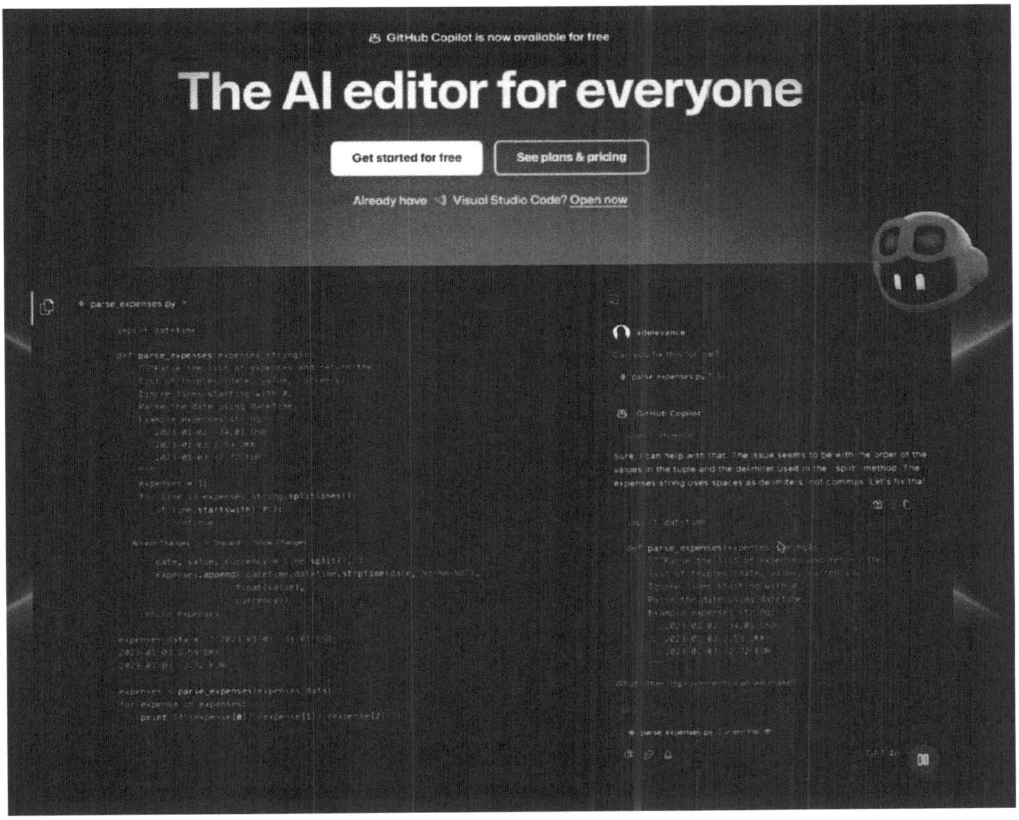

Figure 11.5: *GitHub Copilot Official Website*

Music and Sound Generation

AI models, such as **OpenAI Jukebox**, compose original music and sound effects for various industries.

- **Use Cases**
    - Generating background music for films, games, and commercials
    - Creating personalized music compositions based on user preferences
    - Synthesizing sound effects for digital media production

Synthetic Data Generation

AI-generated data replicates real-world conditions without exposing sensitive or private information.

- **Use Cases**
  - Creating synthetic medical records for AI training in healthcare
  - Generating sample customer data for testing machine learning models
  - Developing synthetic financial transaction data for fraud detection

Personalized Recommendations

Generative AI enhances recommendation engines by predicting user preferences and generating customized suggestions.

- **Use Cases**
  - Personalizing content recommendations in streaming services
  - Generating product suggestions in e-commerce platforms
  - Customizing learning experiences in educational applications

Drug Discovery and Scientific Research

Generative AI accelerates the process of discovering new drugs and materials by predicting molecular structures.

- **Use Cases**
  - Identifying potential drug compounds for medical research
  - Generating new protein structures for biotechnology applications
  - Assisting in materials science for advanced manufacturing

Deepfake Creation and Synthetic Media

AI-driven deepfake technology generates realistic videos, voices, and images, raising both innovative opportunities and ethical concerns.

- **Use Cases**
  - Creating digital avatars for virtual interactions
  - Enhancing visual effects in film production
  - Developing AI-powered language dubbing for media content

Predictive Maintenance and Industrial Automation

Generative AI improves equipment monitoring by analyzing sensor data and predicting failures before they occur.

- **Use Cases**
  - Detecting potential equipment failures in manufacturing plants
  - Enhancing predictive maintenance in transportation and logistics
  - Optimizing operational efficiency in industrial automation

Identifying Responsible AI Considerations for Generative AI

Generative AI has introduced new capabilities in content creation, automation, and decision-making. However, its widespread use also raises ethical, social, and technical challenges. Ensuring responsible AI practices is essential to mitigate risks such as bias, misinformation, and privacy violations.

This section outlines key considerations for the responsible deployment of generative AI, focusing on fairness, transparency, accountability, and security.

Bias and Fairness

Generative AI models learn from large datasets, which may contain **historical biases** related to race, gender, or cultural perspectives. If not properly managed, these biases can influence the outputs generated by AI systems.

- **Challenges**
    - Reinforcement of stereotypes present in training data
    - Unequal representation of different groups in AI-generated content
    - Unintended discriminatory outputs in hiring, lending, or law enforcement
- **Mitigation Strategies**
    - **Using diverse and representative datasets to train AI models**
    - **Implementing bias detection and correction techniques in AI systems**
    - **Conducting fairness audits to evaluate and refine model outputs**

Transparency and Explainability

Many generative AI models operate as **black-box systems**, making it difficult to understand how they generate specific outputs. Lack of transparency reduces trust and limits accountability.

- **Challenges**
    - Difficulty in explaining why a model produces a certain response
    - Lack of user awareness about how AI-generated content is created
    - Potential misuse of AI-generated content in deceptive practices
- **Mitigation Strategies**
    - Providing **clear documentation** on model behavior and limitations
    - Developing **Explainable AI (XAI) techniques** to improve interpretability
    - Implementing **disclosure policies** to label AI-generated content

Misinformation and Deepfakes

Generative AI can create highly realistic images, videos, and text, increasing the risk of **misinformation and deepfake manipulation**. Without safeguards, AI-generated content can be used to deceive the public or spread false narratives.

- **Challenges**
    - Creation of **deepfake videos** that misrepresent individuals
    - AI-generated **fake news articles** influencing public opinion
    - Difficulty in distinguishing real content from AI-generated content
- **Mitigation Strategies**
    - Developing **detection tools** to identify deepfakes and synthetic media
    - Enforcing **AI-generated content disclosures** in media and journalism
    - Promoting **fact-checking partnerships** with AI developers and organizations

Privacy and Data Protection

Generative AI models often process large amounts of data, raising concerns about **privacy violations** and **unauthorized data use**. Protecting user information is hence essential for ethical AI deployment.

- **Challenges:**
  - AI models may **memorize sensitive data** from training datasets
  - Risk of **re-identifying individuals** from AI-generated content
  - Unauthorized use of copyrighted or personal data
- **Mitigation Strategies:**
  - Applying **differential privacy techniques** to protect sensitive data
  - Ensuring **compliance with data protection regulations** (for example, GDPR, CCPA)
  - Using **synthetic data** to reduce reliance on real personal information

Accountability and Governance

Establishing **clear accountability** for AI-generated outputs is critical to prevent misuse and ensure compliance with ethical guidelines.

- **Challenges**
  - Lack of regulatory frameworks governing generative AI
  - Unclear legal responsibility for harmful AI-generated content
  - Difficulty in assigning accountability for AI-related errors
- **Mitigation Strategies**
  - Implementing **AI governance policies** to define accountability
  - Establishing **audit mechanisms** to monitor AI behavior
  - Encouraging **collaboration between regulators, AI developers, and policymakers**

Environmental and Computational Impact

Training large generative AI models requires significant computational resources, which contributes to **high energy consumption** and **environmental impact**.

- **Challenges:**
  - Increased **carbon footprint** due to energy-intensive training processes
  - **Unequal access** to AI capabilities due to high computational costs
  - Scalability challenges in maintaining AI efficiency
- **Mitigation Strategies:**
  - Using **energy-efficient AI models** and optimizing model architectures
  - Encouraging **cloud-based AI solutions** with lower environmental impact
  - Researching **low-resource AI alternatives** for wider accessibility

The responsible deployment of generative AI requires addressing **bias, transparency, misinformation, privacy, accountability, and sustainability**. Organizations and policymakers must collaborate to establish ethical guidelines, improve AI governance, and ensure fair and secure AI applications.

By implementing these responsible AI considerations, generative AI can be leveraged **ethically and effectively** across industries while minimizing potential risks.

Conclusion

This chapter provided a comprehensive overview of Generative AI, covering its foundations, key technologies, and real-world applications. We explored how models like Generative Adversarial Networks (GANs), Transformer-based architectures, and Variational Autoencoders (VAEs) enable AI to generate text, images, music, and other creative outputs. Additionally, we examined its role across various industries, from content creation and marketing to healthcare and software development, while also addressing the ethical considerations and challenges associated with its use.

In the next chapter, we will explore the capabilities of **Azure OpenAI Service**, a powerful platform that operationalizes Generative AI for businesses and developers. We will discuss its core features, integration with Microsoft's cloud ecosystem, and how it enables the creation of intelligent, multimodal, and secure AI solutions that bring generative capabilities into real-world production environments.

Points to Remember

- **Generative AI** creates new content, including text, images, music, and code, by learning patterns from large datasets and generating coherent outputs based on that knowledge.
- **Transformer Models**, such as GPT and BERT, use self-attention mechanisms to capture contextual relevance, enabling accurate text generation, summarization, and translation.
- **Applications of Generative AI** include text generation for chatbots, image synthesis for design and branding, music composition, software development, and personalized recommendations.
- **Generative Adversarial Networks (GANs)** combine a generator and discriminator to produce realistic images and videos, and is widely used for creating digital art and deepfakes.
- **Adaptability and Fine-Tuning** enable Generative AI models to specialize in specific domains such as healthcare, marketing, or customer service.
- **Tokenization** divides text into smaller units (tokens), allowing models to process language effectively for tasks such as machine translation and sentiment analysis.
- **Embeddings** represent tokens as numerical vectors, capturing semantic relationships and enabling tasks such as semantic similarity and information retrieval.
- **Responsible AI Practices** are critical to addressing risks such as bias in outputs, misinformation through deepfakes, privacy violations, and environmental impacts from high computational costs.
- **Challenges of Generative AI** include bias in training data, ensuring transparency in outputs, managing intellectual property issues, and optimizing computational efficiency.

Understanding these points will help effectively leverage Generative AI's capabilities across industries, while addressing its ethical and technical challenges.

Key Terms

- **Generative AI:** A branch of artificial intelligence focused on creating new content, such as text, images, music, and code, by learning patterns from large datasets
- **Transformer Models:** Deep learning architectures such as GPT and BERT that use self-attention mechanisms to improve context-aware text generation, summarization, and translation
- **Generative Adversarial Networks (GANs):** Models consisting of a generator and a discriminator that create realistic outputs, such as images and videos

- **Variational Autoencoders (VAEs):** Models that learn compact data representations to generate new variations, used in music composition and style transfer
- **Tokenization:** The process of breaking text into smaller units, such as words or sub words, for analysis and processing by AI models.
- **Embeddings:** Numerical vector representations of tokens that capture semantic and syntactic relationships, enabling models to process and interpret language more effectively
- **Self-Attention Mechanism:** A feature of Transformer models that evaluates the relevance of each token in relation to others in a sequence, ensuring contextual accuracy
- **Fine-tuning:** The process of adapting a pre-trained generative AI model to a specific domain or task by retraining it with domain-specific data
- **Probabilistic Generation:** A method where generative AI produces outputs based on probability distributions, allowing for creative and varied content generation
- **Multi-Modal AI:** Generative AI systems capable of processing and generating multiple types of content, such as text, images, and audio
- **Synthetic Data:** Artificially generated datasets that replicate real-world conditions, often used to train models without exposing sensitive information
- **Deepfakes:** AI-generated synthetic media, including images, videos, and audio, that mimics real people or content with high realism.
- **Explainable AI (XAI):** Techniques and methods designed to make the behavior and outputs of AI models more interpretable and understandable
- **Differential Privacy:** A method of ensuring that individual data points in a dataset cannot be identified or reconstructed by analyzing model outputs
- **Bias Mitigation:** Strategies used to identify and correct biases in AI models to ensure fairness and avoid discriminatory outputs.
- **Contextual Awareness:** The ability of generative AI models to understand and generate content that aligns with the context of the input data
- **Token-Based Processing:** A text analysis method where input text is divided into tokens, improving the efficiency of natural language processing tasks
- **Energy-Efficient AI Models:** Optimized AI systems designed to reduce computational and environmental costs associated with training and deployment
- **Reinforcement Learning with Human Feedback (RLHF):** A training approach that incorporates feedback from human reviewers to improve the relevance and quality of AI model outputs
- **Scalability in AI:** The ability of generative AI models, especially Large Language Models (LLMs), to handle increased data and computational resources for enhanced performance

Multiple Choice Questions

1. What is Generative AI primarily used for?
   a. Creating new content such as text, images, music, and code
   b. Translating text between languages
   c. Identifying sentiment in customer reviews
   d. Analyzing existing datasets to identify patterns
2. Which models are commonly associated with Generative AI for text and image creation?
   a. Random Forest and Decision Trees
   b. Auto-Regressive Models and k-Means

   c. GPT and DALL-E
   d. SVMs and Clustering Models
3. What distinguishes Generative AI from traditional AI?
   a. It primarily focuses on structured datasets.
   b. It generates new data based on learned patterns instead of only analyzing existing data.
   c. It requires manual input for predictions.
   d. It uses shallow neural networks for output generation.
4. What are the key characteristics of Generative AI?
   a. Predictive modeling, anomaly detection, and classification
   b. Content creation, pattern learning, personalization, continuous improvement, and interactivity
   c. Data summarization, sentiment extraction, clustering, and regression
   d. Static analysis, language parsing, and translation
5. How do Generative Adversarial Networks (GANs) function in Generative AI?
   a. By condensing long documents into concise summaries
   b. By processing data into tokens for analysis
   c. By combining a generator to create new data and a discriminator to evaluate its authenticity
   d. By identifying entities like names and locations in text
6. What are some real-world applications of Generative AI?
   a. Predictive analytics, data clustering, and sentiment analysis
   b. Text generation, image creation, music composition, and code generation
   c. Database indexing, data encryption, and risk management
   d. Video compression, hardware design, and mechanical simulations
7. What is a key challenge in deploying Generative AI models?
   a. Bias in training data and the potential for misuse, such as deepfakes
   b. Lack of access to structured data
   c. Inability to scale for large datasets
   d. Low computational requirements impacting performance

Answers

1. a
2. c
3. b
4. b
5. c
6. b
7. a

Chapter 12
Identifying the Capabilities of Azure OpenAI Service

Introduction

In this chapter, we will explore the fundamentals and practical applications of Azure OpenAI Service capabilities. As the demand for generative AI solutions grows, organizations and developers are eager to leverage these services to transform data into high-value content. Whether it is creating human-like text, generating code snippets, or even producing original images, Azure OpenAI Service offers advanced tools that expand the possibilities for innovation across various fields.

We will begin by examining the natural language generation capabilities, demonstrating how models can produce coherent and contextually relevant content based on natural language prompts. Next, we will discuss the code generation functionalities, highlighting how AI can accelerate software development by automatically suggesting or writing code snippets. Finally, we will delve into the image generation features, showcasing how textual concepts can be transformed into compelling visual representations.

By the end of this chapter, you will have a comprehensive understanding of the key features of Azure OpenAI Service, along with best practices and use cases for each function. With this knowledge, you will be able to integrate these innovative technologies into real-world solutions, while making your projects more efficient and creative than ever.

Structure

In this chapter, we will discuss the following topics:

- Natural Language Generation Capabilities of Azure OpenAI Service
- Code Generation Capabilities of Azure OpenAI Service
- Image Generation Capabilities of Azure OpenAI Service

Natural Language Generation Capabilities of Azure OpenAI Service

The Azure OpenAI Service offers advanced natural language generation capabilities that empower businesses and developers to produce human-like text efficiently. By leveraging state-of-the-art AI models that are built on the Transformer architecture, the service transforms simple prompts into rich, coherent, and contextually relevant content. This enables developers to use it for a wide range of applications, such as in automated report drafting and interactive conversational agents, thereby helping organizations streamline communication and content creation.

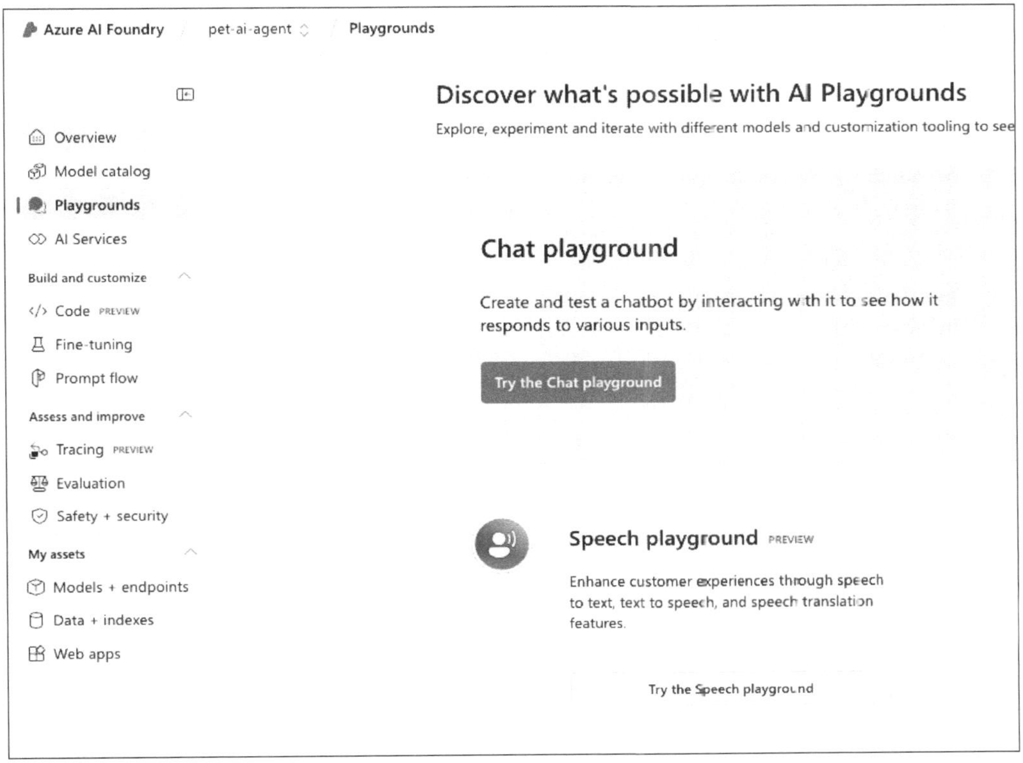

Figure 12.1: *Azure Open AI Service in Azure AI Foundry Portal*

Azure OpenAI Service is a cloud-based platform that seamlessly integrates cutting-edge AI models from OpenAI into Microsoft Azure's secure, scalable infrastructure. Designed for enterprise use, the service allows businesses and developers to harness state-of-the-art generative AI capabilities for a variety of applications like natural language processing, creative content generation, advanced reasoning, and multimodal interactions.

Key Advancements in Azure OpenAI Service

Azure OpenAI Service continues to redefine what's possible in generative AI by introducing innovative updates that enhance model versatility and performance. These advancements empower businesses and developers to tackle a wide range of tasks, such as creating rich, context-aware content and solving complex problems with advanced reasoning. The latest innovations ensure more efficient, accurate, and secure AI solutions that integrate seamlessly into enterprise workflows. They are listed as follows:

- **GPT-5 Preview and Phi-4 Mini:** The newest generation of Azure OpenAI models introduces enhanced reasoning, Retrieval-Augmented Generation (RAG) capabilities, and optimized efficiency for large-scale enterprise workloads. GPT-5 Preview delivers superior contextual grounding and multimodal understanding (text, image, and audio), while Phi-4 Mini provides lightweight, cost-effective intelligence for smaller applications and embedded systems.
- **GPT-4.5 Preview:** A general-purpose model built for advanced reasoning across both text and image inputs. With an expanded context window of 128K tokens, improved multilingual coverage, and more precise creative generation, it is used for conversational copilots, document summarizers, and intelligent writing assistants.

- **GPT-4o and GPT-4 Turbo with Vision:** These multimodal models support text, image, and audio inputs under a unified architecture. GPT-4o delivers seamless cross-modal processing, while GPT-4 Turbo with Vision offers accelerated responses and structured JSON outputs ideal for OCR, real-time visual recognition, and interactive experiences that blend perception and reasoning.
- **Advanced Reasoning Models (o1 and o3-mini):** Purpose-built for technical and analytical workloads that require complex reasoning, scientific computation, and detailed problem-solving. These models deliver measurable improvements in precision, consistency, and reliability across demanding enterprise tasks.
- **Enterprise-Grade Integration and Security:** Running on Microsoft Azure's global cloud infrastructure, the service provides high availability, robust security, and compliance with international standards (ISO 27001, SOC 2, GDPR). Features include Role-Based Access Control (RBAC), private networking, data encryption in transit and at rest, and isolated VNets for sensitive workloads. Integration with Azure AI Studio, REST APIs, SDKs, and Azure AI Foundry simplifies the deployment of generative AI into enterprise systems.
- **Customization and Fine-Tuning:** Azure OpenAI Service supports model customization using proprietary data, enabling organizations to tailor model behavior to their domain, tone, and compliance needs. Fine-tuning and prompt-engineering workflows ensure generated outputs align with brand guidelines and operational objectives, such as delivering enterprise-grade copilots and assistants that address specific business challenges.

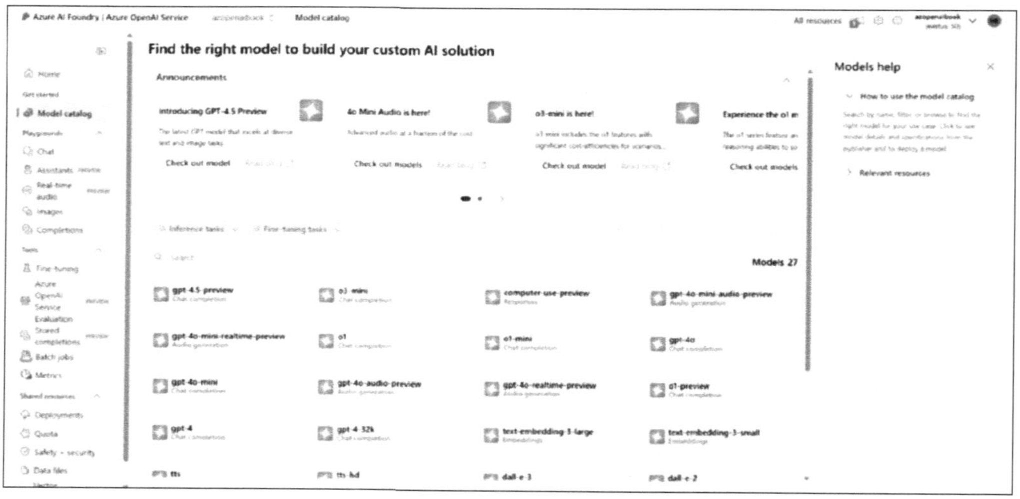

Figure 12.2: *Model Catalog in Azure Open AI Service*

Note: *The models, capabilities, and pricing details mentioned in this overview are subject to change, as Azure OpenAI Service continuously updates its offerings. Customers should always refer to the official Azure OpenAI Service documentation and the Microsoft Azure portal for the latest information on model availability, pricing, and regulatory compliance. Additionally, advanced features such as fine-tuning and multimodal processing may require additional access approvals and may be available only in specific regions.*

Azure OpenAI Service transforms the way organizations innovate by combining state-of-the-art language and vision capabilities with the scalability and security of Microsoft Azure. Whether you are creating interactive chatbots, automating content creation or building intelligent reasoning systems, Azure OpenAI Service offers a comprehensive, future-proof platform for harnessing the full potential of generative AI.

Key Features of Natural Language Generation with Azure OpenAI Service

Azure OpenAI Service provides a comprehensive suite of functionalities designed to create high-quality text that mimics human writing. These features enable organizations to automate content creation, enhance customer engagement, and build intelligent conversational systems.

Context-Aware Text Generation

The service analyzes the context provided in the prompt to produce coherent output and deeply aligned with the desired theme or subject matter. By leveraging extensive pre-training on diverse datasets, the model can generate text that maintains consistency over long passages, making it ideal for drafting detailed reports, essays, or creative narratives.

- **Context Retention:** Remembers earlier parts of a conversation or text, ensuring that the generated content maintains logical continuity and relevance throughout long passages.
- **Thematic Accuracy:** Adapts its responses to the specific subject or theme provided, including detailed explanations, examples, and supporting information when needed.
- **Redundancy Reduction:** Filters out repetitive and extraneous details, ensuring that the output remains clear and focused on the key message.
- **Dynamic Adjustment:** Continuously refines its output in real-time based on evolving input, making it ideal for interactive applications, such as live chat and dynamic report generation.

Customizable Tone and Style

One of the core strengths of the service is its flexibility to adjust tone, style, and formality. Through prompt engineering and parameter tuning, users can generate text that fits specific brand guidelines or audience expectations. For instance, you can tailor outputs to be formal for legal documents or casual for social media posts, ensuring that the generated content aligns with the intended communication strategy.

- **Flexible Output:** Offers a range of stylistic options, from professional and formal to casual and conversational, tailoring content to different contexts, such as legal documents, marketing copy, or social media posts
- **Brand Consistency:** Ensures that the text adheres to predetermined language standards and tone, reinforcing brand identity across various communications
- **User-Defined Parameters:** Allows fine-tuning through adjustable parameters, making it possible to set preferences for sentiment, vocabulary complexity, and sentence structure
- **Adaptive Learning:** Incorporates feedback and iterative adjustments to continually refine the tone and style, ensuring consistent and high-quality outputs over time

Automated Content Creation

Azure OpenAI Service can be integrated into workflows to automatically generate a variety of content types. Whether it is composing emails, drafting articles, summarizing reports, or creating marketing copy, the service reduces the need for manual writing. This not only accelerates the content creation process but also ensures consistency and scalability across large volumes of text.

- **Diverse Content Generation:** Capable of drafting articles, reports, social media posts, summaries, and emails with minimal input, significantly reducing manual writing efforts
- **Scalability:** Produces large volumes of content consistently, making it ideal for enterprises that need to maintain regular communication across multiple channels

- **Consistency and Accuracy:** Delivers uniformly structured and error-free content, reducing the risk of human error and ensuring adherence to style guidelines
- **Time Efficiency:** Automates repetitive writing tasks, freeing up creative and technical teams to focus on higher-level strategic initiatives

Interactive Conversational Agents

The service excels in powering sophisticated chatbots and virtual assistants. Its ability to generate contextually relevant responses over multi-turn conversations allows for the development of systems that can handle complex queries, provide personalized support, and even manage task-oriented dialogues. This results in more natural and engaging interactions with end-users, enhancing overall customer satisfaction and operational efficiency.

- **Multi-Turn Dialogue Management:** Maintains context over a series of interactions, allowing for complex and continuous conversations without losing track of previous exchanges
- **Personalized Responses:** Leverages historical user data and contextual cues to deliver tailored answers, enhancing user engagement and satisfaction
- **Real-Time Interaction:** Processes inputs and generates responses quickly, ensuring smooth and seamless user experiences in customer support and interactive applications
- **Integration Capability:** Easily integrates with various communication platforms, enabling omnichannel support across websites, mobile apps, and messaging services

Domain-Specific Fine-Tuning

For applications requiring high precision, organizations can fine-tune the pre-trained models on domain-specific datasets. This process adjusts the model's parameters so that it better understands industry-specific terminology, contextual nuances, and desired output styles. As a result, the generated content becomes more accurate and tailored to the specialized needs of sectors such as finance, healthcare, legal, and retail.

- **Enhanced Accuracy:** Fine-tuning with domain-specific data helps the model understand specialized terminology, industry jargon, and nuanced context, resulting in more precise outputs
- **Regulatory Compliance:** Customizes outputs to meet specific legal or regulatory standards, essential for sectors like finance, healthcare, and legal services
- **Tailored Use Cases:** Optimizes the model for specific scenarios, whether it is customer support in a technical field or content generation for creative industries
- **Continuous Improvement:** Supports iterative training processes that can adapt to changing industry trends and incorporate new data, while ensuring that the model remains current and effective

Enhanced Creative Expression

Beyond technical applications, the natural language generation capabilities support creative endeavors. Writers, marketers, and content creators can use the service to brainstorm ideas, overcome writer's block, or generate initial drafts that can be refined later. The tool's versatility in handling diverse topics and creative styles makes it a valuable asset for innovation in content production. These capabilities are mentioned in considerable detail as follows:

- **Idea Generation:** Provides a wealth of creative suggestions, storylines, or content themes, helping overcome writer's block and inspiring new ideas
- **Draft Production:** Quickly produces rough drafts or outlines that serve as a foundation for further refinement by human writers, accelerating the creative process

- **Versatility in Expression:** Handles a wide range of topics and creative styles, allowing users to experiment with different tones and narrative structures
- **Collaborative Tool:** Acts as a digital brainstorming partner, offering alternative phrasings and approaches that can be combined with human creativity for optimal results

Use Cases of Azure OpenAI Service: Natural Language Generation

Azure OpenAI Service's advanced natural language generation capabilities can be applied across diverse industries to transform how businesses communicate, create content, and engage with users. By harnessing context-aware text generation, customizable tone and style, and domain-specific fine-tuning, organizations can streamline workflows, improve user satisfaction, and innovate at scale. The following are some key scenarios where Azure OpenAI Service delivers significant value:

- **Enhancing Customer Engagement:** By integrating context-aware text generation into chatbots and virtual assistants, businesses can offer real-time, personalized responses to user queries. This not only improves customer satisfaction but also reduces wait times and operational costs.
- **Automating Content Production:** Enterprises can leverage automated content creation features to draft reports, marketing materials, and social media posts. This significantly accelerates production timelines and ensures consistency in tone, style, and branding across various communication channels.
- **Streamlining Internal Communications:** Internal teams benefit from auto-generated summaries of lengthy documents and meeting notes. This enables quicker decision-making, improves knowledge sharing, and allows employees to focus on high-impact tasks, rather than manual summarization.

Azure AI Foundry: Design, Customize, and Manage AI Apps and Agents

As artificial intelligence continues to advance at breakneck speed, businesses are increasingly looking for efficient and secure methods to integrate cutting-edge technologies into their operations. **Azure AI Foundry** meets that need by offering a centralized environment where technical teams and business units can collaborate seamlessly. This new platform not only simplifies the process of experimenting with, deploying, and monitoring AI models, but also ensures that enterprises can scale their solutions confidently, while adhering to stringent security and compliance standards.

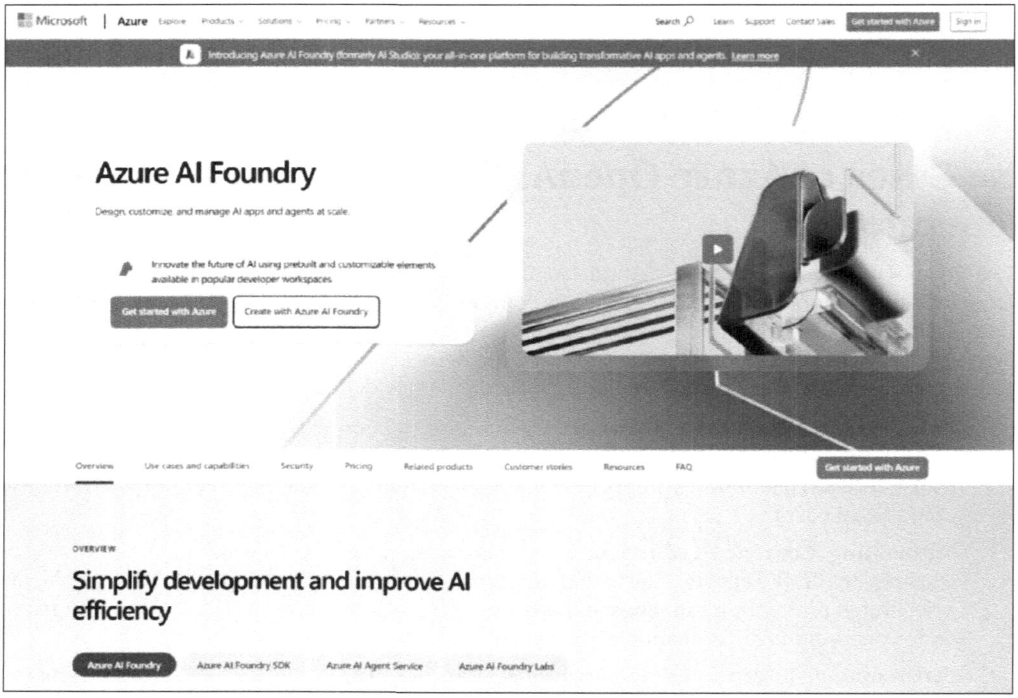

***Figure* 12.3:** *Azure AI Foundry Website*

Azure AI Foundry is more than just a management portal–it is the nerve center for orchestrating advanced AI deployments on Microsoft Azure. It is a platform where you can supervise every aspect of your AI models, right from their initial deployment to ongoing performance monitoring and updates, all in a unified space.

At its core, Azure AI Foundry empowers you to monitor your deployments in real time, providing detailed metrics on token usage, latency, and overall performance. It allows you to configure automatic updates for models, ensuring that your applications always run on the latest, most secure, and most capable versions without constant manual intervention. This flexibility allows you to lock in a specific model version when stability is crucial, or let the system upgrade automatically whenever new features are available.

What makes Azure AI Foundry truly stand out is its deep integration with the broader Azure ecosystem. You can easily link your deployments with Azure Machine Learning, leverage Azure Functions for dynamic scaling, and tap into robust security features like role-based access control, private networking, and advanced encryption. This comprehensive integration ensures that whether you are running small experiments or enterprise-grade AI solutions, everything is built on a foundation of reliability and compliance.

Key Features of Azure AI Foundry

- **Extensive Model Catalog:** Azure AI Foundry provides access to a wide array of models–from foundational and open-source models to task-specific and industry-tailored solutions. This diversity empowers organizations to select and compare the best-fit model for their unique business challenges.

- **Unified SDK and Seamless Developer Integration:** With a centralized Software Development Kit (SDK), developers can create, customize, and test AI applications in their preferred environments, such as GitHub, Visual Studio, or Microsoft Copilot Studio. The platform also offers pre-built templates that accelerate development, reducing time-to-market for innovative solutions.
- **Integrated Visual Dashboard:** The redesigned portal offers an intuitive interface where developers can discover, evaluate, and manage AI models and services. Customizable dashboards provide real-time insights into project performance, resource utilization, and security configurations, making it easier to govern and optimize AI applications.
- **Advanced Model Customization and Fine-Tuning:** Azure AI Foundry includes robust tools for fine-tuning models, such as distillation techniques and adjustments based on enterprise-specific data, thereby ensuring that AI solutions are tailored to meet precise operational needs.
- **AI Agent Management and Orchestration:** The upcoming Azure AI Agent Service enables the creation and orchestration of intelligent agents capable of automating complex business processes. Features like bring-your-own storage and private networking safeguard sensitive data and facilitate seamless integration across enterprise systems.
- **Comprehensive Security and Compliance:** Prioritizing data protection, the platform integrates advanced security measures such as virtual network isolation, granular access controls, and end-to-end encryption. These features ensure that AI solutions meet rigorous compliance standards, while keeping business data secure.
- **Continuous Monitoring and Evaluation:** To maintain optimal performance and reliability, Azure AI Foundry offers tools for continuous monitoring and evaluation. Developers can use these tools to trace model outputs, quickly identify issues, and make real-time adjustments, thereby improving both quality and operational efficiency.

Azure AI Foundry marks a pivotal step in the digital transformation journey, unifying state-of-the-art AI technologies into one user-friendly platform. By streamlining development, deployment, and management processes, this new solution helps organizations reduce costs, accelerate innovation, and maintain competitive advantage in a rapidly evolving AI landscape. Explore Azure AI Foundry today and unlock the full potential of your AI initiatives.

Azure AI Foundry continues to evolve as part of Microsoft's **Copilot Stack**, while integrating seamlessly with **Semantic Kernel** and the upcoming **Azure AI Agent Service** to enable unified orchestration of intelligent, secure, and enterprise-ready AI solutions.

Hands-on Experience: Practical Guide to Deploy a Model Using Azure OpenAI and Azure AI Foundry

In this exercise, you will create an Azure OpenAI resource and deploy a model for generating creative text responses. You will learn how to configure your resource through the Azure Portal, set up a model deployment, and test it using the Azure OpenAI Studio. This hands-on guide demonstrates how to bring generative AI capabilities to your applications and integrate state-of-the-art OpenAI models within Microsoft's secure and scalable cloud environment.

Note: *Before starting this exercise, make sure your Azure subscription includes access to Azure OpenAI Service and that the selected region supports model deployment.*

Step 1: Create an Azure OpenAI Resource

1. Open the Azure portal and log in with your Microsoft account.
2. Create a `New Resource`
   a. Click `+ Create a resource` in the left-hand menu.

   b. In the search bar, type **`Azure OpenAI`** and select **`Azure OpenAI Service`** from the results.

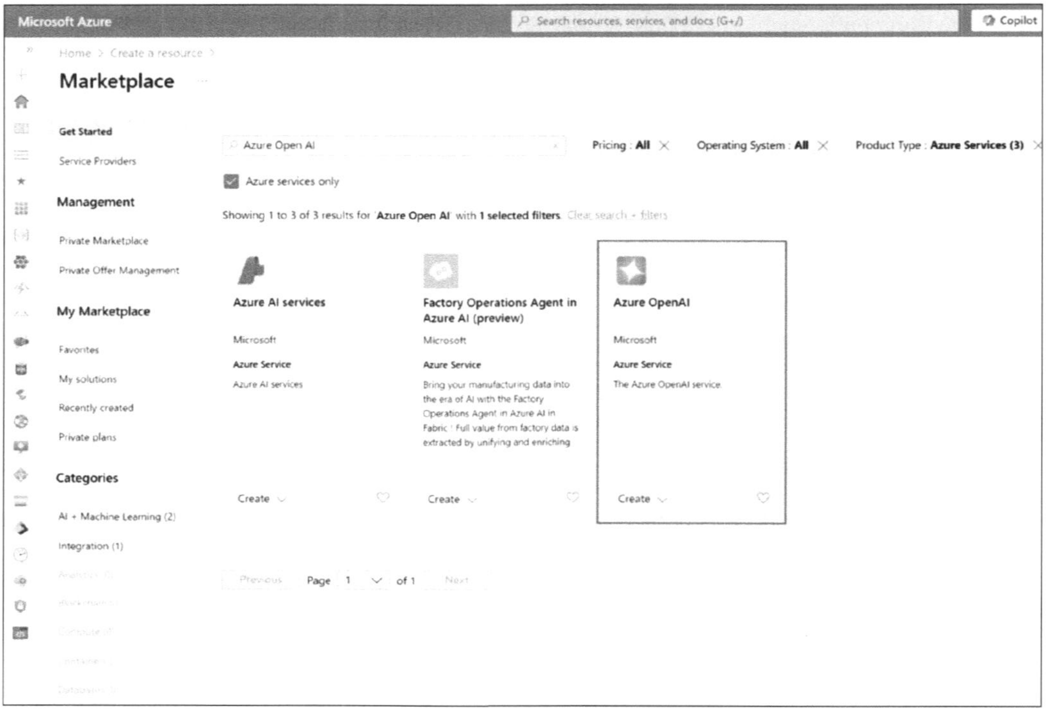

Figure 12.4: *Search for Azure Open AI Service*

3. Configure the **Resource Settings**
   a. **`Subscription`:** Select your active Azure subscription.
   b. **`Resource Group`:** Choose an existing group or create a new one (for example, **`rg-openai`**).
   c. **`Region`:** Pick the nearest supported region (for example, **`East US`** or **`East US 2`**).
   d. **`Name`:** Enter a unique name for your resource (for example, **`myOpenAIBookResource`**).
   e. **`Pricing Tier`:** Select the appropriate pricing tier for your needs (for example, Standard or a free tier, if available).

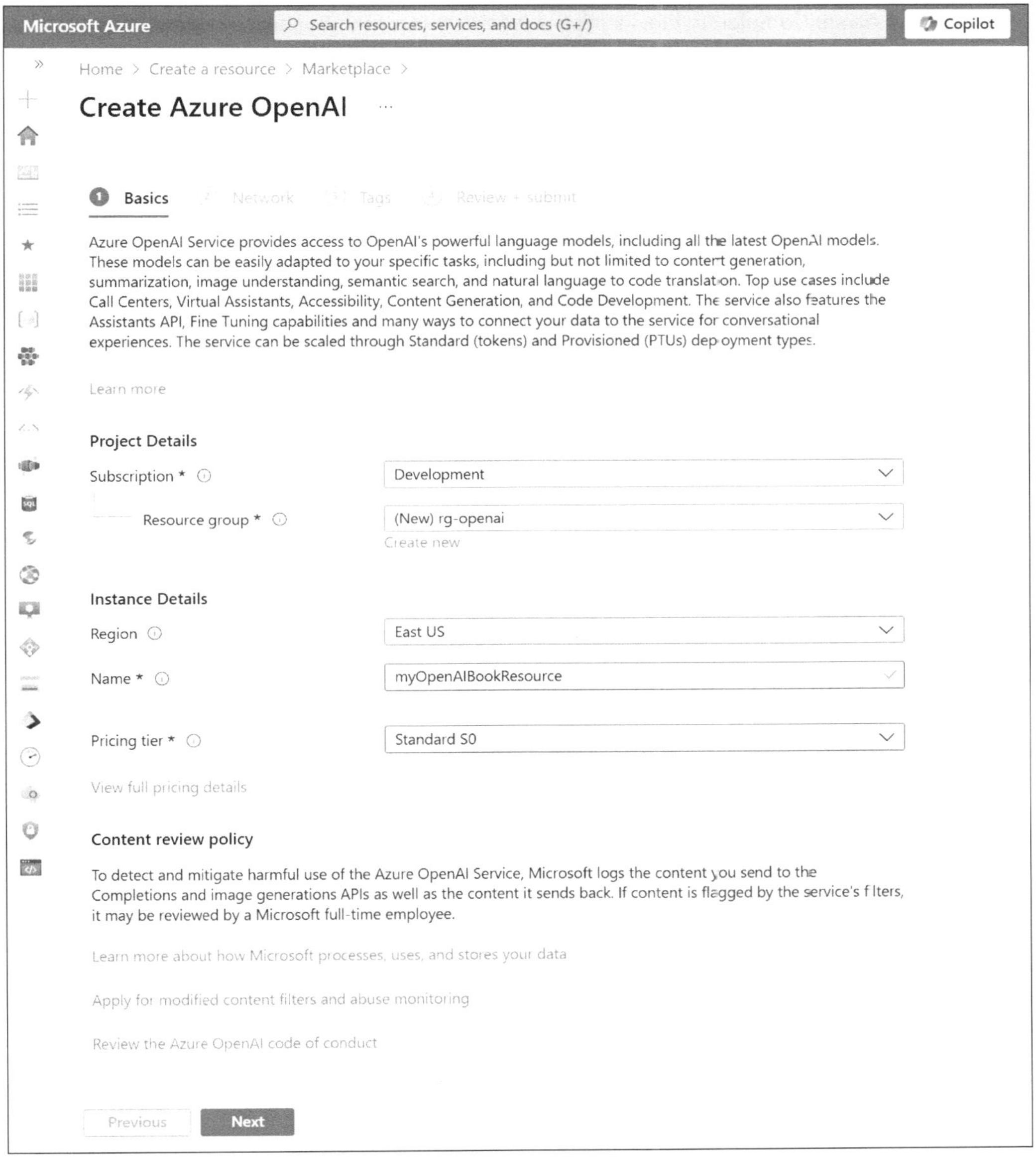

Figure 12.5: *Create Azure Open AI Service in Azure Portal*

4. Click **Next**.
5. In the **Network** tab, you can configure how your Azure OpenAI resource will be exposed or protected from network traffic. In other words, you decide where (and how) the service can be accessed from. These options include:
   a. **`All networks, Including the Internet`:** Allows any network, including the public internet, to access the resource
   b. **`Selected Networks`:** Restricts access to specific networks, applying security rules to limit which IP addresses or networks can reach the service

c. **Disabled:** Completely blocks access from the internet. In this scenario, access typically occurs through private endpoints or other advanced network configurations.

d. For our hands-on exercise, we will keep the All Networks option selected and move forward. Click **Next**.

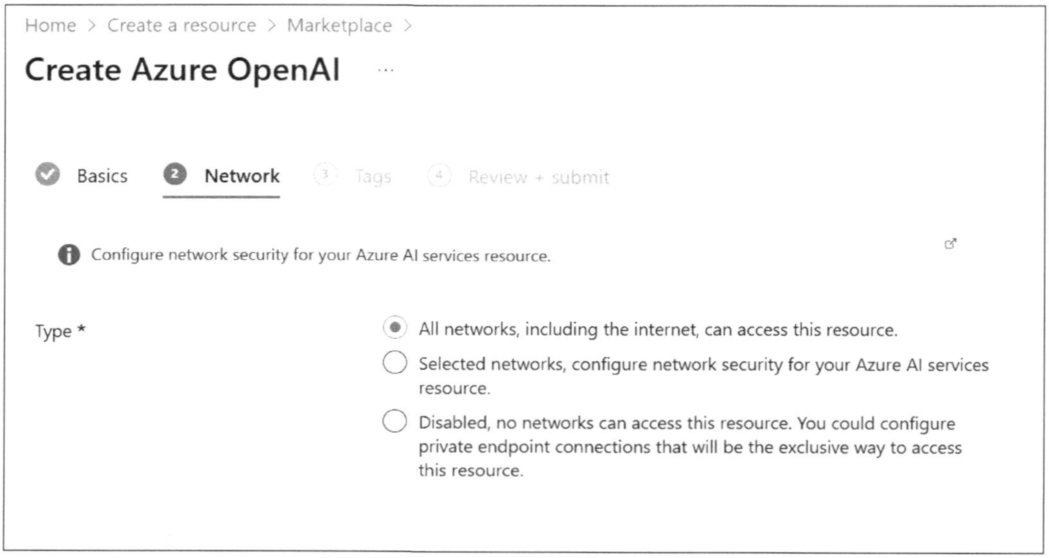

Figure 12.6: *Create Azure Open AI Service in Azure Portal*

6. We do not need to include tags and we can click **Next**.
7. We might have to review the information. By clicking Create, we agree to the terms of use and privacy.
8. Click **Create**.

Note: *Creating an Azure OpenAI resource is subject to availability in specific regions and may require additional access approvals. Always consult the Azure OpenAI Service documentation (https://learn.microsoft.com/en-us/legal/cognitive-services/openai/limited-access) for the latest information on model availability, pricing tiers, and compliance requirements.*

By following this hands-on guide, you will have a fully provisioned Azure OpenAI resource, which is ready to deploy cutting-edge AI models and accelerate innovation within your organization.

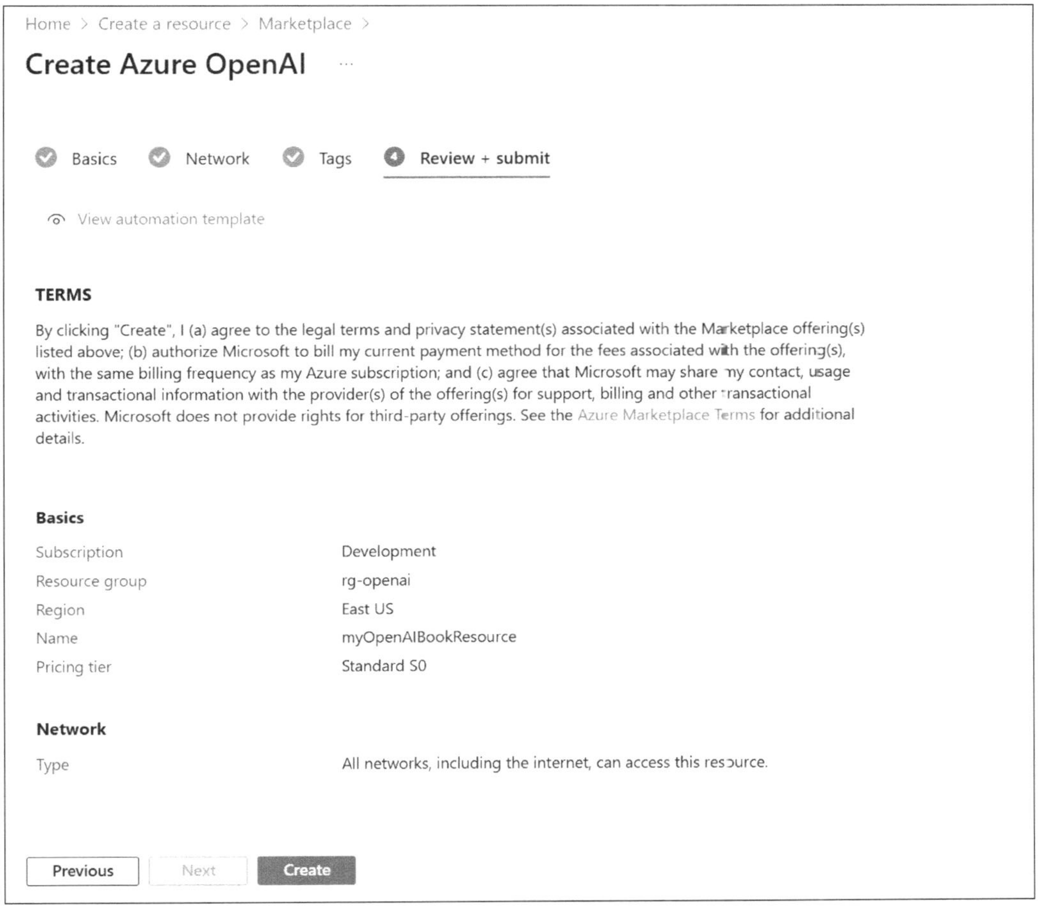

Figure 12.7: *Create Azure Open AI in Azure Portal*

Step 2: Open Azure AI Foundry Portal

1. After finishing creating the Azure OpenAI service, access the resource.
2. On the screen of the created Azure Open AI resource, access the **`Go to Azure AI Foundry portal`** link.

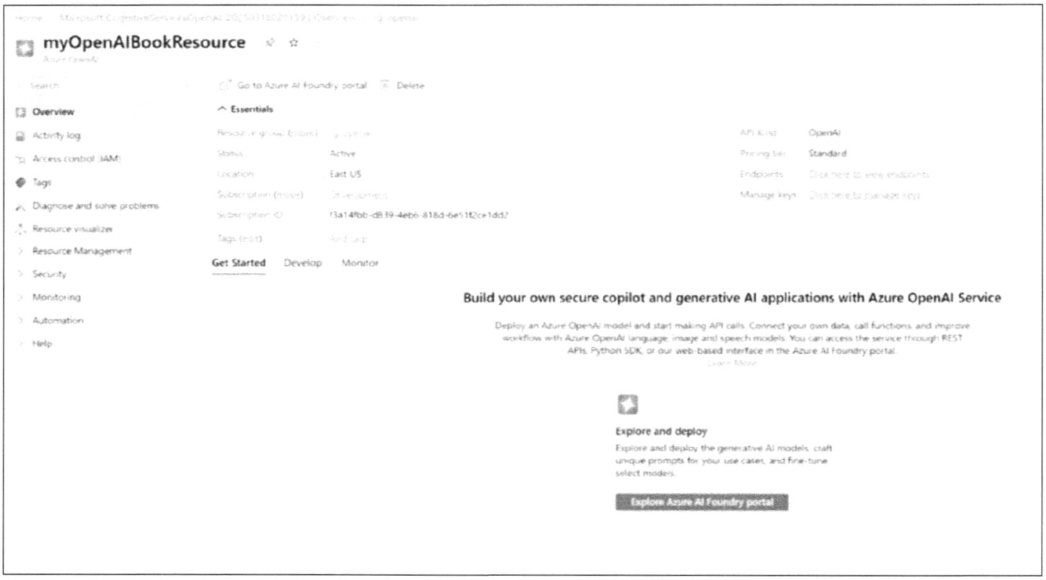

Figure 12.8: *Azure Open AI Resource in Azure Portal*

3. A new tab will open in your browser with the **`Azure AI Foundry portal`**.

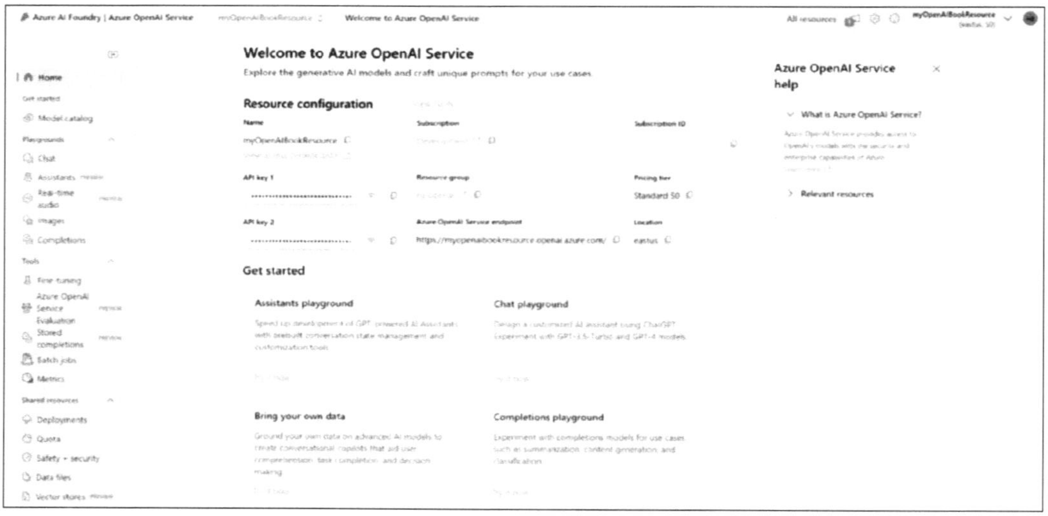

Figure 12.9: *New Azure AI Foundry Portal*

Step 3: Deploy a Deployment in Model Catalog

1. Access **`Azure AI Foundry portal`**.
2. Create a Deployment:
    a. Navigate to the **`Model Catalog`** section.
    b. Navigate to the **`Template Catalog`** section.
    c. Select a **`model`**: Choose a popular model (for example, GPT-4 or o3-mini).

Figure 12.10: *Select a Model to Deploy in Model Catalog*

d. Select the Azure region (for example, East US).

e. Click **Deploy**.

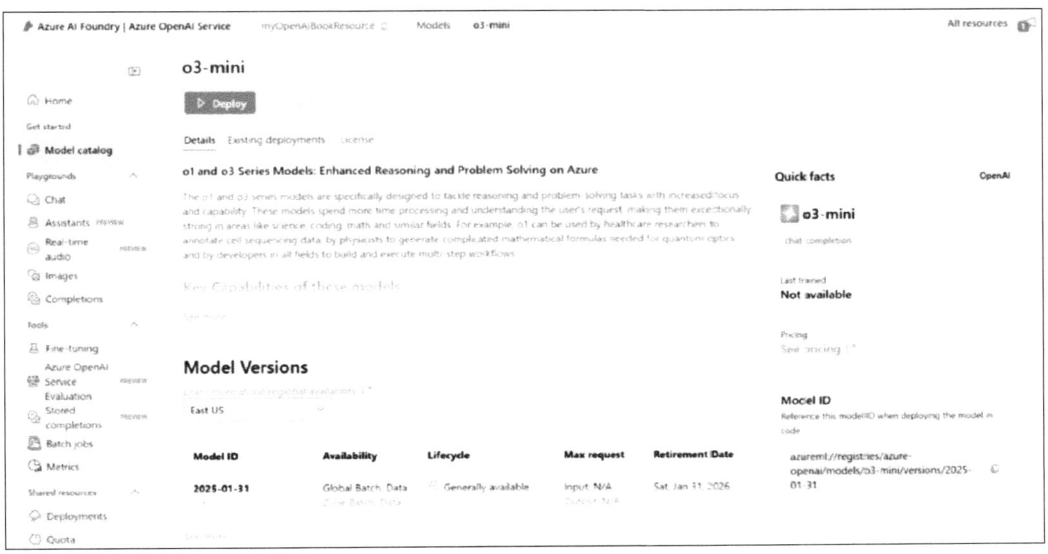

Figure 12.11: *Deploy o3-mini Model in Azure OpenAI Service*

3. In the **Deploy** window, configure model detail.:
   a. **Deployment name:** Enter your Deployment name.
   b. **Deployment type:** Select Global Standard.
   c. **Deployment details:** Configure the deployment details and, if necessary, customize the Tokens per Minute Rate Limit.
   d. **Name:** Provide a unique name.
   e. **Pricing tier:** Select Free F0 or a standard tier.
4. Click **Create resource and deploy**.

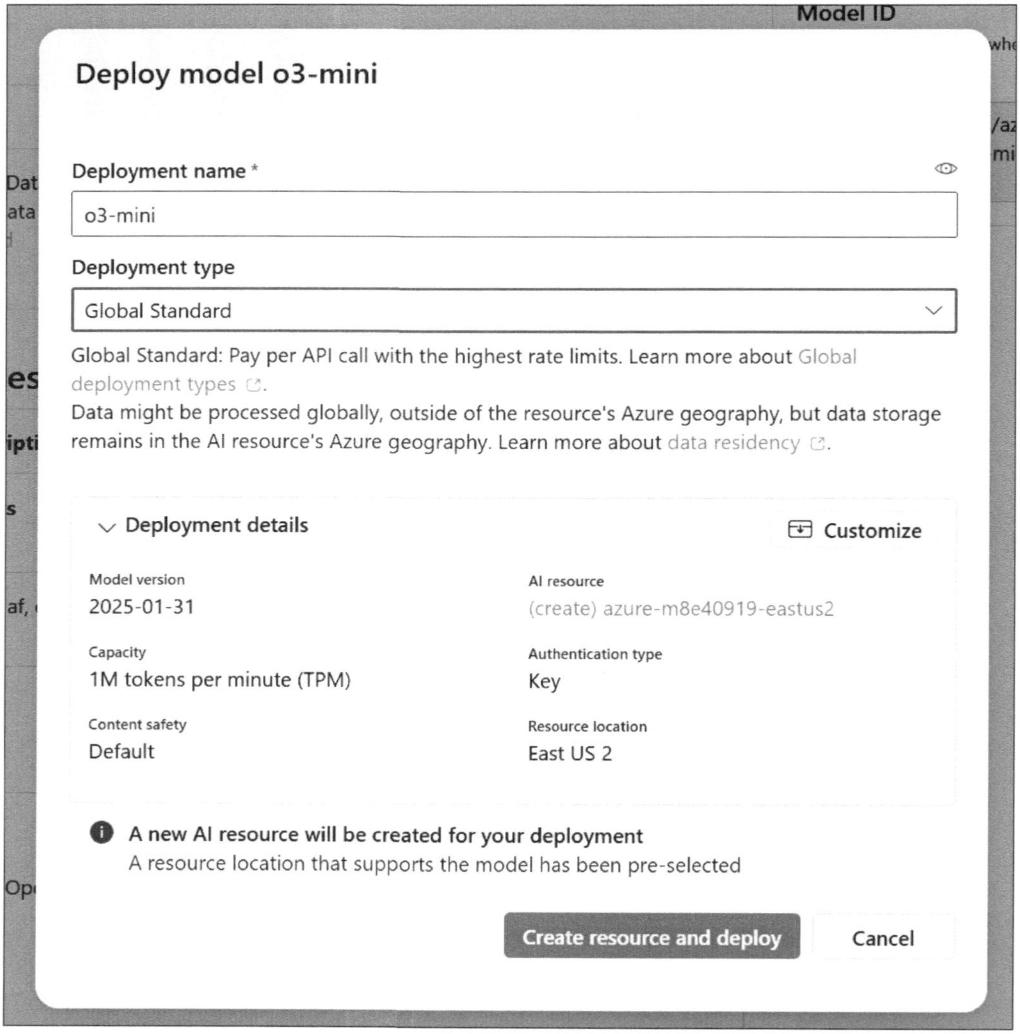

Figure 12.12: Finalize the Deploy Model Configurations

Step 4: Exploring the Chat Playground in Azure AI Foundry

1. Select **`Chat`**.

    a. In the left-hand menu, choose **`Chat`** under **`Playgrounds`**. You should see the Chat Playground interface, similar to the screenshot, as follows:

Figure 12.13: *Finalize the Deploy Model Configurations*

2. Configure Your Deployment

    a. **`Deployment`:** Select your previously created deployment.

    b. **`Give the model instructions and context`:** In the text box, you can set high-level or system instructions. For example: "`You are a friendly AI assistant specializing in career advice. Always provide concise, helpful, and accurate responses.`"

    c. Click **`Apply changes`**.

    d. Confirm to start a new chat session.

    e. **`Generate a prompt` (Optional):** Azure OpenAI will generate a complete prompt from your instruction.

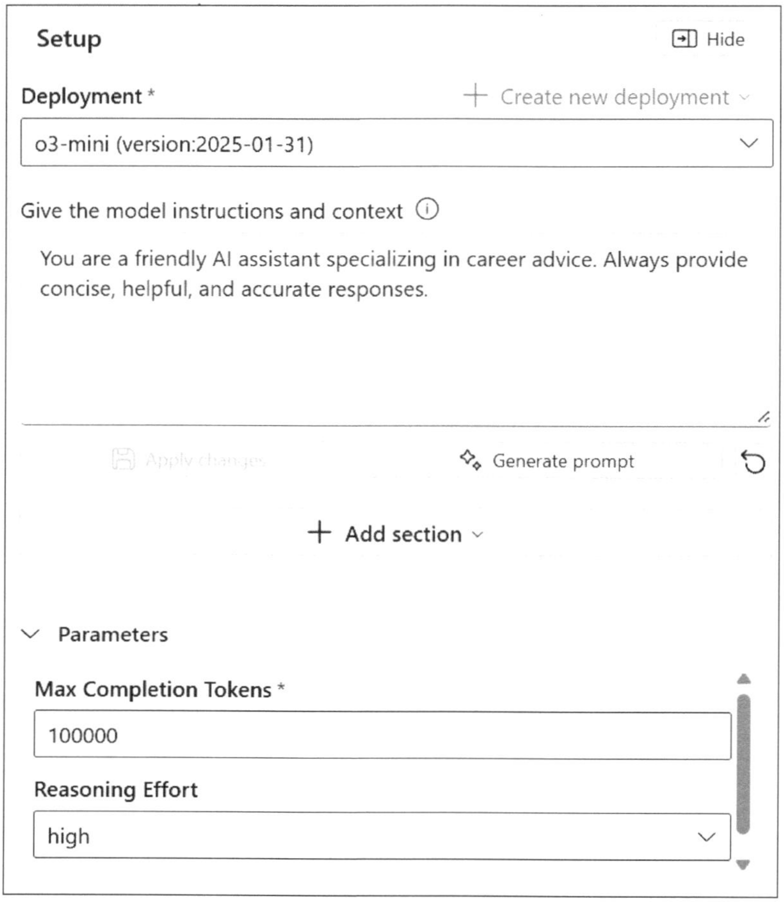

Figure 12.14: *Configure Your Model and Instructions*

3. Adjust these values as needed to match your desired output style.

Step 5: Add Your User Prompt

4. Enter a Prompt.

   a. In the large text area on the right, type the question or command you want the AI model to address. For example, "`I'm preparing for a job interview at a tech startup. Could you provide some tips on how to stand out during the process?`"

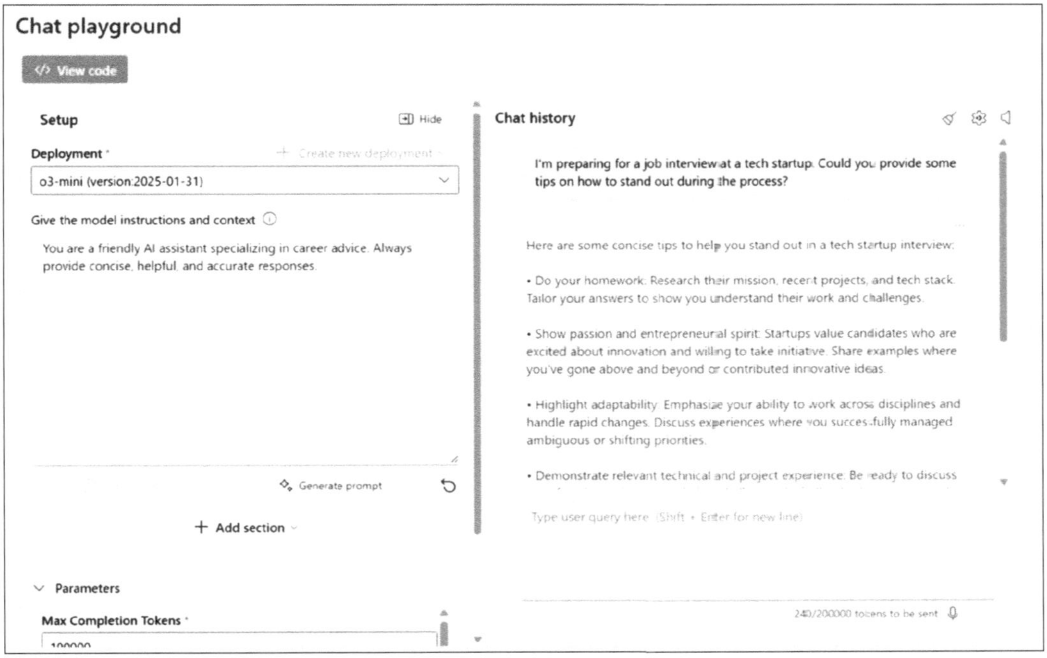

Figure 12.15: *Chat Playground with User Prompt and AI Assistant Response*

Step 6: Refine and Iterate

1. **Review the Assistant's Answer**

   a. Evaluate whether the response meets your needs. If it is too broad or lacks detail, provide more context, or specify your requirements more precisely.

2. **Follow-Up Questions**

   b. Continue the conversation by asking additional questions or requesting clarifications. For instance, "`Could you suggest any common coding challenge patterns I should practice?`"

3. **Adjust Parameters** (Optional)

   c. If the answer is too short, too verbose, or not creative enough, revisit **`Parameters`** and tweak values such as **Temperature** to influence the style and depth of the output.

Best Practices and Tips for Chat Playground

- **Keep Prompts Clear and Specific:** Well-defined questions usually yield more relevant answers.
- **Iterate Through System Instruction:** If the assistant's tone or focus needs to change, update the **Model Instructions and Context**.
- **Use Chat History:** Review or delete previous sessions to maintain clarity in your conversation.

This hands-on exercise demonstrates how we can easily create a new Azure OpenAI resource from the portal. We also learn how to access the new OpenAI portal, called Azure AI Foundry. Additionally, we successfully created a deployment template using our provisioned resource, which allowed us to interact with and test advanced AI models directly from the Chat Playground.

We will continue to use this deployment in upcoming hands-on exercises.

Code Generation Capabilities of Azure OpenAI Service

The Azure OpenAI Service provides sophisticated code generation features that enable developers to **automate coding tasks**, **improve productivity**, and **minimize errors**. Built on state-of-the-art language models fine-tuned for programming tasks, this service can generate code snippets, offer intelligent autocompletion, debug existing code, and even translate code across different programming languages. This functionality not only **accelerates** development workflows but also acts as a **learning resource**, offering best-practice guidance and alternative coding approaches.

Key Features of Code Generation in Azure OpenAI Service

Azure OpenAI Service leverages advanced language models to transform the software development process. It empowers developers by automating repetitive coding tasks, providing intelligent suggestions, and ensuring code quality through real-time error detection. This service not only accelerates development cycles but also is a learning tool, offering insights into best practices and innovative approaches that help teams overcome coding challenges efficiently.

- **Context-Aware Code Completions:** Models like GPT-4 and GPT-3.5 Turbo understand complex code contexts and offer adaptive, intelligent autocompletion suggestions tailored to the structure and logic of your codebase.
- **Multilingual and Cross-Platform Support:** The service supports a wide variety of programming languages—from Python, JavaScript, and C# to specialized languages, thus making it a versatile tool across diverse development environments.
- **Error Detection and Debugging Assistance:** By analyzing syntax and code structure, the models can detect potential errors and provide real-time debugging suggestions, acting as a virtual pair programmer to improve code quality and reduce troubleshooting time.
- **Customizable Code Generation:** Developers can fine-tune models with domain-specific data, ensuring the generated code aligns with industry standards, internal guidelines, or specialized frameworks unique to their projects.
- **Seamless Integration with Development Tools:** Azure OpenAI Service integrates directly into popular development environments and CI/CD pipelines, offering real-time code generation and review support that fits naturally into existing workflows.

These features collectively streamline the coding process, allowing teams to iterate faster, reduce manual errors, and focus on strategic, high-impact development work.

Benefits for Development Teams

Azure OpenAI Service not only accelerates coding workflows but also delivers tangible benefits that empower development teams to work more efficiently and effectively. By automating routine tasks and providing intelligent insights, this service enables teams to focus on higher-level problem-solving and innovation, while maintaining high-quality, robust codebases. We have mentioned more of its benefits as follows:

- **Faster Iterations:** Rapid prototyping and automated code suggestions enable teams to explore multiple approaches quickly, thus reducing the time between ideation and implementation.

- **Enhanced Learning and Best Practice Adoption:** Developers receive real-time insights into coding best practices and design patterns, which improve their skills and elevate the overall quality of the code.
- **Improved Code Quality:** Automated error detection and debugging support ensure that issues are identified and resolved early, leading to more stable and reliable software products.
- **Reduced Cognitive Load:** By automating repetitive tasks, the service allows developers to focus on more strategic aspects of projects, such as architecture design and complex problem-solving.
- **Seamless Workflow Integration:** With integration into popular development tools and CI/CD pipelines, teams can incorporate AI-driven insights into their existing workflows, enhancing collaboration and productivity across the board.

By incorporating Azure OpenAI Service's advanced code generation into your development lifecycle, you can **significantly reduce manual effort**, **enhance code quality**, and **foster innovation**. Whether you're building a large-scale enterprise platform or experimenting with new technologies, these capabilities empower teams to deliver robust, maintainable software faster than ever.

Hands-on Experience: Practical Guide to Code Generation using Azure OpenAI Service

In this exercise, you will explore the code generation capabilities of Azure OpenAI Service. By setting up an Azure OpenAI resource and deploying a model optimized for coding tasks, you will learn how to generate code snippets, get autocompletion suggestions, and even debug existing code through natural language prompts. Follow the steps below to bring AI-powered code generation into your development workflow.

Note: *Before starting this exercise, make sure your Azure subscription includes access to Azure OpenAI Service and that the selected region supports model deployment.*

Step 1: Test Code Generation in Azure OpenAI Studio

1. Open **`Azure Azure AI Foundry`**.
2. Select Your Deployment.
   a. In the AI Foundry portal, choose the **Chat Playground** section.
3. Enter a Sample Code Prompt.
   a. **`Deployment`**: Select your previously created deployment.
   b. **`Give the model instructions and context`**: In the text box, you can set high-level or system instructions. For example: "`Help the developer to create applications using C#.`"
   c. Click **`Apply changes`**.
   d. Confirm to start a new chat session.
4. Enter a **Prompt**.
   a. In the large text area on the right, type the question or command you want the AI model to address. For example: "`Create a function to convert degrees Celsius to Fahrenheit`".

Figure 12.16: *Code Generated by Azure OpenAI*

Step 2: Review and Iterate

- **Examine the Output:** Check the generated code snippet for correctness and readability.
- **Refine the Prompt:** If needed, adjust the prompt to add more context and specify style preferences (for example, include comments or error handling).
- **Follow-up Questions:** Ask additional questions such as, "Explain how the convert Celsius to Fahrenheit works" or "Suggest improvements to the code."

By following this detailed hands-on guide, you have created a code generation model, and tested its capabilities using Azure OpenAI Studio. This process demonstrates how AI-powered code generation can streamline your development workflow, enhance productivity, and serve as a valuable tool for debugging and code optimization in your projects.

Integrating the Azure OpenAI API

The Azure OpenAI API is a powerful interface that lets developers access advanced AI models via simple HTTP calls. It enables functionalities like text generation, summarization, translation, and more, without the need to manage the underlying AI infrastructure.

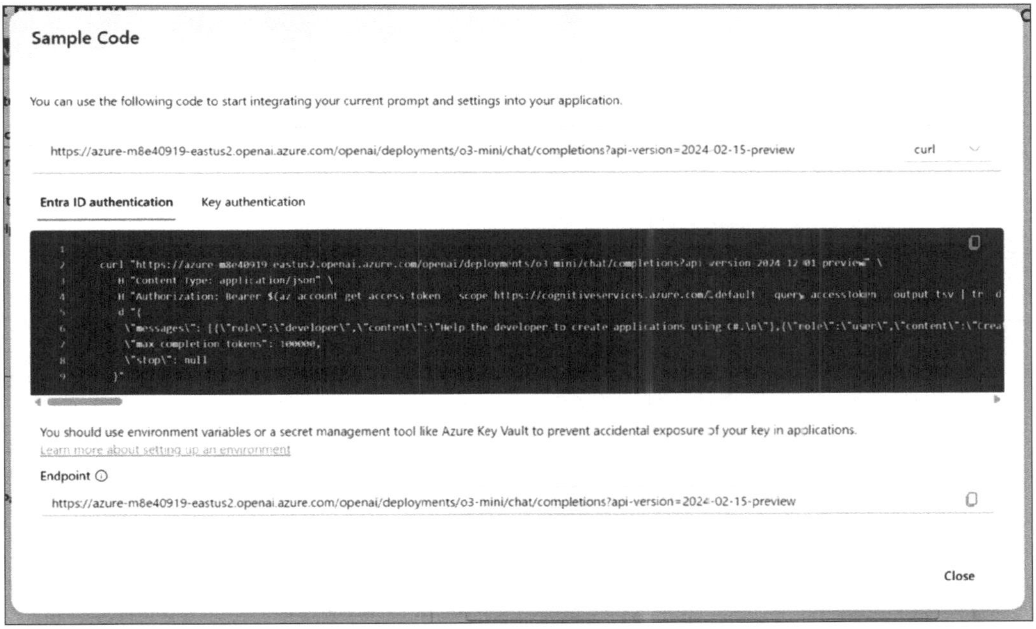

Figure 12.17: *Code Generated by Azure OpenAI to Convert Degrees Celsius to Fahrenheit Using C#*

Accessing the Azure OpenAI API

To start integrating the API into your code, follow these steps:

1. You can click **`View Code`** in Chat Playground and a modal window will open explaining how to integrate the Azure OpenAI API into your application.
2. **Select Your Preferred Programming Language:** Choose from a variety of supported languages such as Python, JavaScript/Node.js, C#, Java, Go, and Ruby.

```
// Install the .NET library via NuGet: dotnet add package Azure.AI.OpenAI --prerelease
using System;
using System.Collections.Generic;
using System.Threading.Tasks;
using Azure;
using Azure.AI.OpenAI;
using Azure.Identity;
using OpenAI.Chat;

using static System.Environment;
using System.Text.Json;

async Task RunAsync()
{
    // Retrieve the OpenAI endpoint from environment variables
    var endpoint = GetEnvironmentVariable("AZURE_OPENAI_ENDPOINT") ?? "https://azure-m8e40919-eastus2.openai.azure.com/";
    if (string.IsNullOrEmpty(endpoint))
    {
        Console.WriteLine("Please set the AZURE_OPENAI_ENDPOINT environment variable.");
        return;
    }

    // Use DefaultAzureCredential for Entra ID authentication
    var credential = new DefaultAzureCredential();

    // Initialize the AzureOpenAIClient
    var azureClient = new AzureOpenAIClient(new Uri(endpoint), credential);

    // Initialize the ChatClient with the specified deployment name
    ChatClient chatClient = azureClient.GetChatClient("o3-mini");

    // Create a list of chat messages
    var messages = new List<ChatMessage>
    {
        new DeveloperChatMessage("Help the developer to create applications using C#.
"),
            new UserChatMessage("Create a function to convert degrees Celsius to Fahrenheit"),
            new AssistantChatMessage("Below is an example of how you can create a function in C# to convert Celsius to Fahrenheit. The con
```

Figure 12.18: *Sample C# Code to Access the Azure OpenAI API*

3. **Choose Your Authentication Method:** Decide whether you want to use Entra ID authentication or Key authentication for secure access to your API.

This interactive experience in the Chat Playground helps streamline the integration process, providing practical code snippets and guidance tailored to your chosen language and authentication method.

Key Benefits of Using the Azure OpenAI API

- **Scalability and Flexibility:** The API allows your application to tap into AI capabilities on demand without investing in dedicated hardware or managing complex infrastructures.
- **Multi-Language Compatibility:** Using standard REST protocols and JSON, the API integrates easily with numerous programming languages like Python, C#, JavaScript, and more, thus making it adaptable to diverse development environments.
- **Cost-Effectiveness:** With consumption-based pricing, you pay only for what you use, which makes the API a cost-effective solution for all types of projects.
- **Easy Integration:** The API's RESTful design and use of common data formats (JSON over HTTPS) simplify integration with your existing systems, tools, and workflows.
- **Continuous Improvement:** Microsoft continuously updates the underlying models and features, so your application benefits from the latest advancements in AI without additional development overhead.

Best Practices for Integration

- **Rate Management and Monitoring:** Configure rate limits to prevent overload and monitor your API usage to manage costs and performance effectively.
- **Error Handling:** Implement robust error handling to manage network failures or unexpected responses, hence ensuring the resilience of your application.
- **Fine-Tuning Parameters:** Experiment with parameters such as temperature, top-p, and maximum token length to adjust the creativity and precision of generated responses for your specific use case.
- **Regular Testing and Validation:** Conduct continuous tests to validate the API responses across various scenarios, ensuring they meet your quality and compliance standards.

Integrating the Azure OpenAI API into your code is a powerful strategy for adding advanced AI capabilities to your applications. With support for multiple programming languages, simple RESTful integration, and a broad array of features–from dynamic content generation to natural language processing–the API offers a scalable, secure, and cost-effective way to modernize your development processes. Additionally, the Chat Playground provides an interactive way to view integration examples, select your preferred language, and choose between Entra ID or Key authentication, further streamlining the setup. With easy access via the Azure portal, comprehensive documentation, and robust security measures, you will be well-equipped to create innovative solutions that stand out in today's competitive market.

Image Generation Capabilities of Azure OpenAI Service

The Azure OpenAI Service goes beyond text generation by incorporating advanced image generation capabilities powered by models like DALL-E. This integration allows developers to transform text prompts into visually compelling images using state-of-the-art AI. By leveraging DALL-E's technology, the service can create detailed, contextually accurate visuals that cater to various creative and practical needs–from marketing assets to design prototypes.

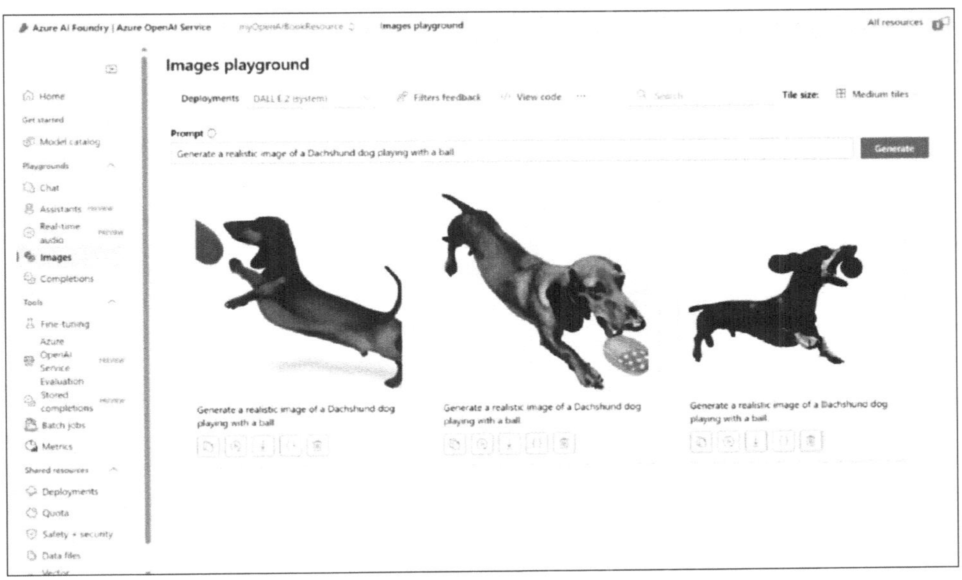

Figure 12.19: *Image Generated Using Prompt and DALL-E on Azure OpenAI*

Working of Image Generation in Azure OpenAI

The image generation process starts when a text prompt is submitted via the Azure OpenAI API. Once received, the underlying DALL-E model analyzes the prompt by tokenizing the descriptive text and mapping it to visual elements based on its extensive training data. The model then generates an image that corresponds to the prompt, using a transformer-based architecture that learns both language and visual patterns. Developers can fine-tune the output by adjusting parameters such as image resolution, style, and creativity level. This process is fully automated and accessible via RESTful API calls, allowing for seamless integration into existing applications.

Before diving into the key features, it is important to understand how DALL-E fits into the picture. Developed by OpenAI, DALL-E uses deep learning techniques to understand and render intricate visual details from textual descriptions. When integrated into the Azure OpenAI Service, DALL-E provides rapid text-to-image conversion with customizable outputs, making it an invaluable tool for automated image creation.

Key Features of Image Generation in Azure OpenAI Service

- **Text-to-Image Synthesis with DALL-E:** Provide a descriptive text prompt, and DALL-E generates an image that reflects the narrative. The model is capable of producing everything from photorealistic scenes to highly imaginative, surreal artworks, depending on the input and specified parameters.
- **Customizable Output:** The API offers options to adjust image resolution, style, and creativity level. This allows you to fine-tune the generated images to match specific project requirements or brand guidelines.
- **Seamless API Integration:** Accessible via RESTful API calls, the image generation capability (including DALL-E) can be easily integrated into your existing applications, websites, or mobile apps. This allows you to create dynamic images as part of your development workflow.
- **Rapid Prototyping and Iteration:** The ability to quickly generate multiple image variations based on different prompts accelerates the creative process. This is particularly beneficial for brainstorming sessions, iterative design, or A/B testing various visual concepts.
- **Enhanced Creative Collaboration:** The tool not only automates the creation of images but also serves as a collaborative platform. Designers and marketers can use AI-generated images as inspiration or starting points, combining human creativity with AI efficiency.

Benefits for Developers and Businesses

Integrating DALL-E powered image generation into your projects offers a host of benefits. It dramatically reduces the time and resources required to produce custom visual content and enables rapid experimentation with various creative concepts. Businesses can scale their visual content production without relying solely on traditional design methods, leading to cost savings and enhanced marketing agility.

- **Time and Cost Savings:** Automating the image creation process minimizes the need for manual design, thus reducing both development time and production costs.
- **Increased Creative Flexibility:** The capability to generate diverse visual outputs on demand empowers teams to explore multiple creative directions and tailor visuals to cater to specific audience needs and campaign objectives.

- **Scalability and Performance:** Leveraging Microsoft's robust cloud infrastructure, the service scales effortlessly to handle large volumes of requests, thus ensuring consistent quality and performance even during peak demand.
- **Improved User Engagement:** Custom, high-quality visuals enhance user interfaces and digital experiences, driving higher engagement and conversion rates across various platforms.

The integration of DALL-E into the Azure OpenAI Service marks a significant advancement in AI-driven creative tools. By transforming text prompts into high-quality, detailed images, this feature opens up new avenues for rapid prototyping, creative exploration, and cost-effective content production. With customizable outputs and seamless API integration, developers and businesses can harness the full potential of DALL-E to innovate and elevate their visual content strategy in today's competitive digital landscape.

Hands-on Experience: Practical Guide to Generating an Image with DALL-E in Azure AI Foundry

In this exercise, you will explore the image generation capabilities of Azure OpenAI Service by using DALL-E in Azure AI Foundry. You will generate an image of a Dachshund dog using a natural language prompt. Follow the steps to create and review your image:

Step 1: Access the Azure AI Foundry Studio

1. Open **Azure Azure AI Foundry.**
2. Select the **`Image`** Section:
   a. In the left-hand menu, click **`Image`**.

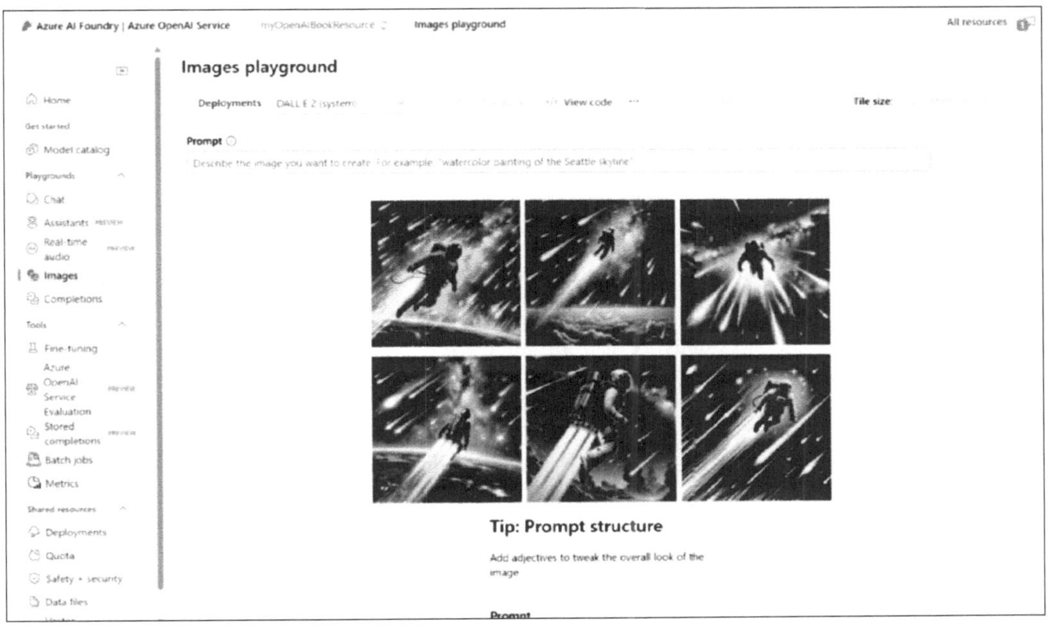

Figure 12.20: *Image Section in Azure AI Foundry*

3. Configure the Image Generation Settings:
   a. **`Deployments:`** Select your previously created deployment. Some deployments are not compatible with DALL-E.

b. **`Prompt`:** In the text box, you can set high-level or system instructions. For example: `"Generate a realistic image of a Dachshund dog playing with a ball."`

c. Click **`Generate`**.

Figure 12.21: *Image Generated with DALL-E on Azure OpenAI*

Step 2: Review the Generated Image

1. **Display the Result:** After a few moments, the generated image will appear on the screen. Examine the image to ensure it reflects the characteristics of a Dachshund dog.
2. **Adjust if Needed:** If the image does not meet expectations, refine the prompt with additional details (for example, "Generate a high-resolution image of a playful Dachshund dog in a sunny park.").
3. **Download Option:** Use the available download or export options in Azure AI Foundry to save the generated image to your local machine.
4. **Review Metadata:** Optionally, review any metadata or settings associated with the image to understand the generation parameters.

Step 3: Clean Up Resources

1. If you do not need the Azure Open AI resource anymore, delete it in the Azure portal to avoid extra costs.
2. Navigate to the resource group, select the Azure Open AI service, and click **`Delete`**.

By following this hands-on guide, you have successfully generated images using **DALL-E** in **Azure AI Foundry**. This exercise demonstrates how natural language prompts can be leveraged to create compelling visuals, integrating advanced generative AI into your creative workflows.

Conclusion

In this chapter, we explored the powerful capabilities of **Azure OpenAI Service** and **Azure AI Foundry**, examining how these platforms enable organizations to build, customize, and manage advanced generative AI solutions. We analyzed how **Natural Language Generation** can create coherent and contextually rich text, how **Code Generation** accelerates software development through intelligent automation, and how **Image Generation** tools like DALL-E transform text prompts into impactful visuals that inspire creativity and innovation.

By mastering these capabilities, you can leverage Azure's ecosystem to integrate automation, enhance communication, and deliver intelligent, scalable AI solutions that align with business goals. Understanding how to apply these tools effectively prepares you to design and deploy real-world solutions powered by Azure's generative AI services.

In the next chapter, we will test your understanding through practice questions and sample scenarios designed to reinforce the key concepts covered throughout this book.

Points to Remember

- **Azure OpenAI Service** seamlessly integrates cutting-edge AI models from OpenAI into Microsoft Azure's secure and scalable infrastructure, enabling enterprises to harness advanced generative AI for text, code, and image generation.
- **GPT-4.5-Preview** introduces support for both text and image inputs, expanded context windows (up to 128K tokens), and improved performance across multiple languages—making it ideal for complex tasks such as document summarization, interactive chatbots, and creative writing.
- **GPT-4o and GPT-4 Turbo with Vision** deliver true multimodal processing by handling text, images, and audio inputs. GPT-4o unifies these input types under a single model, while GPT-4 Turbo with Vision offers faster response times and structured JSON outputs—enhancing advanced visual recognition, OCR, and real-time conversational experiences.
- **New Reasoning Models (o1 and o3-mini)** are engineered for deep reasoning and problem-solving, significantly improving accuracy for complex tasks like coding assistance, scientific computations, and analytical queries.
- **GPT-3.5-Turbo Updates** offer extended context lengths and improved prompt steerability at a cost-effective rate, making them suitable for traditional chat completions, content generation, and coding tasks—while complementing the advanced capabilities of the GPT-4 series.
- **Enterprise-Grade Integration and Security** are built into the Azure platform, featuring role-based access control (RBAC), private networking, and encryption in transit and at rest. These measures ensure robust data protection and compliance for organizations with strict privacy and regulatory requirements.
- **Customization and Fine-Tuning** empower businesses to tailor AI models using proprietary data. This ensures generated content aligns with specific industry requirements, brand guidelines, and business objectives, while improving model accuracy in specialized domains.
- **Azure AI Foundry** serves as a centralized portal for managing AI deployments, providing real-time monitoring, automatic model updates, and deep integration with other Azure services like Azure Machine Learning and Azure Functions.

By understanding and adopting these Azure OpenAI Service features, businesses can capitalize on generative AI to automate tasks, boost creativity, and maintain a competitive edge in an ever-evolving digital landscape.

Key Terms

- **Azure OpenAI Service:** A cloud-based platform that seamlessly integrates advanced AI models from OpenAI into Microsoft Azure's secure, scalable infrastructure. It supports text, code, and image generation, offering enterprise-grade security and compliance features.
- **GPT-4.5-Preview:** The latest general-purpose model is designed to handle both text and image inputs, featuring an expanded context window of up to 128K tokens and enhanced multilingual capabilities for tasks like detailed document summarization and interactive chatbots.
- **GPT-4 Turbo with Vision:** A multimodal model that supports text, images, and audio inputs, offering faster response times and structured JSON outputs—ideal for advanced visual recognition, OCR, and real-time conversational interactions.
- **Reasoning Models (o1 and o3-mini):** Specialized models optimized for complex tasks that require deep reasoning and problem-solving, including coding assistance, scientific computations, and detailed analytical queries.
- **GPT-3.5-Turbo Updates:** Enhanced versions of GPT-3.5 Turbo featuring extended context lengths and improved prompt steerability. These models provide cost-effective solutions for chat completions, content generation, and coding tasks.
- **Enterprise-Grade Integration and Security:** Key features of Azure OpenAI Service include role-based access control (RBAC), private networking, data encryption in transit and at rest, and isolated virtual networks—ensuring robust security and compliance for organizations with strict regulatory requirements
- **Customization and Fine-Tuning:** The ability to adapt AI models using proprietary data, allowing organizations to align model outputs with specific industry requirements, brand guidelines, and business objectives
- **Azure AI Foundry:** A centralized environment for managing AI deployments in Azure. It offers real-time monitoring, automatic model updates, and deep integration with other Azure services like Azure Machine Learning and Azure Functions.
- **Model Catalog:** A feature within Azure AI Foundry that enables users to discover, evaluate, and deploy various AI models—ranging from foundational options to industry-tailored solutions—under a unified interface
- **Chat Playground:** An interactive interface within Azure AI Foundry (or Azure OpenAI Studio) for experimenting with deployed models. Users can test prompts, adjust parameters, and iterate on text, code, or image outputs in real time.
- **Code Generation:** Advanced functionality where models are fine-tuned for programming tasks. Developers can leverage intelligent autocompletion, error detection, and code translation to streamline workflows and improve software quality.
- **DALL-E:** An AI model integrated into Azure OpenAI Service for text-to-image generation, enabling the creation of detailed and contextually relevant visuals from simple prompts; useful for design, marketing, and rapid prototyping

Multiple Choice Questions

1. Which key factor differentiates the Azure OpenAI Service from the standard OpenAI platform?
   a. Azure OpenAI Service only supports older AI models.
   b. Azure OpenAI Service is exclusively for image generation.
   c. Azure OpenAI Service runs on Microsoft Azure's secure, enterprise-grade infrastructure and provides additional compliance, security, and integration features.
   d. Azure OpenAI Service does not support any form of model customization.
2. What feature of Azure OpenAI Service ensures robust security and regulatory compliance for enterprise users?
   a. Expanded context windows of up to 128K tokens
   b. Role-based access control, private networking, and data encryption
   c. Integrated JSON output for structured data
   d. Built-in code debugging and error detection
3. Which capability in Azure OpenAI Service allows organizations to adapt model behavior to specific industry requirements and proprietary data?
   a. Dynamic token rate limiting
   b. Fine-tuning and customization
   c. Multimodal text and image inputs
   d. Structured JSON response outputs

Answers

1. c
2. b
3. b

CHAPTER 13
Practice Test and Sample Questions

Introduction

The AI-900 Exam for Microsoft Azure AI Fundamentals is the gateway for professionals seeking to validate their foundational knowledge in artificial intelligence, machine learning, and Azure's AI services. You have already explored both the theoretical underpinnings and practical applications of these technologies; this chapter brings those learnings together to help you prepare for the exam with confidence.

The exam is designed to assess not only your grasp of key AI concepts, but also your ability to apply them in real-world scenarios that reflect actual business challenges. In today's fast-paced digital landscape, where organizations increasingly rely on AI to drive innovation and efficiency, mastering these fundamentals is essential to stand out in the competitive tech industry.

In this chapter, we will break down the exam's structure, discuss the style of questions you can expect, and review the allotted exam duration along with effective time management strategies. You will also find a detailed example question that illustrates how to leverage your theoretical knowledge to choose the most appropriate Azure service for a given scenario. By the end of this chapter, you will have a clear understanding of what to expect on exam day and practical strategies that help you approach the test with confidence and precision.

Structure

In this chapter, we will discuss the following topics:

- Exam Format and Question Style
- Duration and Time Management
- Useful Links for the AI-900 Exam
- Practical Example of a Question
- Exam AI-900: Microsoft Azure AI Fundamentals Practical Test
- Advanced Preparation Tips

Exam Format and Question Style

The *Exam AI-900: Microsoft Azure AI Fundamentals* is composed primarily of multiple-choice questions, along with some multiple-response items and case studies. Each question is carefully designed to assess both your conceptual understanding and your ability to apply that knowledge in practical scenarios. The exam's structure reflects the diverse nature of AI projects, testing both theoretical fundamentals and real-world problem-solving skills.

Exam Tip: *Carefully read each question's keywords such as "most appropriate" or "best suited." These terms often indicate the precise focus of the question.*

AI and Machine Learning Fundamentals

This section examines your grasp of core AI concepts. You will encounter questions that require you to distinguish between various types of learning–such as supervised learning, where models are trained on labeled data; unsupervised learning, which involves finding hidden patterns in unlabeled data; and semi-supervised learning, which is a hybrid approach combining both methods. Additionally, expect questions on common algorithms and models (like linear regression, decision trees, and neural networks) and key terminologies such as features, labels, training, inference, and evaluation metrics (for example, accuracy, precision, and recall). A solid understanding of these basics is critical as it lays the foundation for more complex scenarios later in the exam.

Azure Services and Solutions

In this segment, you will be tested on your ability to select the most appropriate Azure service to address specific technical challenges. The questions typically present a business or technical scenario and require you to choose between services like Azure AI Vision, Azure Cognitive Services, and Azure Machine Learning. For example, you might need to determine when to use Azure AI Vision for image analysis, Azure Cognitive Services for language or speech processing, or Azure Machine Learning for building custom predictive models. This section challenges you to connect the features of each service with practical applications, so that you can translate theoretical knowledge into actionable solutions.

Ethics and Governance

Responsible AI deployment is a critical component of modern AI solutions. Questions in this category focus on best practices for ensuring transparency, fairness, inclusiveness, and data privacy. You will be asked to evaluate scenarios that require secure and ethical data management, to ensure compliance with regulatory standards, and to demonstrate how to mitigate biases in AI systems. This part of the exam tests your awareness of the broader social and ethical implications of deploying AI technologies, thereby highlighting that technical proficiency must be coupled with responsible implementation practices.

Case Studies

Some questions incorporate brief case studies that simulate real-world scenarios, challenging you to analyze complex situations and decide on the optimal solution. These case studies often involve multiple variables and require a deep understanding of Azure's diverse AI offerings. You might be presented with a scenario describing a business problem, such as improving customer engagement or automating security monitoring, and tasked with choosing the best mix of services to address it. This format not only tests your technical knowledge, but also your critical thinking and problem-solving skills, reflecting the multifaceted challenges faced in a professional environment.

Overall, the AI-900 exam is meticulously designed to ensure that candidates have a comprehensive understanding of both the theoretical underpinnings and practical applications of AI in the Azure ecosystem. Mastering these topics, coupled with effective time management and problem-solving strategies, is the key to pass the exam successfully.

Duration and Time Management

The AI-900 exam is designed to be completed in approximately 60 minutes, with around 40 to 60 questions to answer. Given this tight time constraint, mastering time management is just as important as understanding the syllabus. Effective time management ensures that you answer all questions confidently and have enough time to review your responses.

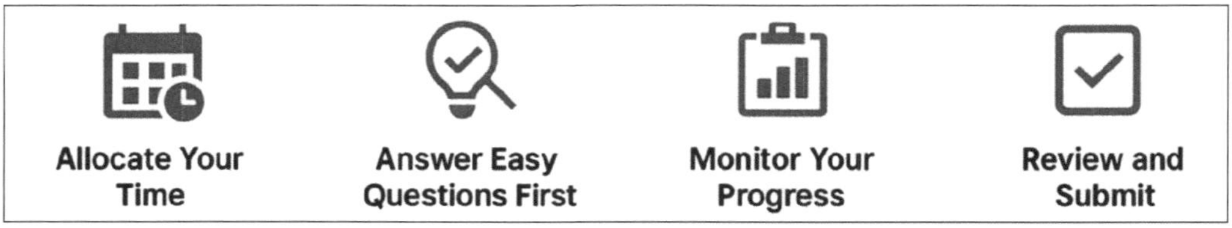

Figure 13.1: *Time Management Strategies for the AI-900 Exam*

Here are several strategies to help you manage your exam time efficiently:

- **Allocate Your Time:** Develop a clear plan before you begin the exam. Aim to spend about 1–1.5 minutes on each question. This initial allocation gives you a baseline for pacing yourself throughout the exam. For questions that seem more complex, reserve a bit of extra time—if necessary, mark them for later review. Having a structured plan minimizes the risk of spending too long on any single question and ensures that you have a buffer for challenging items.
- **Quickly Identify Key Information:** Train yourself to read each question swiftly and effectively by scanning for important keywords and critical details. Focus on understanding what is being asked and identify terms such as "*best suited*," "*most appropriate*," or "*primary objective*" that guide you toward the correct answer. This habit not only saves time, but also helps you distinguish between questions you can answer immediately and those that might require a more careful analysis.
- **Mark for Later Review:** If you encounter a question that appears challenging or confusing, do not get stuck. Instead, mark the question using the exam's built-in flag feature and move on to the next one. This allows you to maintain your pace without sacrificing accuracy on questions you are unsure about. Once you have answered the easier questions, use any remaining time to return to the marked questions. This strategy ensures that no question is left unreviewed and you have the chance to double-check your answers before hitting submit.
- **Practice Under Timed Conditions:** Regularly simulate exam conditions by taking practice tests with strict time limits. This gets you accustomed to the pressure of the exam environment and enables you to refine your time-allocation strategy. Each practice test is an opportunity to identify your strengths and weaknesses—review your performance to determine which types of questions consistently take longer, and adjust your strategy accordingly. Over time, practicing under timed conditions will improve your speed, boost your confidence, and enhance your overall time management skills for the actual exam.

By integrating these strategies into your study plan, you will be able to build the discipline and pacing needed to complete the exam efficiently. Remember, effective time management is a critical component of exam success; it ensures you can answer every question thoughtfully, while also leaving room to review and correct any potential errors.

Useful Links for the AI-900 Exam

We have curated a list of the following official resources and documentation designed to help you prepare effectively for the AI-900 exam. These links provide comprehensive insights into exam objectives, learning paths, study tips, and detailed Azure documentation.

- **AI-900 Exam Overview:** This page offers a complete overview of the AI-900 exam, detailing its objectives, the skills measured, and the structure of the test. It is the perfect starting point to understand what to expect on exam day, including the types of questions and the domains covered.
- **Azure AI Fundamentals Learning Path:** Engage with this official learning path to gain hands-on experience and deepen your understanding of AI concepts as they relate to Azure. It includes interactive labs, video tutorials, and step-by-step guidance to help you master topics such as machine learning, natural language processing, and computer vision.
- **Exam Preparation Tips for AI-900:** This resource provides practical tips and strategies for exam preparation. It covers recommended study materials, practice questions, and effective study techniques to help you tackle the exam confidently and manage your time efficiently.
- **Azure Documentation:** For a deeper dive into specific Azure services, this comprehensive documentation portal is invaluable. It includes detailed technical guides, best practices, and case studies on various Azure services, which are essential for understanding how to apply AI solutions in real-world scenarios.
- **Microsoft Learn:** Explore a wide range of free, self-paced learning modules and interactive exercises on AI and cloud computing. Microsoft Learn is an excellent resource for brushing up on the skills and knowledge required for the AI-900 exam, with content regularly updated to reflect the latest Azure advancements.
- **Azure Certification Community:** Join the Azure Certification Community to connect with other candidates, share study tips, ask questions, and get insights from experts. Engaging with peers can supply you with valuable support and additional resources during the preparation phase.

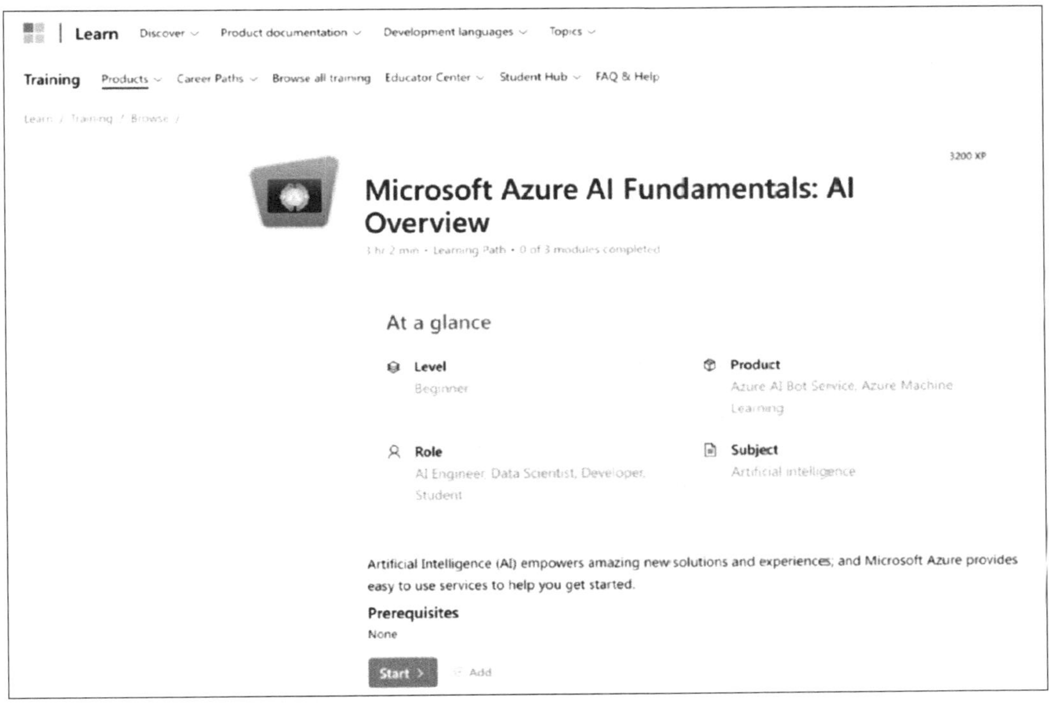

Figure 13.2: Azure AI Fundamentals Learning Path

By leveraging these official resources, you will gain a robust understanding of the topics covered in the AI-900 exam. These links not only provide theoretical knowledge, but also offer practical, hands-on experiences crucial for mastering the material and achieving success in the exam.

Practical Example of a Question

To illustrate the exam's approach, consider the following sample question:

Example Question:

You are developing an AI solution on Azure to analyze security footage. Which of the following services is best suited for detecting and locating objects within an image?

a. Azure AI Vision

b. Azure Cognitive Search

c. Azure AI Language

d. Azure OpenAI Service

Detailed Analysis

The following analysis breaks down the scenario and examines each possible service choice to determine the most suitable solution.

Context:

The scenario involves processing security images to detect and locate objects.

Evaluation of Options:

- **Azure AI Vision:** This service is designed specifically for computer vision tasks. It utilizes advanced image processing techniques, including the use of bounding boxes, to identify and locate objects in images.
- **Azure Cognitive Search:** Although powerful for indexing and searching large volumes of data, it is not optimized for visual content analysis.
- **Azure AI Language:** As it is focused on natural language processing, it does not provide the necessary tools for image analysis.
- **Azure OpenAI Service:** While offering advanced generative and language capabilities, it is not tailored for tasks involving object detection in images.

Conclusion:

The correct answer is **A–Azure AI Vision**. This option is specifically built to handle the type of computer vision tasks required in the scenario.

Exam AI-900: Microsoft Azure AI Fundamentals Practical Test

Q1: Which workload is best suited for detecting anomalies in time-series data?

a. Azure Cognitive Services

b. Azure Machine Learning

c. Azure AI Anomaly Detector

d. Azure Bot Service

Correct Answer: c. Azure AI Anomaly Detector

Explanation: Azure AI Anomaly Detector is designed to identify irregular patterns in time-series data such as sensor metrics or financial transactions. It simplifies anomaly detection using prebuilt algorithms that require minimal setup.

Option A: Provides a wide range of AI models but not specific to time-series data

Option B: Enables building custom models but requires training and maintenance

Option D: Used to build chatbots, not for detecting anomalies

Q2: Select the two key considerations when designing responsible AI workloads. Select Two Answers:

a. Transparency

b. Data Privacy

c. Maximum Model Complexity

d. Cost Efficiency

Correct Answers: a. Transparency and b. Data Privacy

Explanation: Responsible AI prioritizes transparency—explaining how AI makes decisions—and privacy, ensuring the ethical use and protection of user data.

Option C: Complexity is a technical, not ethical, concern.

Option D: Important financially, but not part of responsible AI design.

Q3: Which Azure service is primarily used for content moderation tasks?

a. Azure AI Content Safety

b. Azure AI Vision

c. Azure Cognitive Search

d. Azure Machine Learning

Correct Answer: a. Azure AI Content Safety

Explanation: Azure AI Content Safety detects and filters harmful or inappropriate content, supporting text and image moderation scenarios.

Option B: Focused on computer vision tasks like object detection

Option C: Used for document search and indexing

Option D: A platform for ML experimentation, not moderation

Q4: Select the two workloads that can benefit most from automated anomaly detection techniques. Select Two Answers:

a. Predictive maintenance in industrial IoT

b. Image classification for object recognition

c. Fraud detection in financial transactions

d. Text translation for multilingual applications

Correct Answers: a. and c.

Explanation: Predictive maintenance and fraud detection depend on identifying irregularities or unexpected behaviors within data streams.

Option B: Focuses on identifying objects, not anomalies

Option D: Involves language conversion, not anomaly detection

Q5: Why is it important to split your dataset into training and validation sets?

a. To reduce computation cost
b. To evaluate the model's performance on unseen data
c. To reduce the number of features
d. To increase the training set size

Correct Answer: b. To evaluate the model's performance on unseen data

Explanation: Splitting ensures that a model can be tested on unseen data, validating its ability to generalize beyond what it was trained on.

Option A: Splitting does not lower computational cost.

Option C: Feature selection is unrelated to data splitting.

Option D: Splitting reduces, not increases, training data.

Q6: Select the two main phases in a typical machine learning workflow. Select Two Answers:

a. Training
b. Data Collection
c. Inference
d. Hyperparameter Tuning

Correct Answers: a. and c.

Explanation: Training teaches the model from data; inference applies it to new data for predictions.

Option B: Preparation step, not a main phase

Option D: A subtask within the training phase

Q7: Which Azure service is best suited for building, training, and deploying custom machine learning models?

a. Azure Cognitive Services
b. Azure Machine Learning
c. Azure AI Vision
d. Azure OpenAI Service

Correct Answer: b. Azure Machine Learning

Explanation: Azure Machine Learning provides an end-to-end platform for training, deploying, and managing custom ML models.

Option A: Uses prebuilt AI models

Option C: Specializes in image processing

Option D: Focused on generative AI workloads

Q8: Select the two evaluation metrics most commonly used to measure the performance of a classification model. Select Two Answers:

a. Mean Absolute Error

b. Accuracy

c. Precision

d. Root Mean Squared Error

Correct Answers: b. and c.

Explanation: Accuracy measures overall correctness, while precision evaluates how many predicted positives are correct.

Option A/D: Metrics for regression, not classification.

Q9: What does overfitting refer to in machine learning?

a. Model performs well on both training and unseen data.

b. Model is too simple and underfits the data.

c. Model performs well on training data but poorly on new data.

d. Model uses too many features.

Correct Answer: c. Model performs well on training data but poorly on new data

Explanation: Overfitting occurs when a model memorizes training data patterns but fails to generalize to unseen data.

Option A: Describes ideal behavior

Option B: Refers to underfitting

Option D: Can cause overfitting, but it's not the definition

Q10: Which Azure service is designed for image classification and object detection?

a. Azure AI Vision

b. Azure Cognitive Search

c. Azure AI Language

d. Azure OpenAI Service

Correct Answer: a. Azure AI Vision

Explanation: Azure AI Vision analyzes and interprets image data for classification, object detection, and OCR.

Option B: Handles search, not image analysis

Option C: Used for text understanding

Option D: Focuses on text generation

Q11: Select the two key features crucial for object detection in images. Select Two Answers:

a. Bounding boxes
b. Sentiment analysis
c. Feature extraction
d. Language translation

Correct Answers: a. and c.

Explanation: Bounding boxes identify object locations, and feature extraction detects unique object characteristics.

Option B: Part of NLP

Option D: Related to language tasks

Q12: Which computer vision workload is best used for extracting text from images?

a. Facial recognition
b. Object tracking
c. Optical Character Recognition (OCR)
d. Image segmentation

Correct Answer: c. Optical Character Recognition (OCR)

Explanation: OCR extracts text from images or documents, enabling automation and data digitization.

Option A: Detects identities, not text

Option B: Tracks objects in motion

Option D: Separates image regions without reading text

Q13: Select the two typical applications of computer vision in business scenarios. Select Two Answers:

a. Inventory management through product recognition
b. Customer sentiment analysis
c. Security surveillance for monitoring environments
d. Predicting future sales trends

Correct Answers: a. and c.

Explanation: Computer vision supports automation in product identification and security monitoring.

Option B: Part of NLP workloads

Option D: Based on predictive analytics

Q14: Which Azure service is best suited for sentiment analysis, key phrase extraction, and language detection?

a. Azure AI Language
b. Azure Cognitive Search
c. Azure AI Vision
d. Azure Machine Learning

Correct Answer: a. Azure AI Language

Explanation: Azure AI Language specializes in NLP tasks like text analysis, sentiment classification, and language detection.

Option B: Focused on search

Option C: Handles image data

Option D: Used for model training, not prebuilt NLP

Q15: Select the two main functions of Named Entity Recognition (NER) in NLP. Select Two Answers:

a. Identifying entities in text
b. Translating text between languages
c. Classifying sentiment
d. Categorizing names, locations, and organizations

Correct Answers: a. and d.

Explanation: NER identifies and classifies entities such as people, places, and organizations within text.

Option B: Translation is a separate NLP task

Option C: Focuses on emotional tone, not entities

Q16: What does NLP stand for in the context of Azure AI workloads?

a. Natural Learning Process
b. Neural Language Processing
c. Natural Language Processing
d. Numeric Logic Processing

Correct Answer: c. Natural Language Processing

Explanation: NLP enables machines to understand, interpret, and generate human language.

Option A/B/D: Incorrect definitions of NLP.

Q17: Select the two common tasks performed by Azure AI Language services. Select Two Answers:

a. Sentiment analysis
b. Object detection
c. Text summarization
d. Optical character recognition

Correct Answers: a. and c.

Explanation: Azure AI Language performs sentiment analysis and summarization to derive meaning from large text datasets.

Option B/D: Related to computer vision, not NLP.

Q18: Which Azure service is primarily associated with generative AI for creating new text content?

a. Azure AI Vision

b. Azure Cognitive Services

c. Azure OpenAI Service

d. Azure Machine Learning

Correct Answer: c. Azure OpenAI Service

Explanation: Azure OpenAI Service provides access to advanced generative AI models, such as GPT, for creating human-like text.

Option A: Used for image analysis

Option B: Broader collection of AI APIs, not specialized in generation

Option D: Handles ML model training, not content generation

Q19: Select the two correct statements about prompt engineering in generative AI. Select Two Answers:

a. It involves designing effective input prompts to guide the model's output.

b. It is only applicable to image generation tasks

c. It helps tailor the AI output to meet specific requirements.

d. It eliminates the need for any model training.

Correct Answers: a. and c.

Explanation: Prompt engineering focuses on creating structured and detailed prompts that help AI models like GPT or DALL-E produce relevant and accurate outputs.

Option B: It applies to text, code, and image generation tasks.

Option D: It improves AI usability but does not replace model training.

Q20: Which Azure generative AI feature can transform text prompts into creative images?

a. Azure Cognitive Search

b. Azure OpenAI Service with DALL-E integration

c. Azure AI Language

d. Azure Machine Learning

Correct Answer: b. Azure OpenAI Service with DALL-E integration

Explanation: The DALL-E model within Azure OpenAI Service generates images from text descriptions, enabling creative visual applications.

Option A: Provides enterprise search, not generation

Option C: Designed for text analysis

Option D: Used for ML model development

Advanced Preparation Tips

To further enrich your study plan and ensure you excel on the AI-900 exam, consider these advanced strategies:

- **Focused and Ongoing Review:** Target the most critical topics such as AI fundamentals, Azure service capabilities, and ethical considerations. Use official Microsoft documentation, study guides, and online resources to cover every aspect of the exam content.
- **Simulated Exams:** Regularly take timed practice tests to replicate the exam environment. Analyzing your performance on these tests will help you identify weak areas and refine your time management strategy.
- **Active Participation in Study Groups:** Participate in online forums, discussion groups, or study sessions with peers. Sharing insights and clarifying doubts can deepen your understanding of complex topics.
- **Creation of Visual Aids:** Develop mind maps, flowcharts, and diagrams that illustrate how key concepts connect with each other, especially regarding diverse Azure services and their specific use cases. These visual tools are excellent for quick reviews and long-term retention.
- **Routine Time Management Drills:** Practice answering questions under strict time limits. Establish a rhythm for quickly identifying and answering easier questions, while marking more challenging ones for review to obtain high scores on exam day.

Conclusion

In this chapter, we explored the structure, question style, and time management strategies essential for success in the AI-900 Exam–Microsoft Azure AI Fundamentals We examined the diverse types of questions–ranging from multiple-choice and multiple-response items to case studies–to test your theoretical understanding and practical application of core AI concepts, Azure services, and ethical considerations. We also discussed effective strategies for managing your time during the tight 60-minute time frame of the exam, how to allocate your time to different sections, quickly identify key information, and mark challenging questions for later review. Finally, we provided a practical example of a typical exam question to illustrate how to leverage your knowledge to select the most appropriate Azure service for a given scenario.

By understanding these elements, you are now equipped to navigate the exam format with confidence and precision, apply effective time management techniques to ensure that all questions are answered, and analyze and solve exam scenarios by connecting theoretical knowledge with real-world applications. You can also identify and select the right Azure AI solutions to address diverse business challenges with clarity and accuracy.

As the field of AI and the Azure ecosystem continue to evolve, staying on top of these changes and refining test-taking strategies remains a critical prospect. With the insights and preparation techniques presented in this chapter, you are well-prepared to excel in the AI-900 exam and advance your career in the rapidly evolving world of artificial intelligence.

In the next chapter, we will explore **best practices, future trends, and practical tips** that will help you apply your AI knowledge beyond the exam, enhance real-world implementations, and stay ahead in the ever-changing landscape of artificial intelligence.

Reference Links

The following are the official Microsoft resources and documentation mentioned in this chapter. Use these links to explore the exam objectives, study paths, and Azure AI services in more depth:

- **AI-900 Exam Overview** – https://learn.microsoft.com/en-us/certifications/exams/ai-900
- **Azure AI Fundamentals Learning Path** – https://learn.microsoft.com/en-us/training/paths/get-started-with-artificial-intelligence-on-azure
- **Azure Documentation** – https://learn.microsoft.com/en-us/azure
- **Microsoft Learn** – https://learn.microsoft.com/en-us/training
- **Azure Certification Community** – https://learn.microsoft.com/en-us/users/microsoftcertification/collections/mn5smw9n7d1k7y

CHAPTER 14

Best Practices, Future Trends, and Tips and Tricks

Introduction

This closing chapter connects everything you learned in the book to practical, real-world action. After exploring AI concepts, machine learning fundamentals, and Azure AI services, our goal here is to translate knowledge into effective solutions you can apply on the job and to help you finish your AI-900 preparation with clarity and confidence.

You will see how to turn principles into practice (from responsible AI to scalable deployment), what trends are shaping the near future of Azure AI (generative and foundation models, explainability, edge, low-code, and sustainability), and which exam-smart strategies actually move the needle on test day. By the end of this chapter, you will have a concise set of best practices, a forward-looking perspective, and a focused plan to finalize your certification journey.

Structure

In this chapter, we will discuss the following topics:

- Apply Azure AI Best Practices
- Understand Emerging AI Trends
- Prepare for the AI-900 Exam

Apply Azure AI Best Practices

Implementing AI successfully in real-world scenarios requires more than just technical proficiency; it demands responsibility, strategy, and adaptability on the part of the developer. Microsoft Azure provides a comprehensive ecosystem for building, deploying, and managing intelligent solutions, but true effectiveness comes from applying sound best practices throughout the AI lifecycle.

These practices ensure that your solutions are **ethical**, **scalable**, and **aligned with business goals**, while maintaining transparency and accountability. Whether you are designing a proof of concept, deploying a production model, or preparing for the AI-900 exam, the following principles form the foundation of responsible and effective AI implementation on Azure

Build with Responsible AI Principles

Responsible AI ensures that artificial intelligence systems are designed and deployed in ways that are fair, transparent, and aligned with ethical standards. Microsoft defines six guiding principles that form the foundation for trustworthy AI solutions. These principles are not theoretical, as they are built directly into Azure's tools, frameworks, and governance models.

Principle	Objective	Example or Azure Tool
Fairness	Avoid bias and ensure equitable outcomes.	Use *Fairlearn* to measure and mitigate bias across demographics.
Reliability and Safety	Maintain consistent, predictable model performance.	Apply error analysis and retraining in *Azure Machine Learning*.
Privacy and Security	Protect data and uphold confidentiality.	Implement *Azure Key Vault* and encrypted data pipelines.
Inclusiveness	Design accessible and culturally aware experiences.	Build chatbots with multilingual support in *Language Studio*.
Transparency	Explain how decisions are made.	Use *Responsible AI Dashboard* and SHAP visualizations for model explainability.
Accountability	Ensure human oversight over automated systems.	Establish approval workflows for sensitive decisions.

Table 14.1: *Microsoft Responsible AI Principles*

Note: *Responsible AI is not just a compliance requirement—it is a performance enabler. Fairness, transparency, and accountability build user trust, improve adoption, and directly influence success in the AI-900 exam.*

Design with Business Goals in Mind

A successful AI solution begins with a clearly defined business objective. Before selecting any Azure AI service, you must understand **the problem you are solving**, **who stands to benefit from the solution**, and **how its success will be measured**. Aligning technical implementation with organizational goals ensures that your solution delivers tangible value rather than experimenting without any direction.

While defining your AI project, ask these three key questions:

- What outcome or metric am I trying to improve?
- How will AI support this goal more effectively than traditional automation?
- Which Azure service best fits this scenario?

Business Objective	Azure AI Service	Outcome
Improve customer satisfaction	Azure AI Language	Analyze sentiment in reviews and support tickets.
Optimize inventory and forecasting	Azure Machine Learning	Predict demand using regression models.
Enhance accessibility	Azure Speech Services	Convert speech to text for hearing-impaired users.
Automate document processing	Azure Form Recognizer	Extract structured data from invoices and receipts.
Generate creative content	Azure OpenAI Service	Produce text, summaries, or visuals from prompts.

Table 14.2: *Aligning Azure AI Services to Business Objectives*

Note: *In both real projects and the AI-900 exam, Microsoft expects you to think about the solution first. Identify the business challenge before selecting the Azure service. This approach demonstrates strategic thinking and ensures that AI delivers measurable impact.*

Execute, Test, and Iterate

AI development is an ongoing cycle of experimentation and refinement. Building effective solutions in Azure requires a mindset of **continuous improvement**, where models are tested, evaluated, and enhanced as new data becomes available. This iterative process ensures that performance stays reliable and relevant over time.

A typical implementation workflow includes the following steps:

1. **Start Small:** Use Azure's free or sandbox environments to prototype quickly and validate your idea before scaling.
2. **Train and Validate:** Split your dataset to evaluate model performance on unseen data, ensuring that results generalize beyond the training set.
3. **Monitor Performance:** Track metrics such as accuracy, precision, and recall to detect when retraining is necessary.
4. **Automate Retraining:** Use Azure Machine Learning pipelines to automate updates when data or business conditions change.
5. **Deploy Responsibly:** Apply version control and rollback strategies to ensure model stability and transparency in production.

Note: *Treat AI deployment as a living process, not a one-time event. Regular monitoring, retraining, and feedback loops prevent model drift and maintain fairness, reliability, and accuracy throughout the solution's lifecycle.*

Stay Current and Keep Learning

Artificial intelligence evolves faster than almost any other technology field. New Azure AI services, model updates, and best practices appear regularly, making continuous learning essential for every AI professional. Staying up-to-date not only sharpens your technical skills, but also ensures that your knowledge aligns with Microsoft's latest exam objectives and industry standards.

Practical Ways to Stay Updated:

- **Follow Microsoft's Official Channels:** Subscribe to the *Azure AI Blog* and the *Microsoft AI Newsletter* to keep up with new service releases, case studies, and best practices.
- **Engage with Learning Communities:** Participate in *Microsoft Learn* forums, *LinkedIn groups*, and *GitHub repositories* like Azure ML Examples to collaborate with peers and explore practical implementations.
- **Attend Microsoft Events:** Join *Microsoft Ignite*, *Build*, or *AI Tour* events for hands-on labs, technical deep dives, and direct interaction with Azure experts.
- **Practice Continuously:** Reinforce learning through real use cases. For instance, build a simple model in *Azure ML Designer*, or deploy a chatbot using *Power Virtual Agents* to gain practical insight.

Note: *You can never stop learning about new features and developments in AI. Professionals who stay curious, experiment often, and engage with the community are the ones who translate theory into innovative solutions.*

Understand Emerging AI Trends

Artificial intelligence is currently advancing at an extraordinary pace. Staying informed about the latest developments helps you anticipate new opportunities, adapt to changing technologies, and stay ahead in your career.

This section explores five major trends that are shaping how AI is developed, deployed, and used within the Azure ecosystem. Understanding these trends not only strengthens your expertise, but also prepares you to tackle real-world discussions and scenario-based questions in the AI-900 exam.

Generative and Foundation Models

Generative AI represents one of the most transformative shifts in modern computing. These models can create text, images, audio, and even code by learning patterns from vast datasets. Microsoft Azure provides access to powerful foundation models through the **Azure OpenAI Service**, enabling organizations to integrate creativity and intelligence into their workflows.

Examples of Applications:

- Conversational assistants that understand context and respond naturally
- Automated content creation, from marketing copy to technical documentation
- Developer tools such as *GitHub Coplot*, which translate natural language into code

Note: *For AI-900 scenario questions, when you encounter tasks involving text or image generation, the correct answer typically involves* **Azure OpenAI Service**.

Explainable and Trustworthy AI

As AI becomes more integrated into critical decision-making processes, such as in finance, healthcare, and public policy, the demand for transparency has never been greater. **Explainable AI (XAI)** allows users to understand how and why a model makes its predictions, ensuring both accountability and trust.

Key Tools and Techniques

- **SHAP (Shapley Additive Explanations):** Measures how each input feature contributes to an outcome
- **LIME (Local Interpretable Model-agnostic Explanations):** Explains individual predictions using simple approximations
- **Responsible AI Dashboard:** Provides integrated visualization for fairness, error analysis, and model interpretability in *Azure Machine Learning*

Example: A financial institution uses SHAP values to justify credit approval decisions. By providing clear explanations, customers gain trust in automated systems and regulators become more confident about compliance.

Note: *In the AI-900 exam, questions about interpretability and transparency usually point to tools like* **SHAP** *and* **Responsible AI Dashboard** *in Azure Machine Learning.*

Edge AI and Real-Time Intelligence

Edge AI brings computation closer to where data is generated, enabling faster responses, reduced latency, and improved privacy. Instead of sending all data to the cloud, models run locally on devices like sensors, drones, and industrial cameras.

Benefits of Edge AI

- **Low Latency:** Enables immediate decisions (for example, detecting defects on an assembly line)
- **Data Privacy:** Keeps sensitive information local
- **Bandwidth Efficiency:** Reduces network dependency in remote environments

Azure Edge Technologies

- **Azure Percept:** A development kit for building vision-based edge AI solutions
- **Azure IoT Edge:** Extends cloud intelligence to IoT devices for local analysis

Example: An industrial plant uses Azure IoT Edge to monitor machinery and predict failures in real time, thus preventing costly downtime.

Democratization Through Low-Code AI

AI is no longer limited to data scientists or engineers. With low-code and no-code platforms, professionals from non-technical backgrounds can build intelligent applications visually, while accelerating innovation and reducing dependency on specialized development teams.

Tool	Purpose
Power Virtual Agents	Build chatbots using graphical interfaces.
AI Builder (Power Apps)	Add AI-powered predictions and analysis to business apps.
Azure ML Designer	Create machine learning pipelines with drag-and-drop simplicity.

Table 14.3: *Key Tools*

Example: An HR department uses *Power Virtual Agents* to answer common employee questions about payroll and benefits, thus improving response times while freeing HR staff to take up higher-value tasks.

Note: *Low-code innovation is not only a business trend, but also a democratization movement in AI, which allows every employee to solve and troubleshoot problems effectively.*

Sustainable and Energy-Efficient AI

AI's rapid growth also brings environmental challenges. Training large models consumes significant computational resources and energy. Microsoft and the wider AI community are addressing this through sustainability-focused design and infrastructure.

Key Strategies for Sustainable AI

- Use **model compression** and **efficient architectures** to reduce computational demand.
- Choose **Azure regions powered by renewable energy** to lower your carbon footprint.
- Reuse and fine-tune **existing foundation models** instead of training from scratch.

Example: Organizations use lightweight models such as GPT-4-Turbo to balance performance with energy efficiency. Azure's carbon-neutral data centers further reinforce sustainability goals.

Note: *Expect AI-900 questions referencing "sustainability" or "energy-efficient AI" to connect with* ***model optimization*** *and* ***responsible cloud practices.***

Prepare for the AI-900 Exam

Preparing for the Microsoft Azure AI Fundamentals exam is not only about memorizing concepts, it is about applying them with confidence and understanding how Azure services fit together. This section provides proven strategies, study plans, and practical insights to help you maximize your performance and approach the exam with clarity and composure.

Understand the Exam Format

Before you begin your preparation, you must familiarize yourself with how the AI-900 exam is structured. Understanding the question types and format helps you manage time effectively and anticipate the areas of emphasis.

Exam Characteristic	Details
Official Name	Microsoft Azure AI Fundamentals (AI-900)
Duration	60 minutes
Number of Questions	40–60
Passing Score	700 out of 1000
Question Types	Multiple choice, drag-and-drop, case studies
Coding Required	None
Languages Available	English, Portuguese, Spanish, Japanese, and others

Table 14.4: *AI-900 Exam Overview*

Exam Tip: *Read each question carefully. Watch out for keywords like **"best approach," "most appropriate service,"** or **"responsible implementation."** These phrases often indicate what Azure concept the question is testing.*

Study with the Right Resources

Microsoft provides official materials and practice tools to help you prepare effectively. Start with structured resources and supplement them with hands-on exploration.

Free Resources

- **Microsoft Learn AI-900 Learning Path:** Interactive modules that align directly with the exam objectives
- **Azure Free Trial:** Includes $200 in credits to experiment with real services such as *Azure AI Vision*, *Form Recognizer*, and *Language Studio*
- **Exam Sandbox:** A simulated environment that familiarizes you with the test interface and question formats

Paid Resources

- **Practice Tests:** Platforms such as *MeasureUp*, *ExamTopics*, and *Whizlabs* offer realistic exam simulations.
- **Video Courses:** Options on *Udemy*, *LinkedIn Learning*, and *Microsoft Learn TV* provide guided instruction and visual demonstrations.

Note: *Combine theory with practice. Reading alone will not ensure retention; build something small in Azure to strengthen long-term understanding.*

Hands-On Learning Through Real Scenarios

Practical experience is the most effective way to internalize AI concepts. Small, scenario-driven exercises allow you to connect theoretical knowledge with real Azure implementations.

Suggested Practice Projects

- **Sentiment Analysis:** Use *Text Analytics* to classify customer feedback as positive, neutral, or negative.
- **Image Classification:** Train a *Custom Vision* model to recognize specific products or objects.
- **Document Processing:** Extract structured data from invoices using *Form Recognizer Studio.*
- **Conversational AI:** Create a chatbot with *Language Studio* or *Power Virtual Agents* to handle common support questions.

Note: *The AI-900 exam often presents scenario-based questions. Practicing with real Azure services helps you recognize which solution applies to each situation.*

Use Visual Tools for Review

Visual learning techniques help organize and reinforce knowledge before exam day.

Recommended Tools:

- **Mind Maps:** Use tools such as *Miro*, *XMind*, or *MindMeister* to visualize relationships between Azure AI services.
- **Flashcards:** Create quick questions and answers using *Anki* or *Quizlet* to review concepts like *Responsible AI*, *machine learning types*, or *Azure service functions.*

Example Flashcard:

- **Front:** "What does Azure Translator do?"
- **Back:** "Automatically translates text into over 100 languages using AI models."

Note: *Reviewing 10–15 flashcards daily reinforces short-term memory and boosts recall speed under exam conditions.*

Follow a 14-Day Study Plan

A structured plan helps balance learning, practice, and review. The following schedule provides a manageable framework to cover all major domains in two weeks:

Day(s)	Focus Area
1–2	Responsible AI Principles
3–4	Computer Vision and related services
5–6	Language and Speech Services
7–8	Document Processing with Form Recognizer
9–10	Azure Machine Learning fundamentals
11–12	Practice exams and result analysis
13	Review weak areas and retest
14	Final review and exam-day checklist

Table 14.5: *14-Day Study Plan*

Note: *The day before your exam, review key Azure services and Responsible AI principles; avoid heavy studying. Rest and clarity improve performance more than last-minute memorization.*

Plan Your Next Steps

Earning the AI-900 certification opens the door to more advanced Azure credentials and career opportunities.

Certification	Career Path	Primary Focus
DP-100	Data Scientist	Designing and implementing ML models
AI-102	AI Developer	Building and integrating intelligent applications
AZ-900	Cloud Practitioner	Understanding Azure fundamentals and governance

Table 14.6: *Next-Level Certifications*

Note: *Build a small project portfolio on GitHub showcasing your experiments with Azure ML Designer or Azure OpenAI Service. Real examples will strengthen your professional credibility.*

Conclusion

In this chapter, we connected everything you have learned throughout this book—from understanding core AI workloads, to applying them effectively in real-world scenarios. You explored how to implement best practices when working with Azure AI services, ensuring that every solution you build is responsible, scalable, and aligned with business objectives.

We also looked ahead at the future of artificial intelligence, identifying the key trends shaping the next generation of Azure solutions, such as generative and explainable AI, low-code innovation, edge intelligence, and sustainable computing. These trends will continue to define how AI is created, deployed, and experienced across industries.

Finally, we discussed practical strategies to prepare for the AI-900 exam, emphasizing hands-on learning, structured study plans, and a mindset focused on problem-solving rather than rote memorization. With the tools, insights, and strategies presented here, you will be well-prepared to approach the certification exam confidently and apply your knowledge in impactful projects.

By combining ethical responsibility, technical excellence, and continuous learning, you are not only ready to pass the **AI-900 - Microsoft Azure AI Fundamentals** exam, but also to become a leader in using artificial intelligence responsibly for the future.

Good luck for your exam—and welcome to the next step of your AI journey!

Index

C

O

P

R